The Grammar

The Grammar Level 2

지은이 Nexus Contents Development Team
펴낸이 임상진
펴낸곳 (주)넥서스

출판신고 1992년 4월 3일 제311-2002-2호 2-6
121-893 경기도 파주시 지목로 5
Tel (02)330-5500 Fax (02)330-5555

ISBN 979-11-5752-014-5 54740
979-11-5752-011-4 (SET)

가격은 뒤표지에 있습니다.
잘못 만들어진 책은 구입처에서 바꾸어 드립니다.

www.nexusEDU.kr
NEXUS Edu는 넥서스의 초·중·고 학습물 전문 브랜드입니다.

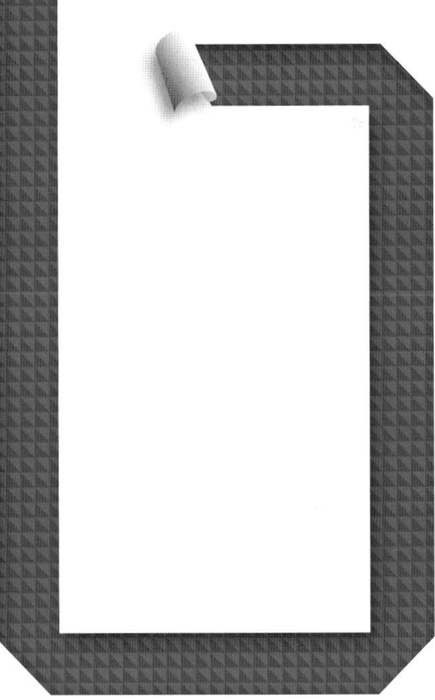

The Grammar

Nexus Contents Development Team

NEXUS Edu

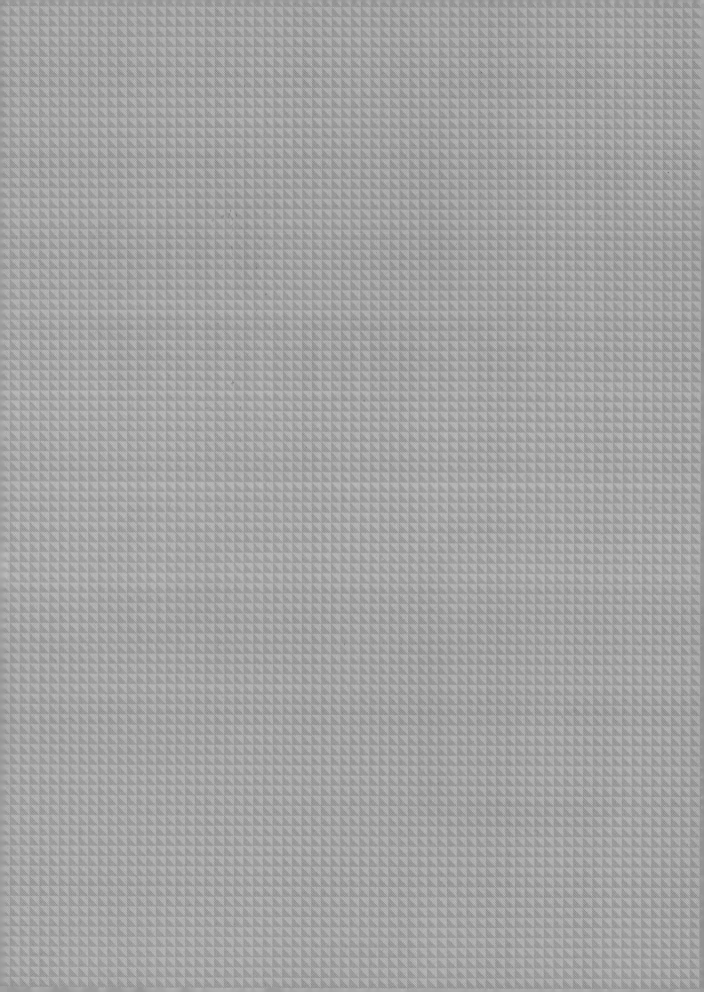

Concise and Core
Grammar Points!

The Grammar Series

Sentence Expansion

기초 문법을 기반으로 문장을 완성,
확장해 가는 학습 방법 적용

Grammar Summary

배운 학습 내용을 차트 및 표로 정리하여
쉽게 암기할 수 있도록 구성

A Variety of Question Types

문법 포인트 확인 ➡ 기초 문법 문제 ➡ 응용 문제 ➡
리뷰 테스트 ➡ 문법 확장 문제 ➡ 종합 문제

Preparation for School Tests

다양한 문제 유형을 통해 내신 대비는 물론
말하기 및 쓰기 실력 향상

Workbook

내신 대비 및 서술형 평가 대비를 위한
충분한 분량의 문제가 수록된 워크북 제공

Concise & Core Grammar

불필요하고 잘 사용하지 않는 문법은 배제하고
핵심적인 부분만을 간결하고 정확하게
예문 중심으로 이해할 수 있도록 구성

Features

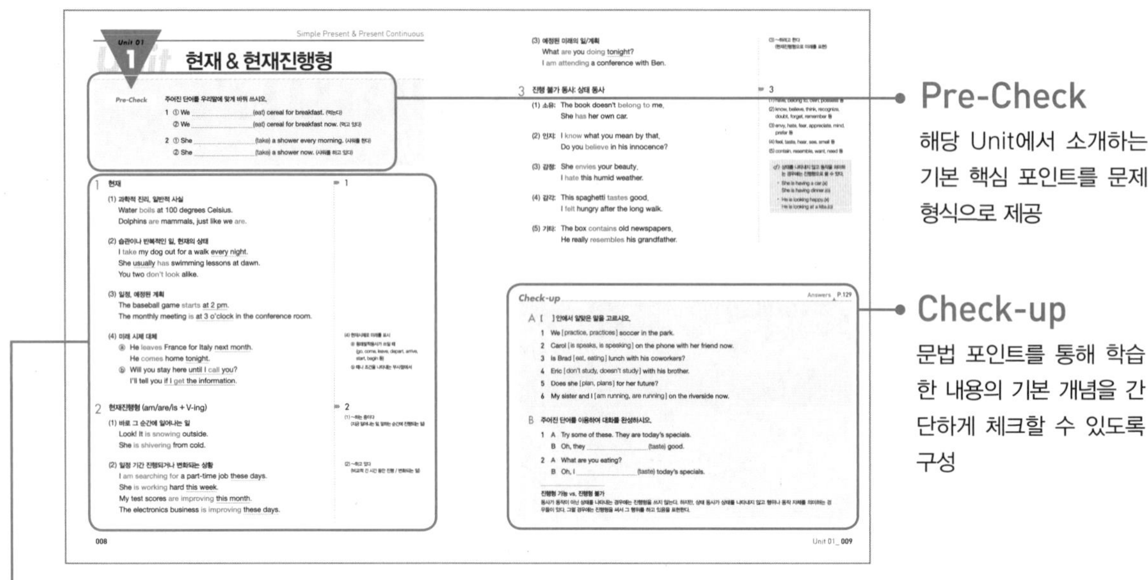

Pre-Check

해당 Unit에서 소개하는 기본 핵심 포인트를 문제 형식으로 제공

Check-up

문법 포인트를 통해 학습한 내용의 기본 개념을 간단하게 체크할 수 있도록 구성

Grammar Point

문법 포인트 설명: 한글 주석과 영문 예문을 분리하여 문장의 예문 패턴을 집중적으로 비교 분석할 수 있도록 구성

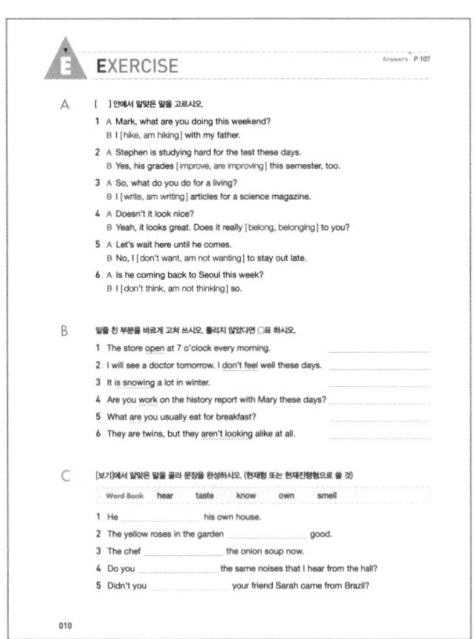

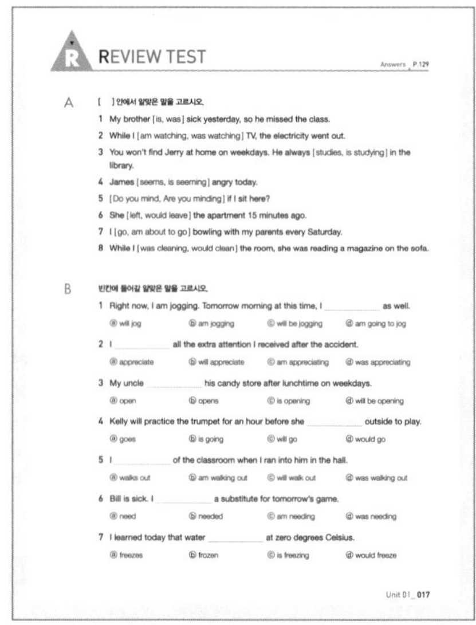

Exercise

배운 내용의 개념과 규칙 등의 확인 연습문제

Review Test

각 단원에서 배운 문제를 총 정리하는 장으로 4가지 유형의 문제 형태로 구성. 각각의 문법 포인트들을 모아 놓아 전체적으로 구성된 문제 풀이를 통해 부족한 부분을 진단

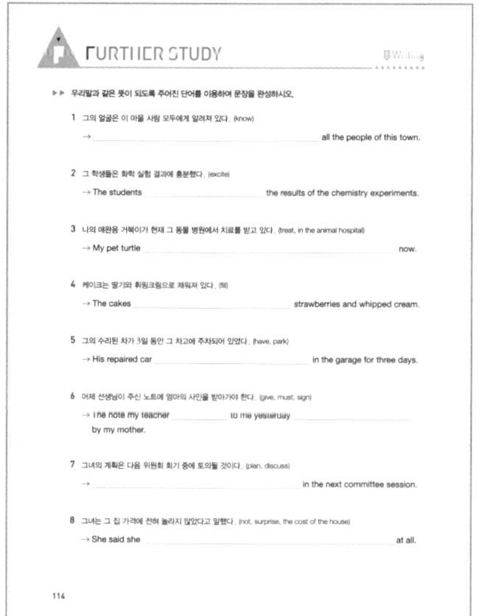

Further Study

짧은 쓰기 문장을 통해 각 단원에서 배운 문법 포인트들을 체크해 볼 수 있도록 문제를 구성하여 영작문 실력 향상 가능

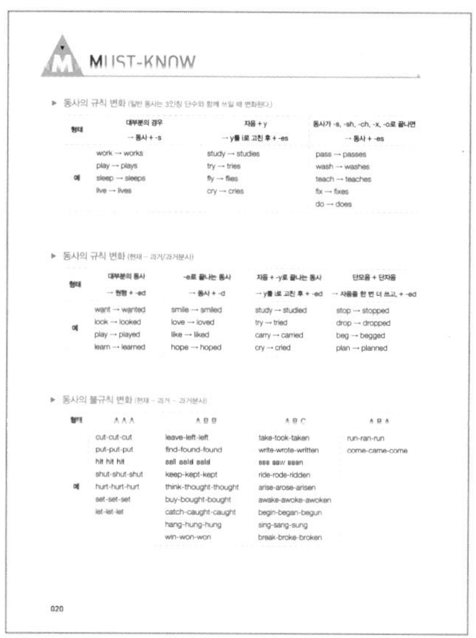

Must-Konw

각 단원에서 배운 기본 문법 포인트들을 표로 정리하여 기본적 문법 사항을 놓치지 않도록 구성. 본문에서 다루지 않은 기본 사항과 보충적인 문법 사항을 수록

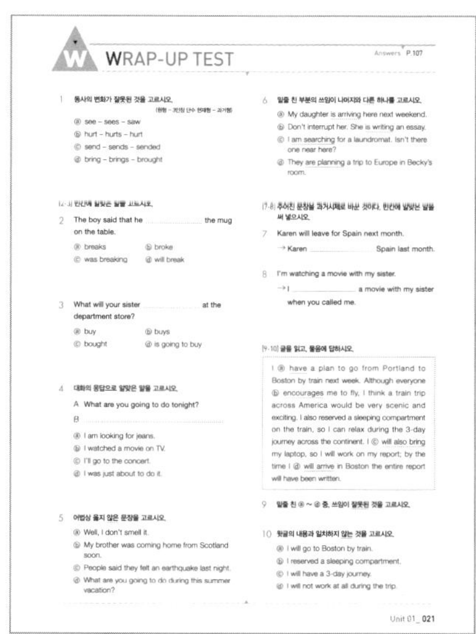

Wrap-up Test

각 단원이 끝나면 내신형 문제를 통해 앞에서 배운 문법 포인트를 확인할 수 있도록 구성하여 학습한 문법을 종합적으로 정리

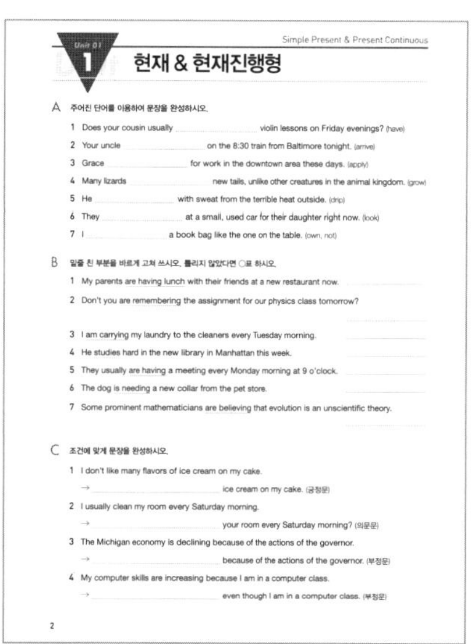

Workbook

기초 문법 확인 문제 외에도 내신 완벽 대비를 위한 객관식, 서술형 문제를 유닛별로 구성하여 자기주도학습을 할 수 있도록 구성

Contents

The Grammar

2
Level

시제

1 현재 & 현재진행형
2 과거 & 과거진행형
3 미래 & 미래진행형

현재 & 현재진행형

Pre-Check 주어진 단어를 우리말에 맞게 바꿔 쓰시오.

1 ① We ________________(eat) cereal for breakfast. (먹는다)
② We ________________(eat) cereal for breakfast now. (먹고 있다)

2 ① She ________________(take) a shower every morning. (샤워를 한다)
② She ________________(take) a shower now. (샤워를 하고 있다)

1 현재

(1) 과학적 진리, 일반적 사실
Water boils at 100 degrees Celsius.
Dolphins are mammals, just like we are.

(2) 습관이나 반복적인 일, 현재의 상태
I take my dog out for a walk every night.
She usually has swimming lessons at dawn.
You two don't look alike.

(3) 일정, 예정된 계획
The baseball game starts at 2 pm.
The monthly meeting is at 3 o'clock in the conference room.

(4) 미래 시제 대체
ⓐ He leaves France for Italy next month.
He comes home tonight.
ⓑ Will you stay here until I call you?
I'll tell you if I get the information.

1

(4) 현재시제로 미래를 표시
ⓐ 왕래발착동사가 쓰일 때
(go, come, leave, depart, arrive, start, begin 등)
ⓑ 때나 조건을 나타내는 부사절에서

2 현재진행형 (am/are/is + V-ing)

(1) 바로 그 순간에 일어나는 일
Look! It is snowing outside.
She is shivering from cold.

(2) 일정 기간 진행되거나 변화되는 상황
I am searching for a part-time job these days.
She is working hard this week.
My test scores are improving this month.
The electronics business is improving these days.

2

(1) ~하는 중이다
(지금 일어나는 일, 말하는 순간에 진행되는 일)

(2) ~하고 있다
(비교적 긴 시간 동안 진행 / 변화되는 일)

(3) 예정된 미래의 일/계획
What are you doing tonight?
I am attending a conference with Ben.

(3) ~하려고 한다
(현재진행형으로 미래를 표현)

3 진행 불가 동사: 상태 동사

(1) 소유: The book doesn't belong to me.
She has her own car.

(2) 인지: I know what you mean by that.
Do you believe in his innocence?

(3) 감정: She envies your beauty.
I hate this humid weather.

(4) 감각: This spaghetti tastes good.
I felt hungry after the long walk.

(5) 기타: The box contains old newspapers.
He really resembles his grandfather.

3

(1) have, belong to, own, possess 등

(2) know, believe, think, recognize, doubt, forget, remember 등

(3) envy, hate, fear, appreciate, mind, prefer 등

(4) feel, taste, hear, see, smell 등

(5) contain, resemble, want, need 등

cf) 상태를 나타내지 않고 동작을 의미하는 경우에는 진행형으로 쓸 수 있다.

- She is having a car.(x)
She is having dinner.(o)
- He is looking happy.(x)
He is looking at a kite.(o)

Check-up

Answers P.2

A [ ] 안에서 알맞은 말을 고르시오.

1 We [practice, practices] soccer in the park.

2 Carol [is speaks, is speaking] on the phone with her friend now.

3 Is Brad [eat, eating] lunch with his coworkers?

4 Eric [don't study, doesn't study] with his brother.

5 Does she [plan, plans] for her future?

6 My sister and I [am running, are running] on the riverside now.

B 주어진 단어를 이용하여 대화를 완성하시오.

1 A Try some of these. They are today's specials.
B Oh, they ________________(taste) good.

2 A What are you eating?
B Oh, I ________________(taste) today's specials.

진행형 가능 vs. 진행형 불가
동사가 동작이 아닌 상태를 나타내는 경우에는 진행형을 쓰지 않는다. 하지만, 상태 동사가 상태를 나타내지 않고 행위나 동작 자체를 의미하는 경우들이 있다. 그럴 경우에는 진행형을 써서 그 행위를 하고 있음을 표현한다.

EXERCISE

Answers P.2

A

[ ] 안에서 알맞은 말을 고르시오.

1 A Mark, what are you doing this weekend?
B I [hike, am hiking] with my father.

2 A Stephen is studying hard for the test these days.
B Yes, his grades [improve, are improving] this semester, too.

3 A So, what do you do for a living?
B I [write, am writing] articles for a science magazine.

4 A Doesn't it look nice?
B Yeah, it looks great. Does it really [belong, belonging] to you?

5 A Let's wait here until he comes.
B No, I [don't want, am not wanting] to stay out late.

6 A Is he coming back to Seoul this week?
B I [don't think, am not thinking] so.

B

밑줄 친 부분을 바르게 고쳐 쓰시오. 틀리지 않았다면 ○표 하시오.

1 The store open at 7 o'clock every morning. ____________

2 I will see a doctor tomorrow. I don't feel well these days. ____________

3 It is snowing a lot in winter. ____________

4 Are you work on the history report with Mary these days? ____________

5 What are you usually eat for breakfast? ____________

6 They are twins, but they aren't looking alike at all. ____________

C

[보기]에서 알맞은 말을 골라 문장을 완성하시오. (현재형 또는 현재진행형으로 쓸 것)

Word Bank hear taste know own smell

1 He ____________ his own house.

2 The yellow roses in the garden ____________ good.

3 The chef ____________ the onion soup now.

4 Do you ____________ the same noises that I hear from the hall?

5 Didn't you ____________ your friend Sarah came from Brazil?

과거 & 과거진행형

Pre-Check 주어진 단어를 우리말에 맞게 바꿔 쓰시오.

1 ① I ________________(watch) TV right before my parents came in. (보고 있었다)
② I ________________(watch) most of the programs on TV last night. (보았다)

2 ① We ________________(go) to the movies last Saturday. (~에 갔다)
② They ________________(go) to the movies when we saw them. (~에 가고 있었다)

1 과거

(1) 역사적 사실

He won the tennis championship in 1972.
The opera was first performed on stage in 1902.
Beethoven wrote the song in the 18th century.

(2) 과거에 일어난 일

I was late for school yesterday.
I read the book last night.
She left the office ten minutes ago.

(3) 과거 시제의 동사 변화

ⓐ 규칙 변화

The rain poured down all day long.
We lived in that apartment 2 years ago.
She stopped her car and asked for directions.
We all tried our best to win the championship.

ⓑ 불규칙 변화

She put the paper on your desk.
I took a piano lesson twice a week back then.
Last night, he came back from a long journey.
I ran to the library to find a book for my report.

1

(1) / (2)
*과거의 때를 나타내는 어구(~ ago, last, yesterday, in the past 등)와 함께 쓰인다.

(3)
ⓐ 규칙 변화 (현재 – 과거)

대부분의 동사	want-wanted
-e로 끝나는 동사	die-died
단모음 + 단자음	beg-begged
모음 + y	play-played
자음 + y	carry-carried

• 과거분사는 과거와 동일함

ⓑ 불규칙 변화 (현재 – 과거 – 과거분사)

A-A-A형	cut-cut-cut put-put-put
A-B-B형	leave-left-left win-won-won
A-B-C형	take-took-taken write-wrote-written
A-B-A형	run-ran-run come-came-come

2 과거진행형 (was/were+V-ing)

(1) 과거 특정 시각에 일어났던 일

It was snowing at that time. It wasn't raining.
I was doing my homework then.
He couldn't call because he was meeting a person from a law firm.

2

(1) (과거의 특정 순간에) ~하고 있었다, ~하던 중이었다

(2) 과거 일정 기간 동안 진행되었던 일

What was she doing last winter vacation?
The U.S. economy was going down during the third decade of the 20th century.

(2)(과거 일정 기간 동안) ~하고 있었다

(3) 과거에 동시 진행되던 일

I was walking the dog when he called me.
(= While I was walking the dog, he called me.)
He was reading the newspaper when she came in.
(= She came in while he was reading the newspaper.)

(3) (…했을 때) ~하고 있었다

Check-up

Answers P.2

A 주어진 단어를 이용하여 문장을 완성하시오.

1 He ________________(fix) the washing machine the other day.
2 Last night, my father ________________(make) dinner for us.
3 My family ________________(prepare) a meal for the homeless on Thanksgiving in 2013.
4 We all ________________(sleep) on the floor last night.
5 Boys from my church ________________(sing) a Christmas carol for us last Christmas Eve.

B 주어진 단어를 이용하여 대화를 완성하시오.

A How was your weekend?
B I didn't do much. I just ① ________________(stay) home and ② ________________(watch) TV.
A Are you sure? I called you in the afternoon, but you didn't answer the phone.
B Oh, that was you? I ③ ________________(take) a shower at that time.

과거 vs. 과거진행형
과거시제는 과거에 끝난 행위를 표현하는 것이고, 과거진행형은 과거의 특정 순간에 하고 있었던 일, 또는 과거의 일정 기간 동안 지속하던 일을 표현할 때 사용한다.

EXERCISE

Answers P.2

A

[ ] 안에서 알맞은 말을 고르시오.

1 A What were you doing there?
B I [have, was having] a meeting with a client.

2 A Where did you go for treats after the game?
B We [were going, went] to the shop over there for ice cream.

3 A I knocked on your door several times, but you didn't answer.
B I [didn't hear, wasn't hearing] you. Jim and I were playing some games.

4 A What did you usually do with your grandfather?
B We usually [go, went] fishing after lunch.

5 A What [are you doing, were you doing] while Marian was knitting a sweater?
B I was studying physics.

B

밑줄 친 부분을 바르게 고쳐 쓰시오. 틀리지 않았다면 ○표 하시오.

1 Were you visit your grandparents last Christmas? ______

2 She receives this cell phone on her last birthday. ______

3 It wasn't raining. It was snow at that time. ______

4 He wasn't doing his homework then. He was emailed his friend. ______

5 They were looking for their seats when I located them in the theater. ______

6 Mozart was writing more than 600 pieces of music. ______

C

주어진 단어를 이용하여 문장을 완성하시오.

1 I was surprised when they ______(visit) my house last Sunday.

2 While he ______ ______(travel) in London, he bought this book.

3 Don't you remember? There ______(be) a cinema here last year.

4 We ______(build) this house four years ago.

5 My favorite soccer team ______(win) the World Cup in 2014.

6 I ______(spend) my teenage years in Canada.

7 They ______ ______(play) games when I entered the room.

Unit 3 미래 & 미래진행형

Pre-Check [보기]에서 알맞은 말을 골라 빈칸에 써 넣으시오.

Word Bank will are going to would

1 They ________________ throw a party this Friday. (파티를 열 예정이다)

2 Sue said she ________________ come to the party. (파티에 오겠다고 말했다)

3 If she doesn't have a ride, I ________________ drive her home. (바래다주겠다)

1 미래의 will

(1) 미래의 일이나 계획

I **will** stay home tonight.
(→ I **am going to** stay home tonight.)
We **will** leave for Brazil this weekend.
(→ We**'re going to** leave for Brazil this weekend.)
We **won't** see him off tomorrow morning.
(→ We**'re not going to** see him off tomorrow morning.)

cf) 〈be going to + V〉
ⓐ *It's rush hour.* Traffic is going to be backed up.
It's so cloudy. It's going to rain sooner or later.
ⓑ They're going to release new games *next Friday*.
The meeting is going to be at *4 pm today*.

(2) 말하는 사람의 의지나 약속

Since you're busy, I'll get the phone.
Don't worry. I **will** take care of him while you're on the trip.

> 1
> (1) will은 be going to로 바꿔 쓸 수 있다.
>
> *cf)* be going to를 쓰는 것이 더 자연스러운 경우
> ⓐ 근거가 있는 미래 예측
> ⓑ 이미 계획되거나 예정된 일

2 미래를 나타내는 기타 표현

(1) be -ing: 곧 ~할 것이다

I **am taking** a big test tomorrow.
Is he **coming** back soon?
The client **is arriving** in an hour.
cf) I'm going to a party tomorrow. (미래시제)
I'm going to the movies now. (현재진행형)

> 2
> (1) 왕래발착동사는 현재진행형 또는 현재형과 미래를 나타내는 부사가 함께 쓰여 미래시제를 나타낸다.
>
> *cf)* 왕래발착동사
> (go, come, arrive, leave, start 등)
> He'll arrive at 7.
> = He's going to arrive at 7.
> = He's arriving at 7.

(2) be (just) about to: (지금) 막 ~하려고 하다

The concert **is about to** begin.

The train **is just about to** leave. Hurry up.

3 미래진행형 (will + be + V-ing)

I can't go there. I **will be working** then.

He'll **be studying** English tomorrow night at this time.

The bus arrives at 5 pm. I **will be waiting** for it.

3
(미래에) ~하고 있을 것이다

4 과거 시점에서의 미래

(1) I told him that I **would** participate in the contest.

He said he **would** send me books from London.

(2) We thought he **was going to** propose to you.

I wasn't satisfied with my report, so I **was going to** rewrite it.

4
(1) would + V
: (과거에) ~하려고 했다
(2) was/were going to V
: (과거에) ~하려고 했다

Check-up

Answers P.2

A 주어진 단어를 이용하여 문장을 완성하시오.

1 She ____________________(will, return) the dress because it does not fit.

2 We ____________________(not, be going to, attend) the meeting this afternoon.

3 She ____________________(will, place an order) for a new book on the Internet.

4 Who ____________________(be going to, prepare) the meal tonight?

5 He ____________________(be -ing, arrive) on the express train tonight.

B 밑줄 친 부분이 현재진행형인지 미래형인지 구분하시오.

A Where are you going?

B ① I'm going to the post office to send a package. What about you?

A ② I'm leaving for the city. ③ I'm meeting my parents tonight.

B Hmm, when are you coming back?

A ④ I'm coming back tomorrow.

진행의 V-ing vs 미래의 V-ing

진행형을 만드는 -ing는 '(현재) ~하고 있는'이라는 뜻 외에 '~할 예정이다'라는 미래의 뜻을 나타내기도 한다. 보통, -ing형이 미래를 나타내는 단어[부사(구)]와 함께 사용되는 경우, 미래의 뜻으로 이해할 수 있다.

EXERCISE

Answers P.2

A

「be going to」를 이용하여 문장을 완성하시오.

1 He will not bring a cake to the party.
→ He ______________________ a cake to the party.

2 We will watch the movies tomorrow night.
→ We ______________________ the movies tomorrow night.

3 She will spend her next winter vacation in Hawaii.
→ She ______________________ her next winter vacation in Hawaii.

4 Will he pick you up at the airport this evening?
→ ______________________ at the airport this evening?

B

[ ] 안에서 알맞은 말을 고르시오.

1 I don't have any plans tonight. I [will stay, stay] home and watch TV.

2 I [am going to, went] the concert with my best friends within a few minutes.

3 The weather [is about to, is going to] be fine for the picnic tomorrow.

4 I [am take, will take] them to a restaurant for dinner tonight.

5 Hurry and sit down! The play [was starting, is about to start].

6 Don't worry. When you get there, she [waits, will be waiting] for you.

7 She promised she [would buy, was buying] me a set of china as a gift.

C

주어진 단어를 이용하여 문장을 완성하시오. (미래시제로 쓸 것)

1 A Look, it's so cloudy.
B Yeah, it ______________(snow) sooner or later, I guess.

2 A It's a surprise party for Daniel.
B OK. I promise I ______________(not, tell) him about it.

3 A You can leave either today or tomorrow.
B We ______________(stay) one more night here.

4 A What is your plan for this Saturday?
B I ______________(see) a movie with my sister. I've already bought the tickets.

Answers P.3

A

[ ] 안에서 알맞은 말을 고르시오.

1 My brother [is, was] sick yesterday, so he missed the class.

2 While I [am watching, was watching] TV, the electricity went out.

3 You won't find Jerry at home on weekdays. He always [studies, is studying] in the library.

4 James [seems, is seeming] angry today.

5 [Do you mind, Are you minding] if I sit here?

6 She [left, would leave] the apartment 15 minutes ago.

7 I [go, am about to go] bowling with my parents every Saturday.

8 While I [was cleaning, would clean] the room, she was reading a magazine on the sofa.

B

빈칸에 들어갈 알맞은 말을 고르시오.

1 Right now, I am jogging. Tomorrow morning at this time, I ____________ as well.

ⓐ will jog ⓑ am jogging ⓒ will be jogging ⓓ am going to jog

2 I ____________ all the extra attention I received after the accident.

ⓐ appreciate ⓑ will appreciate ⓒ am appreciating ⓓ was appreciating

3 My uncle ____________ his candy store after lunchtime on weekdays.

ⓐ open ⓑ opens ⓒ is opening ⓓ will be opening

4 Kelly will practice the trumpet for an hour before she ____________ outside to play.

ⓐ goes ⓑ is going ⓒ will go ⓓ would go

5 I ____________ of the classroom when I ran into him in the hall.

ⓐ walks out ⓑ am walking out ⓒ will walk out ⓓ was walking out

6 Bill is sick. I ____________ a substitute for tomorrow's game.

ⓐ need ⓑ needed ⓒ am needing ⓓ was needing

7 I learned today that water ____________ at zero degrees Celsius.

ⓐ freezes ⓑ frozen ⓒ is freezing ⓓ would freeze

R REVIEW TEST

C

밑줄 친 부분을 바르게 고쳐 문장을 다시 쓰시오.

1 When I get out of the plane, it was raining heavily.

→ ____________________

2 I am going to quit the job because I wasn't happy with my boss back then.

→ ____________________

3 It was amazing that endangered species survives after Hurricane Katrina.

→ ____________________

4 I walk to school with my brother before I got a bike.

→ ____________________

D

(A), (B), (C)의 각 네모 안에서 어법에 맞는 말로 바르게 짝지어진 것을 고르시오.

> Scientists are watching a giant hurricane on another planet. The hurricane is 5,000 miles wide, and its winds (A) [travel / travels] at 350 miles per hour. Researchers are watching this storm on Saturn. The storm is near Saturn's South Pole. Scientists think this storm (B) [continue / will continue] for a long time. They (C) [studied / are going to study] it for as long as they can.

	(A)		(B)		(C)
①	travel	…	continue	…	studied
②	travel	…	will continue	…	are going to study
③	travel	…	will continue	…	studied
④	travels	…	continue	…	studied
⑤	travels	…	will continue	…	are going to study

FURTHER STUDY

▶▶ 우리말과 같은 뜻이 되도록 주어진 단어를 이용하여 문장을 완성하시오.

1 나는 몸이 좋지 않아서 어제 의사의 진찰을 받으러 갔다. (not, feel well, go to the doctor)

→ I ______________________, so I ______________________ yesterday.

2 그녀는 두 대의 자동차를 소유하고 있다. 지금은 빨간색 차를 운전하는 중이다. (own, drive)

→ She ______________________. Now she ______________________.

3 나는 매일 아침 강변으로 조깅하러 간다. (go jogging, along the riverside)

→ I ______________________________________ every morning.

4 곧 콘서트가 시작하려고 해. 자리에 앉자. (be about to, begin)

→ The concert ______________________________. Let's take our seats.

5 그는 다음 달에 우리를 방문할 것이라고 약속했다. (will, visit, next month)

→ He promised that he ______________________________________.

6 내가 비디오를 보고 있는 동안 그는 Julia와 얘기를 하고 있었다. (watch a video, talk to)

→ While I ______________________, he ______________________ Julia.

7 나는 내일 입사면접이 있어서 오늘 밤에 영화를 보러 가지 않을 것이다.
(have a job interview, not, go to the movies)

→ I ______________________, so I ______________________.

8 당신이 사무실에서 일하고 있는 동안 Sam이 우리를 공항까지 태워다 줄 것이다.
(work at the office, will, drive, to the airport)

> While ______________________, Sam ______________________.

MUST-KNOW

▶ 동사의 규칙 변화 (일반 동사는 3인칭 단수와 함께 쓰일 때 변화된다.)

형태	대부분의 경우 → 동사 + -s	자음 + y → y를 i로 고친 후 + -es	동사가 -s, -sh, -ch, -x, -o로 끝나면 → 동사 + -es
예	work → works play → plays sleep → sleeps live → lives	study → studies try → tries fly → flies cry → cries	pass → passes wash → washes teach → teaches fix → fixes do → does

▶ 동사의 규칙 변화 (현재 – 과거/과거분사)

형태	대부분의 동사 → 원형 + -ed	-e로 끝나는 동사 → 동사 + -d	자음 + -y로 끝나는 동사 → y를 i로 고친 후 + -ed	단모음 + 단자음 → 자음을 한 번 더 쓰고, + -ed
예	want → wanted look → looked play → played learn → learned	smile → smiled love → loved like → liked hope → hoped	study → studied try → tried carry → carried cry → cried	stop → stopped drop → dropped beg → begged plan → planned

▶ 동사의 불규칙 변화 (현재 – 과거 – 과거분사)

형태	A-A-A	A-B-B	A-B-C	A-B-A
예	cut-cut-cut put-put-put hit-hit-hit shut-shut-shut hurt-hurt-hurt set-set-set let-let-let	leave-left-left find-found-found sell-sold-sold keep-kept-kept think-thought-thought buy-bought-bought catch-caught-caught hang-hung-hung win-won-won	take-took-taken write-wrote-written see-saw-seen ride-rode-ridden arise-arose-arisen awake-awoke-awoken begin-began-begun sing-sang-sung break-broke-broken	run-ran-run come-came-come

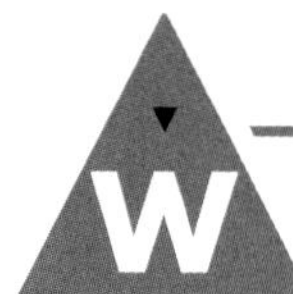

WRAP-UP TEST

Answers P.4

1 동사의 변화가 잘못된 것을 고르시오.

(원형 – 3인칭 단수 현재형 – 과거형)

ⓐ see – sees – saw
ⓑ hurt – hurts – hurt
ⓒ send – sends – sended
ⓓ bring – brings – brought

[2-3] 빈칸에 알맞은 말을 고르시오.

2 The boy said that he ______________ the mug on the table.

ⓐ breaks ⓑ broke
ⓒ was breaking ⓓ will break

3 What will your sister ______________ at the department store?

ⓐ buy ⓑ buys
ⓒ bought ⓓ is going to buy

4 대화의 응답으로 알맞은 말을 고르시오.

A What are you going to do tonight?
B ______________________________

ⓐ I am looking for jeans.
ⓑ I watched a movie on TV.
ⓒ I'll go to the concert.
ⓓ I was just about to do it.

5 어법상 옳지 않은 문장을 고르시오.

ⓐ Well, I don't smell it.
ⓑ My brother was coming home from Scotland soon.
ⓒ People said they felt an earthquake last night.
ⓓ What are you going to do during this summer vacation?

6 밑줄 친 부분의 쓰임이 나머지와 다른 하나를 고르시오.

ⓐ My daughter is arriving here next weekend.
ⓑ Don't interrupt her. She is writing an essay.
ⓒ I am searching for a laundromat. Isn't there one near here?
ⓓ They are planning a trip to Europe in Becky's room.

[7-8] 주어진 문장을 과거시제로 바꾼 것이다. 빈칸에 알맞은 말을 써 넣으시오.

7 Karen will leave for Spain next month.

→ Karen ______________ Spain last month.

8 I'm watching a movie with my sister.

→ I ______________ a movie with my sister when you called me.

[9-10] 글을 읽고, 물음에 답하시오.

> I ⓐ have a plan to go from Portland to Boston by train next week. Although everyone ⓑ encourages me to fly, I think a train trip across America would be very scenic and exciting. I also reserved a sleeping compartment on the train, so I can relax during the 3-day journey across the continent. I ⓒ will also bring my laptop, so I will work on my report; by the time I ⓓ will arrive in Boston the entire report will have been written.

9 밑줄 친 ⓐ ~ ⓓ 중, 쓰임이 잘못된 것을 고르시오.

10 윗글의 내용과 일치하지 않는 것을 고르시오.

ⓐ I will go to Boston by train.
ⓑ I reserved a sleeping compartment.
ⓒ I will have a 3-day journey.
ⓓ I will not work at all during the trip.

The Grammar

2
Level

완료시제

1 현재완료 (I)
2 현재완료 (II)
3 과거완료, 미래완료, 완료진행형

현재완료 (I)

Pre-Check 주어진 단어를 우리말에 맞게 바꿔 쓰시오.

1 ① He ________________(study) English last night. (어젯밤에 공부했다)
② We ________________(study) English for two years. (2년 동안 공부해 왔다)

2 ① I ________________(read) the magazine yesterday. (어제 읽었다)
② I ________________(read) the magazine before. (읽어 본 적이 있다)

1 과거 vs. 현재완료 (-ed vs. has/have p.p.)

I lived in the house in 2003. (Not related to the present)
I have lived in the house since 2003. (Even now)
I chose my major when I was a sophomore.
I have already chosen my major.

> 1
> 과거 vs. 현재완료
> • 과거 – 과거에 행해져서 끝난 일
> • 현재완료 – 과거의 어느 시점부터 현재까지 이어져, 현재에도 영향을 미치는 일
> (* 현재완료는 yesterday, ~ ago, last year, when 등 과거의 특정한 시간을 나타내는 부사와 함께 쓰이지 않는다.)

2 계속

(1) (과거부터) 현재까지 계속된 일

He went to Italy two years ago. He still lives there.
→ He has lived in Italy for two years.

I got a cold last Friday. I'm still sick.
→ I have been sick since last Friday.

I first started collecting stamps when I was 10.
I'm 15 now, and I still collect them.
→ I have collected stamps for five years.

(2) How long ~으로 질문할 때

How long has he lived in Italy?
How long have you been sick?
How long have you collected stamps?

> 2
> (1) (지금까지 계속) ~해 왔다
> (2) 얼마나 오래 ~해 왔는가?
> How long have/has + 주어 + p.p. ~?
> * 함께 쓰이는 시간 표현
> ① for + 기간
> for two weeks, for a month
> ② since + 시점
> since I graduated from school, since the 2014 World Cup

3 경험

(1) 지금까지의 경험을 말할 때

A: Have you ever been abroad?
B: No, I've never been abroad. How about you?
A: I've been to Thailand once.

cf) A: When did you go to England?
B: I went there last year.

> 3
> (1) (지금껏) ~한 적이 있다
>
> *cf)* when은 구체적인 과거의 사실을 물어보는 것이기 때문에 완료시제와 함께 쓰지 않는다.

(2) How many times ~로 질문할 때

A: Have you ever tried shark fin soup?
B: Yes, I've tried it before.
A: How many times have you tried it?
B: I have tried it twice.

cf) A: Did you eat shark fin soup yesterday?
B: No, I didn't. I ate dim sum instead.

(2) 얼마나 많이/몇 번 ~해 봤는가?
How many times have/has + 주어 + p.p. ~?

* 함께 쓰이는 표현
ever, never, once, before, twice, ~ times 등

4 기타 현재완료의 쓰임

(1) This is the greatest movie that I have ever seen in my life.
Bill is the most energetic teacher that I have ever had.

(2) I've told you several times not to bring your dog.
This is the third time that we have taken the quiz.

4
(1) 최상급 + 완료: 지금껏 가장 ~하다
(2) 서수 + 완료: 지금껏 몇 번 ~했다
* 함께 쓰이는 표현
the third time, several times, many times 등

Check-up

Answers P.4

A 주어진 단어를 이용하여 문장을 완성하시오. (현재완료 문장으로 쓸 것)

1 We ____________(construct) a big fort in the snow before.
2 They ____________(attend) the church down the road once.
3 She ____________(not, try) smoked eel or sushi before.
4 ____________(you, ever, visit) Times Square on New Year's Eve?
5 Eric ____________(survive) the earthquake in California.

B 주어진 단어를 이용하여 대화를 완성하시오.

1 A Do you know anyone who can read Japanese?
B I ① ____________(study) Japanese when I was 12. But now, I don't know many of its words. But my sister ② ____________(study) Japanese since she was 11. I'm sure she can read it well.

2 A Do you know Mr. Hong?
B I don't know him personally, but I ① ____________(see) him before. When I went to China last year, I ② ____________(see) him there.

과거 vs. 현재완료 (I)
시제란 시간의 시점을 말한다. 따라서 과거시제는 오직 과거의 사실만 이야기하고, 현재완료시제는 과거에 시작되어 현재의 입장에도 영향을 미치는 일을 나타내고자 할 때 사용한다.

Answers P.4

A

[ ] 안에서 알맞은 말을 고르시오.

1 A I have been to Mississippi once.
B When [have you gone, did you go] there?

2 A Are you going to make a cake for Aunt Betty's birthday?
B Yes, this is my first time. I [have never done, never do] it before.

3 A [Did you see, Have you ever seen] the moon this big and bright?
B I don't think I have.

4 A Is this your 4th year at this company?
B No, I [work, have worked] here for five years.

5 A I don't know how to play the piano. How about you?
B Well, I [played, have played] it since I was 7.

B

밑줄 친 부분을 바르게 고쳐 쓰시오. 틀리지 않았다면 ○표 하시오.

1 I have studied calculus at university <u>since</u> 3 years. ______________

2 Have you <u>ever</u> been to the carnival in Rio de Janeiro, Brazil? ______________

3 I haven't been to San Antonio <u>for</u> 2004. ______________

4 Carol <u>studies</u> French since last April. ______________

5 I <u>haven't paddled</u> the canoe alone last night. ______________

C

현재완료시제를 이용하여 문장을 다시 쓰시오.

1 She sculpted an image of herself in an art class yesterday.
→ She ______________ an image of herself before.

2 I attended a baseball game the other day.
→ I ______________ baseball games several times.

3 Peggy cooked squid for her family yesterday.
→ Peggy ______________ dinner for her family for a month.

4 He traveled the world for over 2 years.
→ He ______________ the world since he graduated from college.

5 Did you take this medicine this morning?
→ How many times ______________ this medicine so far?

Unit 02

2 현재완료 (II)

Pre-Check 밑줄 친 부분에 유의하여 문장을 해석하시오.

1 ① She went to Europe yesterday.
② She has gone to Europe.

2 ① I finished the report an hour ago.
② I have just finished the report.

1 결과

She **has lost** her purse in the mall.
(→ She doesn't have it now.)

I **have locked** my keys in the car.
(→ I can't open the door now.)

I**'ve put** the dog in my room.
(→ Now the dog is in my room.)

cf) Winter came.
(→ Winter came sometime in the past but not the recent past.)
Winter has come.
(→ Winter came, and it is winter now.)

1
결과: (과거에) …해서, (현재) ~했다

cf) 단순 과거 vs. 현재완료 '결과'
• 단순 과거
과거에 일어났던 일만 설명
• 현재완료 '결과'
과거의 일이 현재에 어떤 '결과'로 영향을 미친 것을 설명

2 완료

A: Do you still have to use this copy machine?
B: No, I'm done. I **have just copied** all the articles I needed.

A: Are there any oranges left?
B: No, I **have already eaten** all of them.

A: I'm so hungry.
B: Wait a while. Mom **has not fixed** dinner **yet**.

2
완료: (과거에 시작해서) 현재 끝났다
(과거에 시작된 일이 '현재에 완료'된 상태임을 나타냄)
* 완료와 함께 쓰는 부사
: already, yet, just 등

3 결과 vs. 완료

(1) 결과
A: Where is your computer?
B: I **have sold** it over the Internet.
(→ I don't have it now.)

(2) 완료

A: **Have you built** the fence yet?

B: Yes, we **have already built** the fence.

(→ There is a new fence.)

4 〈have been to/in + 장소〉 vs. 〈have gone to + 장소〉

ⓐ I **have been to** Rome twice.

ⓑ She **has gone to** Turkey.

4

ⓐ 나는 로마에 두 번 가 본 적이 있다. (갔다 왔다.) – 경험

ⓑ 그녀는 터키에 갔다. (지금 여기 없다.) – 결과

Check-up

Answers P.4

A 주어진 단어를 이용하여 문장을 완성하시오. (현재완료 문장으로 할 것)

1 I ______________(not, mention) the new movie to her.

2 She ______________(go) to Thailand. I can't meet her until she comes back.

3 He ______________(leave) his backpack on a bus.

4 They ______________(already, take) the cat to the veterinarian.

5 We ______________(participate) in a psychology experiment at school before.

B 주어진 단어를 이용하여 대화를 완성하시오.

1 A Do you remember the reading assignment that's due today?

B Yeah, I ______________(read) the whole book twice. I guess I'm ready for the class.

A But didn't you tell me that you were busy with other stuff?

B Well, I ______________(read) the book last night after I finished my other assignments.

2 A Is your roommate coming to the party tonight?

B Oh, he ______________(go) on a field trip. He will not be around this week.

A But I thought I saw him in class yesterday.

B Sure, that's because he ______________(go) on the trip right after the class.

과거 vs. 현재완료 (II)

과거시제는 과거의 시점에 국한되어 현재의 입장을 말하지 않으나, 현재완료시제는 과거부터 현재까지 걸쳐 있어서 현재의 입장을 이야기한다. 따라서 현재완료시제가 '완료'와 '결과'를 나타낼 때도 현재의 입장을 표현한다.

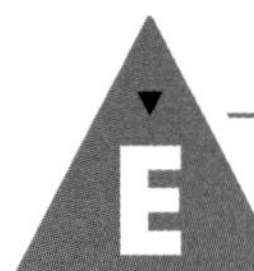

EXERCISE

Answers P.5

A

현재완료시제를 이용하여 하나의 문장으로 완성하시오.

1 He sold his bike a couple of days ago. He doesn't have it now.
→ He ________________________(sell) his bike.

2 I didn't eat lunch. I'm so hungry.
→ I ________________________(not, eat) lunch yet.

3 My older brother went to England to study. He is still there.
→ My older brother ________________________(go) to England to study.

4 He took the train to Busan in the morning. He arrived there a minute ago.
→ He ________________________(just arrive) in Busan.

B

밑줄 친 부분을 바르게 고쳐 쓰시오. 틀리지 않았다면 ○표 하시오.

1 I've just finished the book! You can borrow it. ______________
2 Have you rode the subway lately? ______________
3 Are you talking about the second essay that I have submitted? ______________
4 They have putting off the game several times lately. ______________
5 I am neglected doing my chores lately. ______________

C

현재완료시제를 이용하여 문장을 완성하시오.

1 just / complete
→ I ________________________ my report.

2 break / her favorite glass
→ She ________________________. She can't use it anymore.

3 wash / the car
→ My father ________________________. It is very clean now.

4 just / sign / a contract
→ Max has a job now. He ________________________ to be a stunt man.

5 spend / all of my extra money
→ I ________________________ on piano lessons.

Unit 3 과거완료, 미래완료, 완료진행형

Pre-Check [보기]에서 알맞은 말을 골라 빈칸에 써 넣으시오.

Word Bank will have cooked / have been cooking / had cooked

1 We ______________ dinner for one hour before Mom got home.
2 We ______________ dinner for over one hour by the time Dad arrives.
3 We're still cooking. We ______________ for two hours.

1 과거완료 (had + p.p.)

(1) 과거 이전의 일이 과거까지 영향을 미치는 경우

ⓐ 계속
Jason had lived in Paris for 2 years when I met him there.

ⓑ 경험
I had never tried snails before we went to the restaurant.

ⓒ 결과
I realized that I had lost my keys when I got home.

ⓓ 완료
The game had already started when I came home.

(2) 특정 과거 시점 이전에 일어난 일을 표현하는 경우
He ate the cake that I had bought.
She had cleaned her room before her mom arrived.

1
(1) 과거 기준 시점 이전부터 그 과거 시점까지의 (동작이나 상태의) '계속, 경험, 결과, 완료'를 나타냄
(2) 과거 기준 시점 이전보다 앞선 동작이나 상태를 나타냄

2 미래완료 (will have p.p.)

Denny has visited the Opera House twice.
He will visit the Opera House again next month.
→ He will have visited the Opera House three times by next month.

Meggy has stayed in Seoul for a week.
She will stay here another week.
→ She will have stayed here for two weeks in total.

2
(미래의 그때쯤에는) ~하였을 것이다, ~하고 있을 것이다.
* 미래완료는 미래의 어떤 시점보다 먼저 행해진 일이 미래에 영향을 미치는 것을 표현한다.
* 함께 쓰는 시간 표현: by, until 등

3 완료진행형

(1) She has been eating dinner for one hour.
It has been raining for three days.

cf) I became a baker 5 years ago. I bake cookies every morning.
→ I have baked cookies for 5 years. (상태)

I started baking cookies 2 hours ago. I'm still baking cookies.
→ I have been baking cookies for 2 hours. (동작)

(2) He had been playing tennis for two hours when it began to rain.
She had been sleeping when I called her.

(3) I will have been swimming in the pool.
They will have been studying for exams.

3

(1) 현재완료진행
has/have + been + V-ing
(계속 ~해 오고 있다)

- 현재완료: 일반적인 사실[상태]이 과거부터 현재까지 연결된 경우
- 현재완료진행형: 과거부터 하고 있는 일을 지금까지도 진행하고 있는 경우

(2) 과거완료진행
had + been + V-ing

(3) 미래완료진행
will have been + V-ing
(미래에 진행 중일 동작/일)

Check-up

Answers P.5

A 주어진 단어를 이용하여 문장을 완성하시오.

1 I ______ ______(finish) my homework when you called me.
(네가 전화했을 때 나는 이미 숙제를 끝마쳤었다.)

2 I ______ ______(see) lots of pictures of the Alps before I went to Switzerland.
(나는 스위스에 가기 전에 알프스 사진을 많이 봤었다.)

3 David ______ ______ ______(drive) for three hours.
(David는 3시간째 운전하는 중이었다.)

4 Mr. Crane will retire next month. He ______ ______ ______(work) for 30 years by that time. (Crane 씨가 다음 달에 은퇴할 것이다. 그때쯤 그는 30년 근속이 될 것이다.)

B [보기]에서 알맞은 말을 골라 대화를 완성하시오.

Word Bank	have been waiting	talking	have been talking

A Can I interrupt you for a second?

B I'm sorry. I'm ① ______ to someone at the moment. It won't take long. Could you wait outside for a while?

A But you ② ______ to him for a long time. I ③ ______ here for 30 minutes, so could I just ask you a quick question?

현재진행형 vs. 현재완료진행형

과거시제가 과거의 시점만을 생각하고 말하는 것처럼 현재진행형은 과거와는 상관없이 현재 진행되는 것에만 초점을 맞추어 말을 하는 경우이다. 하지만 현재완료진행형의 경우에는 과거부터 현재까지 걸쳐 진행되고 있는 것을 표현할 때 사용한다.

EXERCISE

Answers P.5

A

완료시제를 이용하여 문장을 완성하시오.

1 I __________ __________(study) painting since I was in the 5th grade.

2 The group __________ __________(plan) the next project before I asked them to.

3 I __________ __________(be) to London three times.

4 The course __________ __________ __________(conclude) by this time next Friday.

5 __________ she __________(order) a meal at the new restaurant today?

6 She __________ __________(feed) the dog when I got home from the office.

7 It's already 8 pm, and I __________ __________(wait) here for almost one hour.

B

밑줄 친 부분을 바르게 고쳐 쓰시오. 틀리지 않았다면 ○표 하시오.

1 I <u>will have</u> finished my homework when you call me. __________

2 The teacher <u>has</u> never taught English before last year. __________

3 He <u>had</u> been sleeping since last night. __________

4 The storm <u>has</u> passed by the time the movie is over. __________

5 The twins <u>had</u> attended the same school since the first grade. __________

6 Kings and queens <u>have</u> worn different crowns for their coronation ceremonies in England. __________

C

주어진 단어를 이용하여 완료시제 문장을 완성하시오.

1 buy / a new house

→ My cousins ______________________________ by the time I fly to see them.

2 know / each other

→ The students ______________________________ since they were on a team together.

3 check / you / the oil

→ ______________________________ before you rented the car?

4 prepare / a special pizza

→ The baker ______________________________ for them right before their arrival.

5 The marathoners / be running

→ ______________________________ for two hours since the race started.

REVIEW TEST

Answers P.5

A

[ ] 안에서 알맞은 말을 고르시오.

1 [How long, How much] have you been talking to your mother on the phone?

2 My family has enjoyed the zoo [for, since] we moved here.

3 The boys have been at camp [for, since] over a week.

4 It has been five years [since, before] they moved to New Zealand.

5 She [has decorated, had decorated] the cake before the party began.

6 We [have seen, have been seeing] the Crown Jewels in London several times.

7 The letter [has reached, will have reached] the post office by 8 o'clock tomorrow morning.

8 It [has been snowing, will have been snowing] for several days.

B

빈칸에 들어갈 알맞은 말을 고르시오.

1 He must be tired. He has been sleeping ______ ten hours.

ⓐ for ⓑ before ⓒ since ⓓ already

2 He had played basketball on the team for two years before he ______.

ⓐ graduate ⓑ graduates ⓒ graduated ⓓ have graduated

3 Don't worry. Your car will have been fixed ______ you need it.

ⓐ for ⓑ once ⓒ since ⓓ by the time

4 I haven't heard from her since we ______ in college together.

ⓐ are ⓑ were ⓒ had been ⓓ have been

5 My grandparents ______ married for 50 years next year.

ⓐ is ⓑ was ⓒ has been ⓓ will have been

6 I ______ trumpet lessons for three months before I entered college.

ⓐ take ⓑ will have taken ⓒ have taken ⓓ had taken

7 She ______ her driver's license yesterday.

ⓐ lost ⓑ has lost ⓒ had lost ⓓ has been losing

REVIEW TEST

C

밑줄 친 부분을 바르게 고쳐 문장을 다시 쓰시오.

1 They had played in the band since they were in high school.

→ ______________________________

2 My youngest cousin is coughing since late last night.

→ ______________________________

3 At the end of the year, he will work for the school for 20 years.

→ ______________________________

4 Jessica has visited me several times since 4 years.

→ ______________________________

5 Do you know how many times he had been working at the company?

→ ______________________________

6 They had stayed in a nice hotel before I meet them.

→ ______________________________

D

(A), (B), (C)의 각 네모 안에서 어법에 맞는 말로 바르게 짝지어진 것을 고르시오.

> Like most working adults of the time, George Stephenson (A) [has never been / had never been] to school. He taught himself to read and learned to be an engineer at a coal mine in northeast England. He (B) [thought / has thought] that there had to be a more effective way of moving coal than using horse-drawn wagons. He decided to improve on the work of Richard Trevithick, who (C) [had built / would built] a simple locomotive railway engine.

	(A)		(B)		(C)
①	has never been	···	thought	···	would built
②	has never been	···	has thought	···	had built
③	had never been	···	thought	···	had built
④	had never been	···	has thought	···	had built
⑤	had never been	···	has thought	···	would built

FURTHER STUDY

Writing

▶▶ **우리말과 같은 뜻이 되도록 주어진 단어를 이용하여 문장을 완성하시오.**

1 나는 그 공원에 몇 번 가봤다. (be, the park, several times)

→ I ______________________________.

2 나는 전에 번지 점프를 딱 한 번 시도해 본 적이 있다. (try, bungee jumping)

→ I ______________________________ only once before.

3 그는 '오페라의 유령'을 두 번 봤다. (see, *The Phantom of the Opera*)

→ ______________________________ twice.

4 네가 나한테 전화했었을 때 나는 한 시간째 숙제를 하고 있는 중이었다. (do, call)

→ I ______________ my homework for an hour when ______________.

5 나는 아직 시험공부를 할 기회가 없었다. (not, have an opportunity, study)

→ ______________________________ for the exam yet.

6 Harold는 이번 3월이 되면 이 회사에 근무한 지 16년째가 될 것이다. (work at, this company)

→ Harold ______________________________ for 16 years this March.

7 그들은 중학생 때 이후로 줄곧 팀 동료였다. (be teammates)

→ ______________________________ since they were in middle school.

8 오후 8시가 되면 그녀는 여기서 한 시간째 기다리는 중일 것이다. (wait, here, for an hour)

→ ______________________________ by 8 pm.

▶ 12시제의 모든 것

시제		시제의 형태	예문
기본시제	현재	• 1, 2인칭 단수, 복수: 동사원형 • 3인칭 단수: -s / -es	I **know** about Cathy. Cathy **eats** breakfast at 7 o'clock.
	과거	• 규칙 변화: -ed • 불규칙 변화	Cathy **washed** her hands and ate breakfast. She **had** a meeting two hours ago.
	미래	• will / be going to + 동사원형 • 현재시제가 미래를 대신	Cathy **is going to travel** around America this summer. She **will come back** when the vacation is over. She **comes** home tonight.
완료시제	현재완료	have/has + p.p.	She **has been** in America for three years.
	과거완료	had + p.p.	She **had been** in LA before she visited her friend.
	미래완료	will have + p.p.	She **will have been** in Washington for two years by next month.
진행시제	현재진행	be동사[am, are, is] + -ing	She **is washing** her hands.
	과거진행	be동사[was, were] + -ing	She **was washing** her hands when the bell rang.
	미래진행	will be + -ing	She **will be working** at her office at 9:30 tomorrow.
	현재완료진행	have/has been + -ing	She **has been eating** breakfast here for an hour.
	과거완료진행	had been + -ing	She **had been eating** breakfast when I visited her.
	미래완료진행	will have been + -ing	She **will have been eating** breakfast for 20 minutes.

▶ 동사시제의 이해 (Time Line)

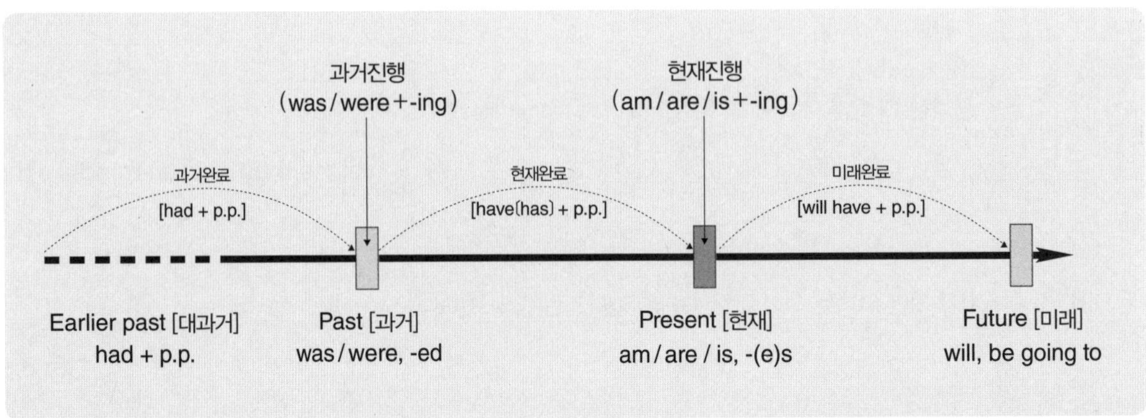

WRAP-UP TEST

Answers P.6

1 밑줄 친 부분의 쓰임이 잘못된 것을 고르시오.

ⓐ How long have you lived in L.A.?
ⓑ I have never met him before.
ⓒ How many times have you took the course?
ⓓ He has worked on the project for a month.

[2-3] 빈칸에 들어갈 알맞은 말을 고르시오.

2 Have you __________ heard about the movie *Transformer*?

ⓐ yet　ⓑ ever
ⓒ ago　ⓓ always

3 Mr. Crane __________ in Seoul since last year.

ⓐ live　ⓑ has lived
ⓒ had lived　ⓓ will have lived

4 빈칸에 알맞은 응답을 써 넣으시오.

A Have you finished cleaning the room?
B No, ____________________.

5 어법상 옳지 않은 문장을 고르시오.

ⓐ Have you ever raised a pet ago?
ⓑ How long have you been in this company?
ⓒ We have never heard about that.
ⓓ Dad has been reading the newspaper for two hours.

6 밑줄 친 부분과 현재완료의 용법이 같은 것을 고르시오.

How long have you taught English in this school?

ⓐ This is the most exciting place I've ever visited.
ⓑ I've never been late for school.
ⓒ My grandmother has been in the hospital since last Wednesday.
ⓓ She has finally got her driver's license after she failed several times.

7 밑줄 친 현재완료의 용법이 나머지와 다른 하나를 고르시오.

ⓐ We have never been abroad.
ⓑ He has driven this car for 5 years.
ⓒ I have never read anything funnier than this.
ⓓ Have you ever participated in this contest before?

8 문장을 한 문장으로 만들 때 빈칸에 알맞은 말을 써 넣으시오.

• Andrew started to search for the information on the Internet two hours ago.
• He is still searching for the information.

→ Andrew ____________________ the information on the Internet __________ two hours.

[9-10] 글을 읽고, 물음에 답하시오.

The best time for the men's 100m race is now less than 10 seconds. The improvement in athletes' technique and fitness is not the only thing that helps them run record-breaking races. Technology has helped, too, in the development of synthetic tracks, aerodynamic clothes, and modern shoes. Starting and timing methods ____________________, and modern electronic systems have helped both athletes and officials ensure that every race has been as fair as possible.

9 빈칸에 들어갈 알맞은 말을 고르시오.

ⓐ improved
ⓑ had improved
ⓒ have been improving
ⓓ will have improved

10 남자 100미터 경주에서 향상된 것이 아닌 것을 고르시오.

ⓐ Athletes' technique
ⓑ Athletes' fitness
ⓒ Better timing methods
ⓓ Highly nutritious food

The Grammar

2
Level

조동사

1 조동사 can, may
2 조동사 will, must, shall
3 기타 조동사

조동사 can, may

Pre-Check [ ] 안에서 알맞은 말을 고르시오.

1 I [can, can't] ride a motorcycle. I've never tried before.

2 Joanna has left for New York. That [can, can't] be her.

3 These are free. You [may, can't] take them.

1 can

(1) 능력

ⓐ I **can** play the piano, but I **can't** play the guitar.
(= I am able to play the piano, but I am not able to play the guitar.)

ⓑ I **could** play the guitar when I was young.
(= I was able to play the guitar when I was young.)

ⓒ I **will be able to** do it again someday.
* I will can do it again someday.(x)

(2) 추측/가능성

He **can** be a progolfer. He plays golf well.
I **could** meet him since he was invited to the party.
It **can't** be true. That makes no sense.
He **cannot** have done such a foolish thing.
It **couldn't** cost that much. It's so ugly.

(3) 부탁, 허락, 허가

Can you give me a ride to work?
Could you give me a ride to school?
Can I use your computer?
You **can** use his computer only if you get his permission.
You **can't** drive a car without a driver's license.

2 may

(1) 추측

He **may** be upset if he finds out you broke it.
He **may** drop by here if he has time.
She said she **might** come here.
She **might** be in the library. I think she is preparing for the exam.

1

(1) 능력: ~할 수 있다

ⓐ 현재: can = is/am/are able to

ⓑ 과거: could = was/were able to

ⓒ 미래: will be able to

* could는 can의 과거이기도 하지만 could 자체가 「가능, 부탁, 허락」 등의 의미를 가진다. 따라서 과거의 능력을 나타낼 때는 could보다 was able to를 더 많이 사용한다.

(2) 추측/가능성: ~일 수 있다, ~일 리가 없다

가능성의 possibility

• **It is possible** that he will forgive us since he is in a good mood today.

• **There's a possibility** that he will forgive us since he is in a good mood today.

(3) 부탁: ~해 주시겠어요?
허가를 구함: ~해도 될까요?
허락: ~해도 좋다
• 공손함 (could>can)
* can't: ~할 수 없다, ~하면 안 된다

2

(1) 추측: ~일 수도 있다, ~일지도 모른다
• 확신 (may>might)

(2) 허가, 허락

May I use the Internet in the library?
= Can I use the Internet in the library?
You may use the library if you have a student card.
(= You can use the library.)
(= You are allowed to use the library.)
You may not create a club if you can't gather more than 5 members for it.
(= You cannot create a club if you can't gather more than 5 members.)

(2) 허가를 구함: ~해도 될까요?
허락: ~해도 좋다
* may not: ~하면 안 된다
* 허락을 구하거나 허락을 해 주는 may는 can과 바꿔 쓸 수 있다.

Check-up

Answers P.7

A 「be able to」를 이용하여 문장을 완성하시오.

1 Kevin says he can swim.
→ Kevin says he ______________________.

2 Cindy cannot play the violin.
→ Cindy ______________________ the violin.

3 Can you read Japanese?
→ ______________________ Japanese?

B 밑줄 친 부분과 바꿔 쓸 수 있는 문장을 [보기]에서 고르시오.

a. There is a possibility that he parks his car here.
b. He is able to park his car here.
c. He is allowed to park his car here.

1 A Ben is a little worried about parking his car here because the parking spaces are narrow.
B He can park his car here. He's been driving for more than 5 years.

2 A I have to catch Ben before he parks his car and leaves. I don't know where he will park his car.
B Don't worry. Since there are not many places to park, he can park his car here.

3 A My client is visiting me in the office. I wonder if he can bring his car here.
B Oh, if you fill out this form, he can park his car here.

1 ____________ 2 ____________ 3 ____________

능력, 가능성, 허락

can은 기본적으로 '~할 수 있다'라는 뜻이다. 그러나 우리말로 해석할 때는 '할 수 있다'가 능력을 이야기하는 것인지, 할 가능성이 있다는 것을 의미하는 것인지, 해도 좋다는 허락을 나타내는 것인지를 생각해야 한다. '능력', '가능성', '허락'과 같이 can의 의미를 구분하는 것은 영어 문제라기보다는 우리말로 그 의미를 구분할 수 있는지를 묻는 것이라 할 수 있다.

EXERCISE

Answers P.7

A

[ ] 안에서 알맞은 말을 고르시오.

1 Will they [be able to, can] come early to the meeting tomorrow?

2 You [were able to, can] drive a car here after you get an international license.

3 I'm really late. [May, Could] you give me a ride home?

4 The bill [can't be, is able to be] paid over the Internet, so I have to go to the bank now.

5 The company [might, be able to] face a serious problem if the chairman doesn't recover from his serious accident.

B

밑줄 친 부분이 의미하는 것을 고르시오.

1 Mom said we could go to the movies when we finished our homework.

ⓐ ability ⓑ permission ⓒ possibility

2 It can't be true that she won the lottery.

ⓐ ability ⓑ permission ⓒ possibility

3 He was able to play soccer very well before his knee surgery.

ⓐ ability ⓑ permission ⓒ possibility

4 If he is not at home, Tom might be at the game with his friends now.

ⓐ ability ⓑ request ⓒ possibility

5 Pardon me, but could you show me the way to the department store, please?

ⓐ ability ⓑ request ⓒ permission

C

주어진 문장을 해석하시오.

1 I'm sorry you can't go to the movies with us this weekend.

____

2 I am allowed to use my brother's computer.

____

3 She might be interested in this magazine.

____

4 Henry is being punished, so he can't talk to you.

____

2 조동사 will, must, shall

Pre-Check [ ] 안에서 알맞은 말을 고르시오.

A: [Will, Should] you get me a glass of water?

B: Sure. But you look so tired. I think you [will, should] get some rest.

A: I know, but I [must, must not] finish this work by tomorrow.

1 will

(1) 미래의 일/예견

He will be twenty next year.

She will arrive on time. She won't be late.

If there is anybody at the office now, it would be Jane.

(2) 의지/약속

Mom, don't worry. I'll be home at least before 8.

I'll not be late for class again.

I said I would finish the work by tomorrow.

(3) 요청

Will you please drop by my house?

Would you please pass me the butter, Mom?

(4) 과거의 습관

We would take a walk after dinner.

During the rainy season, we would sit by the window and talk for hours.

> 1
>
> (1) 미래의 일/예견: ~할 것이다 (단순미래)
> ~일 것이다 (추측)
>
> would
> will의 과거ⓐ vs. 약한 추측ⓑ
> ⓐ He said he would call me.
> ⓑ I think he would win the game.
>
> (2) 의지/약속: ~하겠다, ~할 것이다
>
> (3) 요청: ~해 주시겠어요?
> * 공손함: would > will
>
> (4) 과거의 습관: ~하곤 했다
> (과거에 행해진 습관이나 동작)
> * used to로 바꿔 쓸 수 있다.

2 must

(1) 필요/의무

I'm so tired. I must take a rest.

You must register if you want to take the course.

(= You have to register if you want to take the course.)

I failed the exam, so I had to take it again.

If I fail the exam, I will have to take it again.

(2) 금지

You must not talk to her.

(≠ You don't have to talk to her.)

You must not talk on a cell phone while driving.

> 2
>
> (1) must + V: ~해야 한다 (= have to)
> * must는 과거나 미래형이 없다.
> ∴ 과거 → had to
> 미래 → will have to
>
> (2) must not + V: ~해서는 안 된다 (금지)
> ≠ do not have to: ~할 필요 없다 (불필요)
> (= do not need to)

(3) 추측

It's already 8:30. He **must** be at school by now.
She's going to sell her bike! She **can't** be serious!
He missed the class yesterday. He **must have been** sick.
He looks great. He **must not have been** sick.

(3) 추측: ~임이 틀림없다
• 과거의 추측
must have p.p.: ~했음이 틀림없다
* 부정
(현재) can't/cannot (~일 리가 없다)
(과거) must not have p.p. (~했을 리가 없다)

3 shall & should

(1) 제안/제언

Shall we go to the movies?
What **shall I** do?

(2) 충고/권유

You **should** pay attention to the teacher in the class.
I think you **should** buy this shirt rather than that one.

(3) 의무

You **should** keep quiet in the class.
(= You ought to keep quiet in the class.)
We **should not** forget our mistake.
I **should have apologized** to him. It was my fault.
I **should not have apologized** to him. It was his fault.

3

(1) 제안/제언: (우리) ~ 할까요?
* 보통 1인칭을 써서 Shall I ~?, Shall we ~?와 같이 쓴다.

(2) 충고/권유: ~하는 게 좋겠다

(3) 의무
• should + V: ~해야 한다
should not + V: ~하면 안 된다
• should have p.p.: ~했어야 했다
should not have p.p.: ~하지 말았어야 했다
* should have p.p.의 형태는 과거에 하지 못한 일에 대한 후회를 나타낸다.
[참조] 각 조동사의 용법상의 차이에 대해서는 MUST-KNOW 참조

Check-up

Answers P.7

A 주어진 단어를 이용하여 문장을 완성하시오.

1 Cindy said she ______________(would, bring) cookies to the party.
2 ______________(shall, sit, we) here or over there by the door?
3 ______________(you, will, mail) this letter for me, please?
4 People ______________(not, must, drive) when they are drunk.

B [ ] 안에서 알맞은 말을 고르시오. (복수 정답 가능)

A You don't seem to plan your weekends at all this summer. Did you go out on weekends last summer?
B Well, on sunny weekends, I ① [would, used to] drive to the beach.
A I didn't know you had a car.
B I ② [would, used to] have my own car back then. Anyway, I ③ [would, used to] go there with my dog and spend all day playing with him.

would vs. used to
would는 행위나 동작이 아닌 상태를 나타내는 경우에는 사용하지 않는다. used to는 used to be나 used to have라고 하여 과거의 습관적인 상태를 표현할 수 있지만 would를 쓸 경우 He would be sick.처럼 과거의 습관이 아닌 '그는 아플 것이다'라는 뜻의 미래의 뜻이 될 수도 있다.

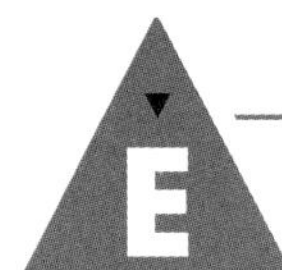

EXERCISE

Answers P.7

A

[ ] 안에서 알맞은 말을 고르시오.

1 Here's good news! We [don't have to, must not] finish the project by next week.

2 When you reach the gate, you [must be, must] show your ID.

3 Everyone [has to, has to not] arrive before we begin the program.

4 Why do I [would, have to] go? I don't want to see it.

5 If you eat spoiled food, you [will have to, will must] see a doctor.

6 You [won't, mustn't] open your book until you are told to do so.

B

밑줄 친 부분을 바르게 고쳐 쓰시오. 틀리지 않았다면 ○표 하시오.

1 You <u>had to</u> watch out when you buy things over the Internet. ____________

2 You <u>don't have to</u> bring a dog to school. It is against the rules. ____________

3 She <u>must be</u> very busy when I called her the other night. ____________

4 You <u>should</u> try this recipe! It is for a delicious mushroom soup. ____________

5 Since I don't have money for a hotel yesterday, I <u>must</u> sleep in the car. ____________

6 John was coughing hard this morning. I <u>should</u> buy him some medicine. ____________

C

주어진 단어를 이용하여 문장을 완성하시오.

1 이 영화는 꼭 봐야 해. 안 보면 후회할 거야. (should, see)
→ You ____________________. You might be sorry if you don't.

2 나는 어렸을 때 몇 시간씩 축구를 하곤 했다. (would, play)
→ As a young child, I ____________________ for hours.

3 우리 내일 뭐 할까? 박물관에 갈까? (shall, do)
→ ____________________ tomorrow? Shall we go to the museum?

4 오하이오로 이사를 간다고? 농담하는 거지? (must, be, kid)
→ You are going to move to Ohio? You ____________________!

5 금요일에 있을 깜짝 파티에 관해 엄마한테 말해선 안 돼. (must, tell)
→ You ____________________ Mom about the surprise party on Friday.

Unit 03

3 기타 조동사

Pre-Check [보기]에서 알맞은 말을 골라 빈칸에 써 넣으시오.

Word Bank would rather / used to / had better

1 There __________ be a tall tree over there.
2 You __________ fasten your seat belt for your own safety.
3 I __________ have juice than coffee.

1 과거의 습관: used to

I used to go to the coffee shop at lunch time.
(→ I don't go to the coffee shop at lunch time anymore.)
She used to drink warm milk before going to bed.
Where did you use to go shopping before you moved?
We didn't use to go swimming in the evening.

cf) I would go to the coffee shop whenever I had nothing to do.
She would drink warm milk when(ever) she couldn't fall asleep.

1
used to + V
: ~하곤 했으나 더 이상 …않는다, 이전에는 ~이었다
• 의문문: Did + S + use to ~?
• 부정문: S + didn't use to

used to/would: 과거의 반복적 행동이나 동작
* 과거의 '상태'를 나타낼 때는 would를 쓰지 않는다.
There ~~would be~~ a school. (x)
There used to be a school. (o)

2 충고: had better

You had better stay home until the rain stops.
Before you leave your room, you'd better clean it.

cf) You should clean your room.
You ought to clean your room.

You'd better not eat junk food.
You'd better not be late for the seminar.
Had I better leave now?

2
had better + V: ~하는 게 좋겠다

cf) had better는 충고를 따르지 않았을 경우 나쁜 결과가 생길 수 있음을 암시한다. 따라서 should나 ought to 보다 의미가 강하다.

• 부정문: S + had better not + V
• 의문문: Had + S + better + V~?

3 선호: would rather ~ (than)

I would rather go with you than stay here with her.
I'd rather stay home and watch TV. It's so cold outside.

I'd rather not go to the meeting this time.
I'd rather not go to the concert. It's terrible.

3
would rather + V (than)
: (~보다) …하는 게 낫다
• 부정문: S + would rather not + V
• 의문문: Would + S + rather + V

4 필요: need

(1) Need we change money into dollars?
(= Do we need to change money into dollars?)
We needn't go to the camp this year.
(= We don't need[have] to go to the camp this year.)

(2) We didn't need to fill in the form.
* We needed not fill in the form.(x)

▶ 4
need + V: ~할 필요가 있다
• 부정문: S + need not[needn't]
* 조동사 need는 부정문과 의문문에서 주로 쓰인다. 긍정문에는 주로 need to 또는 have to를 사용한다.

(2) 조동사 need는 과거형이 없다. 따라서 본동사를 이용한다.

5 과거 추측을 나타내는 조동사

He must have seen me. He turned back and ran away.
She may have taken the bus. I'm not sure how she got there.
If I had had more money, I might have bought a laptop computer than a cell phone.
You could have reached the airport on time if you had taken a taxi.

▶ 5
must have p.p.: ~했음이 틀림없다
may have p.p.: ~했을지도 모른다
might have p.p.: ~했을지도 모르다
could have p.p.: ~했을 수도 있다 (하지 못했다)

Check-up

Answers P.7

A 주어진 문장을 조건에 맞게 바꿔 쓰시오.

1 They would rather come here.
→ They ______________________ here. (부정문으로)

2 You had better not bring rice and chicken.
→ You ______________________ rice and chicken. (긍정문으로)

3 I would rather go to the meeting.
→ I ______________________ go to the meeting. (need를 사용해서 부정문으로)

B [보기]에서 밑줄 친 단어와 바꿔 쓸 수 있는 것을 고르시오.

① a. had better	b. would rather
② a. had better	b. would rather

A Are you having your friends over to your place tonight?
B I have two exams on Monday. So, I ① should not have them over.
A Still, you will have to eat something for dinner, right? I will order some food for you. How about some steak?
B I'm not that hungry now. I ② will have something light instead.

had better vs. would rather
'~하는 편이 낫다'의 had better는 should의 의미이고 '차라리 ~하는 게 좋다'의 would rather는 prefer의 뜻으로 의미상 약간의 차이가 있다.

EXERCISE

Answers P.7

A

[ ] 안에서 알맞은 말을 고르시오.

1 You [had better not, shall not] forget your grandfather's birthday. He would be disappointed.

2 I [need to, would rather] dance to this group's music than any other group's.

3 [You'd better, You'd used to] go to a Broadway show while in New York City.

4 I [would rather, used to] stay home than go to the movies?

5 They [might have opened, mustn't have opened] our mail by mistake because their address is similar to ours.

B

밑줄 친 부분을 바르게 고쳐 쓰시오. 틀리지 않았다면 ○표 하시오.

1 We better get gas for the car tonight, not tomorrow morning. ____________

2 I'd rather not going to the meeting tonight, if you don't mind. ____________

3 I don't know how he found out about it. He might hear about it from my friend. ____________

4 The farmers need to harvest the crops before winter comes. ____________

5 My roommate aced all his courses this semester. He must study hard. ____________

6 You can't afford to pay that much money. You should consider buying the dress. ____________

C

밑줄 친 단어를 참고하고, 주어진 말을 이용하여 문장을 완성하시오.

1 A We took a bus, but it only took us one minute to get there.
B So, you ____________________(need, not) the bus.

2 A Do you go swimming these days?
B Well, I ____________________(used to) regularly, but not these days.

3 A I asked my friends what happened last night. But nobody knew.
B Judy knows what happened. You ____________________(had better) her.

4 A I have not handed in the paper yet. It is not due until tomorrow morning.
B But to be safe, you ____________________(had better, it) today.

5 A Do you want to have either Tom or Jane here tomorrow?
B Since Tom lives closer, I ____________________ him (would rather) here tomorrow.

Answers P.8

A

[ ] 안에서 알맞은 말을 고르시오

1 We [will, need] not be able to complete this project by tomorrow afternoon.

2 Look! There are so many emergency vehicles. The accident [must be, can't be] serious.

3 Excuse me, [may, would] you help me with this?

4 I [would rather not, don't need to] go to the movie. I have tons of work to do.

5 [Must, May] I see your passport and another form of identification, please?

6 We [must not, need not] fill out a new form because I kept a copy of the old one.

7 The cell phone was defective. She [should have returned, must have returned] it, but she didn't.

8 I haven't got my package yet. It [might have been, should be] delivered to the wrong address.

B

빈칸에 들어갈 알맞은 말을 고르시오.

1 He hasn't called me back. He ______________ be angry with me.

ⓐ will　　ⓑ must　　ⓒ have to　　ⓓ had better

2 You ______________ hurry. We have enough time to catch the train.

ⓐ must　　ⓑ can't　　ⓓ may need　　ⓓ don't have to

3 Everyone ______________ master a foreign language if they try hard.

ⓐ can　　ⓑ must　　ⓒ had better　　ⓓ wouldn't be

4 There ______________ a gas station around the corner. But I'm not sure if it's still there.

ⓐ would be　　ⓑ used to be　　ⓒ need to be　　ⓓ would rather be

5 ______________ meet at the movie theater tonight?

ⓐ Let　　ⓑ Shall we　　ⓒ What about　　ⓓ Had you

6 She ______________ shocked to hear about the accident. She fainted.

ⓐ had to　　ⓑ must be　　ⓒ must have been　　ⓓ wouldn't rather not

7 You ______________ prepare dinner for everyone because some people might leave early.

ⓐ shall　　ⓑ have to　　ⓒ wouldn't　　ⓓ need not

R REVIEW TEST

C

밑줄 친 부분을 바르게 고쳐 문장을 다시 쓰시오.

1 Need he <u>pays</u> for this right away?

→ ______________________________

2 I <u>am</u> able to play three instruments when I was in high school.

→ ______________________________

3 Rachel, <u>may</u> you lend me $20?

→ ______________________________

4 I <u>would not rather</u> talk to her in person because she's very rude to everyone.

→ ______________________________

5 We couldn't start the game since there <u>is</u> no ball.

→ ______________________________

D

(A), (B), (C)의 각 네모 안에서 어법에 맞는 말로 바르게 짝지어진 것을 고르시오.

Sometimes people get angry because of politics. But Will Rogers (A) [is able to / was able to] make people laugh about it. He was a famous American. He was a wise and funny cowboy from Oklahoma. He (B) [could / had to] talk about anything and make people think while they laughed. He would not support one political party publicly. He advised all politicians to do the right thing. He said they (C) [should / could] work hard instead of talking so much.

	(A)		(B)		(C)
①	is able to	…	could	…	should
②	is able to	…	had to	…	should
③	is able to	…	had to	…	could
④	was able to	…	could	…	should
⑤	was able to	…	had to	…	could

FURTHER STUDY

Writing

▶▶ 우리말과 같은 뜻이 되도록 주어진 단어를 이용하여 문장을 완성하시오.

1 나는 차라리 다른 버스 스케줄을 알아보겠다. (find, another bus schedule)

→ I'd ____.

2 나는 전등 불빛 때문에 잠을 잘 수가 없었다. (could, because of, the lamplight)

→ I ____.

3 법에 따르면 당신은 그 컴퓨터 소프트웨어를 판매해서는 안 된다. (must, the computer software)

→ The law says that ______________________ the computer software.

4 그는 결코 오후 회의에 제시간에 도착할 수 없을 것이다. (never, be able to, arrive, on time)

→ He ______________________________ for the afternoon meeting.

5 그녀는 토요일까지 새 아파트로 이사 가야 한다. (ought to, move into, her new apartment)

→ She ______________________________ by Saturday.

6 제가 가방을 방까지 옮겨다 드릴까요? (shall, carry your bags)

→ ______________________________ to your room?

7 그녀는 디저트로 호박 파이보다 초콜릿 케이크를 만들고 싶어 한다. (would rather, make, a chocolate cake)

→ ______________________________ for dessert than a pumpkin pie.

8 당신은 그 서류들을 보관할 필요가 없다. 차라리 그것들을 재활용하는 것이 낫다.
(have to, keep, the papers, recycle)

→ You ____________________. You ____________________ them.

MUST-KNOW

▶ 조동사의 의미별 정리

	예문	쓰임
Probability 가능성	• It's already 7:20. They **must be** in Spain by now. • She looks happy. She **must have done** well on the test. • That **must be** John. He said he would come around this time.	〈추측의 정도〉 • 현재의 추측 : must > may/might • 현재 부정의 추측 : can't > may not/might not • 과거의 추측 : must have > may have/might have
	• You **can't be** serious! • They **couldn't have worked** until late.	
	• Jane **could be** at school. • Peter **could have arrived** late.	
	• Joan **may invite** Thomas to the contest. • Edward **might come** this evening. • Jack **might have gone** to Rome.	
Ability 능력	• She **can play** the piano. = She **is able to play** the piano	can: ~할 수 있다 = am/are/is (be의 현재) able to
	• She **could play** the piano. = She **was able to play** the piano.	could: ~할 수 있었다 = was/were (be의 과거) able to
	• I **will** never **be able to lift** the box alone.	can의 미래= will be able to
Necessity 필요	• You **must leave** right away. • You **have to leave** right away. • You **ought to call** your mother. • You **should call** your mother.	must: ~해야 한다 have to: ~ 해야 한다 ought to: ~ 해야 한다 should: ~해야 한다
	• We **don't have to** pay to use it. • We **needn't stay** here.	don't have to: ~할 필요가 없다 needn't +동사원형: ~할 필요가 없다
Permission/ Prohibition 허락/금지	• You **can come in**. = You **are allowed to come in**. • You **may leave** now.	can/may : ~해도 된다, ~해도 좋다
	• You **cannot leave**. • You **must not leave**. = You **are not allowed to leave**. • You **may not leave**.	cannot/must not/may not : ~하면 안 된다, ~할 수 없다
Request 요청	• **May** I **see** your passport, please? • **Could** I **see** your passport, please? • **Can** I **see** your passport, please?	may/could 〉can (May/Could I~?가 공손한 표현)
	• **Would** you **tell** me the way, please? • **Could** you **tell** me the way, please? • **Can** you **tell** me the way, please? • **Will** you **tell** me the way, please?	would/could 〉can/will (Would/Could you ~?가 공손한 표현)

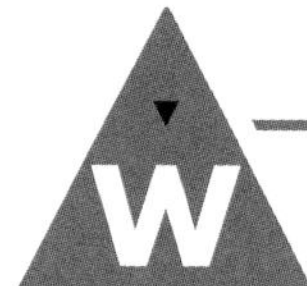

WRAP-UP TEST

Answers P.9

1 빈칸에 들어갈 수 없는 말을 고르시오.

_______ you show me the ticket?

ⓐ Will ⓑ Can
ⓒ Could ⓓ Should

2 밑줄 친 부분과 바꿔 쓸 수 있는 말을 고르시오.

You don't have to whisper. Please say it louder.

ⓐ won't ⓑ can't
ⓒ need not ⓓ had better not

3 우리말과 같은 뜻이 되도록 빈칸에 들어갈 말을 고르시오.

You _______ take a picture here.
(이곳에서는 사진을 찍어서는 안 됩니다.)

ⓐ may not ⓑ must not
ⓒ need not ⓓ don't have to

4 말하는 사람의 의도가 나머지와 다른 하나를 고르시오.

ⓐ The boy should see a doctor.
ⓑ The boy had better see a doctor.
ⓒ The boy ought to see a doctor.
ⓓ The boy might see a doctor.

5 밑줄 친 부분의 쓰임이 잘못된 것을 고르시오.

ⓐ He must be from Italy.
ⓑ That can't be Susan. She has gone to Paris.
ⓒ Don't download the file. It might be infected with a virus.
ⓓ There would be a temple around here.

6 밑줄 친 부분과 쓰임이 같은 것을 고르시오.

My grandfather would take a nap after lunch.

ⓐ Would you use this copy machine?
ⓑ My friend and I would get together after school.
ⓒ I would lock the door if I were you.
ⓓ I said I would tell you later.

7 밑줄 친 부분의 쓰임이 나머지와 다른 하나를 고르시오.

ⓐ Can it be true?
ⓑ May I speak to John?
ⓒ Could you open the door, please?
ⓓ Will you lend me your umbrella?

8 질문에 대한 응답이 될 수 없는 것을 고르시오.

A Do you know where Mark is?
B _______

ⓐ You'd better ask his roommate.
ⓑ He might have gone to the tennis club.
ⓒ He should have been at home.
ⓓ I think he'll be here in ten minutes.

[9-10] 글을 읽고, 물음에 답하시오.

Many people have thought of ways to save energy. One way is to turn off the lights at home that you are not using. Now a new "light emitting diode bulb (LED)" ___ⓐ___ help you to save more energy. If you use one, it ___ⓑ___ use two-thirds less energy. It will last ten times longer, too. People ___ⓒ___ use this new energy-efficient light bulb. If you use ten bulbs, you ___ⓓ___ save over $200 a year in energy costs!

9 질문에 대한 알맞은 답을 쓰시오.

How much money we can save a year if we use LED bulbs?

→ We can save _______ a year.

10 빈칸에 들어갈 말이 바르게 연결되지 않은 것을 고르시오.

ⓐ can ⓑ will
ⓒ used to ⓓ can

The Grammar

2
Level

부정사

1 to부정사의 명사적 쓰임
2 to부정사의 부사적 쓰임
3 to부정사의 형용사적 쓰임
4 기타 부정사의 쓰임

to부정사의 명사적 쓰임

Pre-Check 밑줄 친 말을 이용하여 빈칸에 공통으로 들어갈 말을 써 넣으시오.

- I read comic books. Comic books are fun.

1 ________________ comic books is fun.
2 I want ________________ comic books.
3 My hobby is ________________ comic books.

1 명사처럼 주어 역할을 하는 부정사

English is very important. To learn English is very important. To speak English is very important.

To read detective stories is fun.
To write detective stories is fun.

cf) It is fun to read detective stories.
It is fun to write detective stories.

1
to부정사는 명사처럼 문장에서 주어, 목적어, 보어 역할을 한다. to부정사를 사용함으로써 명사만으로는 부족한 의미를 보충할 수 있다.

to부정사 + V (← 주어 자리)

cf) to부정사 + 동사 ~
= It ~ to부정사

• 주어가 길어질 경우, It을 가주어로 한 It ~ to부정사구를 사용한다.

2 명사처럼 목적어 역할을 하는 부정사

She likes Italian food. She likes to eat Italian food. She likes to cook Italian food.

We need to find a book about the earth's history.
We need to borrow a book about the earth's history.

cf) You'll find it difficult to read the book.

2
S + V + to부정사 (← 목적어 자리)

• to부정사의 부정: not[never] + to부정사

He decided not to play computer games.

• to부정사를 목적어로 취하는 동사 want, like, wish, need, decide, plan, promise 등 [MUST-KNOW 참조]

cf) find, think, believe 등의 동사를 사용한 문장에서 목적어 자리의 to부정사가 길어질 경우, 그 자리에 가목적어 it을 쓰고 to부정사를 뒤로 보낸 것으로 이해할 수 있다.

3 명사처럼 보어 역할을 하는 부정사

His favorite hobby is ice hockey. His favorite hobby is to play ice hockey. His favorite hobby is to watch ice hockey.

I consider her to be a great ballerina.
I believe her to be a world-famous ballerina.

3
• 주격보어: S + V + to부정사
목적격 보어: S + V + O + to부정사
• to부정사가 주어나 목적어를 보충 설명한다.

4 의문사 + to부정사

(1) I'm not sure **what to wear** to the party.
(= I'm not sure what I should wear to the party.)

Please tell me **how to solve** this problem.
(= Please tell me how I should solve this problem.)

(2) Show me **what book to read**.
(= Show me what book I should read.)

I don't know **how many books to buy**.
(= I don't know how many books I should buy.)

4

(1) 의문사 + to부정사
= 의문사 + 주어 + should + 동사원형

〈의문사 + to부정사〉는 명사구로서 주로 know, tell, show, decide 등의 목적어로 쓰인다.

- what to부정사: 무엇을 ~해야 할지
- where to부정사: 어디로 ~해야 할지
- how to부정사: 어떻게 ~해야 할지
- when to부정사: 언제 ~해야 할지

(2) what/which + 명사 + to부정사
: 어떤 것을 ~해야 할지

how many + 명사 + to부정사
: 얼마나 많은 …을 ~해야 할지

Check-up

Answers P.9

A 주어진 문장을 to부정사 문장으로 바꿔 쓰시오.

1 I'm going to a summer camp. It will be exciting.
→ ______________________ to a summer camp will be exciting.

2 I draw paintings. I tend to use many bright colors.
→ I like ______________________ with many bright colors.

3 He put the books on the table for me.
→ Did you ask him ______________________ on the table?

4 There will be a parade this weekend. She likes to watch parades.
→ One of her favorite things to do is ______________________.

B 「의문사 + to부정사」를 이용하여 대화를 완성하시오.

A Don't forget you have a meeting tomorrow. Do you know where you're going to meet your coworkers?

B I'm not sure ① ____________ meet them. I haven't heard anything about the meeting place yet.

A Find out who you should call for information.

B I know ② ______________. Anyway, have you decided which articles you want to read?

A I haven't decided ③ ______________ yet since there are so many.

의문사 + to부정사
to부정사는 미래의 의미를 갖는다. '무엇을 해야 할지', '언제 하는 것이 좋은지', '어떤 것을 하고 싶은지', '어떻게 할 예정인지' 등은 모두 미래의 뜻을 내포하고 있다.

Answers P.9

EXERCISE

A

밑줄 친 단어를 to부정사로 바꿔 문장을 완성하시오.

1 Sally was late for the last meeting, and she doesn't want __________ late this time.

2 I hoped __________ a kitty, but my mom bought me a dog.

3 My uncle can build a house. He plans __________ my mom a new house.

4 He wants to go to Harvard. __________ to Harvard is his dream.

5 He ended up inviting too many people. His original plan was __________ five people.

6 Did you buy a gift for Susan? I don't know what __________ for her.

7 I'm struggling to solve this problem. Please tell me how __________ it.

B

밑줄 친 부분을 바르게 고쳐 쓰시오. 틀리지 않았다면 ○표 하시오.

1 My plan is to bought a dress like this one. __________

2 She expected get a cell phone as her birthday gift. __________

3 It is not possible to move next week. __________

4 To join a club is a good activity for students. __________

5 We decided to not miss the movie this time. __________

6 We don't know how many people invite to the party yet. __________

7 Have you decided where go to for your summer vacation? __________

C

주어진 문장을 「It ~ to부정사」 문장으로 바꿔 쓰시오.

1 To forgive quickly is important.

→ ______________________________

2 To make new friends is exciting.

→ ______________________________

3 To be kind to others is great.

→ ______________________________

4 To eat junk food late at night is bad for your health.

→ ______________________________

5 To exercise regularly is necessary for a healthy life.

→ ______________________________

Unit 2 to부정사의 부사적 쓰임

Pre-Check 주어진 단어를 우리말에 맞게 바꿔 쓰시오.

1 I went to the concert ________________(do) my music homework. (음악 숙제를 하기 위해)

2 My sister came with me ________________(meet) her favorite singer. (가수를 만나려고)

3 It was wonderful ________________(hear) such a beautiful song. (멋진 노래를 들으니)

1 목적을 나타내는 to부정사

(1) I always wear black jeans to look skinny.
He went out of my room to get some fresh air.
I called the hotel to book a room.
(= I called the hotel in order to book a room.)
(= I called the hotel so as to book a room.)

(2) They hurried not to be late for the concert.
He walked on tiptoe not to wake up the baby.
(= He walked on tiptoe in order not to wake up the baby.)
(= He walked on tiptoe so as not to wake up the baby.)

> 1
> (1) ~하기 위해
> = in order to ~
> = so as to ~
> (2) ~하지 않기 위해
> = not[never] + to부정사
> = in order not to ~
> = so as not to ~

2 결과를 나타내는 to부정사

(1) He grew up to be a famous entertainer.
(= He grew up, and he became a famous entertainer.)

(2) She studied hard (only) to fail the exam.
(= She studied hard, but she failed the exam.)

> 2
> (1) …해서 (결국) ~하다
> = A ~, and B ...
> (2) …하지만 결국 ~했다
> = A ~, but B ...
> * only나 never를 써서 to부정사를 강조할 수 있다

3 원인, 조건, 이유, 판단을 나타내는 to부정사

(1) We are happy to hear from you.
He was surprised to meet his ex-girlfriend in the street.

(2) They laughed loudly to see her funny hat.
She must be rich to wear such a nice dress.

(3) You will be astonished to taste this food.
(= You will be astonished if you taste this food.)
You will love to listen to Beatles' songs.
(= You will love them if you listen to Beatles' songs.)

> 3
> (1) 원인: ~하게 되어서 …하다
> * 감정 표현 형용사
> glad, happy, angry, sorry, excited, delighted 등
> (2) 이유: ~하다니, ~하는 것을 보니
> (3) 조건: 만약 ~한다면 …할 것이다
> * 주로 조동사 will과 사용되는 경우가 많다.

4 형용사를 수식하는 to부정사

This book is difficult **to read**.
This food is safe **to eat**.
The river is dangerous **to swim in**.

5 기타 부사적 용법

(1) I'm **too** weak **to** lift these dumbbells.
(= I'm so weak that I can't lift these dumbbells.)

(2) She studied hard **enough to** get an A.
(= She studied so hard that she could get an A.)

(3) We went to the concert **in order to** relieve stress.
(= We went to the concert so that we could relieve stress.)

4
~하기에 …하다, ~하는 데 …하다
(형용사 + to부정사)

5
(1) too ... to ~
= so ... that S can't~
: 너무 …해서 ~할 수 없다

(2) enough to ~
= so ... that S can~
: ~할 정도로 (충분히) …하다

(3) in order to ~: ~하기 위해서
= so ... that S can~
* 주절 동사의 시제와 that절 동사의 시제를 일치시킨다.

Check-up

Answers P.9

A 주어진 문장을 to부정사 문장으로 바꿔 쓰시오.

1 She gives us very special food on holidays.
→ She cooks turkey ________________ us on Thanksgiving Day.

2 The storm lessened and then became worse again.
→ The storm lessened only ________________ worse again.

3 My friends ate at this restaurant, and they were amazed at the food.
→ My friends were amazed ________________ at this restaurant.

4 He has not discovered that she is gone now.
→ He will be sorry ________________ that she is not here any longer.

B 밑줄 친 부분에 유의하여 문장의 의미를 바르게 나타낸 것을 고르시오.

1 They practiced hard, only to lose the game.
ⓐ They practiced hard in order to lose the game. ⓑ They practiced hard, but they lost the game.

2 We ran fast to catch the bus.
ⓐ We ran fast in order to catch the bus. ⓑ We ran fast, but we couldn't catch the bus.

to부정사의 결과 vs. to부정사의 목적
to부정사의 부사적 용법에서 목적인지 결과인지를 구분하는 이유는 자연스러운 우리말 해석을 위해서인데, 그 차이는 문맥에 있다. 경기에 '지기 위해' 열심히 연습하지는 않는다. 열심히 연습했음에도 진 것이다. 이처럼, '목적'이냐 '결과'이냐는 문맥을 잘 살펴 그 문장이 전달하려는 바에 따라 충실하게 해석하는 것이 좋다.

EXERCISE

Answers P.10

A

[보기]에서 알맞은 말을 골라 어법에 맞게 바꿔 대화를 완성하시오.

Word Bank	work	witness	lose	hear	drive	miss	know

1 A Here is a Christmas card from the Smith family.
B Oh, it's great __________ from them again.

2 A He always brings his own computer.
B Yes, he always brings his laptop __________.

3 A What happened to Sam?
B He was shocked __________ the accident near the theater.

4 A They played hard, only __________ the championship game.
B That's too bad. I wish them better luck next year.

5 A What did the teacher say?
B She said everyone might be surprised __________ the results of the exam.

6 A When are you going to get up?
B I'm going to get up early in order not __________ the first bus.

7 A I'm too sleepy __________ any further.
B Why don't you pull over for a while?

B

주어진 표현을 이용하여 문장을 완성하시오.

1 He eats fruit and vegetables to stay healthy. (so that)
→ He eats fruit and vegetables __________.

2 She wears sunglasses to look fashionable. (in order to)
→ She wears sunglasses __________.

3 You are so young that you can't enter the contest this year. (too ~ to)
→ You are __________ this year.

4 My dog is so quiet that he can sleep in my room at night. (enough to)
→ My dog is __________ in my room at night.

5 My aunt arrives on Monday to celebrate my parents' 25th wedding anniversary. (so that)
→ My aunt arrives on Monday __________.

3 to부정사의 형용사적 쓰임

Pre-Check [보기]에서 알맞은 말을 골라 빈칸에 써 넣으시오.

Word Bank	to stay	to drink	cold	available

1 ① I want something ________________. (차가운 것)
② I want something ________________. (마실 것)

2 ① There are no rooms ________________. (이용할 수 있는 방)
② We need a room ________________ in tonight. (머무를 방)

1 형용사처럼 명사를 수식하는 부정사: 명사 + to부정사

There are heavy boxes on the floor.
There are many boxes to carry.

I have good news to share.
He has three books to read this week.

I need someone to help me.
She wanted something cold to drink.

Is there anything to eat?
There is nothing to eat.

2 주의해야 할 형용사적 쓰임

(1) The homeless don't have houses to live in. (live in a house)
He needed someone to talk to. (talk to someone)

(2) I have nothing to write with. (write "with pencils")
I have nothing to write on. (write "on the paper")

3 형용사처럼 주어를 설명하는 부정사

Sue is unhappy with the course.
Sue is to drop it next week.

(1) Everybody is to come in.
(= Everybody can come in.)

(2) She was never to see her roommate again.
(= She was destined never to see her roommate again.)

1
부정사는 명사/대명사 뒤에서 수식한다.

-thing + 형용사 + to부정사
someone, something, anything 등의 대명사 뒤에 형용사가 올 때는 to부정사가 형용사 뒤에서 수식한다.
I want something cold to drink.

2
(1) sit on, talk to, agree with, agree on, consist of 등 한 단어로 취급되는 동사구들은 전치사를 빼먹지 않도록 주의한다.
(2) 전치사에 따라 의미가 달라지는 동사는 문맥에 맞게 사용해야 한다.

3
be to의 용법
(1) 가능: ~할 수 있다 (can)
(2) 운명: ~할 운명이다 (be destined to)

(3) I am to finish the project by this month.
(= I have to finish the project by this month.)

(4) We are to join the club next week.
(= We are going to join the club next week.)

(5) If you are to be there on time, please take a taxi.
(= If you intend to be there on time, please take a taxi.)

(3) 의무: ~ 해야 한다 (have to)
(4) 예정: ~할 예정이다 (be going to)
(5) 의도, 조건: ~하려면 (if)
* be to부정사 용법은 명사적 용법(보어)으로 사용되는 경우와 비슷하므로 문맥을 잘 구별해야 한다.

Check-up

Answers P.10

A 주어진 단어를 알맞게 배열하여 문장을 완성하시오.

1 The little girl wants dolls ______________________(to, with, play).
2 The teacher needs ______________________(to, someone, fix) her computer.
3 Did he decide on ______________________(to, stay in, a hotel)?
4 I have nothing in life ______________________(complain, to, about).
5 They ______________________(to, are, leave) the country next week.

B 빈칸에 들어갈 알맞은 말을 고르시오.

A Can you stay here for a while?
B Well, I have ① ______________________ to take care of at home.
A Then, I will talk to you later since you have ② ______________________ to take care of.

① a. some things urgent b. some urgent things
② a. something urgent b. urgent something

형용사의 명사 수식
형용사는 명사의 앞에서 그 명사를 수식하게 된다. 그리고 to부정사가 형용사와 같이 명사를 수식하는 경우에는 형용사의 뒤에서 그 명사를 수식한다. 하지만 명사와는 달리 명사를 대신하는 대명사의 경우에는 형용사가 그 앞에서 대명사를 수식하지 않는다. I want a cold drink.(o)에서는 cold가 drink를 앞에서 수식하지만 I want cold it.(x)과 같이 cold가 대명사 it의 앞에서 수식하지 않는다. some things라고 할 때 some은 형용사이고 thing은 명사로 some cold things와 같이 사용하지만 something은 대명사이기 때문에 cold something과 같이 사용하지 않는다.

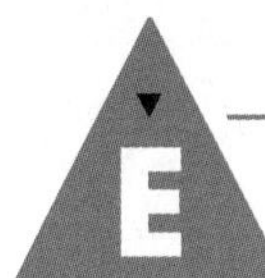

EXERCISE

Answers P.10

A

[보기]에서 알맞은 말을 골라 문장을 완성하시오.

Word Bank about with to for up

1 Mary has nothing but an American history test to study ______________.

2 This part of the highway has a steep hill to drive ______________.

3 The funny TV program was really something to laugh ______________.

4 My mom is my favorite person to talk ______________.

5 Is Peter the best one in the office to work ______________?

B

[보기]와 같이 문장을 완성하시오.

Example Her dream was to own a small restaurant.
→ Her dream <u>to own a small restaurant</u> came true.

1 My teacher told the class to do the assignments over the weekend.
→ I didn't know there were assignments ______________ over the weekend.

2 My plan was to visit my sister during the break.
→ My parents didn't like my plan ______________ during the break.

3 I have to write about something, but I can't think of anything interesting.
→ I'm still looking for a topic ______________.

C

주어진 단어를 알맞게 배열하여 문장을 완성하시오.

1 eat out / to / is / at the Italian restaurant.
→ My family ______________________________.

2 someone / to work with / positive
→ We need ______________________________.

3 is looking for / to stay / a hotel / in
→ He ______________________________ for a couple of days.

4 to leave / for / the train
→ It's time ______________________________.

5 big / for us / to get in / enough
→ Jim's old car is ______________________________.

기타 부정사의 쓰임

Pre-Check 우리말과 일치하도록 빈칸에 알맞은 말을 써 넣으시오.

1 It is very kind ______________ you to help us. (네가 친절하다)
2 It is very difficult ______________ her to prepare things by herself. (그녀에게는 어렵다)
3 My mother made her ______________ the dishes. (설거지를 하게 했다)

1 to부정사의 의미상 주어

(1) 주어가 to부정사의 주어
She wants to lose some weight.
They planned to travel by car.

(2) 목적어가 to부정사의 주어
She wants her boyfriend to be more punctual.
I told her to stop watching TV late at night.

(3) to부정사의 주어가 특정인일 때
It isn't easy for me to finish it in one day.
It is nice of him to help your younger brother.

(4) to부정사의 주어가 일반인일 때
It is always enjoyable (for people) to listen to urban legends.
It is not desirable (for people) to jaywalk.

1

형용사 종류에 따른 의미상의 주어
• 일반 형용사 + for + 목적격
(↑ hard, difficult, important 등)
• 칭찬/비난의 형용사 + of + 목적격
(↑ kind, nice, wise, silly, polite, careful, careless 등)

2 부정사의 시제

(1) He wants us to come to the party.
My mom asked me to do the laundry.

(2) He seems to be hardworking.
(= It seems that he is hardworking.)
It seemed to be raining.
(= It seemed that it was raining.)

(3) Jason is sorry to have been late again.
(= Jason is sorry that he was late again.)
Jason was sorry to have been late.
(= Jason was sorry that he had been late.)

2

(1) 단순 시제: to부정사
(본동사의 시제와 같거나 미래의 시제)
(2) 진행 시제: to be + V-ing
(진행 중인 동작)
(3) 완료 시제: to have + p.p.
(본동사의 시제보다 이전의 시제)

3 사역동사 have, make, let, help

The teacher **had** Harry do the project.
Harry **made** his brother do the project.
Harry's mother **let** Harry help his brother with the project.
Harry's father **helped** him (to) do the project, too.

cf) I **had** my bike repaired.
Larry **had** his hair cut.

4 지각동사 see, hear, feel, smell

I **saw** Daniel come in.
Through the telescope, Ted **watched** the stars move in the sky.
Emily **heard** the dishes rattle in the kitchen.
I **heard** Jake walk out of the room again.
Did you **feel** the ground shake 10 minutes ago?
I **felt** a bug crawl up my arm.

3

사역동사 + 목적어(사람) + 원형부정사
: (누가) ~하게 하다

* help + 목적어 + 원형부정사/to부정사
* get + 목적어 + to부정사

Mr. Fish got him to do another project.

cf) 사역동사 + 목적어(사물) + 과거분사
: (무엇이) ~되도록 하다

목적어가 사물인 경우, 그 사물이 어떤 것으로 인해 특정 행위를 '당하는' 것이므로 원형이 아닌 과거분사형을 쓴다.
「Unit 6. 분사」 참조

4

지각동사 + 목적어 + 원형부정사
(↑ see, look at, watch, observe, hear, listen to, smell, feel 등)

지각동사 + 목적어 + 현재분사

I saw Daniel coming in.

목적어가 사람[동물]인 경우, 그 사람[동물]이 특정 행위를 하는 주체일 때는 진행의 의미를 강조하기 위해 현재분사로 쓰기도 한다.
「Unit 6. 분사」 참조

Check-up

Answers P.10

A 밑줄 친 동사를 이용하여 문장을 완성하시오.

1 James painted the fence. His father had him ______________ it.
2 He said he didn't play the guitar last night. But I heard him ______________ the guitar.
3 My mom is washing the dishes alone. I should help her ______________ the dishes.
4 The dolphins jumped several times, but Karen didn't see them ______________.
5 We have done five experiments this week, but the teacher made us ______________ another one.

B [ ] 안에서 알맞은 말을 고르시오.

1 I had the repairman [fix, fixed] my computer.
I had my computer [fix, fixed].
2 My mom made me [squeeze, squeezed] the orange.
My mom had the orange [squeeze, squeezed].

사역동사의 목적격보어: 동사원형 vs. 과거분사

사역동사를 쓰는 문장에서 목적어의 뒤가 동사원형인지 과거분사가 되는지는 철저히 그 목적어의 입장에 달려 있다. 목적어가 그 행위를 하는 것이면 동사원형을 사용해서 능동의 형태를 만들고, 목적어가 그 행위를 당하는 것이면 과거분사를 써서 수동의 형태를 만든다.

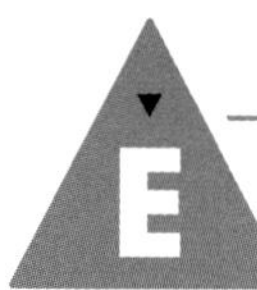

EXERCISE

Answers P.10

A

밑줄 친 단어를 이용하여 대화를 완성하시오.

1 A Did you write in your diary yesterday?
  B Yes, my mom had me ______________ in it last night.

2 A Did he help her move this heavy table?
  B No, he had me help her ______________ it instead.

3 A Can I watch you while you're making the cake?
  B No, I don't want anyone to watch me ______________ it.

B

밑줄 친 부분을 바르게 고쳐 쓰시오. 틀리지 않았다면 ○표 하시오.

1 She let her dog go into the yard. ______________

2 At the museum, she heard him called her name. ______________

3 She made me to take a cooking class. ______________

4 It is so kind for you to lend me the book. ______________

5 She was so happy to helped him when he broke his leg. ______________

6 After the accident, the officer helped the man made an official report. ______________

C

주어진 단어를 알맞게 배열하여 문장을 완성하시오.

1 made / do / me
  → I only did the work because they ______________ it.

2 break into / saw / the man
  → Last night, I ______________ the house.

3 saw / run into / a gray mouse
  → My brother said he ______________ the basement.

4 useful / to participate in / for students
  → It's very ______________ those activities.

5 my sister / heard / talking
  → Early this morning, I ______________ to Jim on the phone.

6 wants / to take / me
  → My brother ______________ his laptop to a computer center to have it fixed.

REVIEW TEST

Answers P.10

A

[ ] 안에서 알맞은 말을 고르시오.

1 Karen had Mike [go, to go] to the store to buy some milk.

2 We [were to read, were read to] the story of the mystery Santa in Kansas City.

3 The diver tried [discover, to discover] a beautiful pearl in an oyster.

4 Would you buy an extra drink [so that, in order to] give it to my brother?

5 Her favorite event [watched, to watch] is the Olympic ice dancing competition.

6 He seems [to be rich, to have been rich] when he was in his early forties.

7 Our hope is [develop, to develop] a team of good soccer players.

8 He didn't ask me [how to play, what to play] this game.

B

빈칸에 들어갈 알맞은 말을 고르시오.

1 He took my lunch money ______________ it.

ⓐ not repay ⓑ never repay ⓒ not repay to ⓓ never to repay

2 I wanted a chance ______________ a scholarship to this school.

ⓐ get ⓑ gotten ⓒ to get ⓓ getting to

3 He may be surprised ______________ the film.

ⓐ see ⓑ saw ⓒ sees ⓓ to see

4 If you ______________ there by noon, please find the subway quickly.

ⓐ be ⓑ were ⓒ are to be ⓓ were let be

5 The teacher ______________ the students help her with a new computer program.

ⓐ let ⓑ got ⓒ wanted ⓓ taught

6 I have many things to talk ______________ with you.

ⓐ by ⓑ to ⓒ as ⓓ about

7 She said she could go to school today, but she still seems ______________.

ⓐ to sick ⓑ to be sick ⓒ to have sick ⓓ having been sick

REVIEW TEST

C

밑줄 친 부분을 바르게 고쳐 문장을 다시 쓰시오.

1 The girl went to the museum so to do her homework.

→ ____________________

2 He opened the door and let the dog to go out.

→ ____________________

3 Would you tell his to ask her about the trip?

→ ____________________

4 There are no chairs left for us to sit at.

→ ____________________

5 I worked hard enough pass the course last semester.

→ ____________________

6 They are to found a new apartment for us today.

→ ____________________

D

(A), (B), (C)의 각 네모 안에서 어법에 맞는 말로 바르게 짝지어진 것을 고르시오.

> People have looked for gold in many places around the world. There are several ways (A) [search / to search] for gold. The first method is (B) [dig / to dig] for and sift through gold dust. This is a difficult and time-consuming way. And this technique results in limited amounts of gold. The second method is more effective. This technique is to float boats to the middle of a river and (C) [vacuums / to vacuum] the gold dust and gold nuggets from the bottom of the river.

	(A)		(B)		(C)
①	search	…	to dig	…	vacuums
②	search	…	dig	…	to vacuum
③	to search	…	dig	…	vacuums
④	to search	…	to dig	…	vacuums
⑤	to search	…	to dig	…	to vacuum

FURTHER STUDY

Writing

▶▶ 우리말과 같은 뜻이 되도록 주어진 단어를 이용하여 문장을 완성하시오.

1 당신이 한 달 만에 탭 댄스를 마스터하는 일은 불가능하다. (impossible, you, master tap dance)

→ It is ______________________________ in a month.

2 추수감사절에 칠면조를 먹는 것은 미국인들의 전통이다. (Americans, eat turkey)

→ It is a tradition ______________________________ on Thanksgiving Day.

3 그녀는 친절하게도 새 옷이 내게 잘 어울린다고 말해주었다. (kind, her, say)

→ It was very ______________________________ that my new dress suited me well.

4 우리는 콘서트를 놓치지 않기 위해서 서둘렀다. (in order to, miss the concert)

→ We hurried ______________________________.

5 우리 축구팀은 우승을 할 만큼 충분히 열심히 연습했다. (hard, win the championship)

→ Our soccer team practiced ______________________________.

6 나는 비행기 시간에 늦지 않으려고 알람을 6시 정각에 맞춰놓았다. (set the alarm, not, be, for the flight)

→ I ______________________________ for 6 o'clock ______________________________.

7 그녀는 고양이 한 마리가 창문가에서 우는 소리를 들었다. (hear, a cat, cry)

→ ______________________________ by the window.

8 나는 내 남편에게 우리의 딸을 공항에서 데려오라고 시켰다. (pick someone up)

→ I had ______________________________ at the airport.

▶ to부정사를 목적어로 사용하는 동사들

소망, 기대	hope, want, wish 등	+ to부정사
의도, 의견	intend, mean, decide, promise, determine, agree, refuse, consent, manage 등	
계획, 준비	plan, prepare 등	
요구, 필요	ask, demand, beg, need, claim 등	

▶ 원형부정사를 목적격보어로 사용하는 동사들

사역동사	have, let, make (* help는 준사역동사로 원형 또는 to부정사를 취함) (* get은 사역의 의미로 쓰일 때 to부정사를 취함)	+ V / -ed
지각동사	see, watch, look at, hear, listen to, feel	+ V / -ing

▶ 관용적으로 쓰이는 독립부정사 구문

- **To tell the truth**, I don't want to go with her. (솔직히 말해서)
- **To be frank with you**, it was my mistake. (솔직히)
- Jenny is, **so to speak** (= as it were), a fashion icon. (말하자면)
- **To speak generally**, people don't like taking others' advice. (일반적으로 말하면)
- **To make [cut] a long story short**, he is just not my type. (간단히 말해서)
- **To begin with**, I'd like to go through what we discussed last meeting. (우선은/먼저 말씀 드릴 것은)
- **To sum up**, we need to change our advertising strategy. (요약하면)
- **To put it another way**, we will not be able to help them. (바꿔 말하면)
- Meg knows Italian, **not to speak** of French. (~은 말할 것도 없이)
  (= to say nothing of, not to mention, let alone)
- **Needless to say**, we're doing this to help you. (말할 필요도 없이)
- **To make matters worse**, Carl was dumped by his girlfriend. (설상가상으로)
- **To make matters better**, I got a job at a company. (금상첨화로)
- **Strange to say**, this place is very familiar to me. (이상하게 들리겠지만)
- **To be sure**, you're not qualified for this job. (확실히)
- **To judge by** his accent, he must be British. (~로 판단하건대)
- **To do her justice**, she is a selfish and narrow-minded person. (정당하게 평가하자면)

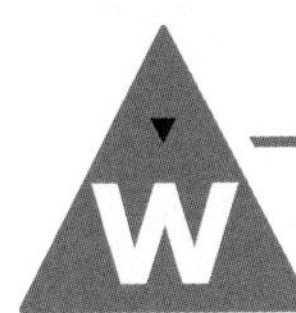

WRAP-UP TEST

Answers P.11

1 주어진 말을 어법에 맞게 바꿔 쓰시오.

I know that you're pretending ______________ (sleep).

2 빈칸에 들어갈 수 없는 말을 고르시오.

I ______________ to visit there once again.

ⓐ hoped ⓑ agreed
ⓒ expected ⓓ postponed

3 대화를 읽고, 밑줄 친 부분의 쓰임이 잘못된 것을 고르시오.

A What about ⓐ going to a movie tonight?
B Sorry, but I can't afford ⓑ go out today. I have tons of work ⓒ to do.
A Don't worry. I'll help you ⓓ do the work.

4 빈칸에 to를 쓸 수 없는 것을 고르시오.

ⓐ I know that he expected us ________ go with him.
ⓑ They made me ________ bring all our luggage.
ⓒ Would you please help me ________ file these papers?
ⓓ We all failed ________ explain the problem clearly.

5 빈칸에 들어갈 말을 바르게 연결한 것을 고르시오.

- It's wise ________ you to make such a decision.
- It's important ________ me to write a diary regularly.

ⓐ of – for ⓑ to – for
ⓒ as – for ⓓ with – of

6 두 문장의 뜻이 같아지도록 빈칸에 알맞은 말을 써 넣으시오.

To find his house was so easy.
→ It was ______________________.

7 주어진 문장과 의미가 가장 가까운 것을 고르시오.

She was too nervous to drive the car herself.

ⓐ She was nervous enough to drive the car herself.
ⓑ She was so nervous, but she could drive the car herself.
ⓒ She was so nervous that she couldn't drive the car herself.
ⓓ She was not as nervous as she couldn't drive the car herself.

8 밑줄 친 부분과 쓰임이 같은 것을 고르시오.

We wanted to reach the top of the mountain.

ⓐ She decided to stop eating any sweets.
ⓑ I visited the website to check the flight schedule to Canada.
ⓒ Are you guys all ready to start?
ⓓ Isn't there anything to eat in the refrigerator?

[9-10] 글을 읽고, 물음에 답하시오.

Filmmaking is an incredibly collaborative form of art. It's not like ⓐ being a photographer or a painter who creates images entirely by himself or herself. A lot of people gather ⓑ makes a movie that tells a story. As a cinematographer, I watch the actors ⓒ rehearse and ⓓ create moods that are correct for each moment in the story. Using light and color, I create a visual language appropriate for the story. I believe films are the most powerful of the visual arts; they are more than just entertainment.

9 밑줄 친 부분의 쓰임이 잘못된 것을 고르시오.

10 질문에 대한 알맞은 답을 쓰시오.

What do I do as a cinematographer?
→ I ______________________ and create moods for the story.

동명사

1 동명사의 여러 가지 쓰임
2 동명사 vs. 부정사
3 동명사의 기타 쓰임

동명사의 여러 가지 쓰임

Pre-Check 주어진 문장을 참고하여 빈칸에 공통으로 들어갈 말을 써 넣으시오.

- Andy is an amateur dancer.

1 He enjoys ________________ . (그는 춤추는 것을 좋아한다)

2 His hobby is ________________ . (그의 취미는 춤추기이다)

3 He thinks ________________ is fun. (그는 춤추는 것이 재미있다고 생각한다)

1 동명사의 역할

(1) 명사처럼 주어 역할을 하는 동명사

The essay is very difficult for students.
Writing an essay is very difficult for students.
Reading an essay is very difficult for students.

(2) 명사처럼 목적어 역할을 하는 동명사

He enjoys instant food.
He enjoys cooking Chinese food.
He enjoys eating Chinese food.

(3) 명사처럼 보어 역할을 하는 동명사

She is a writer.
Her job is writing articles for newspapers.
Her job is writing screenplays for movies.

1

동명사는 명사로 문장에서 '주어', '목적어', '보어' 역할을 한다. 동사의 기능을 더하여 명사만으로는 부족한 의미를 보충할 수 있다.

(1) 동명사(구)는 단수 취급한다.
Collecting coins is his hobby.

(2) 동명사를 목적어로 취하는 동사
like, enjoy, mind, keep, suggest, finish, give up 등

〈동명사 + 명사〉로 굳어진 표현들
a waiting room 대기실
a smoking room 흡연실
a washing machine 세탁기
a sewing machine 재봉틀
a sleeping bag 침낭
a sleeping car 침대차
a dressing room 탈의실
the boiling point 끓는점, 비등점

2 명사로 쓰이는 동명사

(1) 형용사 + 명사/동명사

He wants a creative article.
He wants a piece of creative writing.

We're all surprised at his wonderful performance.
We're all surprised at his wonderful playing.

(2) 소유격 + 명사/동명사

I enjoyed Jim's food.
I enjoyed Jim's cooking.

We all liked his character in the play.
We all liked his acting.

2

V-ing ← 명사적 성질을 띠게 한다.
(1) 형용사의 수식을 받는다.
(2) 의미상 주어는 소유격으로 나타낸다.
* 「Unit 5. 3」 '의미상의 주어' 부분 참조

(3) 전치사 + 명사/동명사

Thank you for your advice.

Thank you for advising me kindly.

I'm thinking of a trip to Jejudo.

I'm thinking of going to Jejudo.

(3) 전치사의 목적어 역할을 한다.

* 동명사의 부정
  = not[never] + 동명사

I'm thinking of not going to Jejudo.

3 동사처럼 쓰이는 동명사

(1) He likes having bagels and coffee every morning.

(2) Being elected chairman was a burden to me.

(3) Having taken his class helped me improve my English.

3

Ⓥ-ing ← 동사에서 왔으므로 동사적 성질을 띤다.

(1) 목적어를 취한다.

(2) '수동태'로 쓰일 수 있다.

(3) 시제를 나타낸다.

* 「Unit 5. 3」의 시제 부분 참조

Check-up

Answers P.12

A 밑줄 친 단어를 동명사로 바꿔 쓰시오.

1 Many people perform magic tricks these days.
→ ________ magic tricks is a lot of fun.

2 My brother reads one or two books a week.
→ He always encourages me in ________.

3 He baked a cake for his brother's birthday.
→ One of his favorite hobbies is ________ cakes.

4 The boy writes various kinds of stories as his hobby.
→ He enjoys ________ detective stories.

B 밑줄 친 부분을 동명사는 G, 분사는 P로 구분하시오.

1 ① My father is working with a computer. ________
② His favorite part of the job is working with his students. ________

2 ① Her hobby is making cakes. ________
② Mom is making cookies with my sister in the kitchen. ________

3 ① The man is training the hockey players. ________
② His job is training the hockey players. ________

동명사 vs. 현재분사

동명사와 현재분사는 모두 〈동사 + -ing〉의 형태이다. 단, 동명사는 동사를 명사화하여 명사로 사용하는 것이고, 현재분사는 동사를 형용사화하여 형용사로 사용하는 것이다. 동명사와 현재분사 둘 다 be동사 다음에 위치할 수 있으므로 해석할 때는 문맥을 살펴 동명사와 현재분사를 구분하여 이해하도록 하자.

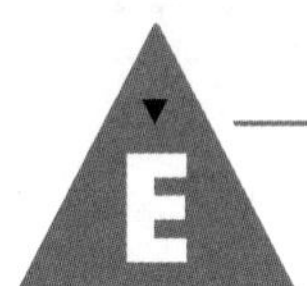

EXERCISE

Answers P.12

A

주어진 단어를 이용하여 문장을 완성하시오.

1 We ______________________ recipes in Mom's old cookbook. (enjoy, read)

2 Thank you for ______________________ with the calculus problem. (help, me)

3 Is your dream ______________________ with other talented musicians? (form, a band)

4 ______________________ with my friends is one of my favorite things to do. (have fun, on weekends)

B

밑줄 친 부분을 바르게 고쳐 쓰시오. 틀리지 않았다면 ○표 하시오.

1 I do not like his watching TV late at night. ______________

2 Thank you for give me this present. ______________

3 He keeps tell me not to waste time. ______________

4 They prefer staying home to playing outside. ______________

5 Cutting patterns are difficult without a pair of sharp scissors. ______________

6 Do you mind sit here? ______________

C

동명사를 이용하여 문장을 완성하시오.

Example I want to be a journalist. It is my dream.
→ Being a journalist is my dream.

1 He likes to collect baseball cards. It is his hobby.
→ ______________________ is his hobby.

2 I had studied Tom's notes. It helped me pass the test.
→ ______________________ helped me pass the test.

3 I am writing an essay. It is difficult homework for me.
→ ______________________ is difficult homework for me.

4 I was chosen president of the club. It was an honor.
→ ______________________ was an honor for me.

5 I saw my baby cousin. It was a joy to me.
→ ______________________ was a joy to me.

동명사 vs. 부정사

Pre-Check 주어진 단어를 어법에 맞게 바꿔 쓰시오.

1 Sam enjoys ________________(play) tennis.
2 I want ________________(watch) the baseball game on TV.
3 I forgot ________________(lock) the door, so I went home.

1 동명사를 목적어로 취하는 동사

She enjoys learning foreign languages.
Lora finished doing her homework.
We postponed going on a picnic.
He practices playing soccer for an hour every morning.
Grandmother gave up knitting after just one scarf.
My brother always puts off cleaning his room.

> 1
> finish, give up, keep, mind, postpone, quit, put off, delay, deny, avoid, practice, suggest, admit, abandon, escape 등

2 to부정사를 목적어로 취하는 동사

I hope to learn Kung-Fu.
I expect to improve my English writing with his help.
Sara plans to attend law school next year.
He decided to join the club.
I didn't mean to hurt your feelings?
The Council agreed not to alter the company's logo.

> 2
> hope, expect, allow, mean, promise, decide, plan, agree, pretend, attempt, choose, wish, desire, determine, refuse, afford 등

3 동명사와 to부정사 모두를 목적어로 취하는 동사

(1) 의미가 같은 경우

He began learning English when he was eight.
He began to learn English when he was eight.

My father hates waking up early as much as he hates going to bed late.
My father hates to wake up early as much as he hates to go to bed late.

> 3
> (1) begin, start, hate, like, love, prefer 등
> * 이들 동사는 목적어로 동명사와 부정사 둘 다를 취하며, 의미상으로도 유사하다.

(2) 의미가 다른 경우

I forgot bringing a swimming suit.
(→ I brought it, but I forgot the fact that I brought it.)
I forgot to bring a swimming suit.
(→ I didn't bring it.)

I regret not studying hard enough.
I regret to say that you have failed the exam.

(2)
- forget + V-ing: ~한 것을 잊다
  forget + to -V: ~해야 하는 것을 잊다
- try + V-ing: 시험 삼아 ~해 보다
  try + to -V: ~하기 위해 노력하다, 애쓰다
- regret + V-ing: ~한 것을 후회하다
  regret + to -V: 유감스럽지만 ~할 것이다

Check-up

Answers P.12

A 주어진 단어를 이용하여 문장을 완성하시오.

1 I hope ________________(be) a doctor after I graduate.

2 My sister enjoys ________________(sit) by the open window.

3 We can't keep ________________(buy) books from the Internet store.

4 Where do you plan ________________(go) on summer vacation?

5 Would you mind ________________(do) the laundry for me?

6 She promised ________________(use, not) my story in the book.

B 주어진 문장의 뜻을 가장 잘 나타낸 것을 고르시오.

1 I remember to visit him.

ⓐ I remember that I visited him.

ⓑ I have to visit him, and I know that I have to.

2 I forgot buying milk and bread on my way home.

ⓐ I forgot the fact that I bought milk and bread on my way home.

ⓑ I had to buy milk and bread on my way home, but I didn't.

동명사 vs. to부정사
어떤 동사는 뒤에 to부정사가 오느냐 동명사가 오느냐에 따라 그 의미가 변한다. 이때 동명사는 명사의 기능에 to부정사는 동사의 기능에 가까운데, 동명사는 동사가 가지는 행위의 의미를 명사로 생각하고, 부정사는 동사의 의미 그대로를 살려서 이해하도록 한다. 특히, 동명사는 과거의 느낌을, to부정사는 앞으로 일어날 일이라는 것을 기억해 두면 도움이 된다.

EXERCISE

Answers P.12

A

[ ] 안에서 알맞은 말을 고르시오.

1 My cousin wanted [having, to have] cherry pie for dessert.

2 I gave up [waiting for, to wait for] her to catch the last train.

3 She decided [writing, to write] a letter before going to bed.

4 Do you mind [putting away, to put away] the box on the other side of the room?

5 I stopped [eating, to eat] hamburgers because I put on so much weight.

6 We all agreed [leaving, to leave] at once.

B

주어진 단어를 이용하여 문장을 완성하시오.

1 Mr. White decided ____________(buy) a diamond ring before ____________(ask) her to marry him.

2 Henry quit ____________(work) last week after his company agreed ____________(let) him retire.

3 The artist attempted ____________(paint) on a building, but he forgot ____________ (get) permission.

4 He planned ____________(delete) the information in the file but delayed ____________ (do) it.

C

주어진 단어를 이용하여 문장을 완성하시오. (과거시제를 사용할 것)

1 deny / inform / me

→ They ________________________________ of the fact.

2 suggest / organize / a new club

→ He ________________________________ this fall semester.

3 mean / infer / by that silly comment

→ What did you ________________________________?

4 give up / participate / in the video game contest

→ The boy ________________________________.

5 pretend / enjoy / her soup

→ He ________________________________, but it was too salty.

동명사의 기타 쓰임

Pre-Check 주어진 단어를 이용하여 빈칸에 알맞은 말을 써 넣으시오.

1 I am looking forward to our lunch.
I am looking forward to ______________________ (have lunch) with him.

2 I'll join you after this.
I'll join you ______________________ (after, finish this work).

1 동명사의 의미상의 주어

(1) 동명사의 주어를 밝히지 않는 경우
ⓐ Drinking milk is good for health.
ⓑ He's afraid of (his) losing the game.
ⓒ She scolded me for (my) breaking her bike.
(= She scolded me because I broke her bike.)

(2) 동명사의 주어를 밝히는 경우
Do you mind my closing the door?
(= Can I close the door?)
Do you mind your closing the door?
(= Would you close the door?)

1
(1) ⓐ 의미상 주어가 일반인일 때
ⓑ 동명사의 주어가 문장의 주어와 같을 때
ⓒ 문장의 목적어가 동명사의 주어와 같을 때
• ⓑ, ⓒ의 경우 동명사의 주어를 넣어서 쓸 수도 있다.

(2) 문장의 주어와 동명사의 주어가 다를 때 〈소유격 + 동명사〉 형태

2 동명사의 시제

(1) -ing: 시제의 구분 없이 사용
ⓐ Georgia spends a lot of her time decorating.
ⓑ Georgia spent a lot of her time decorating.
ⓒ I'm not sure about his coming to the party.
(= I'm not sure if he will come to the party.)

(2) Having + p.p.: 본동사보다 더 이전의 시제 표현
ⓐ We are satisfied having done it perfectly.
(= We are satisfied that we did it perfectly.)
ⓑ We were satisfied having done it perfectly.
(= We were satisfied that we had done it perfectly.)

2
(1) ⓐ 현재 decorating에 시간을 보냄
ⓑ 과거에 decorating에 시간을 보냈음
ⓒ '그가 오는 것'은 미래의 일

(2) ⓐ 과거에 했던 것에 만족함
ⓑ 과거 이전에 했던 것에 만족함

3 전치사 + 동명사

I will call you after arriving home.
She always dreams about going abroad.

3
전치사 뒤에 동사가 필요할 때는 동명사 형태를 취한다. 전치사 뒤에 부정사는 올 수 없다.

He dreams of getting his own car.
You can't leave without finishing the job.
She prefers singing to listening to music.

4 동명사를 이용한 주요 표현

Please forgive me for not telling you the truth.
The boys stopped us from playing baseball.
Heavy fog prevented us from seeing the beautiful scenery.
He is busy classifying those files into two types.
She insisted on doing it herself.
I finally succeeded in uploading the files.
I can't help thinking about the matter.
Let's go shopping.
We kept on talking, ignoring their arrival.
I'm not used to getting up so early.

4

- forgive/apologize ~ for V-ing : ~가 …한 것을 용서하다
- stop/prevent/keep ~ from V-ing : ~가 …하는 것을 막다/금지하다
- be busy V-ing: ~하느라 바쁘다
- insist on V-ing: ~을 주장하다
- succeed in V-ing: ~에 성공하다
- can't help V-ing: ~하지 않을 수 없다
- go V-ing: ~하러 가다
- keep on V-ing: 계속 ~하다
- be used to V-ing: ~에 익숙하다
- feel like V-ing: ~하고 싶다
- be worth V-ing: ~할 가치가 있다
- have trouble V-ing: ~하는 데 문제가 있다
- It is no use V-ing: ~해도 소용없다
- never ~ without V-ing: …없이는 결코 ~하지 않다
- be accustomed to V-ing: ~하는 데 익숙하다

Check-up

Answers P.12

A 주어진 단어를 이용하여 문장을 완성하시오.

1 She and I ______________________(go, shop) the other day.
2 This new laptop computer is ______________________(worth, buy).
3 My brother ______________________(not, feel like, play) soccer with us right now.
4 I ______________________(can't help, complain) about my boss.
5 Thank you ______________________(for, bring) the birthday cake and ice cream.

B [보기]를 참고하여 문장을 완성하시오.

Example Thank you so much for the gift.
→ Thank you so much for sending me the gift. (you sent me the gift)

1 Thank you so much for ______________________. (you bought me the gift)
2 Thank you so much for ______________________. (you wrapped the gift for me)
3 Thank you so much for ______________________. (you paid for the gift)

동명사 vs. 명사

우리말에서도 마찬가지이지만 영어에서도 명사만으로는 말하고자 하는 바를 제대로 표현하기가 어렵다. 그래서 동사를 명사화, 즉 동명사로 바꾸어 표현하게 된다. 명사로 뜻을 전달할 수 있는 경우에도, 좀 더 정확하고 구체적인 의미 전달이 필요한 경우에는 동사처럼 수식도 받고 목적어도 취할 수 있는 동명사를 사용하게 된다. 또한 동명사는 명사의 역할을 하기 때문에 위치상으로는 명사의 자리에 온다.

EXERCISE

Answers P.13

A

밑줄 친 부분을 바르게 고쳐 쓰시오. 틀리지 않았다면 ○표 하시오.

1 Let's go fish at the lake today. ______________

2 I can help you if you have trouble getting in. ______________

3 The rain prevented me to arrive at the office on time. ______________

4 He's not used to study so much for a class. ______________

5 She can't help worried about her daughter in the U.K. ______________

B

주어진 단어를 이용하여 문장을 완성하시오.

1 good at / head

→ Eddie is ______________ the ball.

2 admit / have cheated

→ The boy wouldn't ______________ on the math exam.

3 busy / help others

→ When he's not on the computer, he is ______________.

4 feel like / play badminton / with us

→ Don't you ______________ this morning?

5 it is / no use / blame

→ ______________ the teacher for giving you a lot of homework.

C

[보기]와 같이 문장을 완성하시오.

Example	I'm interested in Mr. Smith's class. I want to take his class. → I'm interested in taking his class.

1 He always grumbles. We're tired of it.

→ We are tired of his ______________.

2 I don't feel well. I won't practice the piano this afternoon.

→ I don't feel like ______________ this afternoon.

3 I'm looking forward to his new movie. I'd like to see his new movie soon.

→ I'm looking forward to ______________.

4 They didn't want to sit in a smoking area.

→ They complained about ______________.

REVIEW TEST

Answers P.13

A

[ ] 안에서 알맞은 말을 고르시오.

1 The teacher postponed [to hear, hearing] the presentations until next Friday.

2 The class expects [to receive, receiving] graduation certificates at the ceremony.

3 I stopped at the shop [to rent, renting] some DVDs for my wife.

4 He gave up [to play, playing] soccer after losing the championship.

5 [To be selecting, Being selected] as your host was an unexpected honor for me.

6 Is one of your joys [taking, taken] trips to other countries?

7 The actress insisted [on, to] performing her own stunts.

8 The girl kept [on, in] singing all night.

B

빈칸에 들어갈 알맞은 말을 고르시오.

1 ______________ is a symptom of the common cold, which is caused by a virus.

ⓐ Coughing ⓑ Be coughing ⓒ To coughing ⓓ For coughing

2 I forgot ______________ the book on time. So I had to pay an overdue charge.

ⓐ returning ⓑ to return ⓒ borrowing ⓓ to borrow

3 What do you ______________ accomplish here by doing that?

ⓐ finish ⓑ want to ⓒ keep on ⓓ quit

4 I'm not accustomed ______________ spicy food.

ⓐ eating ⓑ to eat ⓒ to eating ⓓ for eating

5 Kenny suggested ______________ on a picnic on the last day of school.

ⓐ go ⓑ to go ⓒ going ⓓ should go

6 The students are not used to ______________ classes outdoors.

ⓐ have ⓑ having ⓒ in having ⓓ having on

7 ______________ your teaching methods helped me to become a better teacher.

ⓐ Observe ⓑ Observed ⓒ To observing ⓓ Having observed

R REVIEW TEST

C

밑줄 친 부분을 바르게 고쳐 문장을 다시 쓰시오.

1 He pretended to being busy when I entered the room.

→ ______________________________

2 My best friend promised to not tell my secret to others.

→ ______________________________

3 Haven't you feeling like taking a long walk recently?

→ ______________________________

4 The doctor advised my father to quit to smoke as soon as possible.

→ ______________________________

5 I can help wondering about the gift in the red box.

→ ______________________________

6 She is worried about to changing the schedule after the notice.

→ ______________________________

D

(A), (B), (C)의 각 네모 안에서 어법에 맞는 말로 바르게 짝지어진 것을 고르시오.

> Born in Iran, Ansari came to America when she was 16. She wanted (A) [pursue / to pursue] her passion for the sciences. Now, she may fulfill her dream. She spent lots of her earnings to be the first woman in space. She will be the first woman to take a trip to space. She is expected (B) [to fly / flying] into space on a Russian space mission after (C) [take / taking] a series of tests.

	(A)		(B)		(C)
①	pursue	…	to fly	…	take
②	pursue	…	to fly	…	taking
③	pursue	…	flying	…	take
④	to pursue	…	flying	…	take
⑤	to pursue	…	to fly	…	taking

FURTHER STUDY

Writing

▶▶ **우리말과 같은 뜻이 되도록 주어진 단어를 이용하여 문장을 완성하시오. (동명사를 사용할 것)**

1 나는 너무 피곤해서 오늘 파티에 가고 싶지 않다. (not, feel like, go, to the party)

→ I'm so tired that I ______________________________ today.

2 그 영화 한 번 더 봐도 괜찮겠니? (mind, see, the movie)

→ Do you ______________________________ once again?

3 날씨가 너무 나빠서 나는 운전을 할 수가 없었다. (prevent ~ from ..., drive)

→ The bad weather ______________________________.

4 아버지는 본인이 직접 저녁 준비를 하겠다고 주장하셨다. (insist on, prepare, dinner)

→ My dad ______________________________ himself.

5 숙제를 마친 후에 방을 청소해라. (clean one's room, after, finish one's homework)

→ Please ______________________________.

6 그는 여자 친구와 통화를 하지 않고는 떠나려고 하지 않았다. (leave, without, call)

→ He would not ______________________________ his girlfriend.

7 그녀는 그 상자를 전부 혼자 포장해야 한다는 것에 대해 불평했다. (complain about, wrap, all of the boxes)

→ She ______________________________ alone.

8 그는 어제 탁자 위에 있던 그녀의 머그컵을 깼던 것을 시인했다. (have broken, mug)

→ He admitted ______________________________ on the table yesterday.

MUST-KNOW

▶ 동명사를 목적어로 취하는 동사들

제안, 이해, 계속	suggest, understand, go on, keep on	+ V-ing
인정, 고려, 즐김	admit, consider, enjoy	
부정, 기피	avoid, deny, escape, mind, excuse	
끝냄, 포기, 연기	finish, stop, quit, give up, put off, postpone, delay	

▶ 동명사와 to부정사 모두 목적어로 취하는 동사들

감정, 기호	like, love, hate, regret, prefer	V-ing + 또는 to-V
시작, 계속	start, begin, continue	
마침, 생략	cease	

▶ 동명사와 to부정사 모두 목적어로 취하면서 의미가 달라지는 동사들

stop	to-V	~하기 위하여 멈추다(목적을 나타내는 to부정사의 용법)
	V-ing	~하는 것을 그만두다
try	to-V	~하려고 노력하다
	V-ing	시험 삼아 ~해 보다
regret	to-V	~하려니 유감이다
	V-ing	~했던 것을 후회하다
forget	to-V	~할 것을 잊다
	V-ing	~했던 것을 잊다
remember	to-V	~할 것을 기억하다
	V-ing	~했던 것을 기억하다

▶ 동명사나 to부정사가 오는 구문들 비교

be used to V-ing	~에 익숙하다
used to-V	전에 ~했었다 (과거의 습관)
succeed in V-ing	~에 성공하다
fail to-V	~에 실패하다
despair of V-ing	~에 절망이다, 가망이 없다
hope to-V	~하기를 바라다
be capable of V-ing be able to-V	~할 수 있다
cannot help V-ing cannot but V	~하지 않을 수 없다
be surprised at V-ing be surprised to-V	~에 놀라다
aim at V-ing aim to-V	~에 목표를 두다

WRAP-UP TEST

Answers P.14

1 대화를 읽고, 빈칸에 들어갈 알맞은 말을 고르시오.

A I have a toothache. It really hurts me.

B What about ____________ to the dentist?

ⓐ go ⓑ to go
ⓒ going ⓓ to going

2 밑줄 친 부분의 쓰임이 잘못된 것을 고르시오.

She insisted(ⓐ) on(ⓑ) talk(ⓒ) to the hotel manager(ⓓ).

3 우리말을 영어로 바르게 옮긴 것을 고르시오.

제가 여기 앉아도 될까요?

ⓐ Do you enjoy sitting here?
ⓑ Can you sit here, please?
ⓒ Do you mind my sitting here?
ⓓ Would you like to sit here?

4 어법상 옳지 않은 것을 고르시오.

ⓐ Sam suggested going to a pop concert.
ⓑ Sarah keeps complaining all the time.
ⓒ I decided not giving up the course.
ⓓ The best thing for your health is exercising regularly.

5 주어진 말을 어법에 맞게 바꿔 쓰시오.

• My mother always drinks black coffee right after ____________(eat) dinner.

• You need ____________(study) harder this year.

6 빈칸에 들어갈 말이 바르게 짝지어진 것을 고르시오.

• The man said he can do it ____________ knowing the case.

• I'm not used ____________ making a speech before people.

ⓐ to – with ⓑ for – in
ⓒ without – to ⓓ of – at

7 밑줄 친 부분과 문장에서의 역할이 같은 것을 고르시오.

My teacher said reading a newspaper in English helps you learn English.

ⓐ All of us liked going fishing with Uncle John.
ⓑ I'm not sure of his arriving on time.
ⓒ My favorite hobby is reading comic books.
ⓓ Watching TV dramas is one of my hobbies.

8 주어진 문장과 의미가 통하는 것을 것을 고르시오.

Jim was satisfied that he had finished it successfully.

ⓐ Jim is satisfied to have finished it successfully.
ⓑ Jim is satisfied to finishing it successfully.
ⓒ Jim was satisfied, having finished it successfully.
ⓓ Jim was satisfied finishing it successfully.

[9-10] 글을 읽고, 물음에 답하시오.

> Since I have an important exam next week, I plan to limit my use of the Internet before the exam. I enjoy playing Internet games, but these games can interfere with studying. So I decided not to use my computer at home for a while. If I have to use a computer for studying, I can use one in the library instead. This will help me study rather than surf the Internet.

9 윗글의 내용과 일치하는 것을 고르시오.

ⓐ I am not used to playing Internet games.
ⓑ I think computers prevent me from studying.
ⓒ I prefer Internet games to watching TV.
ⓓ I will not use a computer at home after passing the exam.

10 윗글을 아래와 같이 요약할 때 빈칸에 알맞은 말을 쓰시오.

I ____________ Internet games, but I've decided ____________ my computer at home before taking the exam.

The
Grammar

2
Level

분사

1 현재분사

2 과거분사

3 분사의 다양한 표현

현재분사

Pre-Check 주어진 단어를 우리말에 맞게 바꿔 쓰시오.

1 He has many ________________(interest) books. (재미있는 책)
2 He is ________________(read) a book on the sofa now. (책을 읽고 있다)
3 I saw him ________________(watch) TV. (TV를 보고 있는)

1 현재분사의 역할

(1) 명사 수식

The black dog barks at strangers. The barking dog is mine.

① 명사 앞: 명사 수식
It is an exciting **game** to see.
My older brother heard some earthshaking **news**.
Read all about this fascinating **story**.

② 명사 뒤: 수식어구가 긴 경우 뒤에서 명사 수식
Who is **the guy** wearing the black suit over there?
I know **the guy** talking with the girl.
The girl standing at the cashier is Jane.

(2) 주어, 목적어 설명

The dog is fierce. The dog is barking wildly.

① 주어 설명
The show seems interesting.
cf) **My brother and I** are making doughnuts.

② 목적어 설명
I saw **her** having lunch with her friend yesterday.
The teacher noticed **him** yawning in the back row.

1
분사란 동사에 –ing나 –ed를 붙여 형용사로 쓰는 말이다. 따라서 문장에서 형용사의 역할을 한다.

- 현재분사: V–ing (~하는, ~하고 있는)
  → 능동, 진행의 의미
- 과거분사: V–ed (~ 된, ~하여진)
  → 수동, 완료의 의미

cf) 현재진행형: be+V–ing

• 지각동사를 사용할 경우에는 목적격보어 자리에 동사원형과 현재분사 둘 다 쓸 수 있다.
I saw him play/playing.

지각동사의 종류
보다 see, watch, observe, look at
듣다 hear, listen to
느끼다 feel
냄새 맡다 smell
깨닫다 notice

2 현재분사[ⓐ] vs. 동명사[ⓑ]

ⓐ My grandfather is doing a crossword puzzle.
ⓑ His hobby is doing crossword puzzles.

ⓐ The kids playing in the sand are my cousins.
ⓑ Playing in the sand made them dirty.

ⓐ Look at the sleeping baby in her mom's arms.
ⓑ He wants to buy a new sleeping bag.

2

V-ing: 현재분사 vs. 동명사

단어가 형용사 역할을 하는지 명사 역할을 하는지 구분한다.

ⓐ 현재분사(형용사 역할)
: '~하는, ~하는 중인'으로 해석

ⓑ 동명사(명사 역할)
: '~하는 것, ~하기'로 해석

cf) 동명사(명사) vs 현재분사(형용사)
서로 형태가 같으므로 문맥을 살펴 명사로 쓰였는지 형용사로 쓰였는지를 판단한다.
Look at the sleeping baby.
(잠자는 아기)
He traveled around the world in a sleeping car.
(침대차)

Check-up

Answers P.14

A 밑줄 친 동사를 이용하여 문장을 완성하시오.

1 James called the workers. The workers heard James ________________ them.

2 The wind is blowing hard today. My friend lost her hat in the ________________ wind.

3 Susan always runs at that time, but I didn't see her ________________ this morning.

4 People talk about Jack very often. Jane also heard her mother ________________ about him.

5 The band usually plays soft music, but they were ________________ loudly last night.

B 주어진 단어를 알맞게 배열하여 대화를 완성하시오.

A Excuse me. I'm looking for a guy named Steve.

B Steve is standing over there.

A So, ______________________________ (the guy, by the door, standing) is Steve, right? And who is Matt, by the way?

B He is the host of the party. He is cooking.

A Oh, ______________________________ (man, the, cooking) is Matt? I see. Thanks.

전치 수식 vs. 후치 수식

분사는 형용사처럼 쓰여 명사의 앞뒤에서 명사를 수식한다. 그러나 분사는 원래 동사에서 온 말이기 때문에 목적어나 전치사구를 붙여서 사용하는 경우가 많다. 이렇게 분사에 달려있는 단어들이 많아지게 되면 분사가 어떤 명사를 수식하는지 알기 어려워지므로 명사의 앞이 아니라 명사의 뒤에서 해당 명사를 수식 또는 설명하게 된다.

EXERCISE

Answers P.14

A

밑줄 친 부분을 분사는 P, 동명사는 G로 구분하시오.

1 I enjoyed their <u>fascinating</u> performance. ____________

2 My three cousins dislike <u>running</u> in very long races. ____________

3 Do you know the family <u>living</u> in the next-door apartment? ____________

4 My new teacher doesn't mind <u>using</u> the old English textbooks. ____________

5 The animal trainer heard a very <u>frightening</u> sound coming from the cage. ____________

6 My mom wants to buy a new <u>washing</u> machine. ____________

B

주어진 단어와 현재분사를 이용하여 문장을 완성하시오.

1 The coach called the ____________________ at the stadium. (players, practice)

2 The white cat chased the ____________________ a hole. (mouse, run into)

3 The drama class performed a ____________________. (play, touch)

4 Who was the ____________________ you on the bus? (girl, smile at)

5 I don't know the ____________________ the teacher's desk. (person, lean against)

C

[보기]와 같이 두 문장을 하나의 문장으로 다시 쓰시오.

Example Do you know the man? He is standing at the gate.
→ Do you know the man <u>standing at the gate</u>?

1 I saw the old man. He was walking to the post office.

→ I saw the old man ______________________________.

2 The boy is running after the ball. The ball is rolling into the street.

→ The boy is running after the ball ______________________________.

3 Do you know the two men? They are working on our computers.

→ Do you know the two men ______________________________?

4 She bought the red car. The car was sitting on the dealer's parking lot.

→ She bought the red car ______________________________.

5 Who is the woman? She is speaking at today's meeting.

→ Who is the woman ______________________________?

과거분사

Pre-Check 주어진 단어를 우리말에 맞게 바꿔 쓰시오.

1 ① It was an ________________(excite) game. (흥미진진한 경기)
② Look at their ________________(excite) faces. (상기된 얼굴)

2 ① He is ________________(hang) a picture on the wall. (그림을 걸고 있다)
② The picture ________________(hang) on the wall is from an auction.
(벽에 걸려 있는 그림)

1 과거분사의 쓰임

(1) 명사 수식

① 명사 앞: 명사 수식

The closed **window** is dirty.
This torn **paper** is for scrapbooks.
The recently fixed **computer** broke down again.

② 명사 뒤: 수식어구가 긴 경우 명사 뒤에서 명사 수식

Please pass me **the box** wrapped in red and blue.
Do you see **the items** stocked on the top shelf?
I like **the pictures** exhibited at the art gallery.

(2) 주어, 목적어 설명

① 주어 설명

The red roses are arranged nicely.
The boy was encouraged by the teacher's praise.
The driver was caught by the police officer.

② 목적어 설명

The girl found **a ring** fallen on the grass.
Have you ever seen **a book** written in Hebrew?

2 현재분사 vs. 과거분사

(1) 분사의 형태 비교

① 동사원형 + -ing: 능동

Do you see the smiling boy?
(→ a boy who is smiling)

② 동사원형 + -ed: 수동

Look at the broken bridge.
(→ a bridge which is broken)

1

과거분사 vs. 동사원형
• 목적격보어가 과거분사: 수동의 의미
I had my hair cut.
(머리카락이 잘리도록 하다)
• 목적격보어가 동사원형: 능동의 의미
I had him cut my hair.
(그에게 내 머리를 자르게 하다)

* 목적격보어를 동사원형으로 쓰는 동사에 관해서는 「Unit 4. 4」 참조

(2) 감정을 나타내는 분사형 형용사

① -ing: 감정을 유발하는 '능동'의 뜻

The news was shocking to the people.

This is an entertaining film.

She has an astonishing memory.

② -ed: ~로 인해 감정을 느끼는 '수동'의 뜻

No one was surprised at the news.

We were extremely tired.

Lots of people were disappointed with the play.

(2)

① boring, amazing, surprising 등

② bored, amazed, surprised 등

* 단어의 다양한 예는 〈MUST-KNOW〉 참조

Check-up

Answers P.15

A 주어진 단어를 이용하여 문장을 완성하시오.

1 The ________________(paint) wall isn't a popular tourist attraction.

2 They sent all the ________________(fold) cards.

3 The ________________(deliver) pizza wasn't hot.

4 Do you know anything about the ________________(return) computers?

5 Don't worry. I wasn't ________________(displease) by her unusual comments in the speech.

B [ ] 안에서 알맞은 말을 고르시오.

A You know my partner, Tom, right? I feel ① [boring, bored] when I'm with him.

B I thought he was funny. I met him before, and he was a very ② [exciting, excited] person.

A I once played a game with him. Well, the game was ③ [exciting, excited]. But he didn't look ④ [exciting, excited] at all.

과거분사 vs. 현재분사 (수동태로 쓰이는 경우 vs. 능동태로 쓰이는 경우)

'사람이 주어인 경우에는 bored를 사용하고 사물이 주어일 경우에는 boring을 쓴다'라는 설명은 잘못된 것이다. bore는 '지루하게 하다'라는 뜻의 동사이며, boring은 '지루하게 하는'이라는 뜻의 현재분사이자 형용사이다. bored는 과거분사이며, '지루함을 당하는(수동)'이나, '지루함을 느끼는' 정도의 뜻이 된다. 따라서 어떤 사람이 지루하다면, 그를 두고 He is boring.이라고 할 것이고, 그가 지루함을 느끼고 있다면 He is bored.라고 해야 한다.

EXERCISE

Answers P.15

A

[ ] 안에서 알맞은 말을 고르시오.

1 My brother is [practicing, practiced] pitching in the backyard.

2 The [blocking, blocked] street will be under construction until next week.

3 Fire fighters put out the fire in the [burning, burned] building.

4 The water is leaking from the [breaking, broken] pipe.

5 The students were [amazing, amazed] by the winning score.

6 I couldn't get to the meeting place on time because of the [delaying, delayed] flight.

B

[보기]에서 알맞은 말을 골라 어법에 맞게 바꿔 문장을 완성하시오.

Word Bank	confuse	make	frighten	mend	cancel	invite

1 Some of the musicians ________________ to the party arrived late.

2 He totally forgot about the appointment ________________ last week.

3 The class asked me about the ________________ field trip to the museum.

4 The boy ________________ by the choices couldn't make a decision.

5 She had her old coat ________________.

6 The kids were ________________ by the roaring sound.

C

주어진 단어를 이용하여 [보기]와 같이 문장을 완성하시오.

Example photos / take
→ Let's see the photos taken last Christmas Eve.

1 enter / the event
→ Anyone ________________________ can get a lottery ticket.

2 store / in the wooden boxes
→ He is the one who grew the vegetables ________________________.

3 remove / from the shelf
→ The books ________________________ are on the back table.

4 release / camera
→ I'd like to buy this newly ________________________.

3 분사의 다양한 표현

Pre-Check 두 문장이 같은 의미가 되도록 [ ]에서 알맞은 접속사를 고르시오.
Being sick, I didn't go to school.
→ [Because, So] I was sick, I didn't go to school.

1 분사구문 만들기

(1) 주어가 같을 때
- As I have no money, I can't buy the sofa.

→ ① ~~As~~ I have no money, I can't buy the sofa.
② ~~As I~~ have no money, I can't buy the sofa.
③ Having no money, I can't buy the sofa.

- When we heard the news, we were shocked.

→ ① ~~When~~ we heard the news, we were shocked.
② ~~When we~~ heard the news, we were shocked.
③ Hearing the news, we were shocked.

(2) 주어가 다를 때
- Since it was fine, we took a walk.

→ ① ~~Since~~ it was fine, we took a walk.
② It being fine, we took a walk.

- As his report has been completed on time, he will hand it in immediately.

→ ① ~~As~~ his report has been completed on time, he will hand it in immediately.
② His report having been completed on time, he will hand it in immediately.

▶ 1
(1) 주절과 종속절의 주어가 같으면
① (부사절의) 접속사를 생략하고
② (부사절의) 주어를 생략한 후
③ 남은 동사를 V-ing 형태로 바꾼다.
(2) 주절과 종속절의 주어가 다르면
① (부사절의) 접속사만 생략한 후
② (주어는 그대로 둔 채) 남은 동사를 V-ing형으로 바꾼다.
• 독립분사구문
분사구문의 주어와 주절의 주어가 일치하지 않을 때, 분사 앞에 주어를 밝혀주어야 한다.

주의해야 할 분사구문의 기타 용법
- As I was tired, I went to bed early.
→ (Being) Tired, I went to bed early.
- As you have finished the work, you may go out now.
→ Having finished the work, you may go out now.

• 과거분사가 쓰인 문장에서 Being이나 Having been으로 시작하는 경우 이를 생략할 수 있다. Having p.p.는 주절보다 하나 앞선 시제를 나타낸다.

2 분사구문의 여러 가지 의미

(1) Jumping rope, I sweated a lot.
(= While I was jumping rope, I sweated a lot.)

(2) Not eating enough, we wanted to eat some more.
(= Since we didn't eat enough, we wanted to eat some more.)

▶ 2
(1) 시간: ~할 때, ~하는 동안
(2) 이유: ~이기 때문에, ~ 이므로
(3) 연속상황: ~하고 난 후에, ~한 뒤에
(4) 동시동작: ~하면서, ~과 동시에
(5) 조건: ~라면, ~이면
(6) 양보: ~임에도 불구하고, ~이지만
• 접속사의 의미를 강조할 때는 접속사를 그대로 쓸 수 있다.
After finishing my homework, I went out to play soccer.

(3) Running for an hour, I took a shower.
(= After I ran for an hour, I took a shower.)

(4) Cleaning the computer screen, I talked to her.
(= I talked to her while I was cleaning the computer screen.)

(5) Turning right, you'll find the library.
(= If you turn right, you'll find the library.)

(6) Knowing that it was his fault, he still didn't apologize to her.
(= Although he knew that it was his fault, he didn't apologize to her.)

• 분사구문의 부정: Not[Never] + -ing
Not finishing my homework, I couldn't go out to play soccer.

• 전치사 with를 사용한 부대상황
〈with + 목적어 + -ed/-ing〉
: ~을 하고서, ~ 한 채로
He stood there, and he was folding his arms.
= He stood there, (being) folding his arms.
= He stood there with his arms folded.

3 비인칭 독립 분사

Strictly speaking, we don't believe his thesis.
Judging from his accent, he must be from Germany.
Seeing the circumstances, he should stop doing that.

3
• Judging from ~으로 판단하건대
• Given ~을 고려하면
• Strictly/Frankly/Generally speaking 엄격히/솔직히/일반적으로 말해서
• Depending on ~에 따라
• Speaking of ~에 관해 말하면
• Considering ~을 고려하면
• Concerning ~을 생각하면

Check-up

Answers P.15

A [보기]와 같이 문장을 완성하시오.

Example	Surprised(surprise) by his appearance, she took a step backward.

1 ______________(walk) to the park, he arrived at the picnic.
2 ______________(judge from) her clothes, it must be cold outside.
3 ______________(amuse) by his joke, I laughed until my stomach hurt.
4 ______________(enter) the pipe, the boy was able to rescue the cat.

B 밑줄 친 부분이 의미하는 것을 고르시오.

1 Irritating them all the time, he didn't get an invitation to their party.
ⓐ He irritated them all the time. ⓑ They irritated him all the time.

2 Irritated so much, we didn't invite him to our party.
ⓐ We were irritated so much. ⓑ He was irritated so much.

분사구문의 '능동' vs. '수동'
능동과 수동은 주어가 그 일을 하는 것인지 당하는 것인지를 구분하는 것이다. 분사구문의 경우도 마찬가지이다. 생략된 주어가 그 일을 하는 것인지 당하는 것인지를 고려하여 능동과 수동을 생각하도록 한다.

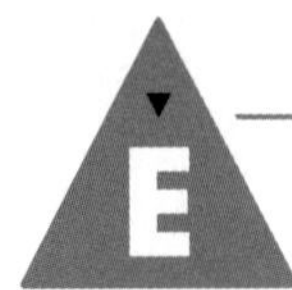

EXERCISE

Answers P.15

A

[ ] 안에서 알맞은 말을 고르시오.

1 [Preparing, Prepared] the holiday meal together, we ate all day long.

2 [Confusing, Confused] so much, he wasn't of help to the other lost hikers.

3 [Came, Coming] to a bus stop, they realized that they had been going in the wrong direction.

4 She ran to the door, [held, holding] her sick puppy in her arms.

5 [Satisfing, Satisfied] with the big success, she cried for joy.

B

[ ] 안에서 알맞은 말을 고르시오.

1 The wrong cake being delivered, I called them to complain.
→ [Because, Although] the wrong cake was delivered, I called them to complain.

2 Having waited for a week, I ordered another pair of shoes.
→ [After, If] I had waited for a week, I ordered another pair of shoes.

3 Watching our grandparents leaving, we cried at the train station.
→ [As, Although] we watched our grandparents leaving, we cried at the train station.

4 Washing the dishes, he talked to a friend on the phone.
→ [Before, While] he was washing the dishes, he talked to a friend on the phone.

5 Arriving late from the airport, he couldn't make it to the meeting on time.
→ [If, Since] he arrived late from the airport, he couldn't make it to the meeting on time.

C

주어진 단어를 이용하여 문장을 완성하시오.

Example find / her lost purse
→ Finding her lost purse, she sighed with relief.

1 be / in school
→ ______________________, she learned to speak Chinese.

2 win / the championship
→ ______________________, they also gained an award.

3 consider / the circumstances
→ ______________________, you should change your travel plan.

4 fold / her arms
→ ______________________, she refused to move away from the door.

REVIEW TEST

Answers P.15

A

[ ] 안에서 알맞은 말을 고르시오.

1 The teacher found the class [fascinated, fascinating] by the history of the Indian tribe.

2 People [amazing, amazed] by the circus clapped for the performers.

3 [While, Although] driving, you should fasten your seat belt.

4 Students found the news article [interesting, interested] enough for their essay topic.

5 They were satisfied with the ceremony [pleasing, pleased] their friends and relatives.

6 [Being, Having] a student, you have to finish your homework before leaving.

7 [If, Although] the wind was bitter, we were refreshed by it.

8 Jack [annoying, annoyed] by her phone call wouldn't answer her question.

B

빈칸에 들어갈 알맞은 말을 고르시오.

1 ________________ the weather, we'd better cancel the meeting and wait here until the rain stops.

ⓐ Considering ⓑ Expected by ⓒ Interrupted in ⓓ Generally speaking

2 The men ________________ in the office are repairing our telephones.

ⓐ work ⓑ working ⓒ worked ⓓ being working

3 ________________ notified, the police arrived too late to arrest the criminals.

ⓐ Have ⓑ Being ⓒ Not having ⓓ Not having been

4 ________________ you leave now, you will encounter less traffic.

ⓐ If ⓑ Even ⓒ While ⓓ Although

5 ________________, the explorers looked for a place to rest in the forest.

ⓐ Tiring ⓑ Have tired ⓒ Being tired ⓓ After tiring

6 ________________ the teachers' conference, she was very thorough.

ⓐ Plan ⓑ Planed ⓒ Planning ⓓ Being planned

7 Was everyone ________________ to meet with them?

ⓐ prepare ⓑ prepared ⓒ to prepare ⓓ have preparing

REVIEW TEST

C

밑줄 친 부분을 바르게 고쳐 문장을 다시 쓰시오.

1 She was so worried that she was forgotten to say that she would be late.

→ ______________________________

2 The missing wallet wasn't stealing. I found it under the bed.

→ ______________________________

3 Speaking general, our class is not prepared to take the test.

→ ______________________________

4 Look at the completing puzzle. It must have been exhausting to put it together!

→ ______________________________

5 The singing bird was fascinating to Sunny. She was satisfying with this amazing discovery.

→ ______________________________

6 The artist drew an interesting woman who was standing by a locking door.

→ ______________________________

D

(A), (B), (C)의 각 네모 안에서 어법에 맞는 말로 바르게 짝지어진 것을 고르시오.

> A Medieval Renaissance Fair was held in Michigan. A reporter attending the fair wrote about his weekend. (A) [While / After] attending the amazing fair, he met many interesting people (B) [pretending / pretended] to be from the 1560s. After encountering the Earl of Sandwich, he was privileged to meet the queen and her court. (C) [Watching / Being watched] a joust between several knights, he wondered if the match had been planned.
>
> *joust 마상 창 시합

	(A)		(B)		(C)
①	While	…	pretending	…	Watching
②	While	…	pretending	…	Being watched
③	While	…	pretended	…	Watching
④	After	…	pretending	…	Watching
⑤	After	…	pretended	…	Being watched

FURTHER STUDY

Writing

▶▶ 우리말과 같은 뜻이 되도록 주어진 단어를 이용하여 문장을 완성하시오. (분사구문을 사용할 것)

1 버스를 쫓아가다가 발이 걸려 넘어졌다. (rush for, the bus)

→ ______________________________, I tripped and fell.

2 그는 파일을 다운로드한 후에 컴퓨터를 껐다. (download the files, turn off)

→ Having ______________________, he ______________________ the computer.

3 첫 번째 모퉁이에서 오른쪽으로 돌면 빵집을 찾을 수 있다. (turn right, at the first corner)

→ ______________________________, you can find a bakery.

4 길을 걷다가 나는 오래된 앨범을 파는 새로 문을 연 가게를 발견했다. (walk down, the street, sell, old albums)

→ ______________________, I noticed a new shop ______________________.

5 그의 강의 내용을 받아 적는 동안, 내게 멋진 생각이 떠올랐다. (take down)

→ ______________________ his lectures, I hit upon a great idea.

6 몇 년간 고국을 떠나있었기 때문에 그녀는 가족이 많이 그리웠다. (be away from one's country)

→ Having ______________________ for years, she missed her family a lot.

7 차를 운전하는 동안 나는 그 누구도 우리 팀이 진 것에 관해 얘기하는 것을 듣지 못했다.
(drive, the car, talk about, our team's loss)

→ ______________________, I heard no one ______________________.

8 Don이 떠나는 것을 알았음에도 불구하고, 나는 그에게 내 일을 도와달라고 부탁했다. (know, ask, help)

→ ____________ Don was leaving, I ______________________ me with the work anyway.

▶ 본동사로서의 분사

현재분사	be + -ing: 진행시제
과거분사	be + -ed: 수동태 have -ed: 완료시제

▶ 형용사로서의 분사

현재분사	과거분사
V-ing (능동, 진행: ~하는, ~하고 있는)	V-ed (수동, 완료: ~당한, ~되어진, ~해 버린)
alarming (놀라는) amazing (놀랄만한, 굉장한) astonishing (놀라운, 눈부신) annoying (성가신, 귀찮은) boring (지루하게 하는, 따분하게 하는) charming (매력 있는) confusing (혼란시키는) depressing (침울하게 만드는) disturbing (불안하게 하는) embarrassing (당황케 하는) encouraging (힘을 북돋아 주는) entertaining (재미있는, 유쾌한) exciting (호기심을 불러일으키는) exhausting (피로하게 하는) fascinating (매혹적인) frightening (깜짝 놀라게 하는) horrifying (무서운, 소름 끼치는) interesting (흥미 있는, 재미있는) irritating (짜증나게 하는, 성가신) moving (감동을 불러일으키는) pleasing (유쾌한, 즐거운) relaxing (긴장을 푸는) satisfying (만족을 주는, 만족스러운) shocking (충격을 주는, 충격적인) surprising (놀랄만한) tiring (피로하게 하는, 고된, 지루한) touching (감동시키는) troubling (걱정을 끼치는, 불안을 야기하는)	alarmed (깜짝 놀란, 겁먹은) amazed (몹시 놀란) astonished (깜짝 놀란) annoyed (성가신) bored (지루한, 따분한) charmed (매혹된) confused (혼란스러운) depressed (낙담한) disturbed (불안한) embarrassed (어리둥절한) encouraged (장려된) entertained (재미있는) excited (흥분한, 자극받은) exhausted (다 써버린, 고갈된, 기진맥진한) fascinated (매료된) frightened (깜짝 놀란) horrified (오싹한, 섬뜩한) interested (호기심이 생긴) irritated (짜증난, 화난) moved (감동한) pleased (기쁜) relaxed (느슨한) satisfied (만족한) shocked (충격을 받은) surprised (놀란) tired (피곤한) touched (감동한, 마음이 움직인) troubled (걱정스러운, 불안해하는)

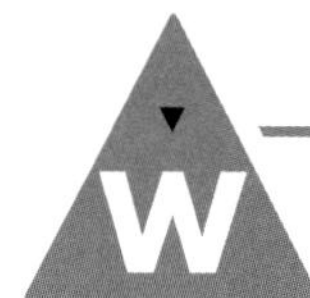

WRAP-UP TEST

Answers P.16

1 빈칸에 들어갈 알맞은 말을 고르시오.

It's ________ how popular American movies are around the world.

ⓐ surprise ⓑ surprises
ⓒ surprising ⓓ surprised

2 대화의 빈칸에 들어갈 말이 바르게 짝지어진 것을 고르시오.

A Have you ________ the news?

B Yes, we're all ________ by his recovery.

ⓐ hear – shock
ⓑ heard – pleased
ⓒ knowing – delighted
ⓓ knew – amused

3 ⓐ~ⓓ 중 given이 들어갈 위치로 알맞은 곳을 고르시오.

Some of the ⓐ patients ⓑ the new ⓒ medicine quickly felt ⓓ better.

4 우리말을 영어로 옮길 때 빈칸에 알맞은 말을 써 넣으시오.

솔직히 말해서, 그의 아이디어는 실현 불가능하다.

________________, his idea is practically impossible.

5 주어진 문장과 의미가 가장 가까운 것을 고르시오.

Considering it, we canceled the meeting.

ⓐ When we consider it, we had to cancel the meeting.
ⓑ After we considered it, we canceled the meeting.
ⓒ Even though we considered it, we didn't cancel the meeting.
ⓓ While we are considering it, we canceled the meeting.

6 밑줄 친 부분의 쓰임이 나머지와 다른 것을 고르시오.

ⓐ Is it raining outside?
ⓑ My brother was fixing the computer then.
ⓒ Matthew was reading a book when the phone rang.
ⓓ I bought a sleeping bag yesterday.

7 밑줄 친 ⓐ, ⓑ를 어법에 맞게 바꿔 쓰시오.

• Some kids ⓐ listen to the classical concert were asleep.
• The car ⓑ steal yesterday was discovered somewhere on the Seoul-Busan highway.

→ ⓐ ________ ⓑ ________

8 어법상 옳지 않은 것을 고르시오.

ⓐ He felt extremely tired after the game.
ⓑ He's not used to driving on the right.
ⓒ Drinking water before meals is not good for health.
ⓓ The cried baby had a high fever.

[9-10] 글을 읽고, 물음에 답하시오.

An unusual art exhibit was ⓐ creating to encourage visitors to listen to art. Listening without seeing was the intention of each artist. Wetland noises were ⓑ played from a speaker behind a plant, for example. Other works of art ⓒ included a phone playing music. 방문객의 의견으로 판단하건대 the reactions were ⓓ mixed. Some people found the sounds pleasant, but some found them unpleasant.

9 밑줄 친 ⓐ~ⓓ 중 쓰임이 잘못된 것을 고르시오.

10 밑줄 친 우리말을 영어로 쓰시오.

→ ________________ the comments of the visitors

The Grammar

2
Level

UNIT 07

수동태

수동태

Pre-Check 우리말을 참고하여 수동태 문장을 완성하시오.

1 They repair the cars in the garage. (수리한다)
→ The cars in the garage ________________ by them. (수리된다)

2 He opened the door. (열었다)
→ The door ________________ by him. (열렸다)

1 수동태 문장 만들기

Karen Smith writes fiction stories.
→ Fiction stories are written by Karen Smith.
(① fiction stories → Fiction stories, ② writes → are written, ③ Karen Smith → by Karen Smith)

People speak English all around the world. (현재)
→ English is spoken by people all around the world.

His behavior shocked us. (과거)
→ We were shocked by his behavior.

She is mowing the lawn now. (현재진행)
→ The lawn is being mowed by her now.

Harris was baking cookies at that time. (과거진행)
→ Cookies were being baked by Harris at that time.

He has set the table in the backyard. (현재완료)
→ The table has been set in the backyard by him.

Our chef will make the wedding cake. (미래)
→ The wedding cake will be made by our chef.

1

능동태를 수동태로 바꾸기
① 능동태 목적어 → 수동태 주어
② 동사 → be + p.p.
③ 문장의 주어 → by + 목적격

* 주의해야 할 수동태의 시제
  - 수동태의 시제는 능동태의 시제에 일치시킨다.
  - 동사의 수는 수동태의 주어의 수에 일치시킨다. 행위자가 일반인 (we, they, people) 일 경우나 불확실할 경우에는 생략할 수 있다.

의문문 수동태
The poem was written by her.
- 의문사가 없는 경우
  → Was the poem written by her?
- 의문사가 있는 경우
  → When was the poem written by her?

2 수동태[ⓐ] vs. 능동태[ⓑ]

ⓐ A: How old is the house?
B: The house was built in 1996.

ⓑ A: Who built the house?
B: My grandfather built it.

2

ⓐ 수동태 문장
: 행위를 '받는' 대상에 초점

ⓑ 능동태 문장
: 행위를 '하는' 주체에 초점

ⓐ A: When will the presentation be?
B: It will be held next Tuesday.

ⓑ A: Who is going to give a presentation?
B: I am going to give one.

3 수동태로 쓰지 않는 동사

(1) They disappeared some time before 2004.
(X) They were disappeared some time before 2004.

(2) You have a nice suit.
(X) A nice suit is had by you.

These shoes fit me well.
(X) I'm fitted well by these shoes.

3
(1) 목적어를 갖지 않는 동사
: appear, disappear 등의 자동사
(2) 목적어를 갖는 동사 중 수동 불가인 동사
: have, own, cost, fit, suit, lack, resemble 등

Check-up

Answers P.17

A [ ] 안에서 알맞은 말을 고르시오.

1 A violent criminal [captured, was captured] by the policemen.
2 The person [spoke, were spoken] to him about the zoo.
3 This cheese cake [bought, was bought] by her last night.
4 Kevin [saw, was seen] at the game by Jim's friends.
5 They [moved, were moved] a piano into my apartment.
6 The wall [didn't repair, wasn't repaired] by the construction company.

B [ ] 안에서 알맞은 말을 고르시오.

A What is this deep bite? Who did this to you?
B My dog. He ① [bit, was bitten] me the other day.
A Are you okay?
B It is not the first time I ② [have bitten, have been bitten] by him.
A So, did you do anything about him?
B Well, this time, I ③ [sent, was sent] him to my parents' house for a while.
A When will he be back?
B He ④ [will send, will be sent] back next week.

수동태 vs. 능동태
수동태와 능동태의 주어는 화자[필자]가 어떤 것을 중점으로 이야기하느냐에 따라 달라진다. 사건을 바라보는 시각[사물]이 '행위를 한 사람[사물]'인지 '행위를 당한 사람[사물]'인지가 기준이다. 특히 행위의 주체(그 행동을 한 사람 또는 사물)를 알 수 없는 경우 행위를 당한 사람[사물]의 입장에서 이야기하는 수동태를 쓴다.

EXERCISE

Answers P.17

A

주어진 단어를 이용하여 문장을 완성하시오.

1 The old school ______________ (demolish) by a flood last week.

2 Nobody ______________ (surprise) about the new project then.

3 Many different online courses ______________ (take) every semester.

4 Nowadays, the Internet ______________ (can, use) for personal advertisement.

5 People ______________ (frighten) because of the earthquake last night.

6 Most credit card bills ______________ (send) via email these days.

B

밑줄 친 부분을 바르게 고쳐 쓰시오. 틀리지 않았다면 ○표 하시오.

1 Has the thief been caught <u>the police</u>? ______________

2 My grandmother <u>was confusing</u> by the notice in the mall. ______________

3 The kid <u>broke</u> the clock, so he replaced it with a new one. ______________

4 The new signs <u>posted</u> on the green bulletin board last night. ______________

5 I was <u>irritate</u> by the barking dog. ______________

6 The music <u>will perform</u> by the new children's choir. ______________

C

주어진 문장을 수동태 문장으로 바꿔 쓰시오.

1 The six brave firefighter put out the big fire.

→ ______________ by the six brave firefighter.

2 My uncle has fixed the broken bookcase.

→ ______________ by my uncle.

3 The waitress is filling the water pitchers.

→ ______________ by the waitress.

4 The doctor will lead the operation on Tom's broken leg.

→ ______________ by the doctor.

5 Will the chef bake three more pies?

→ ______________ by the chef?

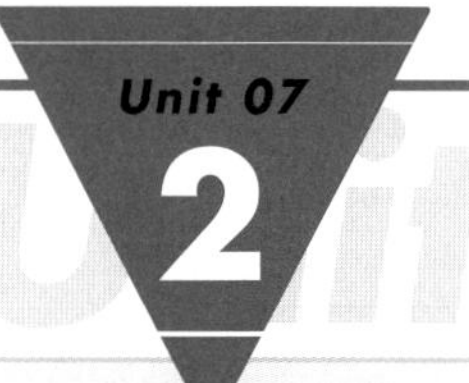

수동태의 여러 가지 형태

Pre-Check 주어진 문장을 수동태로 바꿀 때 빈칸에 알맞은 말을 써 넣으시오.

• He gave the elders computer lessons.

1 ______________________ are given computer lessons by him.

2 ______________________ are given to the elders by him.

1 4형식 문장의 수동태

(1) Jane gave Robby a book.
→ **A book** was given to Robby by Jane.
→ **Robby** was given a book by Jane.

(2) He made me chocolate cake.
→ **Chocolate cake** was made for me by him.
* I was made chocolate cake by him. (x)

2 5형식 문장의 수동태

(1) 목적어와 목적격보어가 있는 문장
Kids called him Uncle John.
→ He was called Uncle John by kids.

(2) 사역동사가 있는 문장
She made us clean the room.
→ We were made to clean the room by her.

(3) 지각동사가 있는 문장
Brandon saw her running away.
→ She was seen running away by Brandon.

Susan saw him sleep on the sofa.
→ He was seen to sleep on the sofa by Susan.

3 동사구의 수동태

The nurse took care of my mother.
→ My mother was taken care of by the nurse.

The truck ran over the poor cat.
→ The poor cat was run over by the truck.

1

4형식 문장은 목적어가 2개이므로
→ 직접목적어를 주어로 만든다.
→ 간접목적어를 주어로 만든다.
* make, buy, write, bring 등은 간접목적어를 주어로 할 경우 의미가 어색할 수 있어 잘 쓰지 않는다.

간접목적어 앞에 쓰는 전치사
(1) to를 쓰는 동사 – write, pass, read, give, teach, sell, send 등
(2) for를 쓰는 동사 – make, buy, get, find 등

2

(1) 목적어를 주어로 하고 목적격보어는 그대로 둔다.
(2) 목적격보어인 동사원형을 to부정사로 바꾼다.
* 사역동사 have와 let은 수동형으로 쓰지 않는다.
She let him go out.
→ He was allowed to go out.
(X) He was let to go out.
(3) 목적격보어가 분사인 경우에는 그대로 둔다. 목적격보어가 동사원형인 경우에는 to부정사로 바꾼다.

3

동사구는 한 단어로 취급한다.
• take care of ~을 돌보다
• take off (옷 등을) 벗다
• put on ~을 입다, 신다
• carry out ~을 수행하다, 실행하다
• look after ~을 돌보다

4 by 이외의 전치사를 쓰는 수동태

My brother is interested in astronomy.
The furniture is covered with white sheets.
Recently lots of paper is made from recycled materials.

5 수동태의 여러 가지 형태

(1) It is said that he falls in love with her.
↑ He is said to fall in love with her.
↑ People say that he falls in love with her.

It is believed that she came from Cuba.
↑ She is believed to have come from Cuba.
↑ People believe that she came from Cuba.

(2) ⓐ Employees wanted to be paid more money.
ⓑ I hate being treated like a child.
ⓒ They might be transferred to other factories.

4

- be satisfied with ~에 만족하다
- be surprised at ~에 놀라다
- be filled with ~로 가득 차다
- be accustomed to ~에 익숙하다
- be made from[of] ~로 만들어지다

5

(1) ~라고 한다

- People say that ~
  → It is said that ~
- People believe that ~
  → It is believed that ~
- that절의 주어가 문장의 주어로 쓰이면, that절의 동사를 to부정사 형태로 바꾼다.

(2) ⓐ to부정사 수동태: to+be+p.p.
ⓑ 동명사 수동태: being+p.p.
ⓒ 조동사 수동태: 조동사+be+p.p.

Check-up

Answers P.17

A [ ] 안에서 알맞은 말을 고르시오.

1 The teacher made the class finish it.
→ The class was made [finish, to finish] it by the teacher.

2 Mom made spaghetti for my friends.
→ Spaghetti [was made, was made for] my friends by Mom.

3 They painted the fence a brown color.
→ The fence was [painting, painted] a brown color.

4 The animals at the zoo fascinated the little kids.
→ The little kids [were fascinated in, were fascinated by] the animals at the zoo.

B [ ] 안에서 알맞은 말을 고르시오.

A What happened to you? Your whole face ① [is tanned, has tanned]!

B Yeah, it's from the beach volleyball game last weekend. Sunscreen didn't really work. My back ② [is burned, was burned] as well. Yet, it's a good thing that my face has recovered in such a short time. My doctor said my back and arms ③ [were healed, would be healed] in a few weeks.

수동태의 시제
어떤 행위의 영향을 받거나 어떤 상태에 빠지게 되는 시점이 언제인가에 따라서 수동태의 시점이 정해진다. ①은 현재의 상태에 대해 이야기하는 것이고, ②는 과거의 상황, ③은 미래의 상황에 대해 언급하는 것이다.

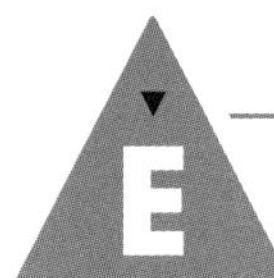

EXERCISE

Answers P.17

A

주어진 능동태 문장을 수동태 문장으로 바꿔 쓰시오.

1 The manager made the cook prepare a German meal.
→ The cook ______________________ a German meal by the manager.

2 My dog found a black squirrel in the park.
→ A black squirrel ______________________ my dog in the park.

3 Peter has bought flowers for his mother.
→ Flowers ______________________ for his mother by Peter.

4 Everyone felt the earthquake in the area.
→ The earthquake ______________________ everyone in the area.

5 The residents heard someone screaming at night.
→ Someone ______________________ at night by the residents.

6 Their good service satisfied the passengers.
→ The passengers ______________________ their good service.

B

밑줄 친 부분을 바르게 고쳐 쓰시오. 틀리지 않았다면 ○표 하시오.

1 A diamond ring was given to Lora of Tom. ______________

2 The building has been managed for five years by him. ______________

3 The bird was looked after him while I was on a trip. ______________

4 The writing will be corrected to the editor. ______________

5 People are said that he traveled around the world for a couple of years. ______________

C

주어진 말을 어법에 맞게 바꿔 문장을 완성하시오.

1 My cousin dislikes ______________(treat) as a careless person.

2 We all pleasantly ______________(hear) the young students playing their violins yesterday.

3 Next month, she will ______________(transfer) to another city by her company.

4 A lecture will ______________(give) by Prof. Kim at 7 pm in the auditorium.

5 Most students don't want to ______________(teach) in boring ways by their teachers.

6 I thought the newcomer ______________(accustom) to working on a computer.

REVIEW TEST

Answers P.18

A

[ ] 안에서 알맞은 말을 고르시오.

1 The factory [was sold, can be sold] by the company in 1995.

2 Many parrots [are trained, are trained to] speak English in three months.

3 The man [has been taught, has taught] to use the new software.

4 The emails were written [to, from] the famous author by the students.

5 The girl was watched [made, making] a phone call by my sister.

6 The students wanted [was taught, to be taught] other languages in class.

7 The little boy [was covered at, was covered with] mud from the wet playground.

B

빈칸에 들어갈 알맞은 말을 고르시오.

1 The store ________________ for the last ten years.

ⓐ had not closed ⓑ is being closed ⓒ will be closed ⓓ has not been closed

2 Many people ________________ by the flood across the country last year.

ⓐ are affected ⓑ were affected ⓒ will be affected ⓓ have been affecting

3 The desserts ________________ by the chef tomorrow.

ⓐ will make ⓑ will be made ⓒ can make ⓓ are being made

4 This research ________________ from November 2013 to April 2014.

ⓐ carried by ⓑ was carried ⓒ is carried by ⓓ was carried on

5 Your expenses will be ________________ completely next week.

ⓐ taken ⓑ taken care ⓒ to take care of ⓓ taken care of

6 Mr. Green ________________ poems since high school.

ⓐ written ⓑ has written ⓒ is writing ⓓ has been wrote

7 If you ________________ photography, don't hesitate to join our club.

ⓐ interest by ⓑ interested to ⓒ are interested in ⓓ are interested for

REVIEW TEST

C

밑줄 친 부분을 바르게 고쳐 문장을 다시 쓰시오.

1 These chocolates are made by the finest cocoa beans.

→ ______________________

2 The children were not let to enter the hall.

→ ______________________

3 I wanted to admire like a movie star by lots of people.

→ ______________________

4 Some books will be given to you with my father.

→ ______________________

5 The party for her grandfather has planned by Rachel.

→ ______________________

D

(A), (B), (C)의 각 네모 안에서 어법에 맞는 말로 바르게 짝지어진 것을 고르시오.

> Two endangered creatures (A) [were studying / were being studied] by an English zoo expert in China last year. He was concerned (B) [by / with] the survival of the slender loris and the Yangtze River dolphin. The slender loris is an endangered animal. The slender loris (C) [is considered / is considering] an evil omen. People are killing it because they fear it. Unfortunately, the zoo expert couldn't find any Yangtze River dolphins. It may be too late to save this dolphin family now.
>
> * slender loris 인디아로리스 원숭이

	(A)		(B)		(C)
①	were studying	…	by	…	is considered
②	were studying	…	with	…	is considering
③	were being studied	…	by	…	is considered
④	were being studied	…	by	…	is considering
⑤	were being studied	…	with	…	is considered

F FURTHER STUDY

Writing

▶▶ **우리말과 같은 뜻이 되도록 주어진 단어를 이용하여 문장을 완성하시오.**

1 그의 얼굴은 이 마을 사람 모두에게 알려져 있다. (know)

→ ______________________________ all the people of this town.

2 그 학생들은 화학 실험 결과에 흥분했다. (excite)

→ The students ______________________ the results of the chemistry experiments.

3 나의 애완용 거북이가 현재 그 동물 병원에서 치료를 받고 있다. (treat, in the animal hospital)

→ My pet turtle ______________________________ now.

4 케이크는 딸기와 휘핑크림으로 채워져 있다. (fill)

→ The cakes ______________________ strawberries and whipped cream.

5 그의 수리된 차가 3일 동안 그 차고에 주차되어 있었다. (have, park)

→ His repaired car ______________________ in the garage for three days.

6 어제 선생님이 주신 노트에 엄마의 사인을 받아가야 한다. (give, must, sign)

→ The note my teacher __________ to me yesterday ____________________ by my mother.

7 그녀의 계획은 다음 위원회 회기 중에 토의될 것이다. (plan, discuss)

→ ______________________________ in the next committee session.

8 그녀는 그 집 가격에 전혀 놀라지 않았다고 말했다. (not, surprise, the cost of the house)

→ She said she ______________________________ at all.

MUST-KNOW

▶ 수동태의 여러 가지 시제

시제	능동태 → 수동태	형태
현재	He writes an email. → An email **is written** by him.	am/are/is + p.p.
과거	He wrote an email. → An email **was written** by him.	was/were + p.p.
미래	He will write an email. → An email **will be written** by him.	will + be + p.p.
현재진행	He is writing an email. → An email **is being written** by him.	am/are/is + being + p.p.
과거진행	He was writing an email. → An email **was being written** by him.	was/were + being + p.p.
미래진행	He will be writing an email. → An email **will be being written** by him.	will be + being + p.p.
현재완료	He has written an email. → An email **has been written** by him.	has/have + been + p.p.
과거완료	He had written an email. → An email **had been written** by him.	had + been + p.p.
미래완료	He will have written an email. → An email **will have been written** by him.	will + have + been + p.p.

▶ 주의해야 할 수동태 구문 (by 이외의 전치사를 쓰는 구문)

전치사의 종류	예	의미
at	be surprised/shocked/amazed/alarmed at	~에 놀라다
	be annoyed at	~에 화가 나다
	be disappointed at	~에 실망하다
with	be satisfied/dissatisfied with	~에 만족하다/불만이다
	be pleased/delighted with	~에 기뻐하다
	be filled with	~로 가득 차다
	be covered with	~로 덮여 있다
	be surrounded with	~으로 둘러싸여 있다
to	be known to	~에게 알려져 있다
	be known for	~로 유명하다
	be known as	~로 알려져 있다
	be known by	~에 의해 알려지다
	be accustomed to	~에 익숙하다
	be married/engaged to	~와 결혼/약혼하다
of	be made of (재료의 형태를 쉽게 알 수 있음) be made from (재료의 형태를 알 수 없음)	~로 만들어지다
	be composed of	~로 구성되다
in	be interested in	~에 흥미가 있다
	be involved in	~에 관련되다
about	be concerned about	~에 대해 걱정하다

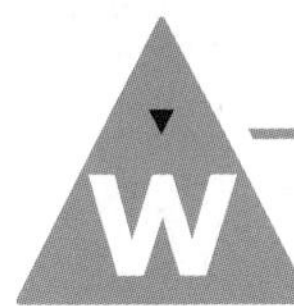

WRAP-UP TEST

Answers P.19

1 대화의 응답으로 알맞은 것을 고르시오.

A When was the poem written?
B ______________________

ⓐ It was written by my little sister.
ⓑ It can be written with a word processor.
ⓒ It was written last night.
ⓓ It was being written about love.

2 주어진 문장을 수동태로 바꿀 때 빈칸에 알맞은 말을 쓰시오.

My boss is introducing the secretary to every staff member.
→ The secretary ______________________ every staff member by my boss.

3 빈칸에 들어갈 말이 나머지와 다른 것을 고르시오.

ⓐ The software was installed ______ Mr. Taylor.
ⓑ Dinner is being cooked ______ Amy.
ⓒ A museum will be built ______ my town.
ⓓ Jane Eyre was written ______ Charlotte Bronte.

4 대화의 빈칸에 알맞은 말을 써 넣으시오.

A When is the due date of the payment?
B It ______________________ (should, pay) by the end of the month.

5 밑줄 친 부분의 쓰임이 잘못된 것을 고르시오.

ⓐ I'm tired of his excuses.
ⓑ Aren't you disappointed with your grade?
ⓒ President Lincoln is well known as Gettysburg Address.
ⓓ The bus is packed with lots of students and workers at rush hour.

6 주어진 문장을 두 가지 형태의 수동태로 바꿔 쓰시오.

Teddy gave me a bunch of roses.
→ I ______________ a bunch of roses by Teddy.
→ A bunch of roses ______________ me byTeddy.

[7-8] 어법상 옳지 않은 것을 고르시오.

7 ⓐ The little boy put on a coat.
ⓑ The dog was let enter the room.
ⓒ This official letter was written to the dean.
ⓓ The theft was seen taking the wallet from the woman's purse.

8 ⓐ The team is planning to finish the course by August 4th.
ⓑ The survey was carrying out from November to December.
ⓒ The wall was broken down because of the storm.
ⓓ All the boys and girls were made to do sit-ups and squats.

[9-10] 글을 읽고, 물음에 답하시오.

Recently, a female deer was stranded on the ice of a frozen Oklahoma lake. The poor animal was almost frozen to death. Soon, a TV news helicopter appeared above the frightened deer. Then an amazing thing happened. The wind from the helicopter began to blow the deer across the slippery ice and towards the shore. When she reached the shore, the deer jumped up and ran away. Everyone ______________ but very happy for the lucky deer.

9 빈칸에 들어갈 알맞은 말을 고르시오.

ⓐ surprises ⓑ surprised
ⓒ is surprised ⓓ was surprised

10 글쓴이의 심정 변화로 알맞은 것을 고르시오.

ⓐ worried → relieved
ⓑ relaxed → nervous
ⓒ shocked → amused
ⓓ frightened → surprised

명사, 관사, 대명사

명사

Pre-Check 명사를 찾아 모두 밑줄을 그으시오. 그 중 셀 수 없는 명사에는 동그라미를 치시오.

1 My sister and I watched a movie last night on TV.
2 Have you ever been to Canada?
3 What would you like to drink, coffee or tea?
4 What is the most important thing in your life?

1 명사의 종류

(1) 보통명사: 사람, 사물에 관한 일반적인 이름
I have a dog and two cats.
The girl is cooking with her brother.

(2) 집합명사: 여러 개체가 모여 집합을 이룬 명사
How many members are there in your family?
The audience liked the musical.

(3) 물질명사: 특정한 형태가 없는 물질
I like coffee without sugar or cream.
How much money do you need?

(4) 추상명사: 형태 없이 머릿속으로 그려지는 추상 명칭
She smiled with happiness.
This will be your last chance.

cf) ① It was a great success.
② The pen is mightier than the sword.

(5) 고유명사: 사람, 장소, 국가명 등 하나뿐인 고유한 이름
Her name is Deborah.
She works in Egypt as an archeologist.

2 셀 수 있는 명사

(1) We have a room for you.
We have two rooms for you.

(2) Do you have any friends in America?
I have several friends in America.
I'll be right back in a few minutes.

1

(1) 단/복수 가능, 복수형은 -(e)s

(2) 단/복수 가능
My family are all well.
가족 개개인 – 복수 취급
My family is going to the beach.
가족 전체 – 단수 취급

〈the + 형용사〉 = 복수명사
the rich = rich people
the young = young people

(3) 단수 취급

* 집합적 물질명사 (단수 형태만 존재)
: furniture, clothing, luggage, baggage 등
: 집합적 성격과 물질명사의 성격을 동시에 지닌다.
The furniture was made in Italy.

(4) 성질, 상태, 개념 등을 가리키는 말
art, life, health, policy, love 등

cf)
① 추상명사의 보통명사적 의미
추상명사가 구체적인 행위나 성질 등을 나타낼 때 a(n)을 붙여 쓸 수 있다.
a beauty (미인)
② 〈the + 보통명사〉 = 추상명사

(5) 세상에 하나 밖에 없는 사람, 사물, 장소 등
Mars, Japan, Seoul, Tom 등

2

셀 수 있는 명사: 보통/집합명사
(1) 단/복수 가능
(2) many, a few 등을 사용한 수 표시

3 셀 수 없는 명사

(1) Milk is good for your health.
The weather is hot and humid.
Water is essential for life.
(x) A water is essential for life.

(2) We have a little time for you.
We have a lot of time for you.
Do you have some time to talk with me?

4 셀 수 없는 명사 세기

Drink two bottles of water every day for your health.
I will give you a piece of advice.
She will buy us four cartons of milk in the afternoon.
We need five pounds of sugar to make chocolate cookies.
Actually, I need six bowls of rice to serve to my visitors, too.

3

셀 수 없는 명사: 물질/추상/고유명사

(1) 항상 단수 취급
: 셀 수 없으므로 a/an을 쓰지 않는다.

(2) much, little 등을 사용하여 양 표시

* 명사 앞에 쓸 수 있는 수량 표시

셀 수 있는 명사 앞	셀 수 없는 명사 앞
many few, a few several	much little, a little
any, some, lots of, a lot of, plenty of	

4

- a cup of (coffee, tea)
- a loaf of (bread)
- a glass of (juice, water, wine)
- a box of (cereal)
- a bottle of (soda, ink, wine)
- a carton of (milk)
- a spoonful of (salt, oil, honey)
- a pound of (sugar, flour)
- a piece of (cake, chalk, advice)
- a slice of (cheese, pizza)
- a bunch of (grapes, bananas)
- a bar of (soap)

Check-up

Answers P.19

A [ ] 안에서 알맞은 말을 고르시오.

1 I'm going to book a [room, rooms] for the Christmas holiday.
2 Jack had only a few [person, people] in his study group.
3 We went to a lot of [play, plays] while we were in New York.
4 This project took over three [hour, hours] to complete.
5 We'll have to bring [many, a lot of] food and drinks to the picnic.

B [ ] 안에서 알맞은 말을 고르시오.

A I'm going to order ① [any, some] juice. What do you want to order?
B I will just have ② [a piece of, a cup of] coffee.
C Make that two.
A Haven't you already had too ③ [much, many] coffee today?
B It's only my third cup today.

셀 수 있는 명사 vs. 셀 수 없는 명사

셀 수 있는 명사와 셀 수 없는 명사의 구분은 영어뿐 아니라 우리말에도 있다. 예를 들어, 우리도 물을 한 개, 두 개라고 하지 않고, 물 한 잔, 물 한 그릇과 같은 단위로 셈을 한다. 다만, 우리말에는 물 두 잔들과 같은 복수를 쓰지 않는 점이 다르다. 또한 영어에서는 셀 수 없는 명사라 하더라도 아주 일반화되거나 상품화된 경우에는 그저 한 종류의 제품으로 개수를 세기도 하는데, 커피가 그 대표적인 경우이다. 커피숍 커피를 생각해 보자. 이마도 누구나 잔에 담겨있는 커피를 생각할 것이다. 이런 경우에 우리는 보통 two cups of coffee 또는 two coffees라고 말하는데, 이때의 coffees가 바로 커피를 하나의 상품으로 취급해 셈을 하는 경우이다.

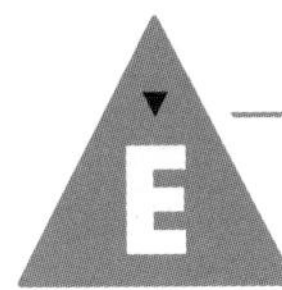

EXERCISE

Answers P.19

A

[ ] 안에서 알맞은 말을 고르시오.

1 I felt [many, a lot of] anger because Suzy didn't keep her promise.

2 Give me [a few, a little] cups of coffee and I'll take them back to the others.

3 I'd like to see you a few [time, times] before you go on your business trip.

4 You can eat as [many, much] as you want at the buffet.

5 Spain wasn't Tim's first [trip, trips] to Europe so he had no problems there.

6 It was a nice park with [much, lots of] beautiful trees and flowers.

7 Can't you give me 3 slices of [cheese, cheeses] so I can share them with the others?

B

밑줄 친 부분을 바르게 고쳐 쓰시오. 틀리지 않았다면 ○표 하시오.

1 Everybody agrees that <u>a water</u> is essential for life. ______________

2 There was one way to see how <u>many</u> wine was left in the bottle. ______________

3 Only <u>a few people</u> gathered to see the movie. ______________

4 I have good <u>news</u> for you. ______________

5 Sandy made <u>much</u> calls to her mother but couldn't get through. ______________

6 He reads <u>a lot</u> books by different authors. ______________

7 There was <u>way</u> to solve the problem but nobody knew what it was. ______________

C

[보기]에서 알맞은 말을 골라 어법에 맞게 문장을 완성하시오.

Word Bank	a teaspoon of	four glasses of	two bowls of	a few slices of
	a bag of	many bottles of	two cartons of	

1 She wanted to take ______________________ water to the soccer team.

2 In-ho had ______________________ rice and got very full.

3 Let's get ______________________ cheese to go with the bread.

4 Lisa and Denny brought ______________________ flour into the kitchen.

5 She put ______________________ sugar into her cup.

6 I've had at least ______________________ juice at the party.

7 My little sister drank ______________________ milk one after the other.

관사

Pre-Check 우리말에 맞도록 빈칸에 a(n), the, Ø 중 하나를 골라 문장을 완성하시오.

1 He cleans his room once ____________ week. (매주 한 번씩)

2 Do you remember ____________ Italian restaurant we used to go to? (그 이탈리아 음식점)

3 Water consists of ____________ oxygen and ____________ hydrogen. (산소와 수소로)

1 부정관사 a/an

(1) I need a pencil.
It's not a good solution.

(2) It may take an hour to finish this assignment.
We couldn't climb the mountain in a day.

(3) He drinks water once an hour.
Jason writes a letter to his parents once a week.

(4) A locust is an insect that flies in large groups and eats crops.

cf) The locust is an insect that flies in large groups and eats crops.
Locusts are insects that fly in large groups and eat crops.

(5) The kids are all of an age.

1

(1) '어떤' : 막연한 것을 가리킬 때
(2) '하나', '한 개' : 개수로 셀 때
(3) '매 ~', '~ 마다'
(4) 종족을 대표할 때

cf) 대표명사 표기의 여러 가지 방법
① a/an + 단수명사 : a dog
② the + 단수명사 : the dog
③ 복수명사 : dogs

(5) '동일한', '같은' : of a(n)~의 형태로 씀

*주의해야 할 a(n)의 사용
an은 철자가 아닌 모음으로 소리 나는 발음 앞에 쓴다.
: an hour, an MP3 player, an FBI agent 등

2 정관사 the

(1) I saw a girl yesterday, and the girl was really cute.
I bumped into a man, and the man stole my wallet.

(2) Mom said, "Turn off the computer."
Please pass me the potatoes.

(3) The hot chocolate in the cup got cold.
The man at the office gave me the directions to the place.

(4) I love to see the North Star in the sky at midnight.
Do you know about the person who first stepped onto the moon?

(5) My friend Susie got the best score on the test.
What is the most important thing in your life?

(6) My sister can play the drums and the guitar.
I go to the movies at least twice a month.

2

(1) 앞에 나온 대상을 언급할 때
(2) 서로 알고 있는 대상에 관해 얘기할 때
(3) 수식어구로 한정될 때
(4) 세상에서 하나뿐인 것
the earth, the sun, the moon 등
(5) 최상급 등의 수식어 앞에
the most, the same, the only, the very 등
(6) 기타
play the piano (악기 이름 앞), the sky, the weather, the Internet, listen to the radio, go to the movies 등

3 무관사

(1) How was your vacation in Singapore?
Good advice is similar to good writing.

(2) I don't think I can live without computers.
He likes to read books about history.

(3) Harry goes to bed early in the evening.
He commutes to work by bicycle.

(4) My family came here by airplane.
We'll have dinner with her in a nice restaurant.

cf) She had a wonderful dinner with him in a nice restaurant.

(5) Sir! What is the value of a human life?
I went to New York with mom.

3

(1) 셀 수 없는 명사 앞
(고유/추상/물질명사 등)

(2) 구체적으로 정하지 않은 불특정 사물

(3) 시설물, 사물 등이 원래의 목적으로 사용될 때

- go to church
: 교회에 '예배 드리러' 가다
go to the church
: 교회라는 '건물에' 가다

(4) 운송 수단, 식사 이름, 운동 경기 등의 앞
cf) a(n) + 형용사 + 식사 이름

(5) 호칭, 가족 관계

Check-up

Answers P.20

A [ ] 안에서 알맞은 말을 고르시오.

1 Come to [an, ø, the] Ireland to visit me if you have time.
2 Where did you put [a, ø, the] report that we discussed last night?
3 I'm going to run three miles [a, ø, the] day to get in shape.
4 We can take only one of [a, ø, the] routes home from Boston.
5 Instead of dreaming about [a, ø, the] future, create it by doing your best now.

B 관사를 이용하여 대화를 완성하시오.

A Where are you going?
B I'm going to ① ___________ school. I'm supposed to see my son's teacher today. How about you?
A I'm going to school, too.
B What is the name of ② ___________ school?
A Long Island High.
B What a coincidence! I'm going to ③ ___________ school, too.

부정관사 a/an vs. 정관사 the
a/an은 셀 수 있는 것으로 특정하지 않은 하나를 가리킬 때 사용하는 관사이다. the는 서로가 알고 있는 것이거나, 앞서 이야기했던 것과 같이 특정한 것을 말할 때 사용한다.

EXERCISE

Answers P.20

A

[보기]에서 밑줄 친 부분과 쓰임이 같은 것을 고르시오.

Example ⓐ I have a plan to invest all of my money.
ⓑ I asked the policeman who was patrolling the neighborhood.
ⓒ An engineer needs a strong knowledge of mathematics.
ⓓ Alice used the same method she always uses.

1 Vernon has a ticket to the show. ______
2 Ralph received the same award that he received two years ago. ______
3 A policeman has the responsibility to protect society. ______
4 Is this the cafe you were talking about? ______

B

밑줄 친 부분을 바르게 고쳐 쓰시오. 틀리지 않았다면 ○표 하시오.

1 Doctors recommend drinking the glass of water at least 8 times per day. ______
2 Lisa is a one in charge of leading the class project. ______
3 I learned how to play a baseball while I was in elementary school. ______
4 Insects are often able to move objects much larger than themselves. ______
5 Use a tool we gave you the other day to complete the job. ______
6 The doctor told Janis that she would be okay. ______

C

[보기]에서 알맞은 말을 골라 어법에 맞게 문장을 완성하시오.

Word Bank	the time	the last person	car	soccer	the only reason

1 Martin can play ______________ but not very well.
2 Please tell me ______________ when you arrived.
3 It took him over six hours to drive by ______________.
4 Love is ______________ that she decided to marry him.
5 Weren't you ______________ to board the ship?

Unit 3 대명사

Pre-Check 다음 표의 빈칸에 알맞은 말을 쓰시오.

인칭		주격	소유격	목적격	소유대명사	재귀대명사
1인칭	단수	I	my	me	①	②
	복수	we	our	③	④	ourselves
2인칭	단수	you	⑤	⑥	yours	yourself
	복수					yourselves
3인칭	단수	he / she / it	⑦	him / her / it	his / hers / -	himself / herself / itself
	복수	⑧	their	them	theirs	themselves

1 인칭대명사

(1) Both you and I have to go there.
They say that helping one another is the first step towards friendship.

(2) I had already told him, but he didn't listen to me.

(3) My friend said he went to Europe with his family last week.

1

인칭대명사의 쓰임

(1) 주격 (주어 자리에 쓰임)
: ~은, ~는, ~이, ~가

(2) 목적격 (목적어 자리에 쓰임)
: ~을, ~를, ~에게

(3) 소유격 (명사 앞에 쓰임)
: ~의

2 소유대명사

(1) This is my book; that is her book.
→ This is mine; that is hers.

These are our products; those are your products.
→ These are ours; those are yours.

It is Charlie's bike.
→ It is Charlie's.

(2) She went shopping with a friend of hers.
He borrowed a comic book of Charlie's.

2

(1) 소유격 + 명사 = 소유대명사
my + 명사 = mine
your + 명사 = yours
her + 명사 = hers
our + 명사 = ours
명사's + 명사 = 명사's

(2) 이중소유격: of + 소유대명사
: a, some, this 등의 한정사는 2개 이상 나란히 쓰지 못하므로 이중 소유격을 써서 나타낸다.
a friend of mine (o)
a my friend (x)

3 재귀대명사

(1) I think I do love myself.
She couldn't forgive herself for what she'd done to them.

(2) Harold did the work (himself).
We (ourselves) should do it.

(3) Can I handle this problem by myself?
Behave yourself in public.

3

(1) 목적어 역할: 생략 불가

(2) 강조 용법: 생략 가능

(3) 관용적 표현

- by oneself 혼자, 스스로
- for oneself 스스로, 자기 힘으로
- in oneself 그 자체로는, 본래는
- of oneself 저절로
- enjoy oneself 즐기다
- help oneself 마음껏 먹다
- behave oneself 예의 바르게 행동하다
- between ourselves 우리끼리 얘기지만
- make oneself at home 집처럼 편하게 있다

4 대명사 it

(1) It's five thirty. The movie starts in ten minutes.
It's 300 meters from here to the White House.

(2) It's shocking that Jim got a grade of 100 on the final test
I made it a rule to wake up early in the morning.

cf) That Jim got a grade of 100 on the final test is shocking. (o)

(3) Jake lost his cell phone yesterday.
→ It was his cell phone that Jake lost yesterday.
→ It was yesterday that Jake lost his cell phone.

> 4
> (1) 시간, 계절, 날씨, 명암, 거리 등을 나타낼 때
> (2) 가주어, 가목적어의 it
> : 주어나 목적어가 길어질 때 사용
>
> *cf)* 가목적어 it
> make, find, think, believe 등의 동사가 to부정사를 목적어로 취하는 경우, 가목적어 it을 사용한다.
> (x) I made to wake up early in the morning a rule.
>
> (3) it ~ that ... 강조 구문

5 지시대명사

(1) This is my picture, and that is my family's.
These are photos, and those are albums.

cf) I'm going to finish this project this week.
These photos were taken by my little sister.

(2) I did my best and this made me the best student.
People in the country are happier than those in the city.

> 5
> (1) 가까운 것을 가리킬 때는 this, 먼 것을 가리킬 때는 that 사용
> • 복수형은 these / those
>
> *cf)* this/these + 명사
> that/those + 명사
> : 이때의 this/these, that/those는 명사를 꾸며 주는 형용사이다.
>
> (2) 앞에 나온 말의 반복을 피해 사용

Check-up

Answers P.20

A 주어진 단어를 이용하여 문장을 완성하시오.

1 Call ________________(she) one more time.
2 ________________(you) books were all over the table.
3 Rose has been talking about ________________(he) all day long.
4 Rachel and ________________(I) heard the story, but we didn't believe it.
5 My mom wanted to buy this because ________________(it) color was unique.

B 밑줄 친 부분이 의미하는 것을 고르시오.

A Hey, I just bought a laptop. It's made by Dell.
B Wow, it looks really awesome. ① They [= Dell, People] make really good computers.
A You think so? Well, for me, it doesn't really matter. I bought it because it was cheaper.
B What are you talking about? ② They [= Dell, People] say your computer determines your performance.

they의 쓰임
they는 두 명 이상의 사람들, 혹은 두 개 이상의 사물을 나타낼 때 사용하기도 하지만, 비인칭 it처럼 총칭적으로 일반 사람들이나 정부, 기관 같은 단체들을 가리킬 때도 사용한다.

Answers P.20

A [ ] 안에서 알맞은 말을 고르시오.

1 The trip [it, itself] took over 4 hours from Boston to New York.
2 No one is listening to [him, his] opinion though I think he is right.
3 Who gave [my, mine] hat to someone else?
4 If I can't find anyone to help me, I'll just do the job [by me, by myself].
5 I took Frank to the park since [he, his] was bored.
6 Harold has not been [him, himself] since his dog died.
7 [She, Her] was the one who was always making trouble.

B [보기]에서 알맞은 말을 골라 문장을 완성하시오.

Word Bank	those	that	he	myself	herself	ours

1 Dana drove a car for the first time all by ________________.
2 I'd like to try on ________________ dress instead of this one, please.
3 Tell ________________ kids in the back of the class to sit down and be quiet.
4 Both you and ________________ will get the job.
5 We tried hard, and the rewards are ________________.
6 I sometimes find ________________ wishing I were vacationing in Bali or some place like that!

C 밑줄 친 부분을 바르게 고쳐 쓰시오. 틀리지 않았다면 ○표 하시오.

1 I'll send the message directly to him email address. ________________
2 Charlene will buy the tickets herself if she has to. ________________
3 Hye-rim showed ourselves how to cook kimchi stew. ________________
4 Let's support us team no matter how they play! ________________
5 My vision is quite different from this of our boss. ________________
6 I'm not sure how to file you papers in the cabinet. ________________
7 You'll have to carry some of these box from the house to the garage yourself. ________________

부정대명사

Pre-Check 다음 보기에서 알맞은 말을 골라 빈칸에 써 넣으시오.

Word Bank	some	none	the others	one	another

Sandy made ① ____________ paper flowers. ② ____________ was purple, ③ ____________ was violet, and ④ ____________ were white. ⑤ ____________ of the flowers were pink.

1 one, the other, another

(1) Look at those bags. I like the black one.
One should keep quiet in the theater.

(2) One is very fresh, but the other is rotten.
He wrote several novels; one was very successful, but the others were little known.
We should pay attention when others speak to us.

(3) That is not enough for me; can I have another?
He has lots of caps; one is white, another is red, and the others are blue.

1

(1) one
: 앞서 언급된 명사와 같은 종류, (일반적인) 사람
* ones: one의 복수형

(2) one, the other
: (둘 중에서) 하나는, 나머지 하나는
• the others: (두 무리 가운데) 나머지 것들
• others: (여럿 중에서) 다른 것들

(3) another (= an + other)
: 또 다른 하나, (셋 이상 중에서) 다른 하나
• one, another, the other(s)
: 하나는, 다른 하나는, 나머지는(나머지 것들은)

2 all, each, no/none

(1) All we can do now is wait for the right time.
That's all. There's nothing more left.

(2) Most of the books are available to students.
She spends most of her time watching TV.

(3) Each of us has our own talents.
They are selling second-hand game CDs for one dollar each.

(4) There were none who did the job voluntarily.
None of our mistakes were criticized.

cf) (1) All the boys in this class are handsome.
(2) Each boy has his own ball in the gym.
(3) Most students prefer comic books to textbooks.
(4) We have no money to buy this magazine.

2

(1) all: 모두, 전부, 다
(2) most: (~의) 대부분
(3) each: 각각, 개개의 것
(4) none: 아무도/누구도 ~않다, 아무것도/하나도 ~아니다

all + (of) + the + 복수/단수 명사
• all (of) the books (o)
• all of books (x)
• all 자리에 most 등이 올 수 있다.
• the 자리에 소유격, this/that, these/those, my 등이 올 수 있다.

cf) 부정형용사 + 명사
• all + 단/복수: 모든 ~
• each + 단수: 각각의/개개의 ~
• no + 단수: 하나의 ~도 없는
• every + 단수: 각각의/개개의 ~
(• every는 대명사로는 쓰지 않는다.)

3 some, any, both, either, neither

(1) Some of the water was spilled.
Someone should clean the table before he arrives.

(2) Don't worry. Take any of the buses. They all go there.
Is there anyone left inside the office?

(3) Both of them eat lunch during their break time.
They both wanted to get the job.

(4) I don't like either of the shirts.
Do either of you play chess?

(5) Neither is welcome at the conference.
Neither of them has any idea about this new construction project.

cf) (1) For some reason, she was very angry.
(2) If you have any questions, don't hesitate to ask me.
(3) Both Daniel and John are my cousins.
(4) I watch dramas either on TV or through the Internet.
(5) Neither Sam nor I am interested in sports.

3

(1) some: 약간, 몇몇
someone: 누군가, 누가 (= somebody)

(2) any: 아무 (것), 어느 (것)
anyone: 아무나, 누구나 (= anybody)

(3) both: 양쪽, 둘 다

(4) either: 둘 중의 하나

(5) neither: 둘 중의 어느 누구[것]도 ~아니다

cf) 부정형용사 + 명사
이때의 some, any, both, either, neither 등은 명사를 수식하는 형용사 역할을 한다.

Check-up

Answers P.20

A [ ] 안에서 알맞은 말을 고르시오.

1 [Each, Every] of us wanted our own room.

2 I don't like this sweater. Please show me [one, another].

3 The ducks walked into the lake one after [other, the other].

4 I can't believe them. [Either, Neither] of them is telling us the truth.

B [ ] 안에서 알맞은 말을 고르시오. (복수 정답 가능)

1 A Who do you want to take with you, James or Susan?
B I want to take as many people as I can on this trip. I can take [both, either] of them with me.
A But you can only take one person. You should take [both, either] of them.

2 A Who do you think can complete the job successfully, James or Susan?
B James is a good organizer. And Susan is a good planner. [Both, Either] of them can complete the job successfully.

both vs. either

either는 기본적으로 '둘 중에 어느 한쪽의'라는 뜻을 가지고 있다. 하지만 문맥에 따라 '각각의'나 '양쪽의'라는 뜻 모두로 쓰일 수 있다. 예를 들어 '어느 쪽이라도 가능하다'라고 한다면 '둘 다 가능하다(both)'라는 뜻이 될 것이고, '어느 한 쪽만 선택하겠다'라고 한다면 '둘 중에 하나'라는 뜻이 되므로 '양쪽 모두(both)'와 다르다.

EXERCISE

Answers P.20

A

[보기]에서 알맞은 말을 골라 문장을 완성하시오.

Word Bank	any	one	another	anyone	none	both

1 Would you like to eat at this restaurant, or to go to ____________ one?

2 I have some sugar left. But there isn't ____________ salt left.

3 Isn't there ____________ who can tell me how to handle this?

4 ____________ of them are writers, although one is more famous than the other.

5 We weren't able to hold the meeting because ____________ of the board members was present.

6 We need to move just ____________ of the tables into the room; we can leave the rest.

B

밑줄 친 부분을 바르게 고쳐 쓰시오. 틀리지 않았다면 ○표 하시오.

1 My mom was very sad because none us remembered her birthday. ____________

2 You can take anything you want. ____________

3 Someone can be a writer if he or she tries hard. ____________

4 I don't read each of the stories in the news. I just choose some of them. ____________

5 They have two dogs; another is a dachshund, and the other is a chihuahua. ____________

6 Neither Andrew nor Lisa is responsible for picking up the groceries from the store. ____________

C

빈칸에 들어갈 알맞은 말을 쓰시오.

1 A Listen! There's something outside.
B Well, I can't hear ____________.

2 A Aren't some of our coworkers coming to the picnic today?
B I don't think ____________ of them are coming because no one's here yet.

3 A Alison is the girl you went to elementary school with, right?
B No, she's not the ____________ I was talking about.

4 A Would you like to see an action movie or a romance?
B ____________ of those genres interests me. Let's see a comedy instead.

REVIEW TEST

Answers P.20

A

[ ] 안에서 알맞은 말을 고르시오.

1 [A, Ø] dolphin (Dolphin) is a highly intelligent and friendly animal.

2 Make [the, this] your last time to come to me with such a problem.

3 I can't believe that [my, mine] words were misunderstood.

4 We should not ignore what [others, the another] think.

5 Some like soccer and [others, the other] like baseball.

6 Jake wouldn't give [her, hers] an opportunity to explain the situation.

7 Please make [it, one] simple and easy.

8 We'll consider some of these travel schedules after we discuss [them, themselves] with the travel agent.

B

빈칸에 들어갈 알맞은 말을 고르시오.

1 My sister and I usually go swimming twice ________ week.

ⓐ a ⓑ the ⓒ that ⓓ Ø

2 I don't know why ________ of you have to be present at the same time.

ⓐ one ⓑ both ⓒ every ⓓ the ones

3 Korea is a peninsula and its geography has affected ________ history.

ⓐ one ⓑ its ⓒ any ⓓ this

4 You can submit ________ form of ID to open your new account at the bank.

ⓐ both ⓑ these ⓒ some ⓓ either

5 I wouldn't argue with Tom anymore because he never agrees with ________.

ⓐ none ⓑ some ⓒ each ⓓ others

6 We all believed ________ pointless to keep insisting on our demands.

ⓐ it ⓑ that ⓒ those ⓓ these

7 This is just another example of why mothers are so important to ________ children.

ⓐ a ⓑ ours ⓒ their ⓓ themselves

REVIEW TEST

C

밑줄 친 부분을 바르게 고쳐 문장을 다시 쓰시오.

1 There are any chocolate cookies here. Please have some.

→ ____________________

2 Don't serve any of the dishes until Sharon and she team arrives to help you.

→ ____________________

3 Betty bought all of these suits for Mark, but he didn't appreciate hers efforts at all.

→ ____________________

4 We put our balls in the storehouse and those suited our coach just fine.

→ ____________________

5 Anyone has his or her chance to speak on these topic before a final decision is made.

→ ____________________

D

(A), (B), (C)의 각 네모 안에서 어법에 맞는 말로 바르게 짝지어진 것을 고르시오.

> A culture is composed of people in a shared territory who embrace a common identity. However, (A) [all / every] cultures may change over time. This may cause problems when people within a culture face challenges connected to such changes. This is particularly the case when change is pressed on them from (B) [others / the others] outside. For example, many nations in Eastern Europe have experienced rapid economic growth since the 1990s, when communism fell. At the same time, these nations have experienced broad cultural stresses caused by their transitions to market economies. Market economies have also challenged (C) [any / some] their traditional religious and family practices.

	(A)		(B)		(C)
①	all	…	others	…	any
②	all	…	others	…	some of
③	all	…	the others	…	some of
④	every	…	others	…	any
⑤	every	…	the others	…	some of

F FURTHER STUDY

Writing

▶▶ **우리말과 같은 뜻이 되도록 주어진 단어를 이용하여 문장을 완성하시오.**

1 내 친구 Fred는 개들이나 다른 동물들을 무서워하지 않는다. (be afraid of, any other)

→ My friend, Fred, ______________________________.

2 우리끼리 얘기지만, Toby는 언제나 잘난 척한다. (ourselves, put on airs)

→ ______________________, Toby always ______________________.

3 나의 조부모님은 시골의 조그만 동네에 산다. (grandparents, small village)

→ ______________________________ in the country.

4 그릇에 밀가루 1파운드와 물 두 컵을 넣어라. (pound, cup)

→ Put ______________ and ______________________ into a bowl.

5 나는 주말마다 테니스를 치기 위해 공원에 간다. (to play)

→ Every weekend, I ______________________________.

6 그녀는 자신의 업무에 서류 작업이 많다고 불평한다. (complain, involve, a lot of)

→ ______________ that her job ______________________ paper work.

7 나는 몇몇 책들은 기억하지만, 그것들 모두가 다 기억나지는 않는다. (some of, not all of)

→ I remember ______________________ but ______________________.

8 이 기사들 중에 시험에 도움이 되는 것은 하나도 없다. (none of, article, helpful for)

→ ______________________________ the test.

MUST-KNOW

▶ 복수 명사를 만드는 방법: 규칙 변화

형태	대부분의 명사	자음 + -y	-f, -fe로 끝나는 명사	-o, -ch, -sh -s, -x로 끝나는 명사
	끝에 -s를 붙임	y를 i로 고친 후 + -es	-f(e)를 -ves로	끝에 -es를 붙임
예시	school → schools girl → girls book → books movie → movies	city → cities fly → flies baby → babies sky → skies	scarf → scarves life → lives knife → knives wife → wives [예외] belief → beliefs chief → chiefs roof → roofs ⋮	potato → potatoes bench → benches dish → dishes glass → glasses fox → foxes

▶ 주의해야 할 명사의 수

단/복수 형태가 같은 명사	뜻	비고
means fish salmon sheep deer series	수단 물고기 연어 양 사슴 연속(물), 시리즈	단/복수의 형태가 같다.
항상 복수 취급하는 명사		
people clergy cattle poultry police army	사람들 성직자들 소떼 조류 경찰 군대	• police, clergy : the와 함께 쓰여 복수 취급 • cattle, people, poultry : 복수 취급 • family, army, people : 집합체를 단위로도 셀 수 있으므로 단수로도 취급 가능하다. ex) a family (한 가족), two families (두 가족)
집합명사		
class club group crowd family committee staff team	학급 클럽, 동호회 그룹, 집단 군중, 무리 가족 위원회 직원 팀	• 전달 내용에 따라 단/복수 모두 가능하다. The audience **was** clapping for 20 minutes. The audience **were** clapping for 20 minutes.

WRAP-UP TEST

Answers P.22

1 밑줄 친 부분과 명사의 종류가 같은 것을 고르시오.

His family went to Italy yesterday.

ⓐ audience ⓑ hamburger
ⓒ friendship ⓓ politeness

2 빈칸에 들어갈 수 없는 말을 고르시오.

My sister drinks ______________ milk a day.

ⓐ many ⓑ a lot of
ⓒ a glass of ⓓ a carton of

3 빈칸에 관사 a(n), the를 쓸 수 없는 것을 고르시오.

ⓐ Her presentation was ________ great success.
ⓑ Kerry and I play ________ badminton after dinner on weekends.
ⓒ Would you mind opening ________ door?
ⓓ She promised to call me twice ________ week.

4 우리말과 일치하도록 빈칸에 알맞은 말을 써 넣으시오.

My sister ate ______________________ cheese cake.
(내 여동생은 치즈 케이크 3조각을 먹었다.)

5 빈칸에 공통으로 들어갈 수 있는 말을 고르시오.

- _____ is 26 degrees in this office now.
- _____ took me seven hours to drive to L.A.
- _____ is certain that he's in the hospital now.

ⓐ It ⓑ This ⓒ That ⓓ They

6 밑줄 친 부분 중 쓰임이 다른 하나를 고르시오.

ⓐ Bill wants to be an astronaut.
ⓑ She is so pleased to get a free ticket to her favorite musical.
ⓒ Your wages will be paid once a week.
ⓓ I bought a cap and sunglasses for the trip next month.

7 밑줄 친 부분을 생략할 수 없는 것을 고르시오.

ⓐ He himself assembled the model airplane.
ⓑ It is said history repeats itself.
ⓒ Mom cut herself with a knife chopping up some cabbage.
ⓓ Don't you think you can solve the problem yourselves?

8 어법상 옳지 않은 것을 고르시오.

ⓐ Every country has its own culture and history.
ⓑ None of the students answered the teacher's question.
ⓒ Some people go abroad during summer vacation.
ⓓ All the emails I got yesterday was infected with viruses.

[9-10] 글을 읽고, 물음에 답하시오.

Hangeul, the Korean system of writing, is the only alphabet in the world whose creation date is known. Devised by ⓐ a King Sejong the Great, Hangeul is both a beautiful art form and a very scientific phonetic system. ⓑ Each of the Hangeul letters was designed to accurately reflect actual human speech. ⓒ This makes the letters ideal for pronouncing foreign words as well. For example, ⓓ the word "Paris" is pronounced "Parii" in Hangeul, which is much closer than English to the actual French pronunciation.

9 밑줄 친 ⓐ ~ ⓓ 중 쓰임이 잘못된 것을 고르시오.

10 윗글의 내용과 일치하지 않는 것을 고르시오.

ⓐ The creation date of Hangeul is unknown.
ⓑ Hangeul was devised by King Sejong the Great.
ⓒ Hangeul letters reflect actual human speech.
ⓓ Hangeul letters are proper for pronouncing foreign words.

형용사, 부사

1 형용사
2 부사
3 비교

형용사

Pre-Check 다음 문장을 참고하여 빈칸에 알맞은 형용사를 써 넣으시오.

1 The flower has a good smell. → The flower smells ________________.

2 You helped me a lot. → You are very ________________.

3 He is a man of wisdom. → He is a ________________ man.

1 형용사의 쓰임과 위치

(1) 서술 용법

① 주어 서술

The writer was upset at the noise outside.

Tony seems satisfied with the result of the exam.

The onion soup smells really good.

② 목적어 서술

We found this new program useful.

The lessons of several failures made him strong.

(2) 한정 용법

① 명사 앞

He is an intelligent man.

His amazing performance surprised the audience.

I made new friends at school.

② 명사/대명사 뒤

She is six feet tall.

Is there anyone capable of speaking French?

My brother is only 14 years old, but he is already six feet tall.

> 1
>
> (1) ① be, become, seem, look 등의 동사 뒤
>
> ② 목적 보어: 목적어 서술
>
> (2) ① 명사 앞: 명사 수식
>
> ② 앞의 명사/대명사 수식
> : 수치, 길이, 나이 등을 나타내는 명사, something, someone, anybody 등의 대명사 뒤에 위치

2 주의해야 할 형용사

(1) 서술 용법으로만 쓰이는 형용사

The man is asleep.

(x) The ~~asleep man~~ is my friend.

→ The sleeping man is my friend.

The woman is alone.

(x) She is an ~~alone woman~~.

→ She is a lone woman.

> 2
>
> (1) 한정 형용사는 명사 수식 용법으로 사용하며, 보어로 사용하지 않는다.
> indoor, elder, inner, outer, live, mere 등
>
> (2) 서술 형용사는 보어로 사용되는 형용사로, 명사 앞에서 수식하지 않는다.
>
> • a-로 시작하는 형용사
> : asleep, alive, ashamed, awake, aware 등
>
> • 그 외 형용사
> : upset, well, ill 등

(2) 한정 용법으로만 쓰이는 형용사

He is my elder brother.

(x) He is ~~elder~~.

→ He is older.

It is the building's main entrance.

(x) The entrance ~~is building's main~~.

→ The entrance is the building's main one.

3 위치에 따라 의미가 달라지는 형용사

ⓐ A certain man gave this flower to you.
ⓑ I'm certain that he will help you.

ⓐ Please write down your present address here.
ⓑ He was not present at the meeting.

3

	ⓐ 한정 용법	ⓑ 서술 용법
certain	어떤	확신하는
present	현재의	출석한
late	죽은(고인의)	늦은
concerned	걱정하는	관계가 있는

4 수량 형용사

(1) Many Europeans speak at least one other language.
I bought so many used books that I should get a new bookshelf.
How much money will we need?
Much effort will be required to complete the task.

(2) A lot of students want to do internships at the company.
It was lots of work, but she enjoyed doing it.

(3) There are some candies in the jar.
Can I get you some cold water?
They don't serve any fresh vegetarian dishes here.
Do you have any money?

(4) He answered a few questions from the audience.
Few students are interested in chemistry.
We had a little ice cream after dinner.
There is little milk in the glass.

(5) Most people want to have their own houses.
The class president won the most votes.

4

종류	수+복수	양+단수
많은	many not a few quite a few no few	much not a little quite a little no little
	lots of, a lot of	
약간의	a few	a little
	some, any	
거의 없는	few	little
매우 적은	only a few	only a little
대부분의	most	

5 형용사를 만드는 접미사

(1) This tastes so bad.
I found a young lady at the door.

(2) People say he is a helpful person.
You should be careful when you chat online.

(3) It was a careless remark.
I'd like to stop this endless debate.

(4) Everybody agrees that she is a capable politician.
We're looking for a portable radio.

(5) He is a very selfish person.
Don't act like a childish boy.

(6) Her voice was so fantastic.
Refer to the words listed in italics.

(7) Unfortunately, the boy has a mental problem.
Sorry, but I have a dental appointment tomorrow.

(8) The girl is so talented.
We're so curious about many things.
He and I went to elementary school together.
How did you come up with such a brilliant idea?

5

형용사를 만드는 접미사

접미사	예
(1) 원형	good, bad, pretty, small, big, fast, slow 등
(2) -ful	careful, useful, hopeful, successful 등
(3) -less	useless, endless, mindless, doubtless 등
(4) -able	lovable, available, portable, probable 등
(5) -ish	foolish, childish, stylish, British 등
(6) -ic	romantic, scientific, fantastic, italic 등
(7) -al	critical, oriental, dental, metal, mental, vital 등
(8) 기타 -ed, -ing, -y, -ous, -ary, -en, -some, -ant, -ent 등	bored, delighted, exciting, interesting, crazy, sleepy, dangerous, anxious, necessary, troublesome, awesome, wooden, brilliant, tolerant, consistent 등

• 예외
revival (부활), survival (생존) 등은 –al로 끝나지만 명사이다.

Check-up

Answers P.22

A [ ] 안에서 알맞은 말을 고르시오.

1 I bought a [used digital camera, digital camera used].
2 The man runs three [miles long, long miles] every morning.
3 He is a [famous writer, writer famous]. He has lots of fans all over the world.
4 Are you going to give out [much, lots of] gifts again at Christmas?
5 You can invite only [a little friends, a few friends] to the show.

B 밑줄 친 부분을 해석하시오.

A I need to talk to you. Do you have some time now?
B Sorry, I have ① little time this morning. Can we make it some other time?
A I don't know. It is kind of urgent.
B Hmm. I think I will have ② a little time in the afternoon between classes.

little vs. a little

little /a little, few /a few는 모두 수량의 적고 많음을 나타내는 수량형용사이나, 그 기준은 객관적이지 않다. 같은 수량이라도 말하는 사람의 입장에 따라 '조금 있다'라고 할 수도 있고, '조금 밖에 없다'라고 할 수도 있다. 즉, 말하는 사람의 주관적인 의견이 반영된다고 볼 수 있다.

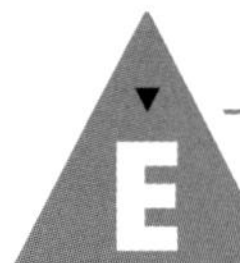

EXERCISE

Answers P.22

A

주어진 단어를 형용사로 바꿔 문장을 완성하시오.

1 Henry is the most ______________ (help) person on our team.

2 I'm so tired of her ______________ (end) worries.

3 Don't approach it. It seems ______________ (danger).

4 Don't get such a ______________ (fool) idea.

5 The concert was ______________ (awe). You should have gone.

6 She was ______________ (delight) at his unexpected gift.

7 He keeps yawning. He must be ______________ (sleep).

B

[ ] 안에서 알맞은 말을 고르시오.

1 Jane is my sister. She is [older, elder].

2 Look at that [sleeping, asleep] dog.

3 We are planning an [indoor, indoors] event.

4 The meeting came [live, alive] when I showed up.

5 The man is [lone, alone].

6 Thomas went [outer, outside] after he ate dinner.

7 You never know what an [upset, unhappy] person would do.

C

주어진 단어를 알맞게 배열하여 문장을 완성하시오.

1 long / seven / feet

→ Is it really ______________________?

2 bitter / tastes

→ This green tea ______________________.

3 exotic / go / somewhere

→ She wants to ______________________ this Christmas.

4 indoor / exercises / some

→ Here's a suggestion for people who are looking for ______________________.

5 your / habit / bad

→ You should be ashamed of ______________________.

부사

Pre-Check 다음 괄호 안에서 알맞은 말을 고르시오.

1 ① Her smile is [beautiful, beautifully].
② She smiles [beautiful, beautifully].

2 ① I'd like to have [water iced, iced water].
② This water is [very icy, icy very].

1 부사의 쓰임과 위치

(1) 동사 뒤에서 동사 수식
Mary sings well.
The kid behaves politely in the class.

(2) 형용사 앞에서 형용사 수식
David is quite clever.
My grandfather is seriously ill now.

(3) 부사 앞에서 부사 수식
She always speaks very nicely.
This car goes very fast.

(4) 문장 앞, 뒤, 중간에서 문장 전체 수식
Strangely, they have met at the same place twice.
She recently won an essay contest.

2 빈도를 나타내는 부사

She is always late for the team meeting.
Dad usually comes home after 8.
I seldom bring my work to the meeting.
I will never be late again.

3 부사를 만드는 접미사

(1) My friend Andrew runs very fast.
(2) Can't you finish the work more quickly?
(3) The meeting is held monthly.
(4) He explained it simply to me.
This copy machine breaks down too easily.

1
- be동사 뒤에 쓰여 주어의 보어 역할을 하지 않는다.
  ex. David ~~is happily~~.
- 명사를 수식하지 않는다.
  ex. David is ~~a happily child~~.

2
빈도부사: be동사/조동사 뒤, 일반동사 앞

• 빈도부사의 빈도 크기
always 〉 usually 〉 often / frequently 〉 sometimes / occasionally 〉 rarely / seldom 〉 never

3

접미사	예
(1) 원형	very, fast, well, always 등
(2) 형용사 +ly	deadly, kindly, smartly 등
(3) 명사 +ly	costly, partly, hourly, timely, weekly 등
(4) 기타	•「자음 + -y」→「자음 + ily」 easy → easily •「-le」→「-ly」 simple → simply

* 예외: lovely, friendly, lonely, daily처럼 일부 형용사 가운데 -ly로 끝나는 것이 있다.

4 부사와 형용사의 형태가 같은 단어

ⓐ I woke up early this morning to catch the first train.
ⓑ I may catch the early train.

ⓐ All the employees have to work hard.
ⓑ Every man in this department is a hard worker.

ⓐ Please speak out loud. I can't hear you.
ⓑ He talked to me in a loud voice because the room was crowded.

ⓐ The snail moves very slow.
ⓑ The traffic is so slow today.

5 두 가지 형태의 부사

(1) 의미는 같으나 형태가 다름
The boys shout out loud.
The woman cried loudly for help.

(2) 형태는 비슷하나 의미가 다름
Everybody was upset because he arrived too late.
I haven't seen him lately.

4

	ⓐ 부사	ⓑ 형용사
early	일찍, 빨리	이른, 빠른
hard	열심히	열심인
	굳게	굳은
loud	큰 소리로	큰 소리의, 시끄러운
slow	느리게, 천천히	느린, 늦은
fast	빨리	빠른
late	늦게, 뒤늦게	늦은, 뒤늦은

5

(1)

부사	의미
loud, loudly	큰 소리로, 크게
slow, slowly	천천히, 느리게
last, lastly	미지막으로

(2)

부사	의미
late	늦게, 지각하여
lately	요즘, 근래
hard	열심히; 굳게, 단단히
hardly	거의/좀처럼 ~않다
near	가까이의
nearly	거의, 가까스로; 대략
high	높이, 높게 (물리적 의미)
highly	대단히, 몹시 (추상적 의미)

Check-up

Answers P.23

A [ ] 안에서 알맞은 말을 고르시오.

1 [Ridiculous, Ridiculously], Ben wore a red shirt and green tie to work.
2 This isn't the [proper, properly] time to eat lunch, is it?
3 Ross and Blake were the ones who [desperate, desperately] objected to the plan.
4 All our attempts to repair the broken truck were [simple, simply] useless.
5 Would you [kind, kindly] bring the tea set into the living room?

B [ ] 안에서 알맞은 말을 고르시오.

1 You [usually, hardly] ever call me. You should call me more often.
2 You should speak [softly, loudly]. The place is so quiet.
3 It's 6 now, and I'm busy until 7. You can visit me an hour [later, before].
4 It is urgent. You must go there [as soon as possible, as often as possible].
5 He was [highly, high] respected as an excellent president.

문장 안에서 부사의 역할
'부수적인 품사'라 불리는 부사는 문장에서 빼더라도 형식상으로는 오류가 생기지 않는다. 그러나 부사가 빠짐으로써 말하고자 하는 바가 분명히 전달되지 못하거나 의도한 것과 달라질 수가 있다. 섬세하고 미묘한 의미 전달에 효과적인 부사, 또는 부사구나 부사절을 잘 활용해서 문상의 맛을 살려 보자.

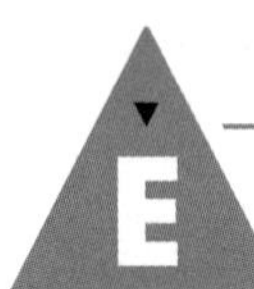

EXERCISE

Answers P.23

A

밑줄 친 부분이 형용사인지 부사인지 구분하시오.

1 Aren't you returning home soon? ____________

2 Beth was quite calm most of the time. ____________

3 It won't be the last time we have to do this. ____________

4 Let's go see an early movie today. ____________

5 I usually go to work late on Friday. ____________

6 He didn't study hard, right? ____________

B

밑줄 친 부분을 바르게 고쳐 쓰시오. 틀리지 않았다면 ○표 하시오.

1 I feel real happy, but I don't know why. ____________

2 I'm not sure what the finally score was. ____________

3 We haven't met the teacher often since graduation. ____________

4 Betty agreed to come after we careful spoke to her. ____________

5 That's the very lastly place that I want to go to. ____________

6 The baby fell fast asleep in her mom's arms. ____________

C

빈칸에 들어갈 알맞은 말을 쓰시오.

Example	She is a good singer.	→	She sings very well.

1 The plane's arrival was early.
→ The plane arrived ____________.

2 His work is very easy.
→ He works very ____________.

3 His word pronunciation is very strange.
→ He pronounces words very ____________.

4 Horace is a capable leader.
→ Horace ____________ leads us.

5 There were slight increases in oil prices.
→ Oil prices were ____________ increased.

Unit 09

Unit 3 비교

Pre-Check 우리말과 일치하도록 빈칸에 알맞은 말을 써 넣으시오.

• Today is so cold. (추운)

1 Today is ________________ than yesterday. (더 추운)

2 Yesterday was ________________ than today. (덜 추운)

3 Today is the ________________ day of this year. (가장 추운)

1 원급, 비교급, 최상급

(1) This desk is cheap.
This desk is cheaper than that one.
This desk is the cheapest one in our store.

(2) This program works quickly.
This program works more quickly than the old one.
This program works most quickly of all the programs.

2 동등 비교

(1) Peter is as old as Jack (is).
└ Peter is 17 and Jack is 17.
She doesn't practice as hard as her partner (does).

Come here as soon as possible.
= Come here as soon as you can.

(2) He has as much money as Carla.
I have as many CDs as him.

3 열등 비교

(1) This is less competitive than that.
= This is not as competitive as that.

(2) This is the least competitive in the market.

4 비교를 나타내는 여러 가지 표현

(1) He is superior to me in writing.
She is 10 years senior to him.

1

• 비교급
: 부사/형용사의 비교급 + than
(~보다 더 …한)

• 최상급
: the 최상급 + of + 복수/집합 명사
: the 최상급 + in + 장소
(~ 중에서 가장 …한)

* 부사의 최상급에는 the를 쓰지 않는다.

2

(1) as + 형용사/부사 + as
(~만큼 …한)
not as [so] + 형용사/부사 + as
(~만큼 …하지 않은)

(2) as much [many / little / few] + 명사 + as (~만큼 많은/적은 …)

3

(1) A... less + 원급 + than ...B
(A는 B보다 덜 ~하다)
→ A... not as + 원급 + as B
(A는 B만큼 ~하지 않다)

(2) the least + 원형 + in/of ~
(가장 덜 ~하다)

4

(1) than 대신 to를 씀
• superior to (~보다 나은)
• inferior to (~보다 못한)
• senior to (~보다 손위인)
• junior to (~보다 손아래인)
• prior to (~보다 우선하는)

(2) She is much older than you.
Your information was a lot more useful than the TV news.

(3) People believe the higher the price is, the more reliable the product is.

(4) The rumor is getting bigger and bigger.

(5) His cell phone is twice as expensive as mine.

(6) They no longer live here.
He has no more than two dollars.

(2) 비교급 강조
- 훨씬 더: 비교급 앞에 much, even, still, far, a lot 등을 붙임
- 약간 더: 비교급 앞에 a bit, a little, slightly 등을 붙임

(3) the + 비교급, the + 비교급 (~할수록 더 …하다)

(4) get/become + 비교급 + and + 비교급 (점점 더 ~해지다)

(5) 배수 + as + 원급 + as (~보다 몇 배 …한)

(6) 기타
- no longer (than) (더 이상 ~ 않다)
- no more than (기껏해야)
- no less than (최소한)

5 최상급의 다양한 표현

This is the funniest movie.
= No movie is as funny as this movie.
= No movie is funnier than this movie.
= This movie is funnier than any other movie.
= This movie is funnier than all the other movies.

5
〈the + 최상급 + 명사〉
= No 명사 + 동사 + as 원급 as (~보다 더 …한 것은 없다)
= No 명사 + 동사 + 비교급 than (어떤 것도 ~보다 더 …하지 않다)
= 비교급 than any other + 단수명사 (~가 다른 어떤 것보다 더 …한)
= 비교급 than all the (other) + 복수명사 (다른 ~보다도 더 …한)

Check-up

Answers P.23

A [ ] 안에서 알맞은 말을 고르시오.

1 The class test was [easy, easier, the easiest] than we had expected.

2 Jimmy was [prepared, more prepared, the most prepared] than I was for the test.

3 Jin-hee is the [selfless, more selfless, most selfless] person I've ever met.

4 I'm [concerned, more concerned, most concerned] than Ally about saving money.

B [ ] 안에서 알맞은 말을 고르시오.

A There are seven cards, numbered 1 to 7. Which one do you want to take?

B Well, I will take card 1 since it is large. It seems ① [larger, the larger] than any other card.
I think it is ② [largest, the largest] of all. It should be the most expensive.

A Actually, card 5 is the most expensive. And cards 1 and 3 are the same in size.
But card 3 is ③ [more, the more] expensive one.

〈the + 비교급〉 과 〈the + 최상급〉

보통 최상급 앞에는 the를 붙이는 것을 공식화하고 있는데, 사실 최상급이나 비교급은 형용사/부사이므로 그 자체로는 정관사 the를 붙일 수 없다 (관사는 명사에만 사용한다). 하지만 최상급의 경우 의미상 '가장 ~한'이 되기 때문에, 어떤 특정한 것을 설명하고 있다고 가정할 수 있다. 따라서 보통은 명사가 생략된 경우에도 관용적으로 〈the + 최상급〉의 형태를 허용하고 있다. 비교급의 경우에도, 앞서 언급한 대상을 이야기할 때는 〈the + 비교급 + 명사〉의 형태로 사용할 수 있다.

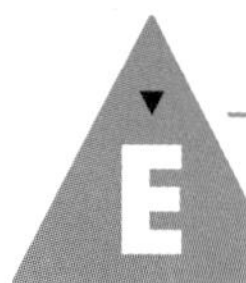

EXERCISE

Answers P.23

A

밑줄 친 부분을 바르게 고쳐 쓰시오. 틀리지 않았다면 ○표 하시오.

1 This is <u>the most exciting</u> suggestion so far. ____________

2 I think this pizza tastes <u>very better</u> than the last one. ____________

3 We should listen to others <u>as much so</u> we talk to them. ____________

4 Central Park is not <u>the more</u> beautiful place in town. ____________

5 The travel guide was <u>the less</u> polite one I've ever met. ____________

B

주어진 단어를 이용하여 문장을 완성하시오.

> **Example** The weather is getting <u>colder and colder</u>. (cold, and)

1 Burt felt ____________ Michael about their plan. (happy, than)

2 Electronics are becoming ____________. (more, and, portable)

3 The idea is not ____________ it sounds. (as, simple)

4 The results just seem to be getting ____________. (bad, and)

5 All the goods in this store are ____________ I remember. (expensive, than)

C

주어진 단어를 이용하여 두 개의 문장을 하나의 문장으로 완성하시오.

> **Example** Jeremy runs 100 meters in 15 seconds.
> His sister runs 100 meters in 13 seconds.
> → Jeremy runs <u>slower than</u> his sister. (slow)

1 Kyle lifted 200 pounds. Barry also lifted 200 pounds.
→ Kyle is ____________ Barry. (strong)

2 Russia is a large country. There is no country in the world as large as Russia.
→ Russia is ____________ in the world. (large)

3 Today's weather is cold. Tomorrow's weather will be colder.
→ The weather will be getting ____________. (cold)

4 Jack finished dinner in 20 minutes. Ralph finished dinner in 10 minutes.
→ Ralph finished dinner ____________ Jack. (quickly)

5 Detroit's crime rate is #2 in the USA. Atlanta's crime rate is #10 in the USA.
→ Detroit has ____________ Atlanta. (high, crime rate)

Answers P.23

A

[ ] 안에서 알맞은 말을 고르시오.

1 He has [few, little] artistic ability.

2 If we don't act now it could be a [cost, costly] mistake.

3 You'd better be [sure, surely] that your decision is right.

4 Kerry [glad, gladly] accepted the position at the new company.

5 No one was [aware, awake] that the leak in the pipe would be so serious.

6 Martin sometimes acts [more childish, much childish] than his younger brother.

7 What will be the [more probable, most probable] outcome of this experiment?

8 Jerry could only [part, partly] lower his head into his jacket to avoid the rain.

B

빈칸에 들어갈 알맞은 말을 고르시오.

1 We tried ______________ ideas for better photographs.

ⓐ a few ⓑ a little ⓒ much ⓓ none

2 ______________ drivers have to go slower when the weather is bad.

ⓐ All ⓑ Every ⓒ Few ⓓ Each

3 Everybody likes him because he behaves ______________.

ⓐ polite ⓑ politely ⓒ politeness ⓓ much polite

4 The last report is almost ______________ the first one.

ⓐ useless ⓑ more useless ⓒ most useless ⓓ as useless as

5 You're going to get into trouble if you aren't ______________ with your words.

ⓐ as careful as ⓑ more careful ⓒ the most careful ⓓ more carefully

6 Bella is determined to be ______________ in her career no matter what problems arise.

ⓐ successful ⓑ as successful ⓒ successful than ⓓ most success

7 Carter is getting ______________ more mindless in both his words and actions nowadays.

ⓐ as ⓑ very ⓒ a lot ⓓ a few

REVIEW TEST

C

밑줄 친 부분을 바르게 고쳐 문장을 다시 쓰시오.

1 Our product is <u>least</u> competitive than our competitor's.

→ ____________________

2 It's more foolish to wait for help than to act <u>quick</u>.

→ ____________________

3 Peter is the more <u>help</u> of the two boys.

→ ____________________

4 He <u>often is regarded</u> as one of the most influential directors in the U.S.

→ ____________________

5 How <u>much</u> states are you going to travel through on your trip?

→ ____________________

D

(A), (B), (C)의 각 네모 안에서 어법에 맞는 말로 바르게 짝지어진 것을 고르시오.

> (A) [Many / Little] lucky dogs find their way home electronically these days. They wear special tags. A tiny microchip fits under each dog's skin, and the microchip contains the owner's information. The microchip can be read by a machine that is (B) [as small as / smaller] a human hand. The information on the microchip is registered with an organization. The organization (C) [quick / quickly] contacts the lost pet's owner.

	(A)		(B)		(C)
①	Many	…	as small as	…	quick
②	Many	…	as small as	…	quickly
③	Many	…	smaller	…	quickly
④	Little	…	smaller	…	quickly
⑤	Little	…	as small as	…	quick

FURTHER STUDY

Writing

▶▶ **우리말과 같은 뜻이 되도록 주어진 단어를 이용하여 문장을 완성하시오.**

1 오늘은 어제만큼 춥다. (as, cold)

→ Today is ______________________________.

2 우리 할아버지는 가난한 사람들에게 아주 친절히 대했다. (treat, the poor, kindly)

→ My grandfather ______________________________.

3 당신이 제 제안을 기쁘게 받아들이니 기쁩니다. (delightfully, accept one's offer)

→ I'm so glad that you ______________________________.

4 더 높이 올라갈수록, 더 춥게 느낄 것이다. (high, cold)

→ ______________ you climb, ______________ you may feel.

5 이것은 내가 지금까지 읽었던 책 중에서 가장 지루한 책이다. (boring, have ever read)

→ This is ______________________________.

6 그녀는 거의 하루도 학교에 결석하지 않았다. (rarely, miss, a day of school)

→ She ______________________________.

7 우리 사무실에서 Stephen보다 컴퓨터에 대해 더 잘 아는 사람은 없다. (know more about)

→ No one in the office ______________________________.

8 이 노트북의 휴대성은 예전 것보다 우수하다. (superior, that of my previous one)

→ This laptop's portability ______________________________.

▶ 비교급 – 최상급 만들기

형용사/부사	비교급	최상급
1음절, 2음절	원급 + -er	원급 + -est
	예) tall - taller - tallest	dark - darker - darkest
어미가 –e로 끝나면	원급 + -r	원급 + -st
	예) nice - nicer - nicest	larger - larger - largest
단모음 + 단자음	자음을 한 번 더 쓰고 + -er	자음을 한 번 더 쓰고 + -est
	예) hot - hotter - hottest	big - bigger - biggest
자음 + –y	y를 i로 바꾸고 + -er	y를 i로 바꾸고 + -est
	예) easy - easier - easiest	pretty - prettier - prettiest
3음절 이상	more + 원급	most + 원급
	예) beautiful - more beautiful - most beautiful	

▶ 주의해야 할 〈비교급 – 최상급〉의 불규칙 변화

good - better - best 좋은
ill - worse - worst 병든
few - fewer - fewest 수가 적은
old - elder - eldest 나이가 위인, 연장자인
far - farther - farthest 거리상으로 먼

well - better - best 건강한
many - more - most 수가 많은
little - less - least 양이 적은
last - later - latest 시간상으로 늦은
far - further - furthest 정도가 더한

bad - worse - worst 나쁜
much - more - most 양이 많은
old - older - oldest 늙은, 낡은
late - latter - last 순서상으로 늦은, 나중의

▶ 여러 가지 수량 형용사

뜻		수/양 형용사	함께 쓰는 명사
수/양	많은	a lot of / lots of / plenty of	+ 복수 가산/불가산 명사
수	많은	many a good [great] many a good [great, large] number of	+ 복수 가산명사
	거의 없는 아주 적은 조금 있는 극히 적은 많은 상당히 많은	few very few a few only a few not a few quite a few	
양	많은	much a good [great] deal [quantity] of a large amount of	+ 불가산명사
	거의 없는 아주 적은 조금 있는 극히 소수의 많은 상당히 많은	little very little a little only a little not a little quite a little	

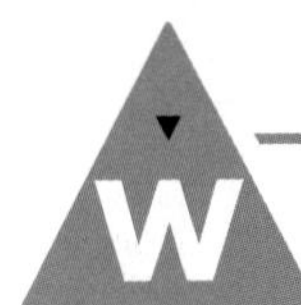

WRAP-UP TEST

Answers P.24

1 [보기]와 같은 관계로 짝지어진 것을 고르시오.

hard – hardly

ⓐ quiet – quietly　ⓑ soft – softly
ⓒ high – highly　ⓓ slow – slowly

2 빈칸에 공통으로 들어갈 말을 고르시오.

• ________ people live alone, and others don't.
• Will you have ________ oranges? They are very delicious.

ⓐ some　ⓑ little　ⓒ a little　ⓓ much

3 어법상 쓰임이 옳지 않은 것을 고르시오.

ⓐ Do you know my eld brother?
ⓑ What happened? Nobody was present at the meeting.
ⓒ Excuse me. Where is the main gate?
ⓓ How cute the sleeping baby is!

4 밑줄 친 부분의 쓰임이 잘못된 것을 고르시오.

ⓐ Look at the frog. It jumps very high.
ⓑ They completed the art work so lovely.
ⓒ Please finish your lunch more quickly.
ⓓ The trouble is that you believe people too easily.

5 빈칸에 공통으로 들어갈 말을 쓰시오.

• He is the best student ________ our class.
• Mr. Walton, the car dealer, was chosen as the best dresser ________ town.

6 두 문장의 뜻이 같아지도록 빈칸에 알맞은 말을 써 넣으시오.

This sketch book is less expensive than that one.
= This sketch book is ________________ as that one.

7 문장의 의미가 나머지와 다른 것을 고르시오.

ⓐ Today was the hottest day of the year.
ⓑ Today was hotter than any other day.
ⓒ No other day was as hot as today.
ⓓ Today was a lot hotter than the other day.

8 빈칸에 들어갈 말이 나머지와 다른 것을 고르시오.

ⓐ Seoul is more polluted ________ all the other cities in Korea.
ⓑ Harmony is prior ________ personal ability in teamwork.
ⓒ Reading books is much more interesting ________ watching TV dramas.
ⓓ The man is funnier ________ any other comedian.

[9-10] 글을 읽고, 물음에 답하시오.

(A) Young people think about saving money, but everyone should save 10 to 15 percent of their total income. (B) The more you save, the more you will earn. The fastest way to begin a savings plan is very simple. You should save a small amount regularly. One young woman gave up expensive coffee each week and saved the money. She saved $12 a week for five years. She received 10 percent in interest on her savings. It surprised her because she had about $4,000 after five years.

9 밑줄 친 (A)에서 rarely가 들어갈 위치를 고르시오.

(A) Young ⓐ people ⓑ think ⓒ about ⓓ saving money, but everyone should save 10 to 15 percent of their total income.

10 밑줄 친 (B)를 우리말로 해석하시오.

→ ________________

전치사

1 전치사 (I)
2 전치사 (II)
3 전치사를 포함한 다양한 표현

전치사 (I)

Pre-Check 우리말에 맞게 빈칸에 알맞은 전치사를 써 넣으시오.

1 The concert will begin ________________ 7 o'clock. (7시에)

2 Let's play soccer ________________ school. (방과 후에)

3 They moved the chairs ________________ the classroom. (교실 안으로)

1 시간 전치사 in, on, at

(1) We made our first trip to Spain in May.
I usually get up early in the morning.

(2) Mary goes to piano class on Thursday afternoon.
We usually eat boiled eggs on Easter Day.

(3) School begins at 8 o'clock and ends at 3:30.
He got a new cell phone from his mom at Christmas.

1

전치사	함께 쓰는 말
in	년, 월, 계절, 오전/오후/저녁 등 하루의 일부
on	요일, 날짜, 특정 시간
at	시각, 시점

기타 예문
(1) in 2014, in July, in winter, in the afternoon 등
(2) on Monday, on my birthday, on the night of June first 등
(3) at the moment, at noon, at that time, at present 등
[주의] • in three days 3일 후에 • on Sundays 일요일마다

2 기타 시간 전치사

(1) She seldom gets phone calls after dinner.
You can get this before Christmas Eve.

(2) We all waited here until 2 o'clock.
She has to complete the assignment by Monday.

(3) Tina played in an orchestra for one year.
I have participated in many activities during my college years.

2

(1) after: ~ 후에
before: ~ 전에

(2) until: ~ 할 때까지
by: ~까지
until은 '계속'을, by는 '끝나는 시점'(동작의 완료)을 나타낸다.

(3) for + 시간/기간: ~동안
during + 특정 기간: ~ 동안

3 장소/위치 전치사 in, on, at

(1) Beth's apartment is in San Diego.
She is sleeping in the next room.

(2) My home is on the corner of Fourth and Yale.
A bird is sitting on a branch.

(3) Will the bus stop at the park?
Now he is at the bus stop.

3

(1) in + 장소/위치(공간)
: ~ 안에, ~ 내부에

(2) on + 장소/위치(표면)
: ~ 위에

(3) at + 장소/위치(지점)
: ~에

4 기타 장소/위치 전치사

Cindy sat behind me.
A tall person stood between Jonathan and me on the bus.
He pointed at the person standing next to the drugstore.
The post office is across from the bakery on Kings Street.
There is a basket under the table.
Take the plant outside the house. I have allergies.
The bridge is over the Thames.

4
- behind: ~ 뒤에
- between A and B: A와 B 사이에
- next to: ~ 옆에 (= by, beside)
- across from: ~의 반대편에
- under: ~의 밑에/아래에
- outside: ~의 바깥에 (↔ inside: ~의 안에)
- over: (위쪽으로 분리되어) ~의 위에

5 방향 전치사

The dog ran into the kitchen.
The cat ran out of the kitchen.
I fell off the bed.
I flew from San Francisco to Miami.
We rode our bikes along the side of the road.
The dog chased the cat up the tree and waited for it to come down.
I drove past the office and forgot to drop off the report.
This route goes through the Rocky Mountains in Colorado.

5
- into: ~의 안쪽으로
- out of: ~의 바깥쪽으로
- off: ~에서 떨어져
- from A to B: A에서 B까지
- along: ~을 따라
- up: ~ 위쪽으로(↔ down: ~ 아래쪽으로)
- past: ~을 지나
- through: ~을 통하여/지나

Check-up

Answers P.25

A [ ] 안에서 알맞은 말을 고르시오.

1 I bumped into my old friend [in, for] New York City.
2 The man doesn't walk to the bus stop [on, at] Sunday mornings.
3 The park opens [during, at] sunrise and closes at 10 pm.
4 He must return the carpet samples [by, until] Saturday.
5 Kelly was on the soccer team [for, by] several months.

B 밑줄 친 부분의 품사를 쓰시오.

1 I have seen it before. ____________
2 I took a shower before dinner. ____________
3 Try to fix it before you have dinner. ____________

다양한 쓰임의 before
before는 after와 같이 부사, 전치사, 접속사로 사용되는 중요한 단어이다. ago는 시간에, in front of는 장소에서만 사용하는 반면 before와 after는 시간, 공간, 순서, 대조 등에서 모두 사용 가능하다.

EXERCISE

Answers P.25

A

[ ] 안에서 알맞은 말을 고르시오.

1 The morning train didn't arrive [at, for] the station because of the broken rail.

2 Did he buy the picture hanging [between, next to] your painting on the wall?

3 I will continue working [by, until] your arrival.

4 We visit our parents [on, in] every major holiday.

5 The policeman looked [through, off] the crowd but couldn't find the criminal.

6 Fortunately, the soccer player kicked the ball [past, up and down] the goalkeeper.

B

[보기]에서 알맞은 말을 골라 문장을 완성하시오.

Word Bank	into	between	out of	during	along	over

1 Did you see the cars stopping when a child's ball rolled ________________ the road?

2 A horse jumped ________________ the fence and ran across the green field.

3 The children ran ________________ the classroom to play in the warm sunshine.

4 The students have made many changes to their project ________________ the semester.

5 We walked ________________ the edge of the beautiful river bank.

6 Sarah sat ________________ us while we watched the scary movie.

C

각 문항의 빈칸에 공통으로 들어갈 전치사를 쓰시오.

1 We're going to finish this report ________________ the end of this month.
I have something to tell you. Come here and sit ________________ me.

2 Why does the brown dog start barking ________________ midnight every night?
Rory was the first shopper ________________ the new store.

3 Sam has worked ________________ England for three years.
My mom is making a dress for me to wear ________________ the spring.

4 My friend's old apartment is ________________ the next block.
I prefer to practice the piano ________________ weekends.

5 I'll drop by your office ________________ 5:00 and 5:30.
Let's keep that secret ________________ you and me.

Unit 10

Unit 2 전치사 (II)

Pre-Check 다음 괄호 안에서 알맞은 말을 고르시오.

1 This is [of, for] you. Congratulations!

2 This is [for, from] Catherine. She said you would like it.

3 I will give this present [to, from] him.

1 전치사 for

(1) She painted it just for me.
(2) The storm has been getting worse for one week.
(3) He left Seoul for Japan.
(4) Mark receives $10 a day for his new part-time job.
(5) Do not punish your students for minor mistakes.
(6) She looks young for her age.
(7) Are students for the classroom remodeling project or against it?

1
(1) ~를 위해서(목적)
(2) ~ 동안(기간)
(3) ~을 향해(방향)
(4) ~의 대가로(대가)
(5) ~ 때문에(이유)
(6) ~에 비해(비교)
(7) ~편인, ~에 호의적인(찬성)
• against: ~에 반대하는

2 전치사 from

(1) She studies 2 hours after school, from 8 to 10.
(2) I suffered from a stomachache last night.
(3) Cake is primarily made from flour and sugar.
(4) This expression is from the movie *Spiderman*.
(5) He was absent from school for two days.

2
(1) ~로부터(시작 시점)
(2) ~ 때문에, ~로 인해(원인)
(3) ~로부터(성분)
(4) ~로부터(출처/기원)
(5) ~에서 떨어져(부재/간격)

3 전치사 of

(1) He is the son of my father's business partner.
(2) The DVDs of his travels were interesting.
(3) The change occurred because of poor planning.
(4) The new water tank was made of steel and concrete.
(5) An old man robbed me of my purse.
(6) The three of us went dancing last night.

3
(1) ~의, ~에 속하는(소유)
(2) ~에 대한, ~에 관한(관계/관련)
(3) ~ 때문에(원인)
(4) ~로 만든(재료)
(5) ~에게서 …을(분리, 박탈)
(6) ~인, ~이라고 하는(동격 관계)

4 전치사 to

(1) Go straight to the church!
(2) He went to Paris to study.
(3) Get up! It's a quarter to seven.
(4) It isn't important to me.

4
(1) ~쪽으로(방향)
(2) ~에(장소)
(3) ~전에(시간)
(4) ~에게는, ~에게 있어서는

5 전치사 with

(1) He drove to work with Jim.
(2) Paint the wall with a paintbrush.
(3) My mom is in bed with a cold.
(4) She stood with her arms folded.
(5) Do you see the woman with the long hair over there?

5
(1) ~와 함께
(2) ~를 가지고(도구)
(3) ~ 때문에(원인)
(4) ~한 채로(동시 동작)
(5) ~이 있는, ~을 가지고 있는(소유)

6 기타 전치사의 의미: in, at, on, by

(1) See the man dressed in black.
Grandmother is in bed. Be quiet.

(2) A strange man is staring at me.
My father is at work now.

(3) He's preparing a new thesis on Sigmund Freud.
This is on sale. You can get it for 30% off.

(4) The train tickets are all sold out. I'd better go by car.
Whom was this article written by?

6
in, at, on, by의 기타 쓰임
(1) ~을 입은,
~ 중인(장소의 기능에 따라)
: in bed 취침 중인, in class 수업 중인
(2) ~을 향하여
~ 중인
: at work 작업 중인
(3) ~에 관한
~하는, ~하는 중(상태)
(4) ~을 타고
~에 의해

Check-up

Answers P.25

A [ ] 안에서 알맞은 말을 고르시오.

1 The middle school students prepared [for, to] the exam on Tuesday.
2 My relatives drove [to, from] San Francisco to Los Angeles for a vacation.
3 The cook isn't baking [of, with] the new pans in the kitchen.
4 The next express bus will arrive at ten minutes [to, for] eight.
5 Was the opinion [of, with] the committee sent to the mayor?

B 밑줄 친 부분이 수식하는 단어가 무엇인지 고르시오.

1 ① I bought the computer on the table. ____________
② I bought a computer in the afternoon. ____________
2 ① She called the police on the public phone. ____________
② She called the police across the street. ____________

전치사구의 수식
전치사가 이끄는 구는 대개 문장에서 부사의 역할(동사 수식)을 하거나 형용사 역할(명사 수식)을 한다. 전치사구가 어떤 단어를 수식하는지를 생각해 보는 과정을 통해 긴 영문을 의미 단위로 이해하는 능력을 기르도록 한다.

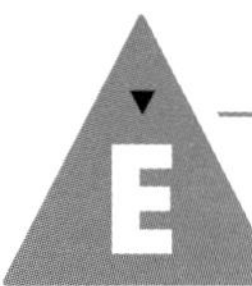

EXERCISE

Answers P.25

A

빈칸에 공통으로 들어갈 알맞은 전치사를 쓰시오.

1 · It's not tasty ____________ an expensive meal in a fancy restaurant.
· I am going to make $5 per hour ____________ the next two weeks.
· Which students must leave early ____________ the science contest?

2 · My coworker was absent ____________ his job for a week.
· Those funny lyrics are ____________ a new song I just wrote.
· He ran ____________ my house to the post office.

3 · My sister is getting married at a quarter ____________ 2 tomorrow.
· As you drive ____________ the school, pick me up at the fast food restaurant.
· My cousin flew ____________ Spain to see the running of the bulls.

4 · The tales ____________ his activities as a young college student were exciting.
· We changed our schedule because ____________ the bad weather.
· She died ____________ lung cancer after suffering from it for a long time.

5 · The excited young coach began yelling ____________ his hands raised.
· The boy searched the tree for the cat ____________ blue eyes.
· My family has dinner reservations ____________ our next-door neighbors for tonight.

B

[보기]에서 알맞은 말을 골라 문장을 완성하시오.

Word Bank	for	from	of	with	to	by	on

1 My sister is ________________ a diet. Don't offer her anything to eat.
2 The rare coins are the property ________________ my brother's new roommate.
3 My room is located ________________ the left of the swimming pool.
4 This stew made ________________ my dad is surprisingly delicious.
5 I assembled the table ________________ a screwdriver and some pliers.
6 Heavy snow has been falling ________________ over a week.
7 Our old products benefited ________________ a new method of installation.

전치사를 포함한 다양한 표현

Pre-Check 다음 빈칸에 공통으로 들어갈 전치사를 써 보시오.

1 They wouldn't account ________________ their mistakes. (실수에 대해 설명하다)

2 We really felt sorry ________________ Ben. (Ben에게 미안하다)

3 He checked ________________ the correct amount of money. (정확한 돈의 양을 조사하다)

1 동사 + 전치사

I forgot about my dentist appointment.
Edward doesn't know about repairing bicycles.
She accounted for her actions.
The child adapted to his new school quickly.
Tom and I don't belong to the same team.
Carol argued with her mom about the way she dresses.
Can he cope with the large amount of homework?
His answers differ from hers.
The test consists of 100 multiple-choice questions.
Can you think of any reasons to change the report?
The result of this test depends on you.
They insisted on paying for dinner for everyone.
He borrowed money from me.
The director explained the difficult role to the actor.

1

- forget about ~에 관해 잊다
- know about ~에 관해 알다
- account for ~의 이유를 밝히다, 설명하다
- adapt to (환경 등에) 적응/순응하다, 익숙해지다
- belong to ~에 속하다
- argue with ~ (about)… …에 관해 ~와 논하다/논쟁하다
- cope with 대처하다/잘 극복하다, 대항하다/맞서다
- differ from ~와 다르다
- consist of ~로 구성되다
- think of ~에 관해 생각하다
- depend on ~에 의존하다, ~에 달려 있다
- insist on ~을 주장하다
- borrow ~ from… …로부터 ~을 빌리다
- explain ~ to… …에게 ~을 설명하다

2 명사 + 전치사

There's a real demand for qualified English teachers.
Did the tornado do any damage to the neighborhood?
Did you send Andy an invitation to the party?
We have a good relationship with our roommates.
He took a photograph of his girlfriend.
We know the cause of the disease is a virus.
I can't see the difference between them.
The police wanted to find a man in connection with the robbery.
The connection between the two victims was very obvious.

2

- demand for ~에 대한 요구/청구
- damage to ~에 대한 손해
- invitation to ~에의 초대
- relationship with ~와의 관계/친척관계
- photograph of ~의 사진
- cause of ~의 원인
- difference between ~ 사이의 차이
- connection with ~와의 관계/관련
- connection between ~ 사이의 관계/관련

3 형용사 + 전치사

I am sorry for Kate.
Texas is famous for its hickory-smoked barbecue.
Who is responsible for the mess in the kitchen?
Why can't you be nice to your parents?
You are very rude to us today.
I was pleased with the present you gave me.
The student was disappointed with his test scores.
You should be ashamed of breaking your promise.
She was proud of her brother.
This newspaper is full of mistakes.
We are short of time and money. We have to shorten our vacation.

3

- be sorry for ~에 대해 미안한, ~이 불쌍한
- be famous for ~로 유명한
- be responsible for ~에 책임이 있는
- be nice to ~에게 친절한
- be rude to ~에게 무례한
- be pleased with/at/by ~이 마음에 드는
- be disappointed with/at/in ~때문에 실망한
- be ashamed of ~이 부끄러운
- be proud of ~이 자랑스러운
- be full of ~으로 가득한
- be short of ~이 부족한

Check-up

Answers P.25

A [ ] 안에서 알맞은 말을 고르시오.

1 My friends and I don't belong [for, to] the same club.
2 Will he be able to cope [of, with] the amount of time the project requires?
3 Did you notice any differences [between, at] the two masked men?
4 There is a high demand [for, of] new televisions in the U.S.
5 The soccer team was proud [of, to] winning the big game.
6 My English test paper wasn't full [for, of] errors this time.

B 빈칸에 들어갈 알맞은 전치사를 쓰시오. 전치사가 필요하지 않으면 X표 하시오.

1 look (보다) → Look ________ me.
2 see (~를 보다) → I saw ________ him talking to you.
3 talk (말하다) → Talk ________ me.
4 tell (~에게 말하다) → What have you heard? Tell ________ me.
5 hear (~이 들리다) → I hear ________ you.
6 listen (듣다) → I'm listening ________ you.

동사와 전치사(look vs. look at)

동사의 자체적인 뜻만으로 표현이 부족한 경우에 동사에 전치사를 붙여서, 보다 정확한 표현을 하게 된다. 따라서 전치사의 의미도 중요하지만 원칙적으로 동사가 어떤 뜻을 가지고 있는지를 잘 이해하는 것이 더욱 중요할 것이다. 예를 들어 look은 '보다'라는 뜻의 동사이다. 이때 주의할 것은 '~을 보다'라는 뜻이 아니라는 것이다. look은 대상을 고려하지 않은 상태에서 그냥 보는 행동 자체를 표현하는 동사이다. 그래서 "이봐, 봐봐"와 같이 말할 때 Look!이라고 말한다. '~을 보라'고 할 때는 look만 가지고는 그 표현을 할 수가 없다. 그래서 지점을 콕 찍어주는 전치사 at을 붙여서 look at~과 같이 사용해야 한다.

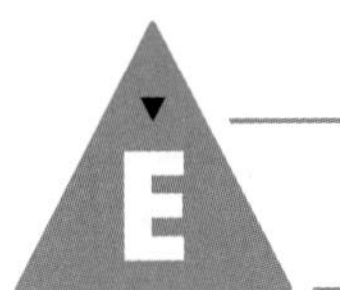

EXERCISE

Answers P.26

A

빈칸에 들어갈 알맞은 전치사를 쓰시오.

1 These policemen have a very positive relationship ________________ the citizens.

2 The rescuers explained the difficult situation ________________ the officials.

3 Why weren't the staff members nice ________________ the new employees today?

4 There is a frequent demand ________________ our steak dinner.

5 The department store clerk knows nothing ________________ the new items.

6 My brother is sorry ________________ his cousin who lost his job.

7 My parents insisted ________________ buying movie tickets for my class.

B

밑줄 친 부분을 바르게 고쳐 쓰시오. 틀리지 않았다면 ○표 하시오.

1 The storms caused lots of damage as the building. ________________

2 The customer argued with the clerk about the high prices. ________________

3 The child was ashamed with being afraid of the dark. ________________

4 My friend borrowed money from his grandfather. ________________

5 Which group is responsible of the new research? ________________

6 I don't understand the connection from the two ideas. ________________

7 The outcome of my report will depend to your cooperation. ________________

C

[보기]에서 알맞은 말을 골라 문장을 완성하시오.

Word Bank	invitation to	rude to	cause of
	forget about	think of	pleased with

1 Mr. Roberts didn't ________________ giving the class more homework. (~에 대하여 잊다)

2 The doctor discovered the ________________ the fever. (~의 원인/이유)

3 Can you ________________ a way to get Gloria to date me? (~에 대하여 생각하다)

4 I have just received a(n) ________________ my best friend's baby shower. (~에 초대를)

5 I'm sure she was ________________ the letter you wrote to her. (~이 마음에 드는)

6 The unfriendly clerk was extremely ________________ my grandparents. (~에게 무례한)

REVIEW TEST

Answers P.26

A

[ ] 안에서 알맞은 말을 고르시오.

1 He accounted [in, for] the big problems at work.

2 My parents will take her [from, to] the park tomorrow.

3 The map indicates a way to get [through, of] the desert.

4 Do they know the man [in, for] the blue baseball jacket?

5 My father just arranged for a taxi [to, on] the airport.

6 I can't believe I forgot [of, about] your birthday again this year.

7 We waited for her outside [until, by] dark.

8 The chapters [of, on] the book were short and very easy to read.

B

빈칸에 들어갈 알맞은 말을 고르시오.

1 Our town is famous ______ its fresh fruit.

ⓐ as ⓑ in ⓒ for ⓓ on

2 My brother knows little ______ electronics, but he is trying to repair my radio.

ⓐ about ⓑ to ⓒ by ⓓ with

3 Our company's most popular Internet service ______ three basic features.

ⓐ copes with ⓑ depends on ⓒ consists of ⓓ borrows from

4 My family is ______ my progress in school this year.

ⓐ accounted for ⓑ pleased with ⓒ demanded for ⓓ belonging to

5 The carpenter found the ______ the holes in our wooden benches.

ⓐ cause of ⓑ explanation to ⓒ difference of ⓓ demand for

6 He ______ buying dinner for all of our guests.

ⓐ insisted on ⓑ pleased by ⓒ was ashamed as ⓓ has an invitation to

7 A hurricane caused significant ______ the houses in the U.S.

ⓐ connection on ⓑ hope for ⓒ cause of ⓓ damage to

REVIEW TEST

C 밑줄 친 부분을 바르게 고쳐 문장을 다시 쓰시오.

1 I was short of coins so I borrowed some <u>of</u> my sister for the parking meter.

→ ______________________________

2 Weren't the boys responsible <u>in</u> throwing the ball through our window?

→ ______________________________

3 The company will have to add new rooms to the hotel <u>at</u> next year.

→ ______________________________

4 I talked <u>on</u> Ben about our exam until school was over.

→ ______________________________

5 The city <u>as</u> Baltimore is famous for its wonderful crab cakes.

→ ______________________________

6 The detective was searching <u>on</u> clues in connection with the suspicious fire.

→ ______________________________

D (A), (B), (C)의 각 네모 안에서 어법에 맞는 말로 바르게 짝지어진 것을 고르시오.

A beautiful sailboat race is held each year just one hour north of Detroit, Michigan. More than 300 sailboats race on Lake Huron to a beautiful island called Mackinac Island. The island is famous (A) [to / for] allowing no motorized vehicles. About 250,000 people attend the Bayview Mackinac Race and festival every year. Children begin the 82-year-old competition with a mini-sailboat race on the night before the big race. The children's race consists of toy sailboats competing (B) [for / against] each other in rain gutters. Everyone is pleased (C) [with / for] the competition.

* rain gutter 빗물을 받는 수로

	(A)		(B)		(C)
①	to	…	for	…	with
②	to	…	against	…	for
③	for	…	against	…	with
④	for	…	for	…	with
⑤	for	…	against	…	for

FURTHER STUDY

Writing

▶▶ 우리말과 같은 뜻이 되도록 주어진 단어를 이용하여 문장을 완성하시오.

1 나는 3시에 고양이를 동물병원에 데려가야 한다. (take the cat, the veterinary hospital)

→ I have to ______________________________.

2 그 개는 울타리를 넘어 낯선 사람을 쫓아갔다. (jump, the fence)

→ ______________________________ and chased the stranger.

3 이제부터 네게 친절하게 대하겠다고 약속할게. (nice, you, from now on)

→ I promise I will ______________________________.

4 그 문제에 대한 당신의 의견은 무엇입니까? (opinion, the matter)

→ What is ______________________________?

5 그 남자는 거리를 가로질러 건물 안으로 달려갔다. (across the street, the building)

→ The man ______________________________.

6 나는 방금 내 남자친구의 사진을 찍었다. (take a photograph, my boyfriend)

→ I have just ______________________________.

7 그들은 20점 차로 경기에 진 것을 부끄러워했다. (ashamed, lose the game)

→ ______________________________ by 20 points.

8 저 두 화가가 그린 그림들 간의 관계는 대단히 주목할 만하다. (connection, the two painters' paintings)

→ ______________________________ is very remarkable.

▶ 전치사의 in, on, at의 여러 가지 의미

종류	예문	의미
in	I lived **in** London for five years. She is **in** class now. My brother is **in** the army. Do you see the man dressed **in** black? My grandfather was born **in** the 1950s. I'll be back **in** ten minutes. Toby is the tallest boy **in** our class. Come on **in**. She is **in** bad condition.	~(안)에서 (장소) ~ 중인, ~ 중에 ~에 (소속, 직업) ~을 입고 있는 ~ 안에, ~ 동안에 (시간) ~이 지나면, ~ 후에 ~ 중에서 ~ 안에, ~ 안으로 (방향) ~의 상태에 있는
on	There is a notebook **on** the desk. There is a bookstore **on** the corner. I met her **on** my way home. My father went to Paris **on** business. We talked a lot **on** the phone. She is **on** a diet. I have an exam **on** Monday. I received a new computer **on** my birthday. I wrote a report **on** American Literature.	~의 위에 (표면) ~에 접하여, ~에 따라 ~의 도중에 ~ 때문에 (용무, 목적) ~으로 (수단, 도구) ~하여, ~하는 중인 (상태, 경과) ~에 (날짜, 시간) ~에 (특별한 날) ~에 관한
at	Turn right **at** the first corner. Let's meet **at** 2 after lunch. The staff members are **at** the meeting now. The boy is good **at** soccer. Look **at** the balloon in the sky.	~에, ~에서 (장소, 위치) ~에 (시점, 시각) ~에 있는, ~에 출석한 (출석, 참석) ~의 점에서, ~을 (능력) ~을 향하여 (방향, 목표)

▶ 쓰임에 따른 여러 가지 전치사

쓰임	종류/예문	의미
도구/수단	I usually go to school **by** bus. He unlocked the door **with** a pin.	~으로 (수송, 전달) ~으로, ~을 가지고 (도구)
관계/관련	They're talking **about** the movie. I submitted a thesis **on** 20th century American literature. He wrote a story **of** a wizard.	~에 관하여, ~에 관한 ~에 관한 ~의, ~에 관한
원인/이유	I was very surprised **at** his sudden death. I feel sorry **for** her. She suffered **from** a bad cold. He died **of** lung cancer. I couldn't say a word **from** fear.	~을 보고/듣고/알고 (감정의 원인) ~ 때문에, ~의 이유로 ~ 때문에, ~으로 ~으로, ~ 때문에 (병, 질병) ~ 때문에
찬성/반대	I voted **for** Mr. Ford. I'm **against** the new policy.	~에 찬성하여 ~에 반대하여
목적/용무	We went shopping **for** the Christmas party. Our class is going to the museum **on** a field trip.	~을 위해 ~의 일로, ~ 때문에

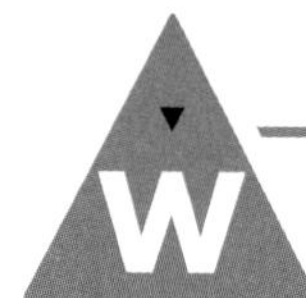

WRAP-UP TEST

Answers P.27

1 빈칸에 들어갈 전치사를 쓰시오.

Jay is leaving for Canada ________ September 4th ________ 3 o'clock ________ the afternoon.

2 빈칸에 들어갈 수 없는 말을 고르시오.

• Dana went ________ the store, but she came back home without buying anything.
• The department store is ________ the theater on 5th Avenue.
• Anyone can take an elevator ________ the Eiffel Tower.

ⓐ to ⓑ up ⓒ across from ⓓ over

3 밑줄 친 부분과 바꿔 쓸 수 있는 말을 고르시오.

Lisa wanted to sit by Bob.

ⓐ over ⓑ next to ⓒ between ⓓ along

4 밑줄 친 부분의 쓰임이 잘못된 것을 고르시오.

ⓐ Please wait here for you're called to come in.
ⓑ The boy saw his cat playing on the roof.
ⓒ Dad has been watching TV for 2 hours.
ⓓ While they were walking along the riverside, they saw a man who was almost drowning.

5 어법상 옳지 않은 것을 고르시오.

ⓐ My mom is poor at cooking.
ⓑ You shouldn't be afraid for the lizard. I'm keeping him as a pet.
ⓒ The huge farm and the five-story house belong to Mr. Walton.
ⓓ Who have you been waiting for?

6 빈칸에 공통으로 들어갈 말을 고르시오.

• If you want, you can send the report ____ mail.
• The package should have been delivered ____ now.

ⓐ by ⓑ in ⓒ for ⓓ up to

7 빈칸에 들어갈 말을 순서대로 나열한 것을 고르시오.

• What happened ________ you and Jennifer?
• I visited a lot of museums ________ the trip.
• What are you going to do ________ those savings?

ⓐ among – by – for
ⓑ between – until – among
ⓒ between – during – with
ⓓ among – after – between

8 빈칸에 전치사가 들어갈 수 없는 문장을 고르시오.

ⓐ It is said there is no life ________ the moon.
ⓑ We really appreciate ________ your cooperation.
ⓒ Phuket is famous ________ its beautiful ocean.
ⓓ The concert was a huge success. The hall was full ________ people.

[9-10] 글을 읽고, 물음에 답하시오.

Some travelers enjoy special Amtrack train rides ⓐ________ the summer months. People buy specially priced tickets to destinations in many parts of the U.S. Families can travel more cheaply, too. An adult can pay for one ticket and get free tickets for two children under the age of 15. This differs from the regular ticket prices ⓑ________ the rest of the year. The demand for these summer tickets is high. Therefore, (A) (planning summer vacations, travelers, should, their tickets, get, quickly).

9 빈칸 ⓐ, ⓑ에 공통으로 들어갈 말을 쓰시오.

→ ________________

10 괄호(A) 안의 단어를 배열하여 문장을 완성하시오.

→ Therefore, ________________

____

The Grammar

2 Level

접속사와 절

1 접속사

2 명사절

3 부사절

접속사

Pre-Check 다음 두 문장을 하나로 연결할 때 빈칸에 들어갈 말을 써 보시오.

1 She is kind. + She is pretty.
→ She is kind ______________ pretty.

2 Jenny will go to Hong Kong tomorrow. + Her sister will go to Hong Kong tomorrow.
→ Both Jenny ______________ her sister will go to Hong Kong tomorrow.

1 등위접속사

(1) The boy is thoughtful **and** understanding.
Tickets for the play **and** the dinner are available now.

(2) The boy was young **but** wise.
She didn't want to buy the pants, **but** her friend insisted she buy them.

(3) Have you seen **or** heard an advertisement about your school?
We can order Chinese food **or** go out to eat.

(4) I had a bad cold, **so** I went to bed early.
We missed the last bus, **so** we had to take a taxi instead.

(5) You can't go out, **for** it is snowing outside.
I ordered my tickets early, **for** I wanted to get good seats.

1

접속사	의미
and	그리고, 그래서
but	그러나, 그렇지만
or	또는
so	그래서, 그러므로
for	왜냐하면 ~이니까

* 접속사 연결 시 주의사항
: '단어와 단어', '구와 구', '절과 절'을 연결한다. 특히, 접속사 so는 보통 문장과 문장을 연결시킨다.

* 명령문, and ~
(~해라, 그러면 ~할 것이다)
Exercise regularly, and you will be healthy.
* 명령문, or ~
(~해라, 그렇지 않으면 ~할 것이다)
Sit up straight, or you will get back pain.

2 상관접속사

(1) **Both** Doris **and** Mark go to the gym.
I think **both** price **and** quality are the key factors for market success.

(2) **Either** he **or** I am responsible for the accident.
Tonight's program is **either** Bach **or** Handel.

(3) **Neither** Mike **nor** Amy wants to take care of the baby.
That bike is **neither** his **nor** mine.

(4) **Not only** you **but also** Carlos came from Spain.
Fruits are **not only** delicious **but (also)** good for one's health.

2

상관접속사: 두 개 이상의 단어가 서로 관련을 맺으며 접속사의 역할을 함.

(1) both A and B
: A와 B 둘 다 (복수 취급)
(2) either A or B
: A 또는 B (둘 중 어느 한 쪽)
(3) neither A nor B
: 둘 중 어느 것도 ~아니다
(4) not only A but (also) B
: A 뿐만 아니라 B도

*B as well as A
: A 뿐만 아니라 B도
She is good at tennis as well as boxing. (복싱뿐만 아니라 테니스도)
*(2) ~ (4)
: 동사의 수는 동사에 가까운 B의 수에 일치

3 종속접속사

(1) It is true that she has not returned home.
(= That she has not returned home is true.)
You'll understand that I had to agree with him.

(2) I often get a runny nose when I'm cold.
Before he came in, I had barely hidden the document.
I can't go out because I'm busy this morning.
After we finished our lunch, we went out for a walk.

3

(1) 명사절: 문장에서 명사(주어, 목적어, 보어)역할
That 절이 주어일 경우 It ~ that ... 구문으로 바꿔 쓸 수 있다.

(2) 부사절: 문장에서 부사(시간, 이유, 조건, 양보, 목적, 결과 등) 역할

Check-up

Answers P.27

A [ ] 안에서 알맞은 말을 고르시오.

1 Roses [and, but] carnations are usually red.

2 Celine is either very careful [and, or] very timid.

3 The lights were turned down [for, and] the audience was able to see more clearly.

4 Should I come before lunch [or, but] after lunch?

5 Not only Karen [and also, but also] Martha is out hiking today.

B 각 문장에 있는 절(clause)의 개수를 쓰시오.

1 Americans have become the wealthiest and the fattest people on the planet. ________

2 How nuclear energy works safely should be taught to all the world's citizens. ________

3 Although it has been criticized, nuclear power has great potential to solve the world's energy problems. ________

4 As Americans grow fatter each year, doctors are warning that a very large percentage of them will suffer from illnesses. ________

절 vs. 문장

문장(sentence)이란 마침표(period)로 끝나는 것을 말하고, 절(clause)은 주어와 동사를 포함하는 하나의 생각(idea)을 말한다. 따라서 단문의 경우에는 절이 곧 문장이 될 수 있다. 그러나 중문이나 복문은 하나의 문장 안에 2개 이상의 절이 존재할 수 있다. 이 2개 이상의 절은 접속사에 의해 연결된다. 접속사는 절(clause) 간의 관계를 이어주는 역할을 하는데, 대등하게 연결하는 경우와 하나의 절이 다른 하나의 절에 종속되는 경우가 있다.

EXERCISE

Answers P.28

A

[보기]에서 알맞은 말을 골라 문장을 완성하시오.

Word Bank	both	and	but	not only	or	neither	either

1 We can order something, ________________ just eat leftovers.

2 Wanda is ________________ selfish nor selfless.

3 She is always ________________ upset or angry about something.

4 Control your anger, ________________ you will succeed at work.

5 We ________________ finished the project on time but also did it less expensively.

6 Julie thought Tom loved her, ________________ he only valued her as a friend.

7 He is famous as ________________ a director and an actor.

B

밑줄 친 부분을 바르게 고쳐 쓰시오. 틀리지 않았다면 ○표 하시오.

1 He has an exam this Thursday, <u>or</u> he is studying hard. ____________

2 We prepared <u>only</u> hot dogs but also soda for the picnic. ____________

3 Jake accepted her proposal, <u>but</u> Susan didn't. ____________

4 Shin-ho could neither sit comfortably in the chair <u>or</u> find a different one. ____________

5 Bob is cautious <u>either</u> wise, which is why he's never made a big mistake. ____________

6 The driver wasn't lost <u>so</u> he wasn't certain if he was on the right road. ____________

C

접속사를 이용하여 두 문장을 한 문장으로 고쳐 완성하시오.

1 Do you go to school by bus? Or do you go to school on foot?
→ Do you go to school ________________________________?

2 He studied hard. He passed the exam with good marks.
→ He studied hard, ________________________________ with good marks.

3 My brother bought a new notebook. He also bought a dozen pencils.
→ My brother bought both ________________________________.

4 They won the baseball game. They practiced hard this time.
→ They won the baseball game ________________________________.

5 Paul plays the saxophone well. He also plays the drums well.
→ Paul plays not only ________________________________ well.

명사절

Pre-Check 다음 문장을 읽고 주어에 해당하는 부분에 밑줄을 그으시오.

1 Thomas made her angry.
2 Her friend made her angry.
3 That her friend told her a lie made her angry.

1 주어, 목적어, 보어로 쓰이는 명사절

(1) 주어 역할

That he will accept the offer is certain.
That he graduated first in his school surprised us.
What they have done was for you.
Where he went is unknown.

(2) 목적어 역할

I know that she works as a curator at a museum.
I didn't know that she was your cousin.
Do you know what these are?
⮤ Do you know? + What are these?
Tell me where I can meet him.
⮤ Tell me. + Where can I meet him?

(3) 보어 역할

The trouble is that I've got a flat tire.
The merit of this system is that it is easily accessible.
This is what I want.
The question is how he opened this lock.

> **1**
> 명사절은 주어, 목적어, 보어의 위치에 오며 명사의 성격을 갖는다.
> (1) 주어: ~하는 것은/것이
> (2) 목적어: ~하는 것을
> (3) 보어: ~하는 것이다

> 간접의문문: 의문문을 명사절로 바꾸기
> • Tell me. + What did you do?
> → Tell me what you did. (의문사 + 주어 + 동사)
> • Tell me. + How old is she?
> → Tell me how old she is. (의문사 + 주어 + 동사)

2 that절의 기타 용법

(1) 동격

There's no proof that there's life on Mars.
The news that he married the millionaire was a rumor.

(2) It ~ that ...

It upset me that she didn't call me last night.
= That she didn't call me last night upset me.
It is certain that he will accept the offer.
= That he will accept the offer is certain.

> **2**
> (1) 동격: ~라는 것; ~은 …이다
> (2) It ~ that ...
> = that절 이하가 ~이다

(3) be + 형용사 + that

My sister was happy that she moved to the city.

He was positive that he would pass the exam.

(3) 주어 + be + 형용사 + that
= that절 이하인 것이 ~ (형용사) 하다

〈자주 쓰이는 구문〉

- be afraid that ~이 두렵다
- be sure/certain that ~이 확실하다
- be worried that ~이 걱정이다
- be pleased that ~이 기쁘다
- be surprised that ~이 놀랍다

3 if, whether 절

(1) I'm not sure if it's true.

I'd like to know if he will come.

(2) She asked whether he was at home.

Whether he'll join the club or not is not certain.

3

(1) if + S + V: ~인지 아닌지
* 이 의미의 if절은 주어 자리에 올 수 없다.

(2) whether + S + V + (or not)
: ~인지 아닌지

Check-up

Answers P.28

A [ ] 안에서 알맞은 말을 고르시오.

1 I don't know [that, what] his name is.

2 It's certain [if, that] Nora is the smartest girl in her class.

3 Barry is wondering [whether, that] the class is still open or not.

4 It is a fact [that, whether] the moon and the sun cause the tides.

5 The man asked the police [if, where] the drugstore was.

B that 또는 what을 이용하여 대화를 완성하시오.

A Your sister was supposed to come to the meeting at 2, but she didn't show up. Do you know ① ____________ she was doing?

B I think ② ____________ she was doing her homework. But I'm not sure exactly ③ ____________ she was doing.

A Maybe she didn't remember ④ ____________ she had a meeting yesterday.

B Maybe. She sometimes forgets ⑤ ____________ she has to do.

명사절을 이끄는 that vs. what

that절의 동사가 목적어를 취하는 경우, 동사가 취하는 목적어를 질문으로 물을 경우나 목적어를 포함하는 경우에는 의문사 what을 이용하여 명사절을 만들 수 있다. what이 이끄는 명사절은 what에 이미 목적어를 포함하고 있으므로 what 절 내에는 별도의 목적어를 가지지 않는다.

EXERCISE

Answers P.28

A

[보기]에서 알맞은 말을 골라 문장을 완성하시오.

Word Bank	that	it	whether	who	where

1 Do they know ____________ will host the party?

2 Do you know ____________ we are supposed to meet this Sunday?

3 We're not certain ____________ they will cancel the soccer game or not.

4 ____________ the cheetah is the world's fastest animal is well-known.

5 ____________ is a fact that each cell phone has its unique serial number.

B

밑줄 친 부분을 바르게 고쳐 쓰시오. 틀리지 않았다면 ○표 하시오.

1 Do you know where did Jane go after lunch? ____________

2 It's certain if they will accept you as an assistant. ____________

3 He told me it he would come if Jack comes. ____________

4 Tanner is wondering what Barbara is holding our tickets or not. ____________

5 This is what I wanted to read. ____________

6 Can you tell me if you'll join the meeting? ____________

C

의문문을 명사절 문장으로 바꿔 쓰시오.

Example What's that machine?
→ I don't know what that machine is.

1 How can I write a good essay?
→ I'd like to know ______________________________.

2 Where will the party be?
→ I'm not sure ______________________________.

3 Who's that person in the red coat?
→ I think I know ______________________________.

4 What was the main topic of the discussion?
→ I don't know ______________________________.

5 Why did the train take so long to get here?
→ I'm not sure ______________________________.

부사절

Pre-Check 우리말과 일치하도록 보기 중에서 알맞은 말을 골라 써 넣으시오.

Word Bank while after although

1 We had dinner ________________ the game was over. (경기가 끝난 후)
2 I felt hungry ________________ I had had dinner. (저녁을 먹었지만)
3 I watched TV ________________ they were playing games. (게임을 하고 있는 동안)

1 부사절

(1) 시간
Please clean the room before they arrive.
We waited outside until they arrived.
I have played tennis since I was eleven.
He was talking on the phone when I entered the office.

(2) 이유
We hurried up since we were late.
He is saving money because he wants to buy his own car.

(3) 대조/양보
She likes ballet, while he likes football.
Even though I knew it was my mistake, I didn't say, "sorry."

(4) 조건
In case you need me, I'll be at Tom's.
If you want my support, tell me exactly what you need.

(5) 결과
The movie was so boring that I fell asleep.
The problem was so difficult that I couldn't solve it by myself.
It was such a hot day that we stayed home all day long.

(6) 목적
We all hurried so that we could catch the last bus.
I practiced hard so that I could win the piano competition.

1

(1) 시간을 나타내는 접속사
when, while, before, after, since, as, as soon as, as long as 등
[주의] 시간부사절에서는 현재시제가 미래시제를 대신한다.
I'll call you if he arrives. (o)
I'll call you if he ~~will arrive~~. (x)

(2) 이유를 나타내는 접속사
since, because, as 등
cf) because S + V
because of + N

(3) 대조를 나타내는 접속사
while, though, although, even though, whereas 등

(4) 조건을 나타내는 접속사
if, in case, unless, whether (or not) 등

(5) 결과를 나타내는 접속사
so 형용사/부사 that
= such (a/an 형용사) 명사 that
(너무 ~해서…하다)

(6) 목적을 나타내는 접속사
so that + S + can/may
= in order that + S + can/may
(~하기 위해[~할 수 있도록] …하다)

2 부사절 vs. 분사구문

When he saw me, he ran away.
→ Seeing me, he ran away.
If you turn right, you'll see the store.
→ Turning right, you'll see the store.
Since she was tired from work, she went to bed early.
→ (Being) Tired from work, she went to bed early.
As I didn't know what to do, I kept quiet.
→ Not knowing what to do, I kept quiet.

2
부사절을 분사구문으로 바꾸어 쓸 수 있다.
[참조] Unit 6

Check-up

Answers P.28

A [ ] 안에서 알맞은 말을 고르시오.

1 The team lost the game [while, because] they didn't practice hard.
2 We met in LA instead [since, while] we couldn't get to San Diego.
3 Don't light the candles [until, because] I signal you.
4 We were still worried [after, although] everything turned out well.
5 [If, Whether] you get behind in your work, you can always ask me for help.
6 [Unless, In case] we get more donations, we can't help them.

B 보기와 의미가 같은 문장을 모두 고르시오.

> His paper was completed this morning. And he submitted it immediately.

ⓐ After his paper was completed this morning, he submitted it immediately.
ⓑ His paper completed this morning, he submitted it immediately.
ⓒ Completed this morning, he submitted it immediately.
ⓓ His paper was completed this morning, and he submitted it immediately.

두 가지 생각(idea)의 연결(접속사)
두 개의 문장을 하나로 연결하는 방법에는 여러 가지가 있다. 위에 주어진 두 문장은 의미상 시간 순서의 관계로 연결될 수 있는데, 이것을 and나 after로 바꾸어 사용할 수 있다. 문장을 하나로 단순화시키고 싶다면 분사구문을 사용할 수도 있다. 분사구문을 만들 경우 주절과 종속절의 주어가 다르면, 분사구문에 주어를 표시해야 함을 잊지 말자.

EXERCISE

Answers P.28

A

[보기]에서 알맞은 말을 골라 문장을 완성하시오.

Word Bank	so that	while	although	unless	but	when

1 There will be more time given to us ________________ we can review our files again.

2 The fair will be almost over ________________ we get there!

3 ________________ he's in Shanghai, he's going to pick up some souvenirs.

4 ________________ a rescue team arrives soon, the travelers may get trapped on the mountain!

5 Bernard was opposed to purchasing a new car, ________________ his wife really wanted to do so.

6 I was unable to find good coffee in the city ________________ there were many cafes there.

B

밑줄 친 부분을 바르게 고쳐 쓰시오. 틀리지 않았다면 ○표 하시오.

1 As if it was cloudy and windy, the school picnic was canceled. ________________

2 Since he said he was full, Martin still wanted to eat dessert. ________________

3 As long as it rains, bring your umbrella. ________________

4 If Allen is not rich, he is always willing to share whatever he has. ________________

5 Judging from his appearance, he'd been outside in the sun for a long time. ________________

C

주어진 단어를 이용하여 두 개의 문장을 하나의 문장으로 완성하시오.

1 Somebody turned the lights off. We couldn't see anything.
→ We couldn't see anything ________________________. (because)

2 My sister went out wearing my new coat. I was sleeping then.
→ My sister went out wearing my new coat ________________________. (while)

3 Nancy studies very hard. Her grades are still poor.
→ ________________________, her grades are still poor. (although)

4 Hye-soo is in charge today. Andy was in charge yesterday.
→ Hye-soo is in charge today, ________________________. (whereas)

REVIEW TEST

Answers P.29

A

[ ] 안에서 알맞은 말을 고르시오.

1 Judy isn't sure [whether, though] she passed the entrance exam or not.

2 He confirmed [that, in case] all of the forms were properly filled out.

3 Burt insisted on his own opinion, and he wouldn't listen to either Peter [or, and] Sally.

4 The project will not succeed [if, unless] we get enough support from everyone.

5 [Before, After] I travelled in India, I had no idea how beautiful the country is.

6 Pick out an English nickname [so long that, as soon as] you sign up for the course.

7 You have to take an additional course [if, unless] you fail this exam.

8 [Since, Even though] he has talent for foreign languages, it was easy for him to master both Spanish and German.

B

빈칸에 들어갈 알맞은 말을 고르시오.

1 The class will be canceled ______________ no more students sign up for it.

ⓐ unless ⓑ despite ⓒ although ⓓ if

2 ______________ Sam is the fastest runner on the Olympic team is undeniable.

ⓐ It ⓑ That ⓒ Since ⓓ While

3 Food customs may seem strange to one culture ______________ quite natural to another.

ⓐ so ⓑ and ⓒ but ⓓ either

4 Please keep your seat belt fastened ______________ you're driving.

ⓐ after ⓑ while ⓒ although ⓓ as soon as

5 I'd like to have a moment with you ______________ you are available.

ⓐ what ⓑ where ⓒ though ⓓ when

6 He felt ______________ Susan nor Paul was following his instructions closely enough.

ⓐ because ⓑ either ⓒ neither ⓓ both

7 Visitors must clean up their campsites, ______________ the forest can be enjoyed by everyone.

ⓐ although ⓑ not only ⓒ so that ⓓ considering from

R REVIEW TEST

C

밑줄 친 부분을 바르게 고쳐 문장을 다시 쓰시오.

1 Neither Jessica nor I <u>are</u> responsible for the accident.

→ ______________________________

2 We don't know whether he went out <u>and</u> stayed inside.

→ ______________________________

3 The main problem is <u>if</u> I don't know what is going on in the meeting.

→ ______________________________

4 Neither Steve nor Simon contacted me, <u>as</u> I'd sent them several emails.

→ ______________________________

5 After <u>driven</u> for more than 14 straight hours, Camille was extremely tired.

→ ______________________________

6 <u>Because</u> the heavy rain, the school was closed for the day.

→ ______________________________

D

(A), (B), (C)의 각 네모 안에서 어법에 맞는 말로 바르게 짝지어진 것을 고르시오.

> Although it has been criticized, nuclear power has great potential to solve the world's energy problems. Judging from its past record, it is much cleaner than using coal or gasoline. Some think (A) [it / that] nuclear energy is not safe, (B) [but / so] this is not true: nuclear energy plants operate safely all over the world. Safety standards have been tightened even further (C) [since / when] the 1980s, when several nuclear accidents did occur. How nuclear energy works safely should be taught to all the world's citizens.
>
> * nuclear power 원자력 발전소 safety standard 안전 기준

	(A)		(B)		(C)
①	it	…	but	…	since
②	it	…	so	…	since
③	that	…	but	…	since
④	that	…	but	…	when
⑤	that	…	so	…	when

FURTHER STUDY

Writing

▶▶ 우리말과 같은 뜻이 되도록 주어진 단어를 이용하여 문장을 완성하시오.

1 그 남자는 은행이 어디에 있는지 알고 싶어 한다. (where, the bank)

→ The man wants to know ______________________________.

2 모든 승객이 버스가 한 시간이나 더 늦는 이유를 물었다. (why, the bus)

→ All the passengers asked ______________________ more than an hour late.

3 인천과 부산 둘 다 한국의 주요 항구 도시이다. (both, major Korean port cities)

→ ________ Incheon ________ Busan ______________________.

4 Jimmy와 그의 동료 모두 회의에 참석하려고 하지 않았다. (were willing to, attend the conference)

→ ________ Jimmy nor his coworkers ______________________.

5 우리가 그의 작품을 망가뜨렸음에도 불구하고, Arnold는 우리를 탓하지 않았다. (ruined, blame)

→ ________________ his work, Arnold ______________________.

6 James나 Jane 둘 중의 하나가 공항으로 너를 데리러 갈 것이다. (pick you up)

→ ______________________________________ at the airport.

7 어느 누구도 한국 축구팀이 월드컵 4강에 가리라고 기대하지 않았다. (nobody, the Korean soccer team)

→ ______________________ would reach the 2002 World Cup semi-finals.

8 내가 전화했을 때 그는 회의 중이라고 말했다. (be in a meeting)

→ He said he ______________________________.

▶ 부사절을 만드는 접속사의 여러 가지 종류

접속사 구분	종류	예문
시간	when ~할 때 while ~하는 동안 before ~하기 전에 after ~한 후에 till/until ~할 때까지 since ~한 이후로 as soon as ~하자마자	**When** he visited me, I was sleeping. Don't speak **while** you are eating. Clean your desk **before** you go out. He arrived **after** everybody had left. She didn't say a word **until** I apologized to her. It has been two months **since** he left us. He stopped the car **as soon as** he saw the dog.
원인/이유	because ~ 때문에 as ~ 때문에 since ~ 때문에 for ~ 때문에 now that ~ 때문에	Jimmy missed the class **because** he had a bad cold. **As** I was full, I skipped dessert. He's good at Chinese **since** he lived in China for 5 years. We stayed inside, **for** it was cold today. **Now that** you are here, please help us to move these.
조건/양보	if 만약 ~하면 unless ~가 아니라면 in case (that) ~인 경우에 although/though ~임에도 불구하고 even if (비록) ~일지라도	**If** you have no special plan, let's go camping together. He'll be there **unless** he forgets the appointment. Bring your umbrella **in case** it rains. **Although** she was tired, she carried on running. **Even if** you insist on that, we will not accept it.
목적/결과 /제한	so that ~하기 위해서 in order that ~하기 위해서 so + 형/부 + that ~해서 …하다 (= such a(n) + 형 + 명 + that) as/so long as ~하는 한은	I go to yoga every day **so that** I can keep in good shape. Study hard **in order that** you can pass the exam. It is **so** noisy here **that** I can't hear anything. It was **such** a sunny day **that** they decided to play soccer. I'll stay here **as long as** you need me.

▶ 혼동하기 쉬운 접속사와 전치사

의미	예문	비고
~ 때문에	We missed the bus **because** we got up late.	• 접속사 + S + V • 전치사 + N
	We missed the bus **because of** you.	
~임에도 불구하고	They kept playing soccer **although** it was raining heavily.	
	They kept playing soccer **despite** the heavy rain.	
~하는 동안	Mr. Ford called you **while** you were away.	
	Mr. Ford called **during** your absence.	
~의 경우에	You should have portable fire extinguishers **in case** there is a fire.	
	You should have portable fire extinguishers **in case of** fire.	
~가 아니라면	I won't go there **unless** he permits me to go.	
	I won't go there **without** his permission.	

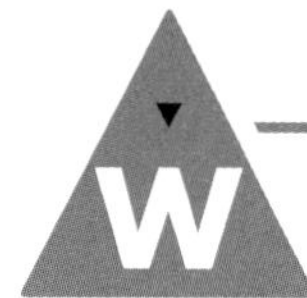

WRAP-UP TEST

Answers P.30

1 빈칸에 공통으로 들어갈 말을 고르시오.

- Jake wanted to act the role of Romeo himself, _____ nobody agreed with his idea.
- Not only Rachel _____ Julie refused to go to the dance party with me.

ⓐ nor ⓑ and ⓒ but ⓓ because

2 어법상 옳지 않은 문장을 고르시오.

ⓐ Both Susan and Donna will make dinner.
ⓑ I like neither spaghetti nor pizza.
ⓒ I couldn't book a room at the hotel, for the hotel is full.
ⓓ Either he or his secretary were prepared for the presentation.

3 밑줄 친 부분의 용법이 나머지와 다른 것을 고르시오.

ⓐ It was you that painted the graffiti on the wall.
ⓑ Please hurry up so that we can make it in time.
ⓒ The problem is that she canceled the appointment without a word as usual.
ⓓ We didn't know that he was a famous singer.

4 밑줄 친 If와 의미가 다른 것을 고르시오.

If you turn right, you may find the bakery.

ⓐ Ask them if it is true.
ⓑ Come to my house if you're not busy.
ⓒ My father will wash the car if it doesn't rain.
ⓓ If you don't make good progress, we may ask you to leave the course.

5 주어진 문장을 부사절로 바꿀 때 빈칸에 알맞은 말을 고르시오.

Leaving the office, he checked his schedule again.
→ ____________ he left the office, he checked his schedule again.

ⓐ While ⓑ Before ⓒ After ⓓ Although

6 문장과 의미가 다른 것을 고르시오.

The kid stood on his tiptoes so that he could reach the top shelf.

ⓐ The kid stood on his tiptoes and he could reach the top shelf.
ⓑ The kid stood on his tiptoes in order to reach the top shelf.
ⓒ The kid stood on his tiptoes to reach the top shelf.
ⓓ The kid stood on his tiptoes although he couldn't reach the top shelf.

7 두 문장의 의미가 통하도록 빈칸에 알맞은 말을 써 넣으시오.

If you don't study hard, you'll fail the course.
→ Study hard, ______________________.

8 두 문장을 한 문장으로 연결하시오.

He is so lazy. Nobody likes to work with him.
→ He is __________ lazy __________ nobody likes to work with him.

[9-10] 글을 읽고, 물음에 답하시오.

> Americans have become not only the wealthiest but also the fattest people on the planet. American diets consist largely of high-calorie and sugary foods. (A) ____________ this problem, not many laws regulate "junk food" in America. (B) As Americans grow fatter each year, doctors warn that within 10 years a very large percentage of Americans will suffer from illnesses such as diabetes or heart problems if this problem is not solved.

9 빈칸 (A)에 들어갈 알맞은 말을 고르시오.

ⓐ As ⓑ Although ⓒ Despite ⓓ Whether

10 밑줄 친 (B)를 우리말로 해석하시오.

→ ______________________________

The Grammar

관계대명사, 관계부사

1 관계대명사

2 관계부사

관계대명사

Pre-Check 다음 밑줄 친 부분을 우리말로 해석해 보시오.

1 Do you see the girl? + The girl is holding an umbrella.
→ Do you see the girl who is holding an umbrella?

2 He has a car. + The car was made in Germany.
→ He has a car which was made in Germany.

1 관계대명사의 역할: 선행사를 한정 / 수식

I know the boy. The boy came from Venice.
→ I know the boy who came from Venice.

I bought a book. The book is about European castles.
→ I bought a book which is about European castles.

2 관계대명사 who, whom, whose

(1) She likes the boy. He lives next door.
→ She likes the boy who lives next door.

(2) Have you ever met the boy? She likes him.
→ Have you ever met the boy (whom) she likes?

This is the man. I saw him at Jessica's house.
→ This is the man (who) I saw at Jessica's house.

(3) She likes the boy. His name is Brian.
→ She likes the boy whose name is Brian.

3 관계대명사 which, whose, of which

(1) I have a book. It was written by James Joyce.
→ I have a book which was written by James Joyce.

(2) I like the book. Nora gave it to me as a gift.
→ I like the book (which) Nora gave to me as a gift.

(3) I like the book. Its cover is leather.
→ I like the book whose cover is leather.
(= I like the book of which the cover is leather.)

1

관계대명사: 접속사와 대명사로 쓰이면서 두 문장을 연결해 주는 것

* who가 뒷문장의 the boy(명사) 대신 쓰이면서 앞 문장과 연결을 시키는 역할을 함

2~3

* 관계대명사의 종류

선행사	주격	목적격	소유격
사람	who	whom	whose
사물	which	which	of which (=whose)

* 목적격으로 쓰인 who(m)과 which는 생략할 수 있다.
  This is the man I saw at Jessica's house.
* 현대에는 whom 대신에 who를 쓰기도 한다.

4 관계대명사 that

(1) I love Jennifer Aniston **that** starred in the sitcom *Friends*.
Jennifer Aniston is the actress **(that)** he likes.

Jack was scared of the cat **that** Susan brought to his house.
The cat **(that)** I bought was a Persian cat.

(2) I saw a boy and a dog **that** were running together.

(3) ⓐ This is the best shirt **that** you can choose.
ⓑ It is the same notebook **that** I wanted to buy.
ⓒ Is there anything **that** I can get you?

4

(1) who, whom, which 를 대신해서 씀

선행사	주격	목적격	소유격
사람	who	whom (= who)	whose
사물	which	which	of which (= whose)
공통	that		x

→ that의 소유격은 없다.

(2) 선행사가 〈사람 + 동물/사물〉

(3) 선행사에 다음과 같은 한정어가 포함될 때
ⓐ 〈the + 최상급〉, 〈the + 서수〉
ⓑ the only ~, the same ~, the very
ⓒ -thing, -one, -body 등으로 끝나는 단어

5 선행사를 포함하는 what

(1) **What** he says is true.
What I want is to get an A on the final exam.
= The thing that I want is to get an A on the final exam.

(2) That's not **what** I wanted to say.
This is **what** he told us.
= This is the thing that he told us.

(3) Tell me **what** you need.
= Tell me anything that you need.
Lend me **what** money you have.
= Lend me all the money that you have.

5

선행사를 포함하는 what

(1) 주어로 쓰임

(2) 보어로 쓰임

(3) 목적어로 쓰임

- what은 선행사를 포함하는 관계대명사이다. (명사절)
- what = the thing which [that]
  = anything that
- what + 명사 = ~하는 것 모두

6 계속적 용법

(1) I met an old friend, **who** didn't recognize me.
= I met an old friend, but he/she didn't recognize me.
We all like Rick, **who** is kind and generous.
= We all like Rick, because he is kind and generous.
I was given a new skirt, **which** was too short.
= I was given a new skirt, but it was too short.

(2) The car, **which** is very old, still runs well.
Billy, **who** came an hour late, treated us to a great dinner.

cf) ⓐ Jim didn't do the assignment which was given by Professor Adams.
ⓑ Jim didn't do the assignment, which made his professor upset.

6

(1) ,(comma) + 관계대명사
= 접속사 + 대명사

- 접속사는 문맥에 따라 and, but, so, because 등을 쓸 수 있다.
- that은 계속적 용법으로 쓰지 않는다.
  Billy, ~~that~~ is a soldier is my son. (x)

(2) 문장 중간에 삽입

제한적 용법ⓐ vs. 계속적 용법ⓑ

ⓐ Jim은 Adam 교수가 내준 숙제를 하지 않았다.

ⓑ Jim은 숙제를 하지 않았고, 그것이 교수님을 화나게 했다.

7 전치사 + 관계대명사

Sam is the man with whom I work.
→ Sam is the man who(m) I work with.
→ Sam is the man (that) I work with.

cf) ⓐ Sam is the man ~~with who~~ I work. (x)
ⓑ Sam is the man ~~with that~~ I work. (x)
ⓒ Sam is the man ~~with ( )~~ I work. (x)

7

〈전치사 + 관계대명사〉
→ 전치사를 문장 뒤로 뺄 수 있다.
→ that으로 대신하거나 that을 생략할 수 있다. (이때 전치사는 생략하지 않는다.)

cf) 전치사가 관계대명사 앞에 올 때
ⓐ 관계대명사는 항상 목적격을 씀
ⓑ 전치사와 that을 나란히 쓰지 않음
ⓒ 전치사만 쓰지 않음

8 whoever, whichever, whatever

Whoever wants to eat the food can taste it.
= Anyone who wants to eat the food can taste it.

Whichever course you choose, it'll be very different.
= No matter which course you choose, it'll be very different.

Whatever happens, don't panic.
= No matter what happens, don't panic.

8

복합관계사
(1) whoever: ~는 누구든지 (= anyone that, no matter who)
(2) whichever: ~은 무엇이든지 (= anything that, no matter which)
(3) whatever: ~은 무엇이든지 (= anything that, no matter what)

Check-up

Answers P.30

A who, which, that을 이용하여 빈칸을 완성하시오.

1 Has he talked to the man __________ repaired the car?
2 I lost the notebook __________ contained my homework assignments.
3 I have some goldfish __________ my uncle bought me.
4 It's the same bread __________ she tasted at the new bakery.
5 He saw the boy __________ jumped over the fence.

관계대명사

관계대명사는 선행사를 수식하는 역할을 하기 때문에 형용사절(Adjective Clauses)라고도 한다. 형용사의 수식을 받는 명사는 특정 의미로 꾸밈을 받는 것, 즉 제한적 의미를 가지는 것으로 이해하면 된다. 그러나 관계대명사는 이런 제한적(수식) 용법 외에도 계속적 용법으로도 사용되는데, 이때는 바로 앞의 선행사가 아닌 문장 전체(절)나 그 일부분(구)에 대한 부가적인 설명으로 이해한다.

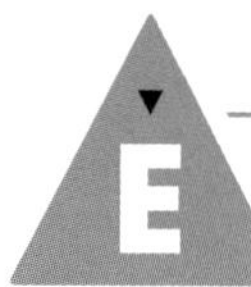

EXERCISE

Answers P.30

A

[ ] 안에서 알맞은 말을 고르시오.

1 Have you seen the play [which, of which] I recommended to you?

2 I enjoy movies [which, whose] major themes are adventurous and exciting.

3 I know the man [who, whose] has just parked his car there.

4 Is there anything [what, that] I should explain to you about this program?

5 [Whatever, Whoever] the results of the test are, don't worry too much about them.

6 That's not [what, which] he bought for your birthday.

7 He was amazed at the award [what, that] was presented to his best friend.

B

밑줄 친 부분을 바르게 고쳐 쓰시오. 틀리지 않았다면 ○표 하시오.

1 She is the girl <u>who</u> bike was stolen. ____________

2 This dog is the worst one <u>what</u> she can select among our dogs. ____________

3 You can choose <u>which</u> you'd like to get. ____________

4 Shawn didn't do the assignment, <u>which</u> has influenced his overall grade. ____________

5 He finally met the woman <u>who</u> wrote this article. ____________

6 Students like the teachers <u>whose</u> perform lots of experiments in class. ____________

C

관계대명사를 이용하여 하나의 문장으로 완성하시오.

1 I read the magazine. The magazine was on the sofa.
→ I read ____________________ was on the sofa.

2 She found a new recipe. The new recipe is for an Italian dish.
→ She found ____________________ an Italian dish.

3 Have they ever heard about the musician? The musician is very popular in our town.
→ Have they ever heard about ____________________ in our town?

4 My father got a new dog yesterday. The new dog was a poodle.
→ The new dog ____________________ was a poodle.

5 I recognized the woman in the raincoat. The woman walked through the park.
→ I recognized ____________________ walked through the park.

Unit 12

2 관계부사

Pre-Check 다음 문장에서 부사 역할을 하는 부분에 밑줄을 그으시오.

1 He visited us yesterday.
2 He visited us on a weekly basis.
3 He visited us the day when he got back from vacation.

1 관계부사의 역할

I will never forget the day. We first visited Spain on that day.
→ I will never forget the day when we first visited Spain.

This is the house. I wanted to live in the house.
→ This is the house where I wanted to live.

2 관계부사 where, when, why, how

(1) The restaurant where I had a blind date was great.
This is (the place) where John took his girlfriend.

(2) The time when we first met was winter.
Today is (the day) when the sun is the lowest in the southern sky.

(3) The reason (why) I visited here is to join the festival.
Do you know (the reason) why so many people in the world learn English?

(4) I don't like how he treats me.
This is the way we can get a good score.

3 관계부사 = 전치사 + 관계대명사

(1) This is the church where Jane and Brad got married.
= This is the church in which Jane and Brad got married.
= This is the church (which) Jane and Brad got married in.

(2) Winter is the time when people go skiing.
= Winter is the time during which people go skiing.

(3) A horror movie was the reason why I couldn't sleep last night.
= A horror movie was the reason for which I couldn't sleep last night.

1

관계부사는 문장 안에서 시간, 장소, 이유, 방법을 나타내는 부사의 역할을 한다.

2

선행사	관계부사
(1) 장소	where
the place (where)	
(2) 시간	when
the time (when)	
(3) 이유	why
the reason (why)	
(4) 방법	how
the way/how	

• the way와 how는 함께 쓰지 않는다.
This is ~~the way how~~ we can get a good score. (x)

• 관계부사의 생략
선행사가 the time, the place, the reason 등의 일반적인 것일 때 생략 가능

• This is the place where we first met.
= This is where we first met.

3

관계부사	전치사 + 관계대명사
where	in/at/on/to which
when	in/at/on/during which
why	for which
how	the way in which, in what way

• 〈전치사 + that〉은 쓸 수 없다.
This is the place ~~in that~~ my father was born. (x)
This is the place that my father was born in. (o)

(4) Show me how the problem is solved.
= Show me the way in which the problem is solved.
= Show me in what way the problem is solved.

4 wherever, whenever, however

(1) Wherever you are, be happy all the time.
= Be happy all the time at any place where you are.

(2) You can use my eraser whenever you need to.
= You can use my eraser at any time when you need to.

(3) However angry he is, he always smiles.
– No matter how angry he is, he always smiles.

4
복합관계부사
(1) wherever: ~하는 곳은 어디든지
(= at any place where, no matter where)
(2) whenever: ~할 때는 언제나
(= at any time when, no matter when)
(3) however: 아무리 ~하더라도
(= no matter how)

Check-up

Answers P.31

A 관계부사를 이용하여 문장을 완성하시오.

1 Tell me the time ________________ the new governor's party started.
2 The reason ________________ I came here is to see wildlife.
3 I don't know ________________ we can complete this chart.
4 Do you know the place ________________ I can get a ticket?

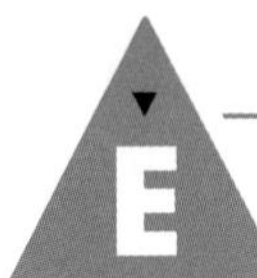

EXERCISE

Answers P.31

A

[ ] 안에서 알맞은 말을 고르시오.

1 She can borrow my brother's car [whenever, any where] she needs it.

2 This is the ship [when, where] famous peace treaties were signed.

3 The time [how, when] we were together was a lot of fun.

4 Do you know [why, what] they canceled the meeting?

5 This isn't the day [when, where] my cousin arrives for a visit.

6 Explain to me [how, in which] the new remote control unit works.

B

밑줄 친 부분을 바르게 고쳐 쓰시오. 틀리지 않았다면 ○표 하시오.

1 The day where my relatives arrived was not very warm. ____________

2 Is this how the way I can get to the subway fastest? ____________

3 You may pick up shells on beaches wherever you walk. ____________

4 Your new friends can choose a location however they want. ____________

5 Whenever you called me, I was there for you. ____________

C

빈칸에 알맞은 관계부사 및 '전치사 + 관계대명사'를 이용하여 문장을 완성하시오.

1 This is the church ____________ Allen and Lori got married.
= This is the church ____________ Allen and Lori got married.

2 Fall is the time ____________ students return to school.
= Fall is the time ____________ students return to school.

3 Tell me ____________ you will correct the mistake.
= Tell me ____________ you will correct the mistake.

4 An illness wasn't the reason ____________ I was absent from class.
= An illness wasn't the reason ____________ I was absent from class.

5 This is the location ____________ the next race begins.
= This is the location ____________ the next race begins.

6 Can you illustrate ____________ the roof is constructed?
= Can you illustrate ____________ the roof is constructed?

REVIEW TEST

Answers P.31

A [ ] 안에서 알맞은 말을 고르시오.

1 Have you ever met the guy [whom, whose] Mary is dating?

2 My father knows a girl [whose, of which] parents run a business in Seoul.

3 [However, Wherever] hard the work is, it's worth the effort to complete the task.

4 The car [which, where] I crashed into the previous week was very expensive.

5 An exam is [the way, the reason] I couldn't go to the movie with you.

6 [However, Wherever] she goes, she takes her dog.

7 I don't like [the way, for what] you talked to my boyfriend.

B 빈칸에 들어갈 알맞은 말을 고르시오.

1 Mrs. Cameron is the only female teacher ______________ I like.

ⓐ how ⓑ what ⓒ whose ⓓ that

2 Do you know the reason ______________ I couldn't attend the opera with you?

ⓐ why ⓑ how ⓒ where ⓓ whatever

3 This is ______________ you can find the airport whenever you return.

ⓐ which ⓑ however ⓒ wherever ⓓ the way

4 I prefer the red cap ______________ my mother bought me.

ⓐ what ⓑ which ⓒ for which ⓓ of which

5 The company chose the applicant ______________ had a master's degree in business.

ⓐ who ⓑ whose ⓒ for what ⓓ for whom

6 This is the school ______________ my sister and I attended.

ⓐ what ⓑ which ⓒ for which ⓓ in where

7 ______________ site you visit, see the play about Native Americans.

ⓐ However ⓑ Wherever ⓒ Whichever ⓓ For whatever

REVIEW TEST

C

밑줄 친 부분을 바르게 고쳐 문장을 다시 쓰시오.

1 Do you know the girl whom lives next door to you?

→ ______________________

2 Will you please explain to me the way how the accident occurred last night?

→ ______________________

3 I think it is the same thing what she planned on studying in school.

→ ______________________

4 My mother found which the old storybook that she used to read to me.

→ ______________________

5 This is the place in where your grandparents moved from England.

→ ______________________

6 Padre Island is a popular location when students spend their spring vacations.

→ ______________________

D

(A), (B), (C)의 각 네모 안에서 어법에 맞는 말로 바르게 짝지어진 것을 고르시오.

> The city of East Lansing, Michigan is about to celebrate a birthday. It's the city's 100th birthday. The city has a year-long celebration planned. The time (A) [when / how] the city began was 1907. Many people will gather downtown which was the birthplace of the city. Many citizens will gather to form the shape of the number "100." Many people will meet friends and neighbors downtown. (B) [However / Whichever] large the crowd is, everyone will have a good time. A special website is available (C) [whatever / whenever] citizens want more information about upcoming events.

	(A)		(B)		(C)
①	when	…	However	…	whenever
②	when	…	Whichever	…	whatever
③	how	…	However	…	whatever
④	how	…	However	…	whenever
⑤	how	…	Whichever	…	whenever

FURTHER STUDY

Writing

▶▶ 우리말과 같은 뜻이 되도록 주어진 단어를 이용하여 문장을 완성하시오. (관계대명사 또는 관계부사를 사용할 것)

1 이것은 뒷바퀴가 펑크 난 자전거이다. (rear tire, flat)

→ This is ______________________________.

2 그가 오늘 아침 당신이 인터뷰한 신입생인가요? (the freshman, interviewed)

→ Is he ______________________________ this morning?

3 이것이 지난번에 내가 너에게 말한 그 핸드폰이다. (cell phone, told you about)

→ This is ______________________________ the other day.

4 교장은 Hansen이라는 이름의 새로 오신 수학 선생님을 소개했다. (introduced, the new math teacher)

→ The principal ______________________________.

5 이 그림이 어떻게 그려졌는지 내게 설명해 주세요. (the picture, be painted)

→ Please describe for me ______________________________.

6 내가 어젯밤에 잠을 못 잔 이유는 시끄러운 이웃 때문이었다. (couldn't sleep well)

→ A loud neighbor ______________________________ last night.

7 네가 원하는 것이면 뭐든 가져도 좋다. (have)

→ You can ______________________________.

8 여름 방학은 많은 아이들이 놀이공원을 찾는 시기이다. (the time, a lot of kids, visit)

→ Summer vacation is ______________________________

the amusement park.

▶ 다양한 that 용법 정리

종류	예문	의미
지시형용사	This computer is more expensive than **that** one.	(조금 떨어진 것을 가리켜) 그, 저
부사	We don't need **that** much money now.	그렇게, 그다지
지시대명사	This is bigger than **that**.	(조금 떨어진 것을 가리켜) 저것
	That's what I wanted to tell you.	(이미 나온 것을 반복하여) 그것
It ~ that 강조 구문	It was yesterday **that** I took a math exam. It was a math exam **that** I screwed up.	It ~ that ... (~) 부분 강조
부사절	He runs an hour every day **so that** he can win the race. = He runs an hour every day **in order that** he can win the race.	so that ~ / in order that ~ (~하기 위해서)
	It's **so** fine today **that** we can go on a picnic. = It's a **such** a fine day **that** we can go on a picnic.	so ~ that / such ~ that (~해서 …하다)
	Put the snow tires on your car **in case (that)** it snows.	in case (that) ~인 경우에
명사절	**That** he won the lottery surprised all of us.	~라는 것은/것이 (주절)
	I didn't know **that** he came from China.	~라는 것을 (목적어절)
	The trouble is **that** I don't remember who he is.	~라는 것이다 (보어절)
	There is no evidence **that** he stole the wallet.	~라는, ~하다는 (동격절)
	It is certain **that** he will quit the job sooner or later.	~라는 것이 …이다
관계대명사	She's carrying a bag **that** was made in Italy.	(주격) - 선행사를 받음
	This is the person **that** I'd like to introduce to you.	(목적격) - 선행사를 받음
	This is the first model airplane **that** I made by myself.	선행사가 특수용법으로 쓰인 것일 때

▶ what을 사용한 관용적 표현

- **what is called, what we/they call** 소위, 이른바
  This is what we call Peter Pan Syndrome.
- **what one used to be** 예전의 인물
  I'm totally different from what I used to be.
- **what one is** 인격, 인물 **what one has** 그가 가진 것
  You should judge a man not by what he has but by what he is.
- **what is worse** 설상가상으로 **what is better** 금상첨화로
  He lost the files. What is worse, he couldn't find the laptop.
  I got an A. What is better, I got a scholarship.
- **A is to B what C is to D** A가 B인 것은 C가 D인 것과 같다
  What exercise is to the body, reading is to the mind.

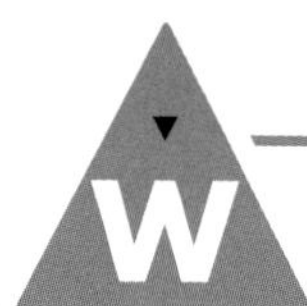

WRAP-UP TEST

Answers P.32

1 빈칸에 공통으로 들어갈 말을 고르시오.

- We all liked __________ he gave us.
- This is __________ he was looking for.

ⓐ who ⓑ that
ⓒ which ⓓ what

2 두 문장을 한 문장으로 바르게 바꾼 것을 고르시오.

He is the one. I really hate him.

ⓐ He is I really hate.
ⓑ He is what I really hate.
ⓒ He is the one I really hate.
ⓓ He is the one I really hate him.

3 밑줄 친 관계대명사를 생략할 수 없는 것을 고르시오.

ⓐ This is the park which we used to play baseball in.
ⓑ I know a girl whose name is Sarah Parker.
ⓒ This is the best way that you can choose.
ⓓ I can't forget the day when we first met.

4 밑줄 친 that과 쓰임이 다른 것을 고르시오.

This is the worst spaghetti that I've ever had.

ⓐ The thing that I really want is travel around the world.
ⓑ This is the best present that I could get you from Japan.
ⓒ She collects color pencils that she buys on her business trips.
ⓓ The man that moved in next door seems very friendly.

5 밑줄 친 부분의 쓰임이 잘못된 것을 고르시오.

ⓐ The day when they arrived in London was rainy and foggy.
ⓑ The reason why I couldn't sleep last night was the crying cat.
ⓒ Could you tell me how you solved the science problem?
ⓓ Nobody knows in when we're supposed to meet.

6 which is가 들어갈 위치로 알맞은 곳을 고르시오.

Do any of you see ⓐ the bike ⓑ parked ⓒ around here? It ⓓ must have been stolen.

[7-8] 밑줄 친 부분이 어법상 옳지 않은 것을 고르시오.

7 ⓐ I have a foreign friend whose comes from Ottawa, Canada.
ⓑ Monica lost one of my books that I lent her.
ⓒ He has a lot of DVDs which he bought in L.A.
ⓓ Joanna always dreams of living in a house whose roof is green, like Anne's.

8 ⓐ You can choose whatever you want to do.
ⓑ Wherever you go, I'll always be with you.
ⓒ Is this the book for that he is looking?
ⓓ One of my friends had a car accident last night, which surprised all the class.

[9-10] 글을 읽고, 물음에 답하시오.

An American company makes roads safer with new technology. Snow and ice don't stick to the new road surface. When salt is spread on the new surface, it works even better. Also, the new surface prevents dangerous "black ice." Black ice is unseen ice on highways. It is the reason many accidents occur in winter. The new surface is ______________ to reduce accidents. The accident rate even dropped to zero on one dangerous bridge. Many states want the new material on their highways now.

9 빈칸에 들어갈 말을 모두 고르시오.

ⓐ how ⓑ the way
ⓒ the how ⓓ the way how

10 밑줄 친 It이 가리키는 것을 고르시오.

ⓐ Black ice
ⓑ Highways
ⓒ An American company
ⓓ The new road surface

The
Grammar

가정법, 일치, 특수 구문

1 가정법 (I)
2 가정법 (II)
3 일치, 특수 구문

가정법 (I)

Pre-Check 다음 밑줄 친 부분에 유의하여 문장을 해석하시오.

1 If you drop a glass, it breaks.
2 If I were you, I would not come along with them.
3 If he had won the lottery, he would have helped the poor.

1 단순 조건문

If the weather **is** fine, we **will meet** outside.
→ It's not certain whether the weather will be fine or not.

If I **am** free tomorrow, I **may stop** by there.
→ I'm not sure whether or not I will be free tomorrow.

cf) If you **don't call** him now, he **will be** disappointed.
→ Call him now, or he will be disappointed.

If you **don't bring** the ticket, you **can't get** in.
→ Unless you bring the ticket, you can't get in.

> 1
> 단순 조건문
> (아직 확정되지 않은 현재나 미래의 일)
> : 만일 ~이면 …일 것이다
>
> *cf)* if절의 부정문
> If 주어 + 동사 not
> = 명령문, or
> (~해라, 그렇지 않으면 …)
> = Unless ~
> (만약 ~하지 않는다면 …)

2 가정법 과거

If I **had** a lot of money, I **could buy** the ring.
= I don't have a lot of money, so I can't buy the ring.

If I **were** rich, I **could buy** a yacht.
= I'm not rich, so I can't buy a yacht.

If I **weren't** busy, I **might play** basketball.
= I'm busy, so I cannot play basketball.

If he **became** rich, **would** she **marry** him?
What **would** you **do** if you **became** rich?
How **would** you **feel** if you **were left** alone?

cf) If I were you, I would talk to the professor.
→ You should talk to the professor.

> 2
> 현재 사실에 반대되는 일
> : 만일 ~라면 …일 텐데

If 절			주절		
If	S	과거 동사	S	would could should might	동사 원형

• if 절에서 be동사는 항상 were

> *cf)*
> • If I were you ~ 구문은 「내가 너라면 ~할 텐데」의 뜻으로 충고나 제안의 의미를 가진다. 따라서 should로 바꾸어 쓸 수 있다.

3 가정법 과거완료

If I had passed the exam, my mom would have been happy.
= I didn't pass the exam, so my mom wasn't happy.

If he had come to the party, I could have met him.
= He didn't come to the party, so I couldn't meet him.

If I had studied harder, I might have gotten an A on the exam.
If it had rained yesterday, would you have stayed at home?

cf) If I had been you, I wouldn't have bought that expensive dress.
= You shouldn't have bought that expensive dress.

3

과거 사실에 반대되는 일
: ~였다면 …였을 텐데

If 절			주절		
If	S	had p.p.	S	would could should might	have p.p.

Check-up

Answers P.33

A 자연스러운 문장이 되도록 <A>와 <B>를 연결하시오.

<A>	<B>
1 If it is sunny,	ⓐ I wouldn't go there alone.
2 If the police were here,	ⓑ we would buy a bigger house.
3 If I were you,	ⓒ he could have passed.
4 If he had studied harder,	ⓓ we will go on a picnic.
5 If we had more money,	ⓔ they could arrest the thief.

B 주어진 문장과 의미상 가까운 것을 고르시오.

1 I don't have a car, so I can't pick you up at 7.
ⓐ If I had a car, I could pick you up at 7.
ⓑ If I have a car, I can pick you up at 7.

2 I might borrow a car, then I can pick you up at 7.
ⓐ If I borrowed a car, I could pick you up at 7.
ⓑ If I borrow a car, I can pick you up at 7.

단순 조건문(Conditional Sentence) & 가정법(Subjunctive Mood)
가정법 과거는 현재 사실에 반대되는 것을 표현하는 것이다. 가정법이란 희망이나 제안, 요청, 명령 등을 표현하기 위해 이용하는 동사의 형태를 말하는 것으로 가정법(동사 형태)으로 과거 사실에 반대되는 표현을 만들 수 있다.

EXERCISE

Answers P.33

A

[ ] 안에서 알맞은 말을 고르시오.

1 If the weather is fine, I [went, will go] swimming at the beach.

2 If I [was, were] stronger, I could move the furniture alone.

3 If I [find, had found] him, I would have called you.

4 If you touch a hot stove, it [burned, will burn] your skin.

5 If she doesn't make it here by 7 tonight, she [won't, wouldn't] be able to see the movie.

6 If he had made any mistakes, it [will be, would have been] a problem.

B

주어진 단어를 이용하여 문장을 완성하시오.

1 If it freezes, I ____________ (cancel) the appointment.

2 If I ____________ (be) younger, I would travel around the world.

3 If I won a Nobel Prize, I ____________ (get) a new laboratory.

4 If it ____________ (snow) last night, we would have driven you home.

C

주어진 문장을 참고하여 문장을 완성하시오.

1 If I had stayed longer, I could have seen him there.
= I ____________ longer, so I ____________ him there.

2 If my computer were up-to-date, I could play the new video game.
= My computer ____________ up-to-date, so I ____________ the new video game.

3 If you had studied the notes, your grade would have been higher.
= You ____________ the notes, so your grade ____________ very high.

4 If I had found my keys earlier, I would not have been late for the conference.
= I ____________ my keys earlier, so I ____________ for the conference.

Unit 13

2 가정법 (II)

Pre-Check 다음 우리말과 일치하도록 빈칸에 들어갈 알맞은 말을 쓰시오.

1 I ________________ I won the contest. (우승하면 좋을 텐데.)

2 I ________________ I had won the contest. (우승했더라면 좋았을 텐데.)

3 He speaks ________________ he were good at snowboarding.
(스노보드를 잘 타는 것처럼 얘기한다.)

1 혼합 가정법

If I had taken the medicine, I would be fine now.
= I didn't take the medicine and I'm not fine now.

If I had gotten a teacher's license, I would be teaching students in middle school now.
= I didn't get a teacher's license, and I am not teaching students in middle school now.

> 1
> If + S + had p.p., S + would + V
> (과거에) ~했다면, (현재) …할 텐데
> : would 대신 could, might, should를 쓸 수 있다.

2 wish 가정법

(1) I wish I knew the man.
→ I don't know the man now.
→ If I knew the man, I would be happy.

I wish I could speak French.
I wish I went shopping.

(2) I wish I had bought the shoes.
→ I didn't buy the shoes in the past.
→ If I had bought the shoes, I would have been happy.

I wish I had taken his advice.
I wish I had learned from him from the start.

> 2
> (1) I wish + 가정법 과거
> : ~라면 좋을 텐데
> 말하는 사람이 현재와 다른 것을 원하고 있을 때
> (2) I wish + 가정법 과거완료
> : ~했다면 좋았을 텐데
> 말하는 사람이 과거와 다른 것을 원하고 있을 때

3 as if 가정법

(1) Mom treats me as if I were a baby.
→ In fact, I'm not a baby.

She acts as if she were a psychologist.
→ In fact, she is not a psychologist.

(2) She acts as if she had been a psychologist.
→ In fact, she was not a psychologist.

> 3
> (1) 주절, as if + 가정법 과거
> : 마치 ~인 것처럼 …하다
> (사실은, 그렇지 않다)
> (2) 주절, as if + 가정법 과거완료
> : 마치 ~였던 것처럼 …하다
> (사실은, 그렇지 않았다)
>
> * as if 절의 동사가 현재일 때
> He behaves as if he is a teacher.
> = I'm not sure whether he is a teacher or not.

They talked as if they had visited New York.
→ In fact, they didn't visit New York.

3 기타 가정법

(1) If it were not for a computer, I couldn't finish it.
= Without a computer, I couldn't finish it.
= But for a computer, I couldn't finish it.

If it had not been for his help, I would not have survived.
= Without his help, I would not have survived.
= But for his help, I would not have survived.

(2) ⓐ I suggested that he (should) be more confident.
ⓑ It is important that people (should) check for viruses.

(3) It's time you went home. It's past 9:30.
It's time you woke up. You are late for school.

3

(1)
- If it were not for ~ + 가정법 과거
  = Without ~,
  = But for ~, (~이 없다면)
- If it had been not for ~ + 가정법 과거완료
  = Without ~,
  = But for ~, (~이 없었다면)

(2) should 생략 가정법
ⓐ 제안, 충고, 주장, 요구의 동사
S + V + that + S + (should) + V
: suggest, propose, ask, request, advise, recommend, decide, insist 등
ⓑ 이성적 판단/필요를 나타내는 형용사
It is + 형용사 + that + S + (should) + V
: important, necessary, natural, essential, right 등

(3) It's time (that) 주어 + 과거동사
: ~해야 할 시간이다, 지금 ~해야 하는데 하고 있지 않다

Check-up

Answers P.33

A 주어진 단어를 이용하여 문장을 완성하시오.

1 I wish you ______________ (help) me. (네가 도와주면 좋을 텐데.)
2 She treats me as if I ______________ (be) very sick. (그녀는 내가 많이 아픈 것처럼 다룬다.)
3 I wish I ______________ (speak) Spanish. (내가 스페인어를 했었더라면 좋을 텐데.)
4 He acts as if he ______________ (buy) this TV. (그는 마치 이 TV를 살 것처럼 행동한다.)

B 밑줄 친 부분과 의미가 같도록 빈칸에 알맞은 말을 넣어 문장을 완성하시오.

A Oh, I'm in big trouble. I have three exams coming this Friday. I definitely need someone who can stay here and help me study.
B Sorry to hear that. (1) I wish I could stay here and help you. But I told you I'm going home for my sister's wedding.
↳ It would be great if ______________.
A That's all right.
B I just wish you good luck on the exams.
A (2) It would be great if we could do well together.
↳ I wish ______________.

wish 가정법
wish 자체에 '희망하다', '~이기를 바라다'라는 뜻을 가지고 있으므로, if 조건문으로 표현하면 It would be great, It would be nice와 같이 '좋겠다'라는 뜻의 표현과 같이 사용하게 된다.

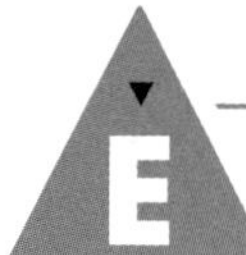

EXERCISE

Answers P.33

A

[ ] 안에서 알맞은 말을 고르시오.

1 I'm not a fool. But my sister thinks of me as if I [was, were] a fool.

2 She isn't from Texas. But she speaks as if she [live, had lived] there.

3 Did you arrive early? I wish you [can call, had called] me then.

4 It's too cold these days. I wish it [were, had been] summer.

5 I was late for school because I woke up late. I wish I [set, had set] my alarm.

B

주어진 문장을 I wish 문장으로 바꿀 때 빈칸에 알맞은 말을 써 넣으시오.

1 I am not smart.

→ I wish I ______________ smarter.

2 I didn't send him the report Jim made for the meeting.

→ I wish I ______________ him the report Jim made for the meeting.

3 I bought expensive sunglasses.

→ I wish I ______________ such expensive sunglasses.

4 I don't know the girl in the picture.

→ I wish I ______________ the girl in the picture.

5 I had a bad cold.

→ I wish I ______________ a bad cold.

C

주어진 문장을 참고하여 문장을 완성하시오.

1 He acts as if he hadn't made any big mistakes at all.

→ In fact, he ______________ a big mistake.

2 She talks as if she were a supermodel.

→ In fact, she ______________ a supermodel.

3 They act as if they didn't care about the results.

→ In fact, they ______________ the results.

4 You act as if you hadn't broken my computer.

→ In fact, you ______________ my computer.

5 He treats me as if I were his girlfriend.

→ In fact, I ______________ his girlfriend.

일치, 특수 구문

Pre-Check 다음 문장을 읽고 생략할 수 있는 부분에 밑줄을 그으시오.

1 Why on earth are you crying?

2 They do believe that there are no errors at all.

3 Steven Spielberg, the director of *Jurassic Park*, is my favorite director.

1 수의 일치

(1) 접속사로 연결되는 주어

Both you and I go to the same school.

He or she is going to organize the party.

Not only you but (also) he speaks French.

(2) 부정대명사 주어

Is there anyone who wants to come?

Somebody is waiting for you.

No one agrees with his new plan.

(3) 학과명, 병명 등의 단수 취급 명사

Physics is my favorite subject.

Diabetes is closely related to obesity.

Is there any good news?

(4) 시간, 거리, 금액 등 하나의 단위로 취급되는 것

Five dollars is all I have now.

It is a two-hour class.

(5) 뒤에 나오는 명사의 수에 따라 단/복수 취급되는 것

Most of his work is valuable.

Most people agree with me.

All the money has been lost.

All of the men in this room are not guilty.

(6) 집합 명사

My family is going to London this summer.

My family (members) are living overseas.

• The two families have dinner together.

My team is hiring a new coach.

My team (members) are spending a lot of time together.

• The national anthems of the two teams are being played.

1

주어 – 동사 일치

주어	동사
(1) and로 연결되는 주어	복수
A or *B* either *A* or *B* neither *A* nor *B* not only *A* but (also) *B*	동사와 가까운 수에 일치(B)
(2) anyone/someone, anything/something, each, every, much, no one, one 등	단수
(3) mathematics, politics, economics, ethics, means, billiards, the Philippines 등	단수
(4) 시간, 거리, 금액 등 하나의 단위로 취급되는 것들	단수
(5) most, all, any, enough, some 등	단/복수
• 명사의 수에 따라 단/복수 취함	
(6) family, class, team 등 • 전달 내용에 따라 단/복수 취함 • 복수 형태로도 쓸 수 있음 (families, classes, teams 등)	단/복수
(7) 분수	명사의 수에 일치
a number of ~ the number of ~	복수 단수

(7) 기타

Three-quarters of the milk was spilt from the mug.
One-third of the members are Jewish.

A number of letters are piled up on the desk.
The number of participants is unknown.

2 시제 일치

(1) ⓐ I think that he is a psychologist.
I think that he was a psychologist.
I think that he will be a psychologist someday.
ⓑ We heard that he built a house.
We heard that he had built a house.

(2) ⓐ The teacher said water freezes below zero.
Mom told us good medicine tastes bitter.
ⓑ I know that Pablo Picasso was born in Spain.
He says that the Korean War broke out in 1950.
ⓒ She said she is learning Japanese nowadays.

2

(1) 시제 일치

주절	종속절
ⓐ 현재	모든 시제 가능
ⓑ 과거	과거 과거진행 과거완료

(2) 시제 일치의 예외

주절(내용)	종속절
ⓐ 과학적 사실, 일반적 진리, 속담, 격언 등	항상 현재
ⓑ 역사적 사실	항상 과거
ⓒ 과거 상황이 현재에도 지속될 때	현재 또는 과거

3 강조

(1) I do know who he is.
She does believe she will pass the exam.

(2) Mark lost the new bicycle.
It was the new bicycle that Mark lost.
It was Mark who lost the new bicycle.

3

(1) do(es) + 동사원형
: 일반동사 강조

(2) It ~ that ... 구문
: '~' 부분 강조
강조 부분이 사람인 경우 that 대신 who를 쓸 수 있다.

4 도치

(1) Never before have I seen such awful behavior.
Little did I think he would become a millionaire.
Only a little later did I realize that I let out a secret.

(2) Into the room came a tall man.
In the square gathered lots of people.

(3) Here comes the bus.
There goes my hero.

(4) A: I'm from Japan. B: So am I.
A: I don't like his plan! B: Neither/Nor do I.

4

주어-동사 도치

(1) 부정어 + be/do/조동사 + S + V
: never, not, only, hardly, little 등 부정의 뜻을 지닌 말 뒤에서

(2) 장소부사(구)가 문장 앞에 올 때

(3) here, there 로 시작하는 문장
: 주어가 대명사인 경우 도치되지 않는다.
Here you are. (o)
There it is. (o)

(4) 동의나 반대를 나타낼 때

5 동격

The question is who will take the role.
I like the idea of his playing the leading role.
Aaron Sorkin, a very famous playwright, lives in my neighborhood.

6 구나 절의 삽입

She is, indeed, not guilty of stealing the money.
This is, I suppose, what he tried to tell you.
Who do you think is the man over there?
= Who is the man over there?

7 생략

(1) While (she was) watching TV, she fell asleep.
Join the meeting, if (it is) possible.
When (I was) young, I liked playing the piano.

(2) Some people like meat, and others (like) fish.
David is a doctor and also his wife (is a doctor).

5
동격
명사(구)와 동일한 관계로 설명하거나 수식하는 문구

6
삽입
부가적으로 보충 설명하기 위해 넣는 삽입 문구

7
(1) 〈주어 + be동사〉의 생략
: (주절의 주어와 같을 때) 접속사 if, when, while, though 등의 다음에서 생략 가능
(2) 반복되는 어휘 생략
: 같은 단어의 반복을 피한다.

Check-up

Answers P.33

A 밑줄 친 부분이 가리키는 것을 고르시오.

1 Isn't your grandmother, the woman in blue, here for a week?
2 Is the biggest shopping day the Friday after Thanksgiving?
3 The school gave her a scholarship, one year of paid tuition.
4 Mr. Benjamin, my teacher, assigned a report for next week.

B be동사를 이용하여 대화를 완성하시오.

A I'm not sure how many people I would need for this group project.
B Well, I think three people ① ________ the best number to work as a group.
A I have five people already. The five ② ________ my close dorm-mates.
B I don't know. For me, five ③ ________ too big, especially when you all have different schedules.

Three people are vs. Three people is
수의 일치의 기본 개념은 화자 또는 필자가 그 대상을 단수로 취급하느냐 복수로 취급하느냐에 따라 결정된다. 특히 돈, 시간, 거리는 항상 하나의 단위로 생각하게 되며, 이외에도 화자가 이야기하고자 하는 의도에 따라 하나의 덩어리로 생각하는지, 아니면 각각의 것을 낱개로 생각하는지에 따라 단수, 복수를 결정하게 된다.

EXERCISE

Answers P.34

A

[ ] 안에서 알맞은 말을 고르시오.

1 My team [is, are] going to different restaurants after the game.

2 Into the arena [came an old horse, an old horse came].

3 Only a while later did I [mention, mentioned] it.

4 The concern [is, are] what could happen to him in the future.

5 [Are, Is] both you and he coming to the new city park this Tuesday?

6 I don't dance in public places, but my parents [are, do].

B

밑줄 친 부분을 바르게 고쳐 쓰시오. 틀리지 않았다면 ○표 하시오.

1 Goes there the last bus to Seoul for the night. ____________

2 Only much later I do discovered my big mistake. ____________

3 Out of the new manager's office came a thin, young woman. ____________

4 He said he didn't like the new assignment. And I did so. ____________

5 Never before has done he such a thoughtful thing for me. ____________

6 She was born in Cleveland, Ohio, and was I so! ____________

7 Some people are catching fish, and others crabs. ____________

C

It~that 강조 구문을 이용하여 문장을 완성하시오.

1 Kevin cooked a Mexican meal for his family.

→ ____________ that cooked a Mexican meal for his family.

2 Out of the principal's office came the young boy.

→ ____________ that came out of the principal's office.

3 Chris, the new boy, kicked the soccer ball.

→ ____________ that Chris, the new boy, kicked.

4 Tina didn't recognize her youngest cousin very quickly.

→ ____________ that Tina didn't recognize very quickly.

5 Jane arrived on the afternoon flight from Kansas.

→ ____________ that Jane arrived from Kansas.

REVIEW TEST

Answers P.34

A

[ ] 안에서 알맞은 말을 고르시오.

1 If they had invited me, I would [go, have gone] with them last night.

2 If the birdcage's door is open, the canary [will fly, flew] away.

3 If I had five dollars, I [can buy, could buy] you some ice cream.

4 She looks as if I [say, had said] something wrong.

5 That is, I imagine, what both Tara and Doris [wants, want] to tell me about.

6 If she had listened to my warning, she [wouldn't be, wouldn't have been] in such trouble then.

7 Most students in our school [disagree, disagrees] with me.

8 Mathematics [is, are] my favorite subject.

B

빈칸에 들어갈 알맞은 말을 고르시오.

1 If I had won the award, my teacher ______________ surprised.

ⓐ was ⓑ will be ⓒ could were ⓓ would have been

2 If the weather isn't good in the morning, my brother and I ______________ swimming.

ⓐ am going ⓑ were going ⓒ went ⓓ will not go

3 Only later ______________ I find out that she had told him about the party.

ⓐ was ⓑ did ⓒ have ⓓ would

4 ______________ was the waiter that found my purse under the table.

ⓐ It ⓑ Who ⓒ That ⓓ There

5 I wish ______________ a new cell phone like his.

ⓐ I have ⓑ I had ⓒ I do get ⓓ I'd like to get

6 People agreed they couldn't accept the expensive gift, and ______________ I.

ⓐ so am ⓑ not do ⓒ neither could ⓓ won't be able to

7 Out of the building ______________ a man with a dog.

ⓐ walked ⓑ both walked ⓒ will walk either ⓓ did walk he

REVIEW TEST

C

밑줄 친 부분을 바르게 고쳐 문장을 다시 쓰시오.

1 If it were not snow, we could go for a drive now.

→ ______________________________

2 Both he and she wears the same sweater to the amusement park yesterday.

→ ______________________________

3 If she arrived on time, we might have gotten a table.

→ ______________________________

4 While he and I were baking bread, the phone rings in the bakery.

→ ______________________________

5 It was the English literature composition what my brother wrote.

→ ______________________________

6 The chemistry teacher, Mr. Cortez, help me with my science project all the time.

→ ______________________________

D

(A), (B), (C)의 각 네모 안에서 어법에 맞는 말로 바르게 짝지어진 것을 고르시오.

> Today is my brother's birthday. I wish I (A) [buy / had bought] a different gift for him. Why? I just found out what he really wants. He wants a new game CD. He treats me (B) [if / as if] I were a mind reader. He makes me guess what he wants for his birthday every year. Then today, the day of his party, he tells me what he wants. It happens this way every year. If I (C) [am / were] older, I would tell him what I think of his yearly birthday gift "guessing game." Instead, I have to go and buy a new game CD before his friends arrive for the party.

	(A)		(B)		(C)
①	buy	…	if	…	am
②	buy	…	as if	…	were
③	had bought	…	if	…	were
④	had bought	…	as if	…	am
⑤	had bought	…	as if	…	were

FURTHER STUDY

Writing

▶▶ 우리말과 같은 뜻이 되도록 주어진 단어를 이용하여 문장을 완성하시오.

1 내가 부자라면 세계 여행을 할 텐데. (rich, travel around the world)

→ If I ______________________, I ____.

2 네가 나와 함께 갔더라면 그를 만났을 텐데. (come, meet)

→ If you ______________________, you ______________________.

3 그들이 그 지도를 봤더라면, 지금쯤 역을 찾을 수 있을 텐데. (read the map, find the station)

→ If they ______________________, they ______________________ by now.

4 내가 스페인어를 할 줄 안다면 좋겠다. (wish, speak Spanish)

→ I ____.

5 그는 하루 종일 도서관에 있었던 것처럼 말했다. (stay)

→ He talked ____ all day long.

6 수학은 내가 제일 좋아하는 과목이다. (favorite, subject)

→ Mathematics ____.

7 10달러가 지금 내가 가지고 있는 전부이다. (all, have)

→ Ten dollars ____ now.

8 그 무료 콘서트에 참가한 사람들의 수는 어마어마했다. (the number of, people at the free concert)

→ ____ amazing.

MUST-KNOW

▶ 가정법의 여러 가지 종류

종류	예문
가정법 과거	If I **had** enough money, I **could buy** the camera. (내게 돈이 충분히 있다면 그 카메라를 살 텐데.) = I don't have enough money, so I can't buy the camera.
가정법 과거완료	If I **had had** enough money, I **could have bought** the camera. (내게 돈이 충분히 있었다면, 그 카메라를 샀을 텐데.) = I didn't have enough money, so I couldn't buy the camera.
가정법 혼합시제	If I **had practiced** driving more, I **would have** my driver's license now. (내가 열심히 연습했더라면, 지금은 운전면허증을 가지고 있을 텐데.) = I didn't practice enough, so I don't have my driver's license now.
wish 가정법 과거	I **wish** I **could join** the party. (내가 파티에 참석하면 좋을 텐데.) = I'm sorry that I cannot join the party.
wish 가정법 과거완료	I **wish** I **had joined** the party. (내가 파티에 참석했더라면 좋았을 텐데.) = I'm sorry that I didn't join the party.
as if 가정법 과거	She **talks as if** she **knew** about it. (그녀는 마치 그것에 대해 아는 것처럼 말한다.) = In fact, she doesn't know about it.
as if 가정법 과거완료	She **talks as if** she **had known** about it. (그녀는 마치 그것에 대해 알았던 것처럼 말한다.) = In fact, she didn't know about it.

▶ 주의해야 할 〈주어 – 동사〉 수일치 정리

수량형용사		명사	동사	비고
some all most a lot	of	+ 복수 명사	복수	* 동사의 수는 앞에 나오는 명사의 수에 따라 결정된다. • 복수 명사 → 복수 동사 • 단수 명사 → 단수 동사
		+ 단수 명사	단수	
many few/a few a number of		+ 복수 명사	복수	
much little/a little		+ 단수 명사	단수	

* 명사에 따른 수일치 부분은 'Unit 8 명사/관사/대명사'편 참조

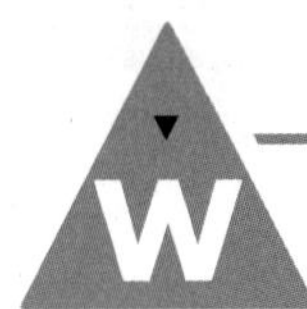

WRAP-UP TEST

Answers P.35

1 대화의 빈칸에 알맞은 말을 고르시오.

A What will you do if it rains tomorrow?
B I ______________ shopping instead of going swimming.

ⓐ will go ⓑ would go
ⓒ had gone ⓓ would have gone

2 빈칸에 공통으로 들어갈 말을 쓰시오.

- If I ______________ you, I would quit the job and go to Rome.
- If it ______________ not for her help, I couldn't get there in time.

3 문장의 종류가 나머지와 다른 것을 고르시오.

ⓐ If you love her, you should propose to her.
ⓑ If I were you, I would buy those shoes.
ⓒ He acts as if he were a CSI agent.
ⓓ I wish I had a camera like yours.

4 빈칸에 들어갈 알맞은 말을 고르시오.

If we had taken the train then, we ______________ at the beach by now.

ⓐ will be swimming
ⓑ would be swimming
ⓒ would have been swimming
ⓓ are swimming

5 어법상 옳은 문장을 고르시오.

ⓐ A year and a half wasn't that a long time to me.
ⓑ Diabetes are one of the most common illnesses these days.
ⓒ Never before I had tried raw fish.
ⓓ Not only Jim and I are good at playing tennis.

6 두 문장의 뜻이 같아지도록 빈칸에 알맞은 말을 써 넣으시오.

She acts as if I had done something wrong to her.
→ In fact I ______________ to her.

7 빈칸에 들어갈 수 없는 말을 고르시오.

Everybody agreed that ______________.

ⓐ his presentation was good
ⓑ the election had been fair enough
ⓒ the politician's speech would be boring
ⓓ they are doing very well

8 어법상 옳지 않은 문장을 고르시오.

ⓐ Most of the oranges that I bought was sour.
ⓑ The number of freshmen is decreasing every year.
ⓒ Mathematics and politics are my favorite subjects.
ⓓ My mom as well as my father is a teacher.

[9-10] 글을 읽고, 물음에 답하시오.

A famous former football star appeared on a popular U.S. TV show. The show was "Survivors." He knew that if he won the show's survival contest, he would get a million dollars. He wanted to win the money. 만약 그가 전직 스포츠 스타가 아니었더라면, he wouldn't have been ready for the contest. He exercised to prepare for the competition. Never before had he eaten termites or acorns, either. While competing, he lost thirty pounds because of the heat and lack of food. Gary Hogeboom, the former star, didn't win, but he was one of the last seven people removed from the Guatemalan "Survivor" series.

9 밑줄 친 우리말을 영어로 쓰시오.

→ ______________________________

(a former sports star)

10 윗글의 내용과 일치하지 않는 것을 고르시오.

ⓐ He ate termites and acorns.
ⓑ He won the million dollars.
ⓒ He was a former football player.
ⓓ He lost some weight while competing.

수준별 맞춤

Vocabulary 시리즈

Grammar 시리즈

The Grammar
Starter
Level 1~3

Concise and Core Grammar Points!

The Grammar

Nexus Contents Development Team

Workbook

NEXUS Edu

The Grammar

Nexus Contents Development Team

Workbook

NEXUS Edu

현재 & 현재진행형

A 주어진 단어를 이용하여 문장을 완성하시오.

1 Does your cousin usually __________ violin lessons on Friday evenings? (have)

2 Your uncle __________ on the 8:30 train from Baltimore tonight. (arrive)

3 Grace __________ for work in the downtown area these days. (apply)

4 Many lizards __________ new tails, unlike other creatures in the animal kingdom. (grow)

5 He __________ with sweat from the terrible heat outside now. (drip)

6 They __________ at a small, used car for their daughter right now. (look)

7 I __________ a book bag like the one on the table. (own, not)

B 밑줄 친 부분을 바르게 고쳐 쓰시오. 틀리지 않았다면 ○표 하시오.

1 My parents <u>are having</u> lunch with their friends at a new restaurant now. __________

2 Don't you <u>are remembering</u> the assignment for our physics class? __________

3 I <u>am carrying</u> my laundry to the cleaners every Tuesday morning. __________

4 He <u>studies</u> hard in the library in Manhattan right now. __________

5 They usually <u>are having</u> a meeting every Monday morning at 9 o'clock. __________

6 The dog <u>is needing</u> a new collar from the pet store. __________

7 Some mathematicians <u>are believing</u> that evolution is an unscientific theory. __________

C 조건에 맞게 문장을 완성하시오.

1 I don't like many flavors of ice cream on my cake.

→ __________ of ice cream on my cake. (긍정문)

2 I usually clean my room every Saturday morning.

→ __________ your room every Saturday morning? (의문문)

3 The Michigan economy is declining because of the actions of the governor.

→ __________ because of the actions of the governor. (부정문)

4 My computer skills are increasing because I am in a computer class.

→ __________ even though I am in a computer class. (부정문)

내신 FOCUS

SCORE:

A 다음 중 동사의 변화가 잘못된 것을 고르시오. (원형 – 3인칭 단수 현재형)

1 ⓐ go – goes ⓑ fly – flys ⓒ read – reads ⓓ leave – leaves

2 ⓐ have – has ⓑ feel – feels ⓒ hate – hatees ⓓ search – searches

B 다음 빈칸에 알맞은 말을 고르시오.

1 The zoo usually ______________ at 7:30 in the morning, except on Sundays.

ⓐ open ⓑ opens ⓒ opening ⓓ is opening

2 We ______________ a very large wedding cake for my family in my apartment now.

ⓐ make ⓑ makes ⓒ making ⓓ are making

C 다음 중 어법상 옳지 않은 문장을 고르시오.

1 ⓐ My company is looking for a new CEO.
ⓑ The Siamese kitten is trembling from fear of the dogs.
ⓒ The weekly presentation is at 4 o'clock in the auditorium today.
ⓓ Are you doubt his memory about the events that night?

2 ⓐ He'll send an email to her if he finds the articles.
ⓑ I prefer the green skirt on the rack in the last store.
ⓒ Are you seeing a movie with Jenny and Greg this afternoon?
ⓓ My teacher change my grade to an "A" now.

D 다음 주어진 단어를 이용하여 문장을 완성하시오.

1 그는 할아버지를 정말 닮았다. (resemble, his grandfather)

He really ____.

2 그 책은 내 것이 아니다. (not, belong to, me)

The book ____.

3 야구 경기는 매주 화요일 오후 2시에 시작한다. (start, at 2 pm)

The baseball game ________________________________ every Tuesday.

4 내가 너에게 전화할 때까지 여기 있을래? (until, call)

Will you stay here ____?

과거 & 과거진행형

A [ ] 안에서 알맞은 말을 고르시오.

1 They [place, placed] the trash in city garbage bags last night.

2 My aunt [receives, received] a wonderful gift from my grandmother on her birthday last week.

3 I [hear, heard] the music on the radio a few minutes ago.

4 Sue [is paying, was paying] for a new hat when Jim was shopping for DVDs this morning.

5 They [are taking, were taking] a walk after dinner every night these days.

B 과거시제로 문장을 다시 쓰시오.

1 He tells her about last night's movie on TV every morning.

→ He ____________________ her about the movie on TV last night.

2 Melody participates in the women's golf championship next week.

→ Melody ____________________ the women's golf championship in 2006.

3 Kurt writes computer programs for my company.

→ Kurt ____________________ computer programs for my company two years ago.

4 We live in a very nice house in the country.

→ We ____________________ a very nice house in the country last year.

5 Why is she opening all of the windows in the kitchen now?

→ Why ____________________ she opening all of the windows in the kitchen then?

6 We eat street snacks for lunch and buy Italian food for supper every day.

→ We ____________________ street snacks for lunch and bought Italian food for supper yesterday.

C 밑줄 친 부분을 바르게 고쳐 쓰시오. 틀리지 않았다면 ○표 하시오.

1 My boyfriend <u>meet</u> my parents for the first time yesterday. ____________________

2 She didn't arrive on time because the car <u>have</u> engine problems. ____________________

3 After a band concert last week, I <u>hear</u> a kitten crying in an alley. ____________________

4 I bought a new skirt. <u>Isn't</u> it beautiful? ____________________

5 The singer <u>returned</u> to his hometown for a concert a few days ago. ____________________

6 The riders shouted at the driver because they <u>want</u> off of the bus. ____________________

내신 FOCUS

SCORE:

A 다음 중 동사의 변화가 잘못된 것을 고르시오. (원형 – 과거형)

1 ⓐ do – did ⓑ sing – singed ⓒ play – played ⓓ sleep – slept

2 ⓐ fix – fixed ⓑ take – took ⓒ build – built ⓓ spend – spended

B 다음 빈칸에 알맞은 말을 고르시오.

1 Tom ______________ to the store to buy some melons when I saw him.

ⓐ walk ⓑ walks ⓒ walking ⓓ was walking

2 The girl was icing the cake when I ______________ to pick it up.

ⓐ arrive ⓑ arrived ⓒ is arriving ⓓ was arriving

C 다음 중 어법상 옳지 않은 문장을 고르시오.

1 ⓐ The large package arrived at my home yesterday evening.
ⓑ The thief is running from the police when I saw him.
ⓒ The new car operates poorly because of the accident.
ⓓ She went to the meeting dressed very appropriately.

2 ⓐ I was listening to the radio while she was emailing friends.
ⓑ What did your brother did during the last summer vacation?
ⓒ My nephew came back from a long trip to the Bahamas.
ⓓ I was thinking about my new invention at that time last year.

D 다음 주어진 단어를 이용하여 문장을 완성하시오.

1 베토벤은 18세기에 그 곡을 작곡했다. (write, song)

Beethoven ________________________________ in the 18th century.

2 그녀는 10분 전에 사무실을 떠났다. (leave, office)

She ________________________________ 10 minutes ago.

3 그때는 눈이 내리고 있었다. 비가 내리고 있지 않았다. (snow, rain)

It ___________________________ at that time. It ___________________________.

4 그는 변호사 사무실에서 온 사람과 회의를 하고 있었기 때문에 전화를 할 수가 없었다. (meet, a person)

He couldn't call because he ________________________________ from a law firm.

미래 & 미래진행형

A 「be going to」를 이용하여 문장을 다시 쓰시오.

1 She and I will rent a new apartment on the first of the month.

→ She and I ________________ a new apartment on the first of the month.

2 Frances will not enter her favorite roses in the flower competition.

→ Frances ________________ her favorite roses in the flower competition.

3 The company will repair the cell phone.

→ The company ________________ the cell phone.

4 Will you make an announcement at 10 o'clock in the morning?

→ ________________ an announcement at 10 o'clock in the morning?

B 밑줄 친 부분이 현재진행형인지 미래형인지 구분하시오.

1 A Does your cousin enter elementary school this fall?
B No, my cousin <u>is going to enter</u> kindergarten this fall. ________________

2 A Where are you meeting tomorrow?
B We <u>are going to meet</u> in the conference room at 2:30 pm. ________________

3 A Where are you going now?
B I <u>am going to</u> the new shopping mall. ________________

4 A When does the new book come out?
B The book <u>is going to come out</u> in bookstores at midnight. ________________

5 A Where are you going now?
B We <u>are going to</u> the show at the Metropolitan Opera House. ________________

C 밑줄 친 부분을 바르게 고쳐 쓰시오. 틀리지 않았다면 ○표 하시오.

1 The veterinarian <u>are going to</u> examine the youngest bear cubs soon. ________________

2 Relax. <u>I'll take care of</u> the dog while you are gone. ________________

3 Hurry! The guide <u>is just about to describe</u> the history of the mansion. ________________

4 Janet says she <u>is going bring</u> me pictures from New York. ________________

FOCUS

SCORE:

A 다음 두 문장의 뜻이 같아지도록 빈칸에 알맞은 단어를 쓰시오.

1 The meeting will be at 4 pm today.

= The meeting ________ ________ ________ ________ at 4 pm today.

2 The diplomat will arrive in an hour.

= The diplomat ________ ________ in an hour.

B 다음 빈칸에 들어갈 수 없는 말을 고르시오.

1 I will go to a concert ____________________.

ⓐ tonight　ⓑ tomorrow　ⓒ this Saturday　ⓓ last night

2 The client is leaving ____________________.

ⓐ now　ⓑ in an hour　ⓒ tomorrow　ⓓ two hours ago

C 다음 중 어법상 옳지 않은 문장을 고르시오.

1 ⓐ It's almost dinner time here.
ⓑ She will hand out new assignments to the class tomorrow morning.
ⓒ Mom finds me a new blue shirt for school tomorrow.
ⓓ I will take care of the order for Mr. Rogers while you're gone.

2 ⓐ I picked him up at the airport for you tomorrow.
ⓑ The sky is very dark. It's going to rain soon.
ⓒ We are going to fly to San Francisco for the weekend.
ⓓ The film company is going to release the movie on DVD next week.

D 다음 주어진 단어를 이용하여 문장을 완성하시오.

1 그들은 여기서 하룻밤 더 묵을 예정이다. (stay, here)

They ______________________________ one more night.

2 서둘러. 버스가 곧 출발하려고 해. (be about to, leave)

Hurry up! The bus ______________________________.

3 네가 그곳에 도착하면 Edward가 널 기다리고 있을 거야. (be, wait)

When you get there, Edward ______________________________ for you.

현재완료 (I)

A [ ] 안에서 알맞은 말을 고르시오.

1 A [Have you ever baked, Did you ever bake] a cake by yourself?
  B Yes, I have.

2 A [Did you lose, Have you lost] your purse on the field trip to the museum that day?
  B Yes, so I had to walk home.

3 A [How long, How many times] have your parents lived there?
  B They have lived in the same house for almost seven years.

4 A Have you and your family ever been to the Hawaiian Islands?
  B Yes, my husband and I [did go, have been] there.

B 밑줄 친 부분을 바르게 고쳐 쓰시오. 틀리지 않았다면 ○표 하시오.

1 I have worked on this project for last Friday. ____________

2 How lately have you been married to each other? ____________

3 My cousin didn't eaten a piece of sausage pizza before. ____________

4 How many times have you played the game since two hours? ____________

5 We have always visit this beach on our vacations. ____________

6 Mike has never been abroad before. ____________

7 My family has live in England for over 14 years. ____________

8 Have you ever been to the restaurant over there? ____________

C 현재완료시제를 이용하여 문장을 다시 쓰시오.

1 My mother purchased a new dress at the mall last week.
→ My mother ____________ new dresses at the mall recently.

2 Bob took photographs of Times Square last summer.
→ Bob ____________ photographs of Times Square many times.

3 My grandparents flew to Amsterdam on an airline once.
→ My grandparents ____________ to Amsterdam on an airline.

4 Mitch and Jeri know each other because they were in middle school together.
→ Mitch and Jeri ____________ each other since they were in middle school together.

내신 FOCUS

SCORE:

A 다음 빈칸에 공통으로 들어갈 말을 쓰시오.

1 My cousin, Andrew, has stayed here ________ two weeks.
I have studied in New York ________ a year.

2 I have worked for this company ________ I graduated from college.
Carlos has played soccer ________ the school year was over.

B 다음 빈칸에 알맞은 말을 고르시오.

1 The artist ________ a mural on a building before.

ⓐ never design ⓑ never designs ⓒ has never designed ⓓ will never design

2 The team has won many games since they ________ a new coach.

ⓐ hires ⓑ hired ⓒ have hired ⓓ will hire

C 다음 중 어법상 옳지 않은 것을 고르시오.

1 ⓐ My dog has eaten my socks before.
ⓑ Did they order the bicycle for Jenny's birthday?
ⓒ How often have the weather reports been incorrect?
ⓓ Charles and Vickie has been to Spain several times.

2 ⓐ They have played on the merry-go-round since Mary gone home.
ⓑ The boy was a teenager when I first met him.
ⓒ Have you been in the hospital for some time?
ⓓ Paul has taught elementary school in Indonesia for almost five years.

D 다음 주어진 단어를 이용하여 문장을 완성하시오.

1 나는 작년 크리스마스 이후로 Fred를 만나본 적이 없다. (not, see, since)
I ________ last Christmas.

2 너는 얼마나 오랫동안 바이올린을 켜왔니? (play the violin)
How long ________?

3 Trudy, 너 전에 초밥 먹어본 적 있니? (ever, try, sushi)
Trudy, ________ before?

현재완료 (II)

A 현재완료시제를 이용하여 두 개의 문장을 하나의 문장으로 완성하시오.

1 I lost my kitty. We can't find him.

→ I ________________ my kitty.

2 I didn't start my homework. I forgot that I had homework.

→ I ________________ my homework yet.

3 She didn't plan the party. The party is tomorrow night.

→ She ________________ the party for tomorrow night.

4 She moved to Florida two months ago. She lives with her grandparents there.

→ She ________________ to Florida to live with her grandparents.

B 밑줄 친 부분을 바르게 고쳐 쓰시오. 틀리지 않았다면 ○표 하시오.

1 Didn't you ride the bus to work this morning? ____________

2 The children has written poems about butterflies. ____________

3 I've lost the study questions. ____________

4 The repairman did not replaced the broken part on the TV yet. ____________

5 Ben has just repair my old bicycle. It works well now. ____________

6 The nurse has gave shots to children in the fifth grade at the school so far. ____________

C 주어진 단어를 이용하여 현재완료 문장으로 완성하시오.

1 purchase / good meat

→ My uncle ______________________________ at that grocery store.

2 prevent / some robberies

→ These policemen ______________________________ at the bank.

3 just / finish

→ The athletes ______________________________ warming up for the competition.

4 not / use / the calculator

→ We ______________________________ for a long time. It may need a new battery.

5 warn / the students

→ The fireman ______________________________ several times not to buy illegal fireworks.

SCORE:

A 다음 단어를 사용하여 빈칸에 알맞게 써 넣으시오.

1 My brother ______________ (go) to Paris to study art last Saturday.

My brother ______________ (go) to Paris to study art. He is not here.

2 I ______________ (not, do) the homework yesterday.

I ______________ (not, do) the homework yet.

B 다음 빈칸에 알맞은 말을 고르시오.

1 The workers ______________ the walls with green paint. It's all green now.

ⓐ paints ⓑ have painted ⓒ will paint ⓓ would have paint

2 We ______________ too much food on our trip so far.

ⓐ eat ⓑ were eating ⓒ have eaten ⓓ will eat

C 다음 중 어법상 옳지 않은 문장을 고르시오.

1 ⓐ Deb found her ring last night.
ⓑ Has she taken the train to New Jersey recently?
ⓒ The contractor delays construction several times until now.
ⓓ They have almost opened the tomb of the recently discovered pharaoh.

2 ⓐ He has not completed the assignment that I gave him.
ⓑ The man has abandoned his dog in the park.
ⓒ It is the best opportunity that they have ever received.
ⓓ When have you and your friends seen this movie?

D 다음 주어진 단어를 이용하여 문장을 완성하시오.

1 내 여자 친구는 영어공부를 위해 영국에 갔다. (그래서 지금 여기에 없다.) (go to, England)

My girlfriend ______________________ to study English.

2 차에 열쇠를 두고 내려서 차 문을 열 수가 없다. (leave, my keys)

I can't open the car because I ______________________ inside it.

3 나는 인터넷을 통해 내 컴퓨터를 팔았다. (그래서) 지금 가지고 있지 않다. (sell, my computer)

I ______________________ on the Internet. I don't have it now.

Unit 3 과거완료, 미래완료, 완료진행형

A 주어진 단어를 이용하여 완료시제 문장으로 완성하시오.

1 Shelly ________________ baking cookies. They smell so delicious. (finish, just)

2 The team ________________ all of their training by this time next week. (complete)

3 The doctor ______________ the surgery many times before he operated on my father. (perform)

4 Ben ________________ hours waiting in the parking lot before Maxine arrived there. (spend)

5 It's already past 8. But Mom ________________ the dinner table yet. (set)

6 The flight ________________ at the airport by 5 pm tomorrow. (land)

B 밑줄 친 부분을 바르게 고쳐 쓰시오. 틀리지 않았다면 ○표 하시오.

1 The criminal had been hiding in a closet in the office for a whole night. ________________

2 I will have moved the package before Henry saw it on the desk. ________________

3 They had graduated from high school when I met them. ________________

4 He will be here for 12 years next month. ________________

5 My little sister has taken piano lessons since two months. ________________

6 I have never heard of my car's problem before my mechanic told me about it. ________________

C 주어진 단어를 이용하여 완료시제 문장으로 완성하시오.

1 destroy / many homes

→ The tornado ____ by the time it is over.

2 study / geography

→ Tina ____ since she was in the third grade.

3 pick up / the cat

→ My parents ________________________________ by the time I get home from work.

4 meet / several times / before

→ The new firefighters ________________________ because they were in training together.

5 be working / already

→ The class ____________________________________ on that project for two hours now.

6 visit / never

→ Gene ________________________________ the Empire State Building before last year.

내신 FOCUS

SCORE: 

A 다음 두 문장을 한 문장으로 만들 때 빈칸에 알맞은 말을 쓰시오.

1 I have seen the movie twice. I'll see it once more this Friday.

→ I ____________________ the movie three times by this Friday.

2 She started doing her homework one hour ago. She is still working on it.

→ She ____________________ her homework for one hour.

B 다음 빈칸에 알맞은 말을 고르시오.

1 The dance academy ____________________ three more classes by next month.

ⓐ opens ⓑ opened ⓒ had opened ⓓ will have opened

2 My brother said he ____________________ his first application for law school.

ⓐ fill out ⓑ fills out ⓒ has filled out ⓓ had already filled out

C 다음 중 어법상 옳지 않은 문장을 고르시오.

1 ⓐ He had never fully recovered his strength before he entered the war.
ⓑ Cheryl said she had never seen a soccer game before.
ⓒ Cora has watched her mother make dresses for many years.
ⓓ She has been waiting in the office for 30 minutes before Scott called.

2 ⓐ They have emailed me long ago.
ⓑ She had noticed the man moments before he stole the painting.
ⓒ They have been talking on their cell phones for over two hours.
ⓓ The judge had just pronounced his sentence on the criminal when chaos erupted in the courtroom.

D 다음 주어진 단어를 이용하여 문장을 완성하시오.

1 그녀는 엄마가 도착하기 전에 방을 청소했다. (clean one's room, arrive)

She ____________________ before her mom ____________________.

2 그는 내년이면 30년 근속이 될 것이다. (work, for 30 years, by next year)

He ____.

3 그녀는 한 시간째 저녁 식사를 하고 있는 중이다. (be eating, for one hour)

She ____.

조동사 can, may

A [ ] 안에서 알맞은 말을 고르시오.

1 Greg, will you [can, be able to] buy some milk on your way home from work?

2 The boss [may, can't] be concerned if you cannot finish the report on time.

3 My cousin [can, be able to] bake wonderful pecan pies.

4 It [could, couldn't] take that much time to do the project. It is a simple project.

5 [May, Could] you bring me the file on the desk in my office?

6 You [may, might be] use my bike if you return it by noon.

B 밑줄 친 부분이 의미하는 것을 고르시오.

1 Your grandfather may take the dog to the park if he has time.

ⓐ ability ⓑ permission ⓒ possibility

2 My brother can play soccer very well, but he can't play basketball well.

ⓐ ability ⓑ permission ⓒ possibility

3 She can go out only when she completes her homework.

ⓐ ability ⓑ permission ⓒ possibility

4 Can you make a cup of hot coffee for me?

ⓐ permission ⓑ request ⓒ possibility

5 Mom said we may not have a dog.

ⓐ ability ⓑ possibility ⓒ permission

C 주어진 문장을 해석하시오.

1 Will you be able to attend the play this weekend?

→ ____________________

2 Could you make a new poster for the school carnival?

→ ____________________

3 Sam might be at the grocery store.

→ ____________________

4 You may park here.

→ ____________________

FOCUS

SCORE:

A 다음 우리말과 일치하도록 빈칸에 공통으로 들어갈 말을 쓰시오.

1 ________________ you describe what it looks like? (그것이 어떻게 생겼는지 설명해 줄래?)

I'm sure he ________________ solve this math problem. (그는 분명히 이 수학 문제를 풀 수 있어.)

2 It ________________ be true. (사실일 리가 없어.)

You ________________ enter the room without a pass. (출입증 없이는 그 방에 들어갈 수 없습니다.)

B 다음 빈칸에 알맞은 말을 고르시오.

1 They ________________ enter the race because they sent their registration in on time.

ⓐ can be ⓑ could ⓒ allowed to ⓓ was able to

2 Tim said we ________________ learn rock climbing from him after dinner.

ⓐ can ⓑ may be ⓒ could ⓓ was able to

C 다음 중 어법상 옳지 않은 것을 고르시오.

1 ⓐ Can I make a phone call on your cell phone?
ⓑ She was able to say the alphabet in English when she was four years old.
ⓒ Molly might become a teacher. She communicates information very effectively.
ⓓ Students may participate not in the games without the proper equipment.

2 ⓐ Steve will can play football after his broken leg heals.
ⓑ Lucy might have your pen. She was writing with it a few minutes ago.
ⓒ Mrs. Baker, can I open the birthday gifts here now?
ⓓ You cannot drive a car without a driver's license.

D 다음 주어진 단어를 이용하여 문장을 완성하시오.

1 그에게 시간이 있다면 여기 들를지도 모른다. (drop by)

He ____ if he has time.

2 공항까지 태워다주시겠어요? (give me a ride)

____ to the airport?

3 그렇게 비쌀 리가 없다. 정말 이상하게 생겼는데. (cost, that much)

It ____. It's so ugly.

조동사 will, must, shall

A [ ] 안에서 알맞은 말을 고르시오.

1 Darlene, [have, would] you please pass the pepper to Joe?

2 He [had to, shall] get a new hat for his band uniform because he had lost his.

3 People [have not, must not] smoke in public buildings in many U.S. cities.

4 I [will not, must be] swim in such polluted river water again!

5 She [must be, must] at the airport since it is noon now.

6 They [shall have, should have] let us leave, but they didn't.

B 밑줄 친 부분을 바르게 고쳐 쓰시오. 틀리지 않았다면 ○표 하시오.

1 My mom thinks we should read storybooks instead of comic books. ____________

2 Vickie thought she have to prepare the presentation by Friday. ____________

3 If you forget the map, you had to stop and ask for directions. ____________

4 They shall not tell Larry about it, or he will be upset. ____________

5 I will take my dog for a walk tonight. ____________

6 I think she would be twenty-six on her next birthday. ____________

C 주어진 문장을 해석하시오.

1 Will you please take the package to the post office for me?

→ ____

2 You must not distract the bus driver while he is driving.

→ ____

3 Is he going to become a cook? I can't believe it!

→ ____

4 You should notice how the software is operating.

→ ____

5 Shall we buy tickets to the opera on Wednesday night?

→ ____

FOCUS

SCORE:

A 다음 밑줄 친 부분과 바꿔 쓸 수 있는 말을 고르시오.

1 We <u>should not</u> download music from the Internet without paying for it.

ⓐ must not ⓑ will not ⓒ don't have to ⓓ should have not

2 <u>Will</u> you please install this software on my computer?

ⓐ Can ⓑ Have to ⓒ Should ⓓ Must

B 다음 빈칸에 알맞은 말을 고르시오.

1 You ______________ open the door for a stranger.

ⓐ should ⓑ don't have to ⓒ couldn't ⓓ shouldn't

2 He parked the car illegally, so he ______________ move it again.

ⓐ must to ⓑ need to ⓒ had to ⓓ should have to

C 다음 중 어법상 옳지 <u>않은</u> 문장을 고르시오.

1 ⓐ You will be wait in the reception area before the doctor sees you.
ⓑ She decided she would not work with him ever again.
ⓒ Don't be concerned about it. I will make the changes before nine tonight.
ⓓ Denise will be the leader of her class this spring.

2 ⓐ He ought to sign a contract before he sells his invention.
ⓑ Julia missed the bus this morning. She must have overslept.
ⓒ What shall we do after we eat at the Mexican restaurant?
ⓓ We must go to the clinic last week.

D 다음 주어진 단어를 이용하여 문장을 완성하시오.

1 우리는 저녁 식사를 한 후에 산책을 하곤 했다. (take a walk, after dinner)

We ______________________________________.

2 운전 중에는 휴대 전화로 전화해서는 안 된다. (talk on the cell phone)

You ______________________________________ while driving.

3 그건 내 잘못이었어. 내가 그에게 사과를 했어야 했는데. (apologize, to him)

It was my fault. I ______________________________________.

기타 조동사

A [ ] 안에서 알맞은 말을 고르시오.

1 You [need not, don't have] bother to come. I can do it myself.

2 We [had better, ought] read the instructions before we put the bookcase together.

3 I [used to, had better] eat pepperoni pizza on Sunday nights in college.

4 Jackson [need have, could have] saved money if he had shopped more carefully.

5 The dog [must have, better have] seen me because it barked at me.

B 밑줄 친 부분을 바르게 고쳐 쓰시오. 틀리지 않았다면 ○표 하시오.

1 She rather not ask him for his help with the project. ____________

2 Harry wouldn't use to be a member of the club. ____________

3 There would be an airport there when I lived in that city. ____________

4 Gina would rather meet with the tutor than with the professor. ____________

5 The cheerleaders need not buy sweaters for the upcoming season. ____________

6 You ought find your book and return it to the library. ____________

C 주어진 단어를 이용하여 대화를 완성하시오.

1 A Mom will arrive in less than 30 minutes. But Adam hasn't cleaned up his room yet.
B Oh, you and I ____________ the room then. (had better)

2 A What would you rather do for fun tonight, go shopping or watch movies?
B I ____________ than watch movies. (would rather)

3 A Denis must have been angry with me. He passed me without saying hello.
B Well, he ____________ you. He's not such a guy. (must, not, see)

4 A You must have told her about the birthday party, right? She's not surprised at all.
B No, she ____________ about the party herself. (must, find out)

5 A Brandon is the worst soccer player I've ever seen.
B He ____________ baseball than soccer. I can't believe he chose that sport. (had better)

FOCUS

SCORE:

A 다음 문장을 괄호 안의 지시대로 바꿔 쓰시오.

1 You'd better cancel the meeting.

→ ______________________________ the meeting. (부정문으로)

2 I would rather drink coffee.

→ ______________________________ coffee. (부정문으로)

B 다음 밑줄 친 부분과 바꿔 쓸 수 있는 말을 고르시오.

1 I'd rather have ice cream for dessert this time.

ⓐ would　　ⓑ should　　ⓒ need to　　ⓓ prefer to

2 You'd better not keep the dog in the house. Children easily develop allergies to dogs.

ⓐ should not　　ⓑ didn't use to　　ⓒ used to not　　ⓓ might have not

C 다음 중 어법상 옳지 않은 문장을 고르시오.

1 ⓐ They had better change the oil in the car before they drive into the mountains.
ⓑ She didn't need arrive so early for the interview.
ⓒ The waitress may have taken the order from the back table already.
ⓓ Melinda used to ignore us at school.

2 ⓐ I am warning you! You'd better not drive too fast.
ⓑ I used to take the subway to work when I lived in Manhattan.
ⓒ Need we make more rice cakes for the New Year's party?
ⓓ They could had reached an agreement with the company if they had tried harder.

D 다음 주어진 단어를 이용하여 문장을 완성하시오.

1 우리 엄마는 젊었을 때는 날씬했었다. (be, slim)

My mom ______________________________ when she was young.

2 집에 혼자 있느니 차라리 너와 함께 가는 게 낫겠다. (go with you)

I ______________________________ than stay home alone.

3 그는 나를 본 게 틀림없다. 그는 뒤돌아서 도망갔다. (see, me)

He ______________________________. He turned back and ran away.

to부정사의 명사적 쓰임

A 밑줄 친 단어를 to부정사로 바꿔 문장을 완성하시오.

1 I love swimming. I like ____________ at the beach on sunny days.

2 They told him about the accident, but he's not sure what ____________ his little sister.

3 Minnie collects coins. ____________ coins is her favorite hobby.

4 Chester is playing a board game with his friends. He loves ____________ games with them.

5 I can't find a good auto mechanic. Do you know where ____________ a repair shop?

B 밑줄 친 부분을 바르게 고쳐 쓰시오. 틀리지 않았다면 ○표 하시오.

1 I've asked you repeatedly not to wore shoes in the house. ____________

2 My dad tried fix my car, but he failed. ____________

3 He has finally decided to mail the letter to her. ____________

4 Own stock in the company is a good idea, I believe. ____________

5 Jackie is not convinced of how change the design. ____________

6 She wants to be a great scientist someday. ____________

C 주어진 문장을 「It ~ to부정사」를 이용하여 다시 쓰시오.

1 To choose which way to go is difficult.

→ ____________

2 To hear Tom's ideas is wise in these circumstances.

→ ____________ in these circumstances.

3 To send an email is easy with this software.

→ ____________ with this software.

4 To speak slowly to non-native speakers is sometimes important.

→ ____________

5 To become astronauts is challenging for young men and women.

→ ____________

내신 FOCUS

SCORE: 

A 다음 괄호 안의 말을 이용하여 빈칸에 알맞은 말을 쓰시오.

1 Would you like ________________ (come) to the meeting?

2 My younger brother wants ________________ (raise) a dog.

B 다음 빈칸에 알맞은 말을 고르시오.

1 My family wants ________________ in a hotel for the night.

ⓐ stay ⓑ to stay ⓒ how to stay ⓓ how should stay

2 Carolyn's favorite task is ________________ the books for the school library.

ⓐ order ⓑ to order ⓒ what to order ⓓ how order

C 다음 중 어법상 옳지 <u>않은</u> 문장을 고르시오.

1 ⓐ The committee is not sure of what to do about the problem.
ⓑ His teacher chose not change the grade for him.
ⓒ To study police techniques is popular on TV in the U.S.
ⓓ Tell me which plants to grow in the sunny areas of the yard.

2 ⓐ Uncle Jacob plans to attend the wedding next Saturday afternoon.
ⓑ The engineers tried to improve the sound of the speakers.
ⓒ To participate in club activities is very important for most American students.
ⓓ She doesn't know how make the icing for the cake.

D 다음 주어진 단어와 to부정사를 이용하여 문장을 완성하시오.

1 추리 소설을 읽는 것은 굉장히 재미있다. (read, a detective story)

It's a lot of fun ________________________________.

2 우리는 그녀가 훌륭한 선생님이라고 생각한다. (be, great)

We consider her ________________________________.

3 그녀는 이탈리아 요리하는 것을 좋아한다. (cook, Italian food)

She likes ________________________________.

4 나는 댄스파티 때 무엇을 입어야 할지 결정하지 못했다. (haven't decide, wear)

I ________________________________ to the dance party.

to부정사의 부사적 쓰임

A [보기]에서 알맞은 말을 골라 어법에 맞게 바꿔 대화를 완성하시오.

Word Bank be read get stay receive start

1 A Where is Melinda this summer?
  B She left ____________ with her friends in America for the summer.

2 A What happened to the woman we saw?
  B She turned out ____________ a dangerous criminal and was arrested.

3 A What is the problem?
  B The battery is too weak ____________ the car.

4 A What are you reading?
  B It's a mystery story. You will be interested ____________ it for yourself, too.

5 A Where did Betty go?
  B She went to the beauty shop ____________ her hair cut.

6 A Is there something wrong?
  B They were surprised ____________ the new price list.

B 주어진 표현을 이용하여 문장을 완성하시오.

1 My brother is so tired that he cannot drive to the park now.
  → My brother is ________________________ now. (too ~ to)

2 The class will be excited to see the aquarium.
  → The class will be excited ________________________. (if)

3 The man is so late that he cannot see the doctor.
  → The man is ________________________. (too ~ to)

4 The manager called her so that he could discuss the complaint with her.
  → The manager called her ________________________. (in order to)

5 He is too worried about the exam to think about the party.
  → He is ________________________. (so ~ that...)

FOCUS

SCORE: 

A 다음 우리말과 일치하도록 빈칸에 알맞은 말을 쓰시오.

1 Your daughter is smart ____________________ to become a lawyer someday.
(당신의 딸은 충분히 똑똑해서 언젠가 변호사가 될 거예요.)

2 The ink on the paper is ____________________ faded to read well.
(종이 위에 잉크가 너무 흐려서 잘 읽을 수 없다.)

B 다음 빈칸에 알맞은 말을 고르시오.

1 She decided to do yoga ____________________ in shape.

ⓐ keep　ⓑ to keep　ⓒ so to keep　ⓓ enough to keep

2 I'm so happy ____________________ my lost bag.

ⓐ find　ⓑ to find　ⓒ in order to find　ⓓ so as to find

C 다음 중 어법상 옳지 <u>않은</u> 문장을 고르시오.

1 ⓐ It is too complex for me to explain the situation to you.
ⓑ Steve is so full to eat any pumpkin pie.
ⓒ Was she happy to hear from her friends in Canada?
ⓓ He didn't say anything about his mistake in order not to upset the boss.

2 ⓐ The group will be pleased to change their reservations to a better hotel.
ⓑ They worked willingly to build new homes in the New Orleans area.
ⓒ The woman yelled to warn the boys about the broken glass.
ⓓ Janice is too angry that she can't talk to you right now.

D 다음 주어진 단어를 이용하여 문장을 완성하시오.

1 그는 아기를 깨우지 않으려고 발꿈치를 들고 걸었다. (wake up, the baby)

He walked on his tiptoes ____.

2 사람들은 그녀의 이상한 모자를 보고는 크게 웃었다. (laugh, loudly, see, funny hat)

People ____.

3 그녀는 A학점을 받을 만큼 열심히 공부했다. (hard, get an A)

She studied ____.

to부정사의 형용사적 쓰임

A [보기]에서 알맞은 말을 골라 어법에 맞게 바꿔 문장을 완성하시오.

Word Bank	fill out	play with	talk about

1 The cute puppies have nothing safe ______________.

2 The little fight between us is nothing ______________.

3 Do you know which of these forms we are ______________?

B [보기]와 같이 문장을 완성하시오.

Example The plan was to drive the car the whole distance.
→ The plan to drive the car the whole distance didn't work out.

1 My teacher's lecture was to remind us about the test.

→ My teacher's lecture ______________________________ was effective.

2 My goal was to collect 100 baseball cards of old players.

→ My goal ______________________ of old players was not successful then.

3 I have an important meeting tomorrow. We'll talk about a new agenda in the meeting.

→ The important meeting ____________________ has been put off to next week.

C 주어진 단어를 알맞게 배열하여 문장을 완성하시오.

1 sit down / is to

→ Nobody in the wedding party ______________________________ yet.

2 are to / to / fly

→ They ______________________________ New Jersey next summer.

3 has / to discuss / nothing

→ Her boyfriend says he ______________________________.

4 something / to eat / sweet

→ Everyone in the afternoon meeting wants ______________________________.

내신 FOCUS

SCORE:

A 다음 빈칸에 알맞은 말을 쓰시오.

1 Will you lend me a pen? I have nothing to write ____________.

2 Some wild birds choose other birds' nests to live ____________.

B 다음 빈칸에 알맞은 말을 고르시오.

1 His new fiction book ____________ this weekend.

ⓐ publishes ⓑ to publish ⓒ to be published ⓓ is to be published

2 The police need ____________ them with the search.

ⓐ someone help ⓑ someone to help ⓒ to help someone ⓓ help someone

C 다음 중 어법상 옳지 않은 문장을 고르시오.

1 ⓐ The girls say they have nothing nice to put on.
ⓑ If you are to keep a pet, please pay the pet fee with your rent.
ⓒ The record company is release this CD by that time.
ⓓ The astronauts were never to see the weather satellite again.

2 ⓐ Everyone needs someone worthwhile to believe in.
ⓑ After our discussion, I have nothing to worry about anymore.
ⓒ The bored children want fun something to play.
ⓓ No one is to open the gate and come in.

D 다음 주어진 단어를 이용하여 문장을 완성하시오.

1 여러분에게 말해줄 좋은 소식이 있어요. (good news, tell)

I have ______________________________ you.

2 그녀에게는 얘기할 누군가가 필요했다. (need, someone, talk to)

She ______________________________.

3 그 선수는 뭔가 차가운 마실 것을 원했다. (want, something, cold, drink)

The player ______________________________.

4 노숙자는 살 집이 없는 사람을 말한다. (have, houses, live in)

The homeless are the people who don't ______________________________.

기타 부정사의 쓰임

A 밑줄 친 단어를 이용하여 대화를 완성하시오.

1 A Can we eat sweets?
B It is not good ____________ too many sweets.

2 A Did the boss seem pleased with the factory's organization?
B Yes, the boss ____________ be pleased with the factory's organization.

3 A Did the firefighter allow the bystander to help rescue the cat?
B Yes, the firefighter let the bystander ____________ with the rescue of the cat.

4 A Did you hear a loud hitting noise this morning?
B It was John's car. I heard his car ____________ a tree this morning.

B 밑줄 친 부분을 바르게 고쳐 쓰시오. 틀리지 않았다면 ○표 하시오.

1 Nancy made her younger sister do her chores around the house. ____________

2 It isn't hard of him to consider your request. ____________

3 This economics book is too difficult for me understand. ____________

4 Daniel heard the reporters to describe the heroism of the officers. ____________

C 주어진 단어를 알맞게 배열하여 문장을 완성하시오.

1 seem / be completing / to
→ The workers ____________ the project on time.

2 not good / to spend / for dogs
→ It is ____________ many hours alone every day.

3 smelled / burn / something
→ The family next-door said they ____________.

4 her / taking / to keep
→ The doctor told ____________ the medicine until the next morning.

5 to the party / to come / everyone
→ The neighbors want ____________.

6 me / helped / do
→ My best friend ____________ my homework last night.

내신 FOCUS

SCORE:

A 다음 중 밑줄 친 부분의 쓰임이 잘못된 것을 고르시오.

1 It's very lucky of you to find the lost bag.
ⓐ very ⓑ lucky ⓒ of ⓓ to find

2 The old pop-song made me to feel sad.
ⓐ made ⓑ me ⓒ to feel ⓓ sad

B 다음 빈칸에 들어갈 수 없는 말을 고르시오.

1 I __________ the cat chase the mice in the barn again.

ⓐ let ⓑ heard ⓒ wanted ⓓ saw

2 Jack's sister __________ him do the cleaning without her help last night.

ⓐ made ⓑ had ⓒ let ⓓ asked

C 다음 중 어법상 옳지 않은 문장을 고르시오.

1 ⓐ It is nice for you to let your younger sister have the cake.
ⓑ Your old bike is too rusty for me to fix.
ⓒ Did you instruct her to stop eating peanuts until the results were known?
ⓓ The restaurant manager saw Eddie and his girlfriend come in.

2 ⓐ The students were embarrassed to have been unprepared for the class.
ⓑ Did the men want to close their accounts with us?
ⓒ Adrian let his friends do all the hard work.
ⓓ During the tour with a guard, Jane noticed him checked everyone's bags.

D 다음 주어진 단어를 이용하여 문장을 완성하시오.

1 저에게는 그 일을 하루 안에 끝내기가 쉽지 않습니다. (easy, finish, the work)

It's not __________________________ in one day.

2 Jason은 또 다시 늦은 것에 대해 미안해했다. (late again)

Jason was sorry __________________________.

3 교사는 학생들에게 짐을 나르도록 시켰다. (have, carry, the luggage)

The teacher __________________________.

4 방원경을 통해 Ted는 하늘에서 별들이 움직이는 것을 관찰했다. (watch, move)

Through the telescope, Ted __________________________ in the sky.

동명사의 여러 가지 쓰임

A 주어진 단어를 동명사로 바꿔 문장을 완성하시오.

1 Doesn't he want a part of ____________ (create) a new business?

2 The manager offered him a job. It is ____________ (clean) the movie theater.

3 He quit ____________ (read) science fiction stories at bedtime.

4 ____________ (make) a cake is fun for me.

5 ____________ (have) seen the effects of the storm made me appreciate my warm bed.

6 The people cheered his ____________ (perform) the difficult magic trick.

B 밑줄 친 부분을 바르게 고쳐 쓰시오. 틀리지 않았다면 ○표 하시오.

1 He warned me about enter the building without permission. ____________

2 Being known as a hero was a new experience for her. ____________

3 Her young children loved to feeding the little yellow kittens. ____________

4 Own a car is very costly in New York City. ____________

5 The members of the football team appreciated his kicking. ____________

C 동명사를 이용하여 문장을 완성하시오.

1 She reads mystery novels. It is her way to relax.

→ ____________ is her way to relax.

2 My daughter became a veterinarian. It was her dream.

→ ____________ was my daughter's dream.

3 The woman teaches sculpture at an art school. She enjoys it.

→ The woman enjoys ____________ at an art school.

4 I am buying a new cell phone. It is a difficult process.

→ ____________ is a difficult process.

5 My brother likes repairing broken cars. It is one of his hobbies.

→ One of my brother's hobbies is ____________.

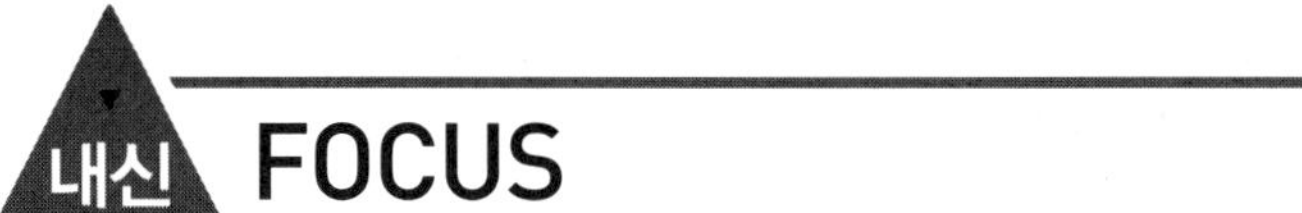

SCORE:

A 다음 중 밑줄 친 부분의 쓰임이 잘못된 것을 고르시오.

ⓐ Taking pictures are my favorite activity.
ⓑ I can't imagine buying my own car.
ⓒ Their hobby is playing basketball.
ⓓ My father enjoys doing jigsaw puzzles.

B 다음 빈칸에 알맞은 말을 고르시오.

1 The director congratulated him for ____________ the role well.

ⓐ perform ⓑ performs ⓒ performing ⓓ to perform

2 Their responsibility ____________ a good substitute for the medication.

ⓐ develops ⓑ to develop ⓒ developing ⓓ is developing

C 다음 중 어법상 옳지 않은 문장을 고르시오.

1 ⓐ Being treated effectively in the hospital was a great help to him.
ⓑ She added to the disaster by put the ice cream on the hot stove.
ⓒ The director continued leading the marching band for another year.
ⓓ Does she prefer studying with people from her school?

2 ⓐ She thanked him for calling after the accident on Monday.
ⓑ The new art teacher asked about an unusual painting.
ⓒ Having watched the program made me more aware of the environment.
ⓓ Don't you want owning your own shop?

D 다음 주어진 단어를 이용하여 문장을 완성하시오.

1 우리는 모두 그의 연기를 좋아했다. (like, acting)

We all ____________________________.

2 제게 사실대로 말씀해 주셔서 감사합니다. (tell, the truth)

Thank you for ____________________________.

3 그의 직업은 영화 시나리오를 쓰는 것이다. (be, write, scenarios)

His job ____________________________ for movies.

4 에세이를 쓰는 것은 학생들에게 무척 어렵다. (write, an essay, be)

____________________________ very difficult for students.

동명사 vs. 부정사

A [ ] 안에서 알맞은 말을 고르시오.

1 The authorities do not expect [to solve, solving] the case in a few days.

2 The sign prohibits [to swim, swimming] in the pool without a lifeguard.

3 The dog gave up [to chase, chasing] the cats in the alley.

4 The professor denied [to speak, speaking] about a controversial subject on campus.

5 Did his mother keep [to make, making] desserts for him during college?

6 The plumber refused [to change, changing] his bill for the repairs.

7 Steve hopes [to ski, skiing] in Breckenridge, Colorado next winter.

B 주어진 단어를 이용하여 문장을 완성하시오.

1 He gave up ____________(take) the position, and he choose ____________(remain) at his old job.

2 She resented ____________(have) her purse examined, but promised ____________(cooperate).

3 She happened ____________(see) the accident, but failed ____________(report) it to the police.

4 This system prevented us from ____________(identify) the person who attempted ____________ (access) the information on the computer.

C 주어진 단어를 이용하여 문장을 완성하시오. (과거시제로 쓸 것)

1 request / modify / the contract

→ His ________________________________ was refused by the company.

2 practice / run / for a marathon

→ The team members ________________________________.

3 decide / build / a new building

→ The church ________________________________ in the suburbs.

4 suggest / park / in a parking lot

→ The policeman ________________________________ on another street.

내신 FOCUS

SCORE: 

A 다음 빈칸에 알맞은 동사를 고르시오.

1 The students ________________ talking as the teacher came into the classroom.

ⓐ agreed ⓑ stopped ⓒ pretended ⓓ refused

2 The boy ________________ making fun of his little brother.

ⓐ wanted ⓑ planned ⓒ attempted ⓓ regretted

B 다음 빈칸에 알맞은 말을 고르시오.

1 She couldn't recall ________________ those words to anyone in her family.

ⓐ saying ⓑ to say ⓒ be saying ⓓ said

2 She demanded ________________ the reasons for the sudden change.

ⓐ hear ⓑ to hear ⓒ heard ⓓ hearing

C 다음 중 어법상 옳지 않은 문장을 고르시오.

1 ⓐ They couldn't afford to buy a car.
ⓑ Imagine sky diving from a plane.
ⓒ He decided to go to Paris to see her.
ⓓ She feared to go out at night.

2 ⓐ What do you intend to do with the old radio?
ⓑ The man threatened to hurt them.
ⓒ The young child denied to throw the ball through the window.
ⓓ You should avoid spending too much money on clothes.

D 다음 주어진 단어를 이용하여 문장을 완성하시오.

1 그는 여덟 살 때 영어 공부를 시작했다. (begin, learn)

He ________________________________ when he was eight.

2 내 남동생은 항상 자신의 방 청소하는 것을 미룬다. (put off, clean one's room)

My brother always ________________________________.

3 나는 수영복을 가져오는 것을 깜박 잊어버렸다. (forget, bring, a swimming suit)

I ________________________________.

동명사의 기타 쓰임

A [ ] 안에서 알맞은 말을 고르시오.

1 The morning traffic prevented [my, me] from arriving at the office on time.

2 The content of the article was certainly worth [to discuss, discussing].

3 He's not used [to make, to making] breakfast for the whole family.

4 Please excuse me for [informing not, not informing] you that the museum was closed.

5 Would you mind my [to try, trying] to open the window?

6 Don't you feel like [to eat, eating] some light dish for a change?

B 밑줄 친 부분을 바르게 고쳐 쓰시오. 틀리지 않았다면 ○표 하시오.

1 The old woman rewarded <u>he</u> for finding her lost dog. ____________

2 Did your late flight prevent you <u>attending</u> the meeting? ____________

3 Do you like <u>I</u> wearing this kind of perfume? ____________

4 He will never change without <u>realizing</u> his unfortunate error. ____________

5 <u>Making</u> a good decision is important at this time in your life. ____________

6 <u>Fished</u> with good friends is a wonderful and relaxing activity. ____________

C 주어진 단어를 이용하여 문장을 완성하시오.

1 can't help / look at

→ She ____________________ her beautiful, new baby boy.

2 succeed in / complete

→ After many long hours, they've finally ____________________ the puzzle.

3 keep / on / complain

→ She ____________________ about her own troubles last night.

4 fearful of / change

→ The officer is ____________________ the schedule.

5 feel like / do more homework

→ I don't ____________________ this evening.

내신 FOCUS

SCORE:

A 다음 중 밑줄 친 부분의 쓰임이 잘못된 것을 고르시오.

1 We are all accustomed(ⓐ) on(ⓑ) his(ⓒ) living(ⓓ) with us.

2 I am(ⓐ) afraid of(ⓑ) speak(ⓒ) in(ⓓ) front of others.

B 다음 빈칸에 알맞은 말을 고르시오.

1 We're not sure of ______________ for Europe on Friday.

ⓐ leave　ⓑ their left　ⓒ their leaving　ⓓ to leave

2 The team prefers ______________ to running around the football field.

ⓐ practicing　ⓑ practices　ⓒ for practice　ⓓ to practice

C 다음 중 어법상 옳지 않은 문장을 고르시오.

1 ⓐ My friends will help you if you have difficulty in navigating.
ⓑ Does he trust their taking over the project?
ⓒ It is no risk calling them on your cell phone.
ⓓ The storm prevented we from going to the beach.

2 ⓐ He's busy organizing the boxes into several large stacks.
ⓑ Let's go to bowl with the rest of the P.E. class.
ⓒ The security guard stopped him from entering the mysterious building.
ⓓ Are you not used to driving such long distances?

D 다음 주어진 단어와 동명사를 이용하여 문장을 완성하시오.

1 집에 도착한 후에 네게 전화할게. (after, arrive, home)

I will call you ______________________________.

2 그녀는 언제나 해외에 가는 것을 꿈꾼다. (dream about, go abroad)

She always ______________________________.

3 그 소년은 스스로 그 일을 하겠다고 주장했다. (insist, do it)

The boy ______________________________ himself.

4 안개가 심해서 우리는 아름다운 경치를 볼 수 없었다. (prevent, from, see)

Heavy fog ______________________________ the beautiful scenery.

현재분사

A 밑줄 친 부분을 현재분사는 P, 동명사는 G로 구분하시오.

1 The boy running with the ball is my youngest son. ____________

2 Typing too much on the computer can result in wrist problems. ____________

3 The appliance repairman is coming to fix the washing machine. ____________

4 Listen for the interesting sound of the red bird. ____________

5 She is learning to change the baby's diaper. ____________

6 The man's passion is repairing cars. ____________

7 The company is doing well this fiscal year. ____________

B 주어진 단어를 이용하여 문장을 완성하시오.

1 The water from the faucet ____________ again tonight. (be, drip)

2 We saw many athletes ____________ the next Olympics. (compete for)

3 The ____________ river carried away many cars and homes. (flood)

4 The university astronomer pointed out the small, ____________ star. (shine)

5 The technician ____________ the old computer program now. (be, reload)

C 두 개의 문장을 하나의 문장으로 완성하시오.

1 Do you hear the cat? It is calling from the hallway.
→ Do you hear the cat ____________________?

2 I waved to Mike. He was coming toward me.
→ I waved to Mike ____________________.

3 Who is the woman? She is knitting on the park bench.
→ Who is the woman ____________________?

4 Did you see the movie? It is showing at the theater.
→ Did you see the movie ____________________?

FOCUS

SCORE:

A 다음 문장을 아래와 같이 바꿀 때 빈칸에 알맞은 분사를 써 넣으시오.

1 I was bored with this book.
→ This book was so ________________.

2 I was confused with the manual for the program.
→ The manual for the program was ________________ to me.

B 다음 빈칸에 알맞은 말을 고르시오.

1 My younger sister met some ________________.
ⓐ people interested ⓑ people interesting ⓒ interesting people ⓓ interest people

2 My teacher created ________________ near the school building this spring.
ⓐ a tutoring center ⓑ tutoring a center ⓒ centered tutoring ⓓ a center tutoring

C 다음 중 어법상 옳지 않은 문장을 고르시오.

1 ⓐ My best friend is solving a difficult math problem.
ⓑ The results of the survey of the students were very encouraging.
ⓒ The World Cup is an excite event to attend.
ⓓ The man's bleeding hand was treated by the nurse at the hospital.

2 ⓐ Who is the man standing in the doorway with your boss?
ⓑ He told her about the graduating seniors at the school.
ⓒ I saw her to have lunch with her friends yesterday.
ⓓ The sights in New York were amazing to the young girl.

D 다음 주어진 단어를 이용하여 문장을 완성하시오.

1 나는 아주 중대한 소식을 들었다. (earthshake, news)
I heard ________________________________.

2 그 TV 쇼는 무척 재미있어 보였다. (very, interest)
The TV show seemed ________________________________.

3 저기 검은색 양복을 입고 있는 남자는 누구니? (wear, the black suit)
Who is the guy ________________________________ over there?

과거분사

A [ ] 안에서 알맞은 말을 고르시오.

1 I was [looked, looking] for the batteries for my calculator.

2 The engineer was [disappointed, disappointing] by the failure of the bridge.

3 Her children picked up some [fallen, falling] apples in the orchard.

4 The German rider got his damaged racing bike [fixed, fixing].

5 Have you ever [hearing, heard] any traditional Korean music?

6 She waved to the girl [worn, wearing] a pair of glasses.

B [보기]에서 알맞은 말을 골라 어법에 맞게 바꿔 문장을 완성하시오.

Word Bank	trust	fly	hold	lose	hide

1 She asked the receptionist about her ______________ purse.

2 The winter party will be ______________ at a luxury hotel.

3 The ______________ symbols describe life in the early centuries of civilization.

4 I have a picture of a UFO ______________ over the field.

5 The girl is not one of my ______________ friends anymore.

C 주어진 단어를 이용하여 문장을 완성하시오.

1 open / box

→ The ______________________ was full of old papers from my high school days.

2 speak / to the team

→ Have you ever ______________________ about your injury?

3 take / to the tent

→ Children ______________________ got a free bottle of orange juice.

4 scare / kitten

→ The ______________________ jumped out of the water in the bathtub.

5 flowers / paint / on every advertisement

→ The graphic artist liked ______________________________ in the store.

FOCUS

SCORE:

A 다음 빈칸에 알맞은 말을 고르시오.

1 The three-hour lecture was really ____________.

ⓐ tire ⓑ tires ⓒ tired ⓓ tiring

2 We're all ____________ with his knowledge of movie history.

ⓐ amaze ⓑ amazes ⓒ amazing ⓓ amazed

B 다음 빈칸에 알맞은 말을 고르시오.

1 The horses were ____________ by the noise from the car.

ⓐ surprise ⓑ surprises ⓒ surprised ⓓ surprising

2 Did you watch the DVD ____________ over by my sister?

ⓐ bring ⓑ brings ⓒ brought ⓓ bringing

C 다음 중 어법상 옳지 않은 문장을 고르시오.

1 ⓐ The pictures taken with this camera are wonderful.
ⓑ Have you ever checked out a book describing the early Christians?
ⓒ The taxi driver was giving change to the young man.
ⓓ Please look the sat cat on the sofa.

2 ⓐ The policeman saw a thief ran away from the store.
ⓑ Didn't you see the mug stocked on the top shelf.
ⓒ Who is the army officer wearing the dress uniform?
ⓓ It was a recently stolen truck in the neighbor's alley.

D 다음 주어진 단어를 이용하여 문장을 완성하시오.

1 최근에 수리한 컴퓨터가 또 고장 났다. (fix, break down, again)

The newly ____.

2 소녀는 잔디밭에 떨어진 반지를 발견했다. (a ring, fall, on the grass)

The girl found ____.

3 너는 일본어로 쓰인 책을 읽어 본 적이 있니? (a book, write, in Japanese)

Have you ever read ____?

분사의 다양한 표현

A [ ] 안에서 알맞은 말을 고르시오.

1 [Waiting, Waited] in the office, I heard about the change in locations.

2 [Found, Finding] the sick cat, we were shocked at her condition.

3 It [was, being] the afternoon, they left for the market.

4 [Depending, Depended] on its performance, the customer may want to return it.

5 [Having, Since] my roommate left the room, I took a nap.

6 [Not knowing, Not known] his name, she wanted to meet him quickly.

B [ ] 안에서 알맞은 말을 고르시오.

1 Turning right, you will see the new bank.

→ [Although, If] you turn right, you will see the new bank.

2 Swimming in the pool with friends, she learned how to play water polo.

→ [While, If] she was swimming in the pool with friends, she learned how to play water polo.

3 Moving the heavy furniture, the old man became very exhausted.

→ [After, When] he moved the heavy furniture, the old man was very exhausted.

4 Typing for two hours, the secretary felt so tired.

→ [Because, Although] the secretary typed for two hours, she felt so tired.

C [보기]와 같이 주어진 단어를 이용하여 문장을 완성하시오.

Example eat / street snacks
→ Eating street snacks, the students shared them with their friends.

1 generally / speak

→ ______________________, this television is too expensive for our family.

2 pass / the market

→ ______________________, she remembered to stop for some milk.

3 consider / the alternatives

→ ______________________, his choice was a very good one.

4 Judge from / his fans' response

→ ______________________, his concert was a success.

FOCUS

SCORE:

A 다음 문장을 아래와 같이 바꿀 때 빈칸에 알맞은 말을 고르시오.

1 Arriving home, she went to bed.

→ __________ she arrived home, she went to bed.

ⓐ If ⓑ While ⓒ As soon as ⓓ Because

2 Crossing the street, you can take a bus to the library.

→ __________ you cross the street, you can take a bus to the library.

ⓐ If ⓑ Since ⓒ While ⓓ Although

B 다음 빈칸에 알맞은 말을 고르시오.

1 We walked in the park together, __________ about our future.

ⓐ talk ⓑ talked ⓒ talking ⓓ talks

2 __________ the answer, we looked up the word in the dictionary.

ⓐ If knowing ⓑ Not known ⓒ Not knowing ⓓ Knowing not

C 다음 중 어법상 옳지 않은 문장을 고르시오.

1 ⓐ Given that Americans love football, we should go to see a game.
ⓑ Have not excuse, the boy accepted his punishment and stayed home.
ⓒ After the rain stopped, we went to the market.
ⓓ Strictly speaking, his survey is very questionable.

2 ⓐ Planting the trees, my father sang a song.
ⓑ Judging on his looks, he must be a soldier.
ⓒ Considering that he is not coming, let's invite one more person.
ⓓ Talking about mistakes, I can tell you about one that I made.

D 다음 주어진 단어를 이용하여 문장을 완성하시오. (단, 분사구문을 사용하시오.)

1 우리는 돈이 없어서 그 소파를 살 수가 없다. (have, no money)

__________, we can't buy the sofa.

2 줄넘기를 하는 동안 나는 땀을 많이 흘렸다. (jump rope)

__________, I sweat a lot.

3 나는 컴퓨터 스크린을 닦으면서 그녀와 얘기했다. (clean, the computer screen)

__________, I talked to her.

수동태

A 주어진 단어를 이용하여 문장을 완성하시오.

1 The girl's temperature ______________ by a nurse at the hospital yesterday. (take)

2 The children said they ______________ of the tiny bug on the wall. (scare)

3 Next Friday, the music class ______________ by a guest lecturer. (teach)

4 The copier ______________ by our supervisor a month ago. (purchase)

5 In the future, the park ______________ by many volunteers. (maintain)

B 밑줄 친 부분을 바르게 고쳐 쓰시오. 틀리지 않았다면 ○표 하시오.

1 The famous movie was <u>releasing</u> by the studio in 1941. ______________

2 The building will <u>design</u> by the young architect. ______________

3 The scores will <u>list</u> early in the morning. ______________

4 Cindy's old car has <u>owned</u> by me for several months so far. ______________

5 The children's book <u>is being read</u> by the author today. ______________

C 주어진 문장을 수동태 문장으로 바꿔 쓰시오.

1 The contractor prepared the foundation of the large building.
→ ______________ by the contractor.

2 She was using the computer in the library.
→ ______________ by her.

3 They are baking a special cake for their parents.
→ ______________ by them for their parents.

4 The teacher will present a new curriculum to students.
→ ______________ to students by the teacher.

5 Sandra has filled the vase with flowers.
→ ______________ with flowers by Sandra.

6 All people in the office know the good news about her.
→ ______________ to all people in the office.

내신 FOCUS

SCORE:

A 다음 문장의 빈칸에 들어갈 말을 고르시오.

1 The song ______________ by Mozart in the 1780s.

ⓐ wrote ⓑ is written ⓒ was written ⓓ can be written

2 Nobody knew why the actor ______________ suddenly.

ⓐ disappears ⓑ disappeared ⓒ is disappeared ⓓ was disappeared

B 다음 빈칸에 알맞은 말을 고르시오.

1 His family was surprised ______________ the condition of his clothes.

ⓐ in ⓑ by ⓒ on ⓓ for

2 A promotion ______________ to her at the meeting yesterday.

ⓐ offered ⓑ is offered ⓒ was offered ⓓ would be offered

C 다음 중 어법상 옳지 않은 문장을 고르시오.

1 ⓐ The meal was being made by my niece then.
ⓑ The marching band will appear at half time of a New Year's Day football game.
ⓒ The frame will being repaired by the carpenter.
ⓓ The early planning was done by the committee in 2006.

2 ⓐ I had a lot of fun experience last weekend.
ⓑ The posters will see everywhere next Monday.
ⓒ The land for the university was donated by Mr. Brown in 1855.
ⓓ My cousin has placed the basket on the porch.

D 다음 주어진 단어를 이용하여 문장을 완성하시오.

1 그 건물은 1996년에 건설되었다. (build, in 1996)

The building ______________________________.

2 이 소설은 어제 Karen이 쓴 것이다. (write)

This novel ______________________________ yesterday.

3 2020년 올림픽 게임은 도쿄에서 개최될 것이다. (hold)

The 2020 Olympic games ______________________________ in Tokyo.

수동태의 여러 가지 형태

A 주어진 문장을 수동태 문장으로 바꿔 쓰시오.

1 Father allowed me to drive his car.
→ I ______________________ my father's car.

2 My son writes me a letter once a month.
→ A letter ______________________ by my son once a month.

3 The worried mom was watching the child for any new symptoms.
→ The child ______________________ for any new symptoms by his worried mom.

4 The clerk sold the woman a copy of a new novel.
→ A copy of a new novel ______________________ to the woman by the clerk.

5 Mom made us take off our wet clothes.
→ We ______________________ take off our wet clothes by Mom.

6 The young scientist will teach the class in computer engineering.
→ The class in computer engineering ______________________ by the young scientist.

B 밑줄 친 부분을 바르게 고쳐 쓰시오. 틀리지 않았다면 ○표 하시오.

1 The coach had the team <u>ran</u> early in the morning. ____________

2 The names might <u>written</u> down in his notebook. ____________

3 A delicate oriental rug was given <u>for</u> me by a friend. ____________

4 The men heard someone <u>moving</u> equipment from the unlocked office. ____________

5 The kid <u>called</u> Nikola after his mother Nika. ____________

C [보기]에서 알맞은 단어를 골라 어법에 맞게 바꿔 문장을 완성하시오.

Word Bank	pay	smell	give	find

1 It is said that natural gas ______________________ like rotten eggs.

2 Everyone with a full-time job has to ______________________ a minimum wage by the company.

3 The report about the wetlands can ______________________ in the library.

4 A mountain bike ______________________ to Don as a birthday present yesterday.

FOCUS

SCORE:

A 다음 빈칸에 들어갈 알맞은 전치사를 쓰시오.

1 Chocolate is made ________________ cacao.

2 A coupon will be given ________________ every participant.

B 다음 빈칸에 알맞은 말을 고르시오.

1 This electric guitar needs to ________________ to the new amplifier.

ⓐ plug ⓑ plugging ⓒ be plugged ⓓ be plugged in

2 His punishment ________________ a monetary fine and three days in jail.

ⓐ makes up ⓑ makes of ⓒ is made up ⓓ is made up of

C 다음 중 어법상 옳지 않은 문장을 고르시오.

1 ⓐ My friend does not want to be treated like her twin sister.
ⓑ The trash on the street is taken care of by the janitor.
ⓒ The snake was seen sliding down a hole.
ⓓ He was dreamed about marrying her.

2 ⓐ He called Uncle John by kids.
ⓑ The boxes will be picked up by the delivery man.
ⓒ He was pleased to accept a scholarship to the university.
ⓓ His advisor chose some classes for him.

D 다음 주어진 단어를 이용하여 문장을 완성하시오.

1 나는 Jane에게 책 한 권을 받았다. (give, a book)

I ____.

2 간호사가 우리 할머니를 돌봐주었다. (take care of)

My grandmother ________________________________ the nurse.

3 엄마가 우리에게 방 청소를 하라고 하셨다. (make, clean our room)

We ________________________________ our mother.

명사

A [ ] 안에서 알맞은 말을 고르시오.

1 The woman called the store with [some, any] complaints about the service.

2 The young man wants to have [a slice of, a loaf of] pizza and some ice cream.

3 [The pieces of, The basket of] flowers is my favorite arrangement in this store.

4 He knew the meeting was the project's last [hope, hoping].

5 I have [much, several] books for you from the library.

6 Could you get [a bottle of, a box of] chalk for the teacher?

7 Kyle is going to study in [the Europe, Europe] for the summer.

B 밑줄 친 부분을 바르게 고쳐 쓰시오. 틀리지 않았다면 ○표 하시오.

1 Darrin and his friends from school will visit the Australia next month. ______________

2 I'd like a bowl rice with my meal. ______________

3 The boy is sorry that he has very few time to spend with the dog. ______________

4 Eating correctly is important for your good health. ______________

5 Do you need many salt for the beef stew? ______________

6 She gave him an golden opportunity to advance in the company. ______________

C [보기]에서 알맞은 말을 골라 문장을 완성하시오.

Word Bank	a slice of	many	a carton of
	a cup of	a tablespoon of	two pounds of

1 He ordered ______________ hot chocolate.

2 She ate ______________ bread as a snack.

3 How ______________ older sisters does she have?

4 Would you pick up ______________ flour at the market for me?

5 He added ______________ applesauce to the cake mixture.

6 She prefers ______________ milk with her meal.

내신 FOCUS

SCORE: 

A 다음 문장에서 명사가 아닌 것을 고르시오.

My brother, David, always goes swimming after school.
ⓐ My ⓑ brother ⓒ David ⓓ school

B 다음 빈칸에 알맞은 말을 고르시오.

1 I have discovered __________ beautiful stones in the shallow river.

ⓐ a ⓑ much ⓒ a lot of ⓓ a little

2 How __________ will the new project cost the company?

ⓐ any ⓑ much ⓒ a lot of ⓓ few

C 다음 중 어법상 옳지 않은 문장을 고르시오.

1 ⓐ Linda Gray is the name of my new neighbor.
ⓑ The pound of milk spilled onto the kitchen floor.
ⓒ He bought a house from his best friend in college.
ⓓ The group of critics enjoyed the director's new movie.

2 ⓐ Take a aspirin for your symptoms and call me in the morning.
ⓑ The sushi chef prepared the fish for the guests.
ⓒ Will they have a little time to visit us during their trip?
ⓓ He will return in a few days.

D 다음 주어진 단어를 이용하여 문장을 완성하시오.

1 나는 설탕이나 크림을 넣지 않은 커피를 좋아한다. (without, or)

I like coffee ______________________________.

2 이것이 네 마지막 기회가 될 것이다. (last, chance)

This will be ______________________________.

3 그녀는 이집트에서 고고학자로 일을 한다. (as, archaeologist)

She works ______________________________ in Egypt.

4 건강을 위해서 매일 물 2병을 마셔라. (bottle)

Drink ______________________________ every day for your health.

관사

A [보기]에서 밑줄 친 부분과 쓰임이 같은 것을 고르시오.

Example
ⓐ Each person can take a piece at a time.
ⓑ I talk to the manager at the coffee shop every week.
ⓒ I ordered a part for my bike last week, and the part came in today.
ⓓ Do you have a pencil to lend me?
ⓔ The advantage of a dog is the loyalty it shows its master.

1 The map will take a week to finish correctly. ____________

2 A squirrel is an animal that climbs trees and has a bushy tail. ____________

3 I looked at a car this morning, and I bought the car this afternoon. ____________

4 I want a good camera to take pictures of my family. ____________

5 Is he the man who proposed to her? ____________

B 밑줄 친 부분을 바르게 고쳐 쓰시오. 틀리지 않았다면 ○표 하시오.

1 A papers on your desk are ready to sign. ____________

2 My mother exercises with her friends once the day. ____________

3 The project could require two week of your time. ____________

4 She'll have black tea with a spoonful of sugar and no cream. ____________

5 My brother is member of the math club and the basketball team. ____________

6 Have you spoken to your boss about the office space? ____________

C [보기]에서 알맞은 단어를 골라 문장을 완성하시오.

Word Bank Alaska / a computer program / Korean kings / a classical music concert / the park

1 I have to buy ____________ for my work.

2 I walk to ____________ with my dog almost every day.

3 My grandmother enjoys hearing stories about ____________.

4 Shall we go to ____________? I have two tickets.

5 Did you see any whales on the cruise to ____________?

SCORE:

A 다음 빈칸에 공통으로 들어갈 말을 써 넣으시오.

1 I have ______________ idea.

It was a rumor that Michael was once ______________ FBI agent.

2 My father can play ______________ electric guitar very well.

______________ Pacific Ocean is the largest of the world's five oceans.

B 다음 빈칸에 알맞은 말을 고르시오.

1 I'm looking for ______________ MP3 player online, and I will buy one tomorrow.

ⓐ Ø ⓑ an ⓒ the ⓓ some

2 What is the most valuable lesson to learn in ______________ life?

ⓐ Ø ⓑ a ⓒ an ⓓ some

C 다음 중 어법상 옳지 않은 문장을 고르시오.

1 ⓐ My uncle saw interesting show on television last night.
ⓑ You know I can't rest without finding the answer.
ⓒ Do you understand the role of the drummer in *pansori*?
ⓓ Dad said, "Take out the trash and recycle the bottles."

2 ⓐ Please pass me the green peppers.
ⓑ Tropical fish can't live in a cold freshwater tank.
ⓒ The new books all look the same to me.
ⓓ The electric car was traveling at speeds near sixty miles hour.

D 다음 주어진 단어를 이용하여 문장을 완성하시오.

1 이 숙제를 끝내는 데 한 시간이 걸릴 것이다. (take)

It may ______________ to finish this assignment.

2 그녀는 한 시간마다 한 번씩 물을 마신다. (once)

She drinks water ______________.

3 내 컵에 담긴 핫초콜릿이 식었다. (hot chocolate)

______________ in my cup got cold.

4 나는 어떤 남자와 부딪혔는데, 그 남자가 내 지갑을 훔쳐갔다. (steal, wallet)

I bumped into a man, and ______________.

대명사

A [ ] 안에서 알맞은 말을 고르시오.

1 She called [he, him] last night, but he wasn't home.

2 My cousin sold [her, him] old bike to me, and she bought a new one.

3 I should do the work on the project [me, myself].

4 [It, That] is ten feet deep in this swimming pool.

5 [The, These] boxes contain my books, and those contain my clothes.

6 [They, Them] say that "Honesty is the best policy."

7 I used a sleeping bag and a tent of [Steven, Steven's].

B 밑줄 친 부분을 바르게 고쳐 쓰시오. 틀리지 않았다면 ○표 하시오.

1 Ted's actions are similar to that of his uncle's. ____________

2 It is amazing that the flying squirrel glides between the tops of trees. ____________

3 Both he and her are required to sign the contract. ____________

4 I found mine bus pass in my locker. ____________

5 Remember to watch out for yourself in the big city. ____________

6 I went dancing with a my old friends last night. ____________

C [보기]에서 알맞은 말을 골라 문장을 완성하시오.

Word Bank	those	she	this	ourselves	him	it

1 We ____________ should be thankful for the development in procedures.

2 She bought ____________ a new laptop computer.

3 The school teaches ____________ curriculum in the fifth grade.

4 ____________ is preparing for a trip to South Africa in the fall.

5 These are our bags, and ____________ are their bags.

6 She made ____________ a requirement to complete the form before entering the room.

SCORE:

A 다음 문장을 아래와 같이 바꿀 때 빈칸에 알맞은 한 단어를 쓰시오.

1 My friend and I are going hiking this Friday.

→ ____________ are going hiking this Friday.

2 This red cap is my cap, but that blue cap is Brandon's cap.

→ This red cap is ____________, but that blue cap is ____________.

B 다음 빈칸에 알맞은 말을 고르시오.

1 According to the director, the actor never understood ____________ role.

ⓐ he ⓑ his ⓒ him ⓓ himself

2 This is a picture of ____________ climbing a mountain in the park.

ⓐ me ⓑ I ⓒ mine ⓓ myself

C 다음 중 어법상 옳지 않은 문장을 고르시오.

1 ⓐ This is our car, and that is yours.
ⓑ He went rollerblading with his good friends from the university.
ⓒ Lucy warned him, but he refused to listen to hers.
ⓓ It's getting late. We should go home now.

2 ⓐ She carried the heavy luggage to the train herself.
ⓑ This mistake is my fault, but that mistake is Dan.
ⓒ My cousins planned a graduation party for my sister.
ⓓ I think they brought the bad circumstances upon themselves.

D 다음 주어진 단어를 이용하여 문장을 완성하시오.

1 그녀는 친구 중 한 명과 쇼핑을 갔다. (a friend of)

She went shopping ____________.

2 내 친구 Jim은 지난주에 그의 가족과 유럽에 갔다. (family, last week)

My friend, Jim, went to Europe ____________.

3 우리 집에서 학교까지는 1km이다. (from, house)

It's one kilometer ____________ to the school.

4 시골 사람들이 도시 사람들보다 더 행복하다. (those, city)

People in the country are happier than ____________.

부정대명사

A [보기]에서 알맞은 말을 골라 문장을 완성하시오.

Word Bank none either one both another some

1 They ______________ needed to find the information before the meeting.

2 ______________ should look for the best in every circumstance.

3 Do you want ______________ of the oranges?

4 All the pieces are gone. There's ______________ in the box now.

5 I don't like this hat. Would you show me ______________?

6 ______________ of you has a contribution to make to this country.

B 밑줄 친 부분을 바르게 고쳐 쓰시오. 틀리지 않았다면 ○표 하시오.

1 Any my daughter and son often call home to talk to me. ______________

2 Put on the new parts, but keep the old others. ______________

3 No of the games were canceled due to bad weather. ______________

4 He takes all of his used clothing and donates it to the homeless shelter. ______________

5 I enjoy watching this one, but my favorite is one other. ______________

6 He used all his energy at work. ______________

C [보기]에서 알맞은 말을 골라 대화를 완성하시오.

Word Bank the other another most some

1 A Will either of them join us for dinner tonight?
B One will, but ______________ can't because of work.

2 A May I help you pick those up?
B Yes, thank you. Oh, ______________ papers are under the table, too.

3 A What are you doing this summer?
B I am spending ______________ of my time reading books for classes in the fall.

4 A Are your friends coming over for supper?
B They can't come tonight. We will eat together ______________ night.

SCORE:

A 다음 빈칸에 알맞은 말을 쓰시오.

1 I have two dogs; __________ is a Chihuahua, and __________ is a poodle.

2 I don't like this shirt. Could you show me __________ one?

B 다음 빈칸에 알맞은 말을 고르시오.

1 He told __________ about the new schedule in the spring.

ⓐ every ⓑ each ⓒ another ⓓ us

2 The field trip is for __________ student in middle school.

ⓐ every ⓑ all ⓒ other ⓓ anyone

C 다음 중 어법상 옳지 않은 문장을 고르시오.

1 ⓐ May I have one of the books for my father?
ⓑ I bought this new pairs of socks for three dollars.
ⓒ Any of the clerks will help you with your purchase.
ⓓ Neither of them is going to the theater this week.

2 ⓐ I want one of the new cell phones from the company.
ⓑ He knows where each of the remodeled buildings is.
ⓒ He turned on some of the lights, but not none of them worked.
ⓓ You have no transportation to the amusement park on Monday.

D 다음 주어진 단어를 이용하여 문장을 완성하시오.

1 도서관에 있는 대부분의 책은 학생들에게 이용 가능합니다. (most of)

__________ in the library are available to students.

2 하나는 신선한데, 다른 하나는 썩었다. (other, rotten)

One is fresh, but __________.

3 우리들의 실수 중 어떤 것도 비난 받지 않았다. (none, mistakes)

__________ were criticized.

4 그가 도착하기 전에 누군가가 테이블을 닦아야 한다. (should, clean)

__________ before he arrives.

형용사

A 주어진 단어를 이용하여 문장을 완성하시오

1 This article is ____________________ to read for the final exam. (use)

2 The ____________________ woman wore a yellow scarf and smiled. (cheer)

3 The firemen were ____________________ as they fought the fire. (caution)

4 The movie star is always very ____________________. (style)

5 I saw a ____________________ nature program on Sunday night. (fantasy)

6 My sister is ____________________ to go to the mall with me. (delight)

B [ ] 안에서 알맞은 말을 고르시오.

1 She seems rather [shy, shyness].

2 He bought his wife an [oriental, oriented] rug for their anniversary.

3 His tire was [useless, used] after the blowout on the highway.

4 She was [succeeded, successful] in school this year.

5 The [love, lovely] dog was living in a box in the parking lot.

6 Nobody at work knows that he is a [qualified, qualifying] electrician.

C 주어진 단어를 배열하여 문장을 완성하시오.

1 flowers / colorful

→ Mom picked some ____ from the rose garden.

2 new / a / card game

→ I have learned ____ from him.

3 restaurants / any / Mexican

→ Do you have ____ in your town?

4 dental / a / appointment

→ I have ____ in the morning.

5 experience / much / at

→ I don't think she has ____ this job.

FOCUS

SCORE:

A 다음 주어진 문장을 참고하여 빈칸에 알맞은 형용사를 써 넣으시오.

1 I believe the work will certainly succeed.

→ I believe the work will be ______________________.

2 He sometimes acts like a child.

→ He is sometimes ______________________.

B 다음 빈칸에 알맞은 말을 고르시오.

1 Have you caught ______________ fish in the lake recently?

ⓐ few ⓑ any ⓒ lots ⓓ a lot

2 My ______________ never went to school with him.

ⓐ sister older ⓑ elder sister ⓒ sister old ⓓ old sister

C 다음 중 어법상 옳지 않은 문장을 고르시오.

1 ⓐ The TV program doesn't contain much singing or dancing.
ⓑ My new boss seems to be a very confidence person.
ⓒ She spoke to him in a soft voice because it was during the meeting.
ⓓ Everyone at school knows she is a thoughtful teacher.

2 ⓐ She rode to the grocery store in her new car.
ⓑ The latest lecture by the speaker was very scientific.
ⓒ Would you and your friends like much cookies and juice?
ⓓ Is there anyone available to help me with these heavy boxes?

D 다음 주어진 단어를 이용하여 문장을 완성하시오.

1 그 작가는 밖에서 나는 소음 때문에 화가 났다. (upset, at the noise, outside)

The writer ______________________________________.

2 우리들은 이번 새 프로그램이 유용하다는 것을 알았다. (this new program)

We found ______________________________________.

3 누구 프랑스어를 할 줄 아는 사람 있나요? (anyone, capable of, French)

Is there ______________________________________?

4 여기 당신의 현 주소를 써 주십시오. (present, address)

Please write down ______________________________ here.

부사

A 밑줄 친 부분이 부사인지 형용사인지 구분하시오.

1 The coach is rarely home on Monday nights. ________

2 The man wondered if he should be less selfish towards his girlfriend. ________

3 The slow turtle crawls across the beach to lay eggs in the sand. ________

4 The cowboy walked carefully away from the hissing snake. ________

5 She often has coffee with me at this coffee shop. ________

6 The friendly children welcomed their new classmate from Boston. ________

7 The tomato soup I made tastes so awful! ________

B 밑줄 친 부분을 바르게 고쳐 쓰시오. 틀리지 않았다면 ○표 하시오.

1 The woman looked for an early bus to Seoul. ________

2 My son's new electric guitar has a lovely sound. ________

3 The class needed to work more quiet because of the guests. ________

4 They sometime get street snacks after school on Fridays. ________

5 My mom bought any delicious chickens at the market today. ________

6 The woman was unhappy because the mail was delivered too lately. ________

7 All the young football players have practiced hardly. ________

C 다음 문장을 완성하시오.

Example His behavior is so bad. → He behaves so badly.

1 We take our usual walk along the shore and watch the boats.
→ We ________ walk along the shore and watch the boats.

2 The vicious woman in the story did many bad things.
→ The woman in the story ________ did lots of bad things.

3 She was the last person out of the office that night.
→ ________ she came out of the office that night.

4 The fast car went around the new race track.
→ The car went around the new race track ________.

SCORE:

A 다음 괄호 안에서 알맞은 말을 고르시오.

1 All the students should study ______________.

ⓐ hard ⓑ hardly ⓒ diligent ⓓ diligence

2 We haven't seen her ______________.

ⓐ late ⓑ later ⓒ recent ⓓ recently

B 다음 빈칸에 알맞은 말을 고르시오.

1 The runner ______________ reached for a bottle of water.

ⓐ slow ⓑ slowly ⓒ slowed ⓓ slowing

2 The ______________ popular player will join the soccer team on Monday.

ⓐ high ⓑ highs ⓒ highed ⓓ highly

C 다음 중 어법상 옳지 않은 문장을 고르시오.

1 ⓐ She slept late this morning because of her illness.
ⓑ My mother occasional brings home some mangoes for dinner.
ⓒ We have just moved into a new apartment in Seoul.
ⓓ The children waited eagerly for Santa Claus to appear.

2 ⓐ Please speak more quickly.
ⓑ Can the science teachers make the homework assignments practical?
ⓒ Recently, very important computer data was lost, too.
ⓓ Every player on this team has to practice diligent.

D 다음 주어진 단어를 이용하여 문장을 완성하시오.

1 우리 할아버지가 지금 많이 편찮으시다. (seriously, ill)

My grandfather ______________________________ now.

2 아빠는 보통 8시 이후에 집에 오신다. (usually)

Dad ______________________________ after 8.

3 나는 첫 기차를 타기 위해 아침 일찍 일어났다. (early)

I woke up ______________________________ to catch the first train.

4 그가 너무 늦게 도착했기 때문에 모두들 걱정을 했다. (arrive, too late)

Everybody was worried because ______________________________.

비교

A 주어진 단어를 이용하여 문장을 완성하시오.

Example I think the best football team in the conference won the game. (good)

1 The days are getting ______________________ now that it's fall. (short, and)

2 This new video game is not ______________________ the old one. (as, challenging)

3 The boy was ______________________ his brother at climbing the rocks. (good, than)

4 He asked me to arrive ______________________ for the meeting. (as, fast, possible)

5 The car is ______________________ than I thought. (much, expensive)

6 Our family's new home is ______________________ than our previous one. (cheap)

B 밑줄 친 부분을 바르게 고쳐 쓰시오. 틀리지 않았다면 ○표 하시오.

1 My sister has collected as much shells as my cousin. ______________________

2 The kit contains not more than five nuts and bolts. ______________________

3 It is the fastest way to lose weight. ______________________

4 The river moved very swiftly than the tour group had expected. ______________________

5 Is the paint peeling off of the wood much and more these days? ______________________

C 주어진 단어를 이용하여 두 개의 문장을 하나의 문장으로 완성하시오.

1 I like vanilla ice cream. I like chocolate ice cream more.
→ I like chocolate ice cream ______________________ vanilla ice cream. (good, than)

2 The play is a success. It is a growing success.
→ The play is becoming ______________________ successful. (more, and)

3 I have three dollars. My sister has two dollars.
→ I have ______________________ my sister. (money, than)

4 David is six feet tall. His brother is also six feet tall.
→ David's brother is ______________________ he is. (as, tall)

FOCUS

SCORE:

A 다음 두 문장을 한 문장으로 바꿀 때 빈칸에 알맞은 말을 써 넣으시오.

1 My school is 10 minutes away from home.
My church is 20 minutes away from home.
→ My church is ________________ my school from home. (far)

2 My sister is 17 years old. My brother is 13 years old.
→ My sister is ________________ my brother. (senior)

B 다음 빈칸에 알맞은 말을 고르시오.

1 These comics are humorous. No comics are ________________ these.

ⓐ humorous than
ⓑ more than humorous
ⓒ much humorous than
ⓓ more humorous than

2 She skates ________________ an Olympic champion.

ⓐ as well as ⓑ as better than ⓒ much best than ⓓ so well

C 다음 중 어법상 옳지 않은 문장을 고르시오.

1 ⓐ Are they feeling better since the train stopped for the night?
ⓑ Students know the harder the class is, the more difficult the test is.
ⓒ Make plans for your summer vacation as soon as can.
ⓓ He didn't bring as many kites as I did for the competition.

2 ⓐ He no longer keeps his bicycle in the garage.
ⓑ Your directions were a lot more helpful than the map.
ⓒ The product is superior than any other on the market today.
ⓓ That lecture was the most interesting that I've had this semester.

D 다음 주어진 단어를 이용하여 문장을 완성하시오.

1 나는 Cathy만큼 많은 CD를 가지고 있다. (as, many CDs)
I have ________________________________ Cathy does.

2 그의 핸드폰은 내 것보다 2배나 비싸다. (twice, as)
His cell phone is ________________________________ mine.

3 손해가 점점 커지고 있다. (big, and)
The damage is getting ________________________________.

전치사 (I)

A [ ] 안에서 알맞은 말을 고르시오.

1 How many days is it [until, for] your next birthday?

2 I found the English grammar book [between, behind] the cabinet.

3 The couple traveled [from, to] California to the Hawaiian Islands.

4 I have an appointment [at, in] 2 o'clock, so I have to leave before 1 pm.

5 He spoke to me [during, along] the break between our classes.

6 He put the empty glass [on, in] the kitchen table.

7 He rode the horse [on, through] the river to catch the calf.

B [보기]에서 알맞은 말을 골라 문장을 완성하시오.

Word Bank	next to	down	at	out of	into	after

1 The child climbed __________ the car to go for a ride.

2 The class had a party __________ their exams.

3 He sat __________ a young man with a mustache.

4 Please put the vase __________ on the living room table.

5 The squirrel took a nut __________ a hole in the tree.

6 Many people try to avoid shopping __________ the mall during the Christmas season.

C 각 문항에 공통으로 들어갈 전치사를 쓰시오.

1 He placed the new files __________ the green chair.
She will return from Chicago __________ Friday afternoon.

2 Will this express train stop __________ Hyde Park?
Are you going to leave for San Antonio __________ one o'clock?

3 She saw many fish swimming __________ the clear stream.
I will return from the store __________ a few minutes.

4 He's supposed to send the column __________ 9 o'clock.
She's so nervous about the presentation __________ the class.

5 The ice cream store may not open __________ next month.
I waited for him __________ 2 o'clock.

SCORE:

A 다음 중 밑줄 친 부분의 쓰임이 잘못된 것을 고르시오.

1 ⓐ I'll be there in a minute.
ⓑ We all stood in line to get tickets.
ⓒ She often wakes up in the middle of the night.
ⓓ He promised to visit me in my birthday.

2 ⓐ The result is uncertain at present.
ⓑ At that time, I was going scuba diving.
ⓒ Does this bus stop at Sang-am Stadium?
ⓓ One of my friends lives at New York City now.

B 다음 빈칸에 알맞은 말을 고르시오.

1 The garden gate was left open __________ several hours.

ⓐ on ⓑ for ⓒ opposite ⓓ in

2 The mysterious people were sitting __________ the window.

ⓐ next to ⓑ out of ⓒ after ⓓ over

C 다음 중 어법상 옳지 않은 문장을 고르시오.

1 ⓐ The coffee shop is across from the train station.
ⓑ The Broadway play begins at seven o'clock by night.
ⓒ The thief ran out of the bank with the money.
ⓓ My sharpened pencil fell behind my brother's desk.

2 ⓐ We have to take the TV to the repair shop on Tuesday afternoon.
ⓑ My mother is flying from New York to Detroit on the first of May.
ⓒ The boy sat outside the two women on the bus.
ⓓ She earned a promotion from her company because she worked so hard.

D 다음 주어진 단어를 이용하여 문장을 완성하시오.

1 나는 자다가 침대에서 떨어졌다. (fall)

I __________ while sleeping.

2 이 루트는 콜로라도의 로키 산을 통과해 지나갑니다. (go)

This route __________ the Rocky Mountains in Colorado.

3 나는 대학 시절 동안 많은 활동에 참여했다. (my college years)

I participated in many activities __________.

전치사 (II)

A 각 문항에 공통으로 들어갈 전치사를 쓰시오.

1 He has just called ____________ a repairman to come.
The path has been rebuilt ____________ a month. Isn't it nice?
Would you like some sugar ____________ your iced tea?

2 My cousin lives ____________ two other women and a dog.
The baseball player is standing ____________ his bat on his shoulder.
I am having lunch today ____________ Susie and Jane.

3 Do you know what this cheese is made ____________?
The next train goes ____________ Baltimore to Washington, D.C.
I learned ____________ my friend that the store is closing late tonight.

4 The young man went ____________ London to meet his friends.
Is it time to go ____________ the beach, yet?
He asked me to call him at ten ____________ seven.

5 The accident happened because ____________ a broken step.
The pie contained two cups ____________ cherries and some pineapple.
A mutual friend of ours told me ____________ your good fortune.

B [보기]에서 알맞은 말을 골라 문장을 완성하시오.

Word Bank	for	from	at	of	to	by	in	on

1 The bus arrives ____________ half-past eight in the morning.
2 The new students at the school are ____________ green shirts.
3 He received a letter ____________ the university about his classes.
4 The patience ____________ his mother was amazing.
5 She put the sign ____________ her desk this afternoon.
6 The food is not ____________ the dog and the cat.
7 Is this a new movie produced ____________ the famous director from Hollywood?
8 My mom took my eldest brother ____________ football practice.

내신 FOCUS

SCORE:

A 다음 중 밑줄 친 부분의 쓰임이 잘못된 것을 고르시오.

1 ⓐ I brought this for you.
ⓑ He looked too old for his age.
ⓒ I've never been absent for school.
ⓓ Are you guys all for his suggestion or against it?

2 ⓐ I got this idea from an Internet website.
ⓑ Coal is mainly made up from carbon.
ⓒ Katherine is from London, England.
ⓓ The country is suffering from a severe food crisis.

B 다음 빈칸에 알맞은 말을 고르시오.

1 A young man helped me ________ my bags at the airport.

ⓐ on ⓑ at ⓒ of ⓓ with

2 The email ________ my teacher is about my grades.

ⓐ from ⓑ on ⓒ with ⓓ of

C 다음 중 어법상 옳지 않은 문장을 고르시오.

1 ⓐ She bought a ticket of the train at Penn Station.
ⓑ Americans learn to read from left to right.
ⓒ My baby brother is in the study with Dad.
ⓓ The sad news of his illness was not welcomed.

2 ⓐ The bike is on sale today at the bike shop.
ⓑ The waves had been getting higher for a few minutes.
ⓒ You can buy the luggage for 200 dollars.
ⓓ It isn't very important of me at this time.

D 다음 주어진 단어를 이용하여 문장을 완성하시오.

1 나는 어젯밤 복통으로 고생했다. (suffer)

I ________________ a stomachache last night.

2 폭풍이 일주일째 계속 악화되고 있다. (one week)

The storm has been getting worse ________________.

3 일어나세요! 벌써 7시 15분 전이에요. (a quarter, seven)

Wake up! It's already ________________.

전치사를 포함한 다양한 표현

A 전치사를 이용하여 문장을 완성하시오.

1 The man wanted to take a photograph ________________ the Empire State Building.

2 The two women realized that they belong ________________ the same gym.

3 I am ashamed ________________ my immature behavior.

4 Who can you depend ________________ in troubled times?

5 Can she cope ________________ the sudden change in schedule?

6 The teacher discussed the difference ________________ the two classes.

7 The suspect finally accounted ________________ his actions during the crime.

B 밑줄 친 부분을 바르게 고쳐 쓰시오. 틀리지 않았다면 ○표 하시오.

1 The manager was proud at clearing up the misunderstanding. ________________

2 The package is full of supplies for the camp. ________________

3 My new friend insisted to buying our dinner last night. ________________

4 They have a wonderful relationship by their parents. ________________

5 My cousin borrowed a shirt of me for the party. ________________

6 The coach was disappointed for the performance of the team. ________________

C [보기]에서 알맞은 말을 골라 문장을 완성하시오.

Example	in connection with	pleased with	cause of
	forget about	responsible for	damage to

1 Who is ________________ getting the tickets to the party?

2 The fireman found the ________________ the fire.

3 There was a lot of ________________ people's homes because of the heavy rain.

4 It was successful. You have to be ________________ the results of the survey.

5 Don't ________________ taking the dog for a walk.

6 I'd like to see you ________________ a new offer.

FOCUS

SCORE:

A 다음 빈칸에 들어갈 말을 쓰시오.

1 Every student can borrow books ____________ the school library.

2 I can easily adapt ____________ the new circumstance.

B 다음 빈칸에 알맞은 말을 고르시오.

1 The strategy consists ____________ hard work and good luck.

ⓐ with ⓑ of ⓒ to ⓓ for

2 The information in the chart ____________ the data significantly.

ⓐ differs from ⓑ differs to ⓒ differs about ⓓ differs at

C 다음 중 어법상 옳지 않은 문장을 고르시오.

1 ⓐ Don't feel sorry for Matt.
ⓑ The teenager was extremely rude to his elder brothers.
ⓒ Can the students cope for a noisy classmate?
ⓓ The director couldn't answer any of her questions.

2 ⓐ The old restaurant is famous for its Chicago-style pizza.
ⓑ The workmen were short on hammers and nails.
ⓒ The solution to the problem depends on your group.
ⓓ The connection between the two incidents is under investigation.

D 다음 주어진 단어를 이용하여 문장을 완성하시오.

1 나는 내 치과 예약에 관해 잊어버렸다. (forget)

I ____________ my dental appointment.

2 그 시험은 100개의 객관식 문제로 구성되어 있다. (consist)

The test ____________ 100 multiple-choice questions.

3 너는 약속을 깨뜨린 것에 대해 부끄러워해야 한다. (ashamed)

You should ____________ breaking your promise.

4 경찰은 절도와 관련된 한 남자를 찾고 싶어 한다. (connection)

The police want to find a man ____________ the robbery.

접속사

A [보기]에서 알맞은 말을 골라 문장을 완성하시오.

Word Bank	neither	and	but	or	either	not only

1 ____________ Jack, but also Mary came to the party last night.

2 ____________ the dog nor the cat woke up during the storm.

3 May I have pancakes ____________ syrup for breakfast in the morning?

4 You may select ____________ green tea or coffee.

5 I bought a new book bag, ____________ the zipper is broken.

6 Steve ____________ Joan will bring the desserts for the meal.

B 밑줄 친 부분을 바르게 고쳐 쓰시오. 틀리지 않았다면 ○표 하시오.

1 The box is not ready to be mailed, <u>for</u> the label is not on it. ____________

2 Both Kevin <u>or</u> Grace go to the same school. ____________

3 Either Pete <u>nor</u> Cindy knows the man by the window. ____________

4 Sue can't join the fencing club <u>but</u> she has a class when it meets. ____________

5 The program on TV is either *Medical Crimes* <u>and</u> *Lost*. ____________

6 My mom felt tired, <u>or</u> she was not sick. ____________

C 접속사를 이용하여 두 개의 문장을 하나의 문장으로 완성하시오.

1 Jim runs very fast. Sam also runs very fast.

→ ____________________ run very fast.

2 We flew to Ireland. We wanted to go to the Blarney Stone.

→ We flew to Ireland ____________________.

3 I had a terrible headache. I took an aspirin.

→ I had a terrible headache, ____________________.

4 I am at the doctor's now. The teacher knows it.

→ The teacher knows ____________________.

5 I don't want to go camping. My sister doesn't want to go camping, either.

→ ____________________ want to go camping.

내신 FOCUS

SCORE:

A 다음 빈칸에 알맞은 말을 고르시오.

1 All the people at the party ate ______________ drank.

ⓐ and ⓑ but ⓒ so ⓓ or

2 I was bored, ______________ I went to sleep.

ⓐ so ⓑ but ⓒ for ⓓ or

B 다음 빈칸에 알맞은 말을 고르시오.

1 My friend can't buy a new bike ______________ he doesn't have enough money.

ⓐ and ⓑ but ⓒ because ⓓ or

2 Did you climb the mountain ______________ go to the beach?

ⓐ for ⓑ or ⓒ after ⓓ so

C 다음 중 어법상 옳지 않은 문장을 고르시오.

1 ⓐ I have a car and a new motorcycle.
ⓑ She forgot that she had to ask about the assignment.
ⓒ Do you want Coke or a different soft drink?
ⓓ He believes both Max and Gene is great businessmen.

2 ⓐ I couldn't get the phone, for the doorbell rang.
ⓑ He is good at soccer as well as running.
ⓒ You can choose either this hat or that tie.
ⓓ The play is neither Hamlet and Macbeth.

D 다음 주어진 단어를 이용하여 문장을 완성하시오.

1 그 소년은 어렸지만 영리했다. (young, wise)

The boy was ______________________________.

2 우리는 중국 음식을 배달시키거나 외식하러 나갈 수 있다. (go out)

We can order Chinese food ______________________________ to eat.

3 David 또는 나, 둘 중 하나가 그 사고에 책임이 있다. (either)

______________________________ responsible for the accident.

명사절

A [보기]에서 알맞은 말을 골라 문장을 완성하시오.

Word Bank	it	that	where	who	whether	what

1 ____________ the committee will meet tomorrow or not is unknown.

2 ____________ is good that the tree will be planted here.

3 The fact ____________ the baseball cap is hers is revealed.

4 This is the person ____________ prescribed the medicine for your uncle.

5 Can you show me ____________ the office is now?

6 Please tell me ____________ exactly you want from me.

B 밑줄 친 부분을 바르게 고쳐 쓰시오. 틀리지 않았다면 ○표 하시오.

1 My mother was pleased that I brought her some flowers. ____________

2 That she made was a sweater and a scarf. ____________

3 Do you understand whether my vacation is next week? ____________

4 Do they read that he sends them each week? ____________

5 I believe that the interesting gentleman could become the next president. ____________

C 주어진 문장을 참고하여 명사절 문장을 완성하시오.

1 Where is the new city park?

→ I don't know ________________________.

2 What is that spot on his arm?

→ Do you know ________________________?

3 Who is the race car driver on TV?

→ I don't know ________________________.

4 What do you want to do now?

→ I don't know ________________________.

5 Where can I buy that book?

→ My sister told me ________________________.

SCORE:

A 다음 두 문장을 한 문장으로 만들 때 빈칸에 알맞은 말을 써 넣으시오.

1 Tell me. + What are you looking for?

→ Tell me ______________________________ looking for.

2 I'm not sure. + Is he coming to the party?

→ I'm not sure ______________________________ to the party.

B 다음 빈칸에 알맞은 말을 고르시오.

1 The mystery is ______________ the magician escaped from the box.

ⓐ where that ⓑ whether or ⓒ what ⓓ how

2 The teacher was worried ______________ the books would not arrive.

ⓐ that ⓑ what ⓒ how ⓓ whether or

C 다음 중 어법상 옳지 않은 문장을 고르시오.

1 ⓐ I'm not sure if she will travel this week.
ⓑ What the woman did for you was very kind.
ⓒ The problem with this car is what it uses a lot of gas.
ⓓ I haven't decided whether I'll go to college or not.

2 ⓐ Let me know where I can see the movie.
ⓑ If he is guilty or not is uncertain.
ⓒ It worried me that the dog kept barking last night.
ⓓ Where he works is in a very large office building.

D 다음 주어진 단어를 이용하여 문장을 완성하시오.

1 나는 그녀가 네 사촌이라는 것을 몰랐다. (your cousin)

I didn't know ______________________________.

2 화성에 생명체가 산다는 증거는 없다. (life, on Mars)

There's no proof ______________________________.

3 그가 그 제안을 받아들일 것이 확실하다. (accept, the offer)

It's certain ______________________________.

부사절

A [보기]에서 알맞은 말을 골라 문장을 완성하시오.

Word Bank	so	while	although	unless	but	when

1 She was making a cake ________________ I got home.

2 I wanted to watch the movie, ________________ I fell asleep on the couch.

3 The seashore was ________________ wonderful that I didn't want to return.

4 You can have this money ________________ you are going to spend it foolishly.

5 Please sit down ________________ I get you something to drink.

6 ________________ it was time to go home, I worked late.

B 밑줄 친 부분을 바르게 고쳐 쓰시오. 틀리지 않았다면 ○표 하시오.

1 In case anybody wants me, call me on my cell phone. ________________

2 The computer was not working, so it is fixed now. ________________

3 He called me unless he needed my permission to go on the field trip. ________________

4 That the tickets are more than five dollars, how will you pay for them? ________________

5 Even though they were hungry after hiking, I gave them some food. ________________

6 As possible, tell me about the agenda in ten minutes. ________________

C 주어진 단어를 이용하여 두 개의 문장을 하나의 문장으로 완성하시오.

1 Hold onto the string. The balloon will not pop.

→ The balloon will not pop ________________. (if)

2 The lake was very beautiful. We took many pictures.

→ ________________, we took many pictures. (as)

3 It was a large box. I couldn't move it.

→ It was ________________ move it. (such, that)

4 We ran very fast. We could get to the train station on time.

→ We ran very fast ________________. (so that)

5 My brother fixed my car quickly. I thanked him by buying him a Chinese dinner.

→ ________________, I thanked him by buying him a Chinese dinner. (since)

내신 FOCUS

SCORE:

A 다음 우리말과 일치하도록 빈칸에 들어갈 알맞은 말을 쓰시오.

1 ____________ he was waiting for her, he read a book at the cafe. (그녀를 기다리는 동안)

2 Don't start the meeting ____________ I get to the office. (사무실에 갈 때까지)

B 다음 빈칸에 알맞은 말을 고르시오.

1 ____________ he finished the work, he went out for coffee.

ⓐ After ⓑ Whether ⓒ Such ⓓ In order to

2 She has played the piano ____________ she was four.

ⓐ in case ⓑ since ⓒ even though ⓓ as soon as

C 다음 중 어법상 옳지 않은 문장을 고르시오.

1 ⓐ She prayed kneeling in church until the bell rang.
ⓑ I like to play badminton, whereas my brother likes to play soccer.
ⓒ The book was such difficult to read that I returned it to the library.
ⓓ In case anyone calls, I'll be in my office.

2 ⓐ I walked slowly so that my little dog wouldn't get tired.
ⓑ I cleaned up my room before my grandparents arrived.
ⓒ If the chair was pretty, it was very uncomfortable.
ⓓ The case was so strange that the TV shows covered it.

D 다음 주어진 단어를 이용하여 문장을 완성하시오.

1 내 도움을 원한다면 네가 필요한 게 뭔지 정확히 얘기해 줘. (want, support)

____________________________, tell me exactly what you need.

2 그는 자신의 차를 사고 싶어서 돈을 모으고 있다. (want, own)

He is saving money ____________________________.

3 나는 내 실수인줄 알았으면서도 미안하다는 말을 하지 않았다. (know, mistake)

____________________________, I didn't say "sorry."

관계대명사

A [ ] 안에서 알맞은 말을 고르시오.

1 I know the woman [that, whose] car is at the corner.

2 I want the man [who, whom] took the file to return it.

3 That's not the plan [what, that] the committee created.

4 [Whoever, Whichever] is here may have some pumpkin pie now.

5 [Whatever, Whichever] way you decide to go, you will find a nice restaurant.

6 She has an apartment [which, of which] is located in Lakewood.

7 [Whatever, However] you choose to do is fine with us.

B 밑줄 친 부분을 바르게 고쳐 쓰시오. 틀리지 않았다면 ○표 하시오.

1 Do you know <u>whose</u> to contact about the problem? ______________

2 I would like to marry a person <u>whom</u> I have a lot in common. ______________

3 <u>Whichever</u> courses you take, you will be challenged. ______________

4 Has he ever seen the man <u>whose</u> I have hired? ______________

5 The author spoke with the girl <u>whom</u> wrote to him. ______________

6 This is not <u>what</u> I bought for him. ______________

C 관계대명사를 이용하여 두 개의 문장을 하나의 문장으로 완성하시오.

1 The bank is open. It is a new bank in town.

→ The bank, ______________ is new in town, is open.

2 He likes the books. He bought them for himself yesterday.

→ He likes ______________ he bought for himself yesterday.

3 This is my new car. Its top is blue.

→ This is ______________ top is blue.

4 I have many new customers. They live in other cities.

→ I have many ______________ live in other cities.

5 The salesman told her about the TVs. Any one she selected would be a good one.

→ The salesman told her ______________ she selected would be a good one.

FOCUS

SCORE:

A 다음 빈칸에 들어갈 수 있는 말을 모두 고르시오.

1 The book ________________ my aunt wrote was the best-seller of the year.

ⓐ who ⓑ which ⓒ what ⓓ that

2 We couldn't believe ________________ she told us.

ⓐ who ⓑ which ⓒ what ⓓ anything that

B 다음 빈칸에 알맞은 말을 고르시오.

1 You can do ________________ you want about replacing the carpet.

ⓐ which ⓑ whatever ⓒ whose ⓓ whom

2 Henry is the scientist ________________ the government has made a contract.

ⓐ whom ⓑ with whom ⓒ that ⓓ whoever

C 다음 중 어법상 옳지 않은 문장을 고르시오.

1 ⓐ Is there anything that I can do for you right now?
ⓑ Whoever has a permission slip may go on the field trip.
ⓒ The swimming pool, which is very new, is my favorite place to swim.
ⓓ This is the girl whom I told you.

2 ⓐ Write down that you want from the grocery store.
ⓑ She appreciated the musician who appeared there for the first time.
ⓒ He was amazed by the dog that he had rescued from the river.
ⓓ Whatever you discover there, you won't have to worry about the outcome.

D 다음 주어진 단어를 이용하여 문장을 완성하시오. (단, 관계대명사를 이용하시오.)

1 그녀는 옆집에 사는 소년을 좋아한다. (next door)

She likes the boy ________________________________.

2 그 공연에는 우리를 흥미롭게 할 만한 것이 거의 없었다. (excited)

There was little ________________________________ at the show.

3 나는 옛 친구를 만났는데, 그 친구는 나를 기억하지 못했다. (recognize)

I met an old friend, ________________________________.

4 내가 원하는 것은 기말 고사에서 A학점을 받는 것이다. (want)

________________________________ to get an A on the final exam.

관계부사

A [ ] 안에서 알맞은 말을 고르시오.

1 Do you know the reason [how, why] you were asked to come here?

2 That is the restaurant [where, when] we had the wedding reception.

3 [However, Wherever] you go, I will be thinking of you.

4 Can you tell me [however, how] the parts are assembled?

5 It was the moment [when, why] she had expected to discover the truth.

6 He used my computer [whenever, however] he needed to email her.

7 The choir was singing [when, whatever] the new conductor arrived.

B 밑줄 친 부분을 바르게 고쳐 쓰시오. 틀리지 않았다면 ○표 하시오.

1 <u>Whichever</u> he visits me, he brings comic books to read. ______________

2 The gravity of Jupiter is the reason <u>why</u> it is struck by many space objects. ______________

3 This tropical location is the place <u>when</u> we spent our spring break. ______________

4 Tell him <u>in what ways</u> the group members will improve their grades. ______________

5 <u>Wherever</u> difficult the circumstances might be, remember to smile. ______________

C 예시의 내용을 참고하여 문장을 완성하시오.

Example That is the chair where my grandfather sat.
→ That is the chair <u>on which</u> my grandfather sat.

1 They can see my results whenever they wish.

→ They can see my results ______________ they wish.

2 Wherever he travels, I know that he will be careful all the time.

→ I know that he will be careful all the time ______________ he travels.

3 However interested she was, she didn't enroll in the cooking class.

→ ______________ interested she was, she didn't enroll in the cooking class.

4 Tell me how the case was concluded in the Supreme Court.

→ Tell me the way ______________ the case was concluded in the Supreme Court.

SCORE:

A 다음 문장의 밑줄 친 부분을 〈전치사 + 관계대명사〉로 바꿔 쓰시오.

1 This is the store where I bought my notebook computer.

→ This is the store ____________ I bought my notebook computer.

2 How he went to Africa is unknown.

→ The way ____________ he went to Africa is unknown.

B 다음 빈칸에 알맞은 말을 고르시오.

1 ____________ he comes, we will be happy to have him.

ⓐ Whenever ⓑ Where ⓒ In what way ⓓ However

2 A traffic jam is the reason ____________ I was late this morning.

ⓐ in which ⓑ for which ⓒ during where ⓓ how

C 다음 중 어법상 옳지 않은 것을 고르시오.

1 ⓐ This is the time when I miss my friends the most.
ⓑ The third period is the hour during which students go to P.E.
ⓒ A flat tire was the reason for which I couldn't ride my bike.
ⓓ Describe to me the way how he will change.

2 ⓐ This is how I can improve my grade in his class.
ⓑ He can borrow my dictionary whatever he needs to.
ⓒ I'll never forget the evening she first shared her stories.
ⓓ No matter how difficult the work becomes, she always tries her hardest.

D 다음 주어진 단어를 이용하여 문장을 완성하시오.

1 우리가 처음 만난 때는 겨울이었다. (the time)

____________ we first met was winter.

2 이곳이 Jane과 Brad가 결혼한 교회이다. (the church)

This is ____________ Jane and Brad got married.

3 이것이 우리가 좋은 점수를 얻을 수 있는 방법이다. (the way)

This is ____________ get a good score.

가정법 (I)

A [ ] 안에서 알맞은 말을 고르시오.

1 If the boat [arrived, had arrived] on time, we would have ridden it.

2 If the road [was, were] better, we could take it.

3 What [would, did] she do if she changed schools again?

4 How [do, would] you survive if you lost your job?

5 If you don't [make, made] the cake, we can buy one at the bakery.

6 If the man [worked, had worked] harder, he might have gotten a promotion.

B 주어진 단어를 이용하여 문장을 완성하시오.

1 If they had the package, they ____________________ it today. (send)

2 If he ____________________ her soon, he will be very sad. (see)

3 If she weren't still so weak, she ____________________ with us. (go shopping)

4 If I were healthy, I ____________________ you now. (play with)

C 주어진 문장을 참고하여 빈칸에 알맞은 말을 써 넣으시오. (단, 축약형을 이용하시오.)

1 If they don't call the doctor's office, they won't get an appointment.

→ Unless they ______________ the doctor's office, they ______________ an appointment.

2 If the weather were better, I could go hiking.

→ The weather ______________ good, so I ______________ hiking.

3 If she had a car, we could drive to the mountains.

→ She ______________ a car, so we ______________ to the mountains.

4 If she had brought the book, she could have returned it.

→ She ______________ the book, so she ______________ it.

5 If the policeman weren't here, people might speed.

→ The policeman ______________ here, so people ______________ speed.

FOCUS

SCORE: 

A 다음 주어진 문장을 참고하여 빈칸에 알맞은 말을 써 넣으시오.

1 I woke up late, so I missed my school bus.

→ If I ______________________ earlier, I could have taken my school bus.

2 I am busy, so I can't go to the movies with you.

→ If I ______________________ busy, I could go to the movies with you.

B 다음 빈칸에 알맞은 말을 고르시오.

1 If we ______________________ some different clothes, we could change now.

ⓐ were　　ⓑ had　　ⓒ would have　　ⓓ do

2 If you ______________________ tell her today, she will make a mistake.

ⓐ don't　　ⓑ didn't　　ⓒ were　　ⓓ weren't

C 다음 중 어법상 옳지 않은 것을 고르시오.

1 ⓐ If I am smarter, I would invent something very useful.

ⓑ If she weren't injured, she might play volleyball this semester at school.

ⓒ If they are not busy tomorrow, they may come here.

ⓓ If she had completed the assignment, her teacher would have been satisfied.

2 ⓐ If the car is fixed in the morning, I will pick you up.

ⓑ We're not in school now, so we can't participate in school clubs.

ⓒ If it snowed last night, I would have made a snowman.

ⓓ How would you feel if you were asked to sing?

D 다음 주어진 단어를 이용하여 문장을 완성하시오.

1 날씨가 좋으면 우리는 밖에서 만날 것이다. (meet)

If the weather is fine, we ______________________ outside.

2 만약 네가 부자라면 넌 뭘 할 거니? (rich)

What would you do ______________________?

3 내가 공부를 좀 더 열심히 했었다면, 아마도 시험에서 A를 받았을 텐데. (study, harder)

If I ______________________, I might have gotten an A on the exam.

가정법 (II)

A [ ] 안에서 알맞은 말을 고르시오.

1 Isn't Mary home? I wish she [can play, could play] with me now.

2 He talked to me about it. Without his advice, I [couldn't have, wouldn't had] done it.

3 He didn't want the hat, but she insisted that he [buy, bought] it.

4 Didn't she take any medicine? I wish I [gave, had given] some to her last night.

5 Thank you for your dictionary. But for the dictionary, I [can't, couldn't] finish my homework.

B 주어진 문장을 「I wish」 문장으로 다시 쓰시오.

1 I don't have a big dog at home.
→ I wish I ____________ a big dog at home.

2 I can't find the old book in the library.
→ I wish I ____________ the old book in the library.

3 I didn't go swimming with my friends from school.
→ I wish I ____________ swimming with my friends from school.

4 I didn't lock the door to my house before I left.
→ I wish I ____________ the door to my house before I left.

C 주어진 문장을 참고하여 빈칸에 알맞은 말을 써 넣으시오.

1 She acts as if everything were all right between us.
→ In fact, it ____________ all right between us.

2 She looks as if she had all the money in the world.
→ In fact, she ____________ very little money.

3 He acts as if he were our teacher.
→ In fact, he ____________ our teacher.

4 They act as if they had visited here before.
→ In fact, they ____________ here before.

5 It seems as if they wanted to play with us.
→ In fact, they ____________ play with us.

FOCUS

SCORE:

A 다음 주어진 문장을 참고하여 빈칸에 알맞은 말을 써 넣으시오.

I wish I had such a beautiful house.

→ In fact, I ______________ such a beautiful house.

B 다음 빈칸에 알맞은 말을 고르시오.

1 I wish I ______________ a better picture of my boyfriend.

ⓐ can have ⓑ have ⓒ had ⓓ have gotten

2 If she ______________ today, she would have been at the meeting.

ⓐ work ⓑ working ⓒ had worked ⓓ worked

C 다음 중 어법상 옳지 않은 문장을 고르시오.

1 ⓐ He insisted that you will send for the doctor.
ⓑ I wish I knew the answer to that question.
ⓒ If they had removed the items from the shelf, it would have been OK.
ⓓ If it had not been for my cat, I couldn't have survived breaking up with him.

2 ⓐ It's time he showed up. He's very late.
ⓑ He suggested that she buy the yellow dress in the store window.
ⓒ If I gone to school this year, I would have graduated.
ⓓ Without a flashlight, I couldn't find the missing pen.

D 다음 주어진 단어를 이용하여 문장을 완성하시오.

1 내가 그의 충고를 들었더라면 좋았을 텐데. (take his advice)

I wish I ______________________________.

2 그녀는 마치 심리학자였던 것처럼 행동했다. (a psychologist)

She acted ______________________________.

3 내가 그때 그 약을 먹었었더라면, 지금쯤 몸이 괜찮을 텐데. (take the medicine)

If I ______________________ then, I would be fine now.

4 컴퓨터가 없다면 나는 그 일을 끝내지 못할 것이다. (finish)

If it were not for a computer, I ______________________ it.

일치, 특수 구문

A [ ] 안에서 알맞은 말을 고르시오.

1 Three dollars [is, are] all the money that I have.

2 A number of fans [appear, appears] suddenly.

3 Into the basket [came, comes] a small cat and a mouse.

4 He [was, is], I suppose, trying to change for the better at that time.

5 We believe that she [is, will be] a good mother someday.

6 I know that the Civil War [fought, was fought] between the North and the South.

B 밑줄 친 부분을 바르게 고쳐 쓰시오. 틀리지 않았다면 ○표 하시오.

1 She doesn't like the schedule. <u>Or</u> do we. ____________

2 Little did I <u>knew</u> that we would become relatives after their wedding. ____________

3 I heard that she <u>had completed</u> the course work. ____________

4 The three clubs <u>meet</u> together for the first time yesterday. ____________

5 <u>Are</u> there anyone who needs a new sheet of paper? ____________

6 Both Jade and Matt <u>was</u>, I suppose, waiting for the doctor. ____________

7 Most of the apples <u>were</u> rotten. ____________

C 주어진 문장을 「It ~ that ...」을 이용하여 다시 쓰시오.

1 Mr. Johnson from his office won the lottery.

→ ____________ that won the lottery.

2 Economics was my least favorite subject in school this year.

→ ____________ that was my least favorite subject in school this year.

3 I saw David playing with the puppy in the park.

→ ____________ that I saw David playing with the puppy.

4 Tom gave the card with a bunch of flowers on my birthday.

→ ____________ who gave me the card with a bunch of flowers on my birthday.

내신 FOCUS

SCORE:

A 다음 중 밑줄 친 부분의 쓰임이 잘못된 것을 고르시오.

My little brothers told(ⓐ) me that he(ⓑ) found(ⓒ) a wallet on their(ⓓ) way home.

B 다음 빈칸에 알맞은 말을 고르시오.

1 Some people like to wear shoes, ________________ prefer sandals.

ⓐ other ⓑ others ⓒ the other ⓓ the ones

2 The biggest problem was who ________________ here first.

ⓐ is ⓑ are ⓒ will be ⓓ would be

C 다음 중 어법상 옳지 않은 문장을 고르시오.

1 ⓐ I know that she were a teacher years ago.
ⓑ While cooking dinner, he got a phone call from her.
ⓒ This was a tiring two-hour trip up the mountain.
ⓓ Steve is a real estate lawyer, and so is his sister.

2 ⓐ I like the thought of her coming to live with us next year.
ⓑ Only a little later I did discover what I had done.
ⓒ He knows everyone in the test group already.
ⓓ The sailor said the tide comes in and goes out twice a day.

D 다음 주어진 단어를 이용하여 문장을 완성하시오.

1 5달러가 현재 내가 가진 전부이다. (five dollars)

________________________________ all I have now.

2 이 방에 있는 사람들 모두 죄가 없다. (all of the men, in this room)

________________________________ not guilty.

3 참석자의 수는 알려지지 않았다. (the number of, the participants)

________________________________ unknown.

4 그녀는 요즘 일본어를 배우고 있다고 말했다. (learn, Japanese)

She said ________________________________ nowadays.

Concise and Core Grammar Points!

The Grammar

Nexus Contents Development Team

Answers

NEXUS Edu

The Grammar

Nexus Contents Development Team

Level 2

Answers

NEXUS Edu

Answers ▸▸

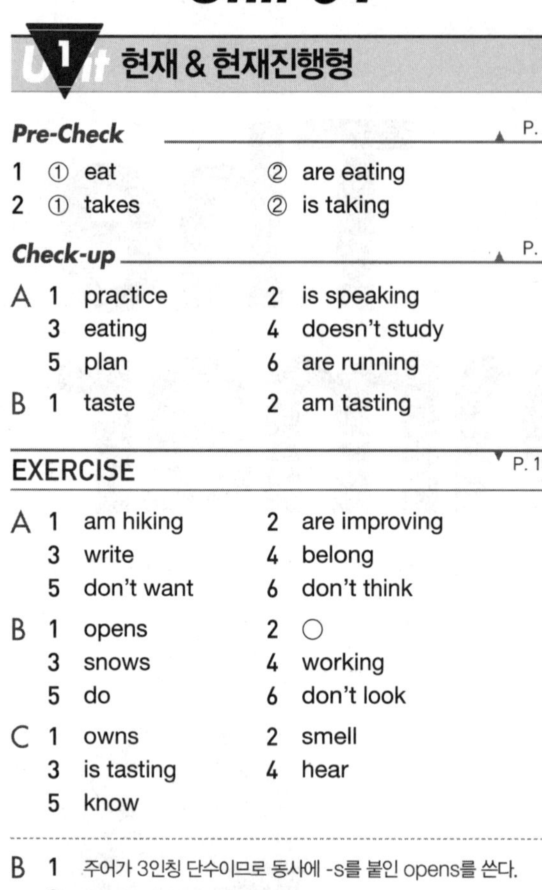

Unit 01

Unit 1 현재 & 현재진행형

Pre-Check P. 8

1 ① eat ② are eating
2 ① takes ② is taking

Check-up P. 9

A 1 practice 2 is speaking
3 eating 4 doesn't study
5 plan 6 are running

B 1 taste 2 am tasting

EXERCISE P. 10

A 1 am hiking 2 are improving
3 write 4 belong
5 don't want 6 don't think

B 1 opens 2 ○
3 snows 4 working
5 do 6 don't look

C 1 owns 2 smell
3 is tasting 4 hear
5 know

B 1 주어가 3인칭 단수이므로 동사에 -s를 붙인 opens를 쓴다.
3 '겨울에는 눈이 많이 온다'는 일반적인 사실이므로 현재시제를 쓴다.
4 〈be동사 + -ing〉이므로 working을 쓴다.
5 일상적인 습관이므로 단순 현재를 쓴다.
6 상태동사는 진행형으로 쓸 수 없다.

Unit 2 과거 & 과거진행형

Pre-Check P. 11

1 ① was watching ② watched
2 ① went ② were going

Check-up P. 12

A 1 fixed 2 made
3 prepared 4 slept
5 sang

B ① stayed ② watched
③ was taking

EXERCISE P. 13

A 1 was having 2 went
3 didn't hear 4 went
5 were you doing

B 1 Did 2 received
3 snowing 4 emailing
5 ○ 6 wrote

C 1 visited 2 was traveling
3 was 4 built
5 won 6 spent
7 were playing

B 1 '지난 크리스마스'는 과거이므로 Did you visit ~?로 써야 한다.
2 과거의 일이므로 과거로 써야 한다.
3 과거진행형이므로 snowing을 쓴다.
4 then은 특정한 때를 가리키므로 진행형을 쓴다.
6 과거의 특정 순간에 진행되는 일이 아니므로 단순 과거를 쓴다.

Unit 3 미래 & 미래진행형

Pre-Check P. 14

1 are going to 2 would
3 will

Check-up P. 15

A 1 will return
2 are not going to attend
3 will place an order
4 is going to prepare
5 is arriving

B ① 현재진행형 ② 현재진행형
③ 미래 ④ 미래

EXERCISE P. 16

A 1 is not going to bring
2 are going to watch
3 is going to spend
4 Is he going to pick you up

B 1 will stay 2 am going to
3 is going to 4 will take
5 is about to start 6 will be waiting
7 would buy

C 1 will[is going to] snow

2 will not[am not going to] tell
3 will[are going to] stay
4 will[am going to] see

B 1 오늘밤의 일에 대한 계획이다.
2 현재진행형의 표현이다.
3 내일의 날씨를 예상하는 것이므로 be going to를 쓴다.
4 오늘 일에 대한 예정이므로 will이 자연스럽다.
5 금방 일어날 일에 대해서 말하고 있다.
6 '도착하면 (미래), 기다리고 있을 것이다'이므로 미래진행형을 쓴다.
7 과거 시점에서의 의지를 나타내므로 would를 쓴다.

R REVIEW TEST

P. 17

A
1 was
2 was watching
3 studies
4 seems
5 Do you mind
6 left
7 go
8 was cleaning

B
1 ⓒ 2 ⓐ 3 ⓑ 4 ⓐ
5 ⓓ 6 ⓐ 7 ⓐ

C
1 When I got out of the plane, it was raining heavily.
2 I was going to quit the job because I wasn't happy with my boss back then.
3 It was amazing that endangered species survived after Hurricane Katrina.
4 I walked to school with my brother before I got a bike.

D ②

A 1 내 남동생은 어제 아파서 수업에 빠졌다.
▶ 어제의 일이므로 was가 적절하다.
2 내가 TV를 보고 있는 동안 전기가 나갔다.
▶ 과거에 동시에 일어났던 일을 얘기하고 있다.
3 평일에는 집에서 Jerry를 찾지 못할 것이다. 그는 항상 도서관에서 공부를 한다.
▶ always라는 부사구가 있으므로 현재시제를 고른다.
4 James는 오늘 화가 난 것 같다.
▶ 상태동사는 진행형으로 쓰지 않는다.
5 제가 여기 앉아도 될까요?
▶ 상태동사는 진행형으로 쓰지 않는다.
6 그녀는 15분 전에 아파트를 떠났다.
▶ 15분 전의 일이므로 단순 과거인 left를 쓴다.
7 나는 매주 토요일 부모님과 볼링을 치러 간다.
▶ '매주 토요일'에 일어나는 반복적인 일이므로 현재시제를 쓴다.
8 내가 방을 청소하고 있는 동안, 그녀는 소파에서 잡지를 읽고 있었다.
▶ 과거에 동시에 일어난 일이므로 과거진행형을 쓴다.

B 1 나는 지금 조깅을 하고 있다. 내일 아침 이 시각에도 나는 조깅을 하고 있을 것이다.
▶ 내일 진행되고 있을 일이므로 미래진행형을 쓴다.
2 사고 후에 여러 가지로 배려해 주신 모든 일에 대해 감사드립니다.
▶ 상태동사는 진행형으로 쓰지 않는다.
3 우리 삼촌은 주중에는 점심시간 후에 사탕 가게 문을 연다.
▶ 평소에 일어나는 반복적인 일이므로 현재를 쓴다.
4 Kelly는 밖에 놀러 나가기 전에 한 시간 동안 트럼펫을 불 것이다.
▶ 때를 나타내는 부사절에서는 현재시제로 미래를 대신한다.
5 나는 그와 복도에서 마주쳤을 때 교실 밖으로 나가는 중이었다.
▶ 과거의 특정한 때의 일을 나타내고 있다.
6 Bill이 아프다. 나는 내일 경기에 대신 출전할 선수가 필요하다.
▶ 상태동사는 진행형으로 쓰지 않는다.
7 나는 오늘 물이 0도에서 언다고 배웠다.
▶ 과학적 사실이나 불변의 진리는 항상 현재시제이다.

C 1 내가 비행기에서 내렸을 때 비가 심하게 내리고 있었다.
▶ 과거의 일이므로 got으로 고친다.
2 그때는 사장님과 편하게 지내지 못했기 때문에 직장을 그만두려고 했었다.
▶ 과거의 일이므로 was going to로 고친다.
3 멸종 위기의 종들이 허리케인 카트리나 이후에도 살아남았다는 사실이 놀랍다.
▶ 과거의 일이므로 survived로 고친다.
4 나는 자전거가 생기기 전에는 남동생과 학교에 걸어 다녔다.
▶ 과거의 일이므로 walked로 고친다.

D

과학자들이 다른 행성의 거대 허리케인을 지켜보고 있다. 이 허리케인은 너비가 5,000마일에 이르고 풍속은 시간당 350마일이다. 연구원들은 토성의 이 폭풍을 지켜보고 있다. 폭풍은 토성의 남극 근처에 위치하고 있다. 과학자들은 이 폭풍이 오랫동안 계속될 것이라고 생각한다. 그들은 될 수 있는 한 오래 이것을 관찰할 것이다.

▶ (A) 주어가 복수(its wind)이므로 travel (B) 폭풍이 계속되는 것이므로 will continue (C) 될 수 있는 한 오래 관찰할 것이라는 의미이므로 are going to study

FURTHER STUDY [Writing]

P. 19

1 did not feel well, went to the doctor
2 owns two cars, is driving a red car
3 go jogging along the riverside
4 is about to begin
5 would visit us next month
6 was watching a video, was talking to
7 have a job interview tomorrow, will not go to the movies tonight
8 you are working at the office, will drive us to the airport

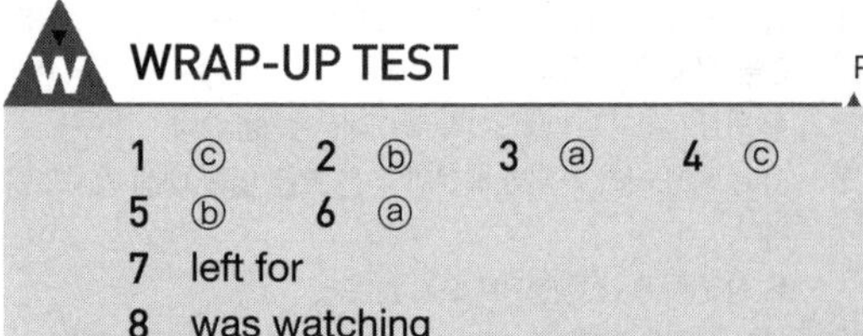

WRAP-UP TEST

P. 21

1 ⓒ 2 ⓑ 3 ⓐ 4 ⓒ
5 ⓑ 6 ⓐ
7 left for
8 was watching
9 ⓓ 10 ⓓ

1 ▶ send의 과거형은 sent이다.

2 그 소녀은 테이블 위에 있는 컵을 깨뜨렸다고 말했다.
▶ 주절의 동사가 과거(said)이므로 과거형(broke)이 와야 한다.

3 네 여동생이 백화점에서 무엇을 살거니?
▶ 앞에 조동사 will이 있으므로 현재형(buy)이 와야 한다.

4 A: 오늘 밤에 무엇을 할 예정이야?
B: ⓐ 청바지를 찾고 있어요. ⓑ TV로 영화를 봤어요. ⓒ 콘서트를 보러 갈 거예요. ⓓ 그것을 막 하려던 참이었어요.
▶ 오늘밤에 무엇을 할지 물었으므로 미래시제로 답해야 한다.

5 ⓐ 음, 나는 냄새가 안나. ⓑ 내 남동생이 스코틀랜드에서 곧 돌아올 거야. ⓒ 사람들이 지난밤에 지진이 나는 것을 느꼈다고 말했다. ⓓ 이번 여름휴가 때 무엇을 할 예정이야?
▶ 미래 부사(soon)가 왔으므로 was는 is가 돼야 한다.

6 ⓐ 내 딸이 다음 주에 여기 도착할 거야. ⓑ 그녀를 방해하지 마. 에세이를 쓰는 중이야. ⓒ 세탁소를 찾고 있어요. 이 근처에 하나 있지 않나요? ⓓ 그들은 Becky의 방에서 유럽 여행을 계획하고 있다.
▶ ⓐ 가까운 미래를 나타내는 미래시제이다. ⓑⓒⓓ 현재진행형이다.

7 Karen은 다음 달에 스페인으로 떠날 것이다.
▶ 과거를 의미하는 부사(last month)가 있으므로 과거시제로 써야 한다.

8 나는 여동생과 영화를 보고 있다.
▶ 과거 동사(called)가 있으므로 과거진행형이 와야 한다.

[9-10]
나는 다음 주에 포틀랜드에서 보스턴까지 기차 여행을 할 계획이다. 모두들 비행기를 타고 가라고 권하지만 미국을 횡단하는 기차 여행을 하는 것이 경치도 즐길 수 있고 흥미로울 것이라고 생각한다. 나는 또 기차의 침대칸도 예약해 두었기 때문에 3일간의 대륙 여행을 편하게 할 수 있다. 나는 노트북을 가지고 가서 보고서도 쓸 것이다. 보스턴에 도착할 때쯤에는 보고서를 다 끝냈을 것이다.

9 ▶ 시간의 나타내는 부사절에서 미래시제 대신에 현재시재를 쓴다.

10 ⓐ 나는 기차를 타고 보스턴으로 갈 것이다. ⓑ 나는 침대칸을 예약했다. ⓒ 나는 3일간 여행할 것이다. ⓓ 나는 여행 동안 전혀 일을 하지 않을 것이다.
▶ 기차 안에서 보고서를 쓴다고 했으므로 일을 전혀 안 하는 것은 아니다.

Unit 02

Unit 1 현재완료 (I)

Pre-Check

P. 24

1 ① studied ② have studied
2 ① read ② have read

Check-up

P. 25

A 1 have constructed 2 have attended
3 has not tried 4 Have you ever visited
5 has survived

B 1 ① studied ② has studied
2 ① have seen ② saw

EXERCISE

P. 26

A 1 did you go
2 have never done
3 Have you ever seen
4 have worked
5 have played

B 1 for 2 O
3 since 4 has studied
5 didn't paddle

C 1 has sculpted 2 have attended
3 has cooked 4 has traveled
5 have you taken

B 1 기간이 왔으므로 for가 돼야 한다.
3 시점이 왔으므로 since가 돼야 한다.
4 지난 4월 이래로 현재까지 이어지는 일이므로 현재완료를 쓴다.
5 과거 특정 시점의 일이므로 과거시제를 쓴다.

Unit 2 현재완료 (II)

Pre-Check

P. 27

1 ① 그녀는 어제 유럽으로 갔다.
② 그녀는 유럽에 갔다. (그래서 지금 여기 없다.)

2 ① 나는 한 시간 전에 보고서를 끝냈다.
② 나는 방금 보고서를 끝냈다.

Check-up

P. 28

A 1 have not mentioned 2 has gone
3 has left 4 have already taken
5 have participated

B 1 have read, read 2 has gone, went

EXERCISE

P. 29

A 1 has sold 2 have not eaten
3 has gone 4 has just arrived

B 1 ○ 2 ridden
3 ○ 4 put off
5 have

C 1 have just completed
2 has broken her favorite glass
3 has washed the car
4 has just signed a contract
5 have spent all of my extra money

B 2 현재완료의 형태는 〈has/have + p.p.〉이다.
4 '여러 차례 경기를 연기했다'라는 의미이므로 현재완료를 쓴다.
5 lately라는 단어는 과거부터 지금까지를 모두 포함하는 단어이다. 따라서 현재완료를 쓴다.

Unit 3 과거완료, 미래완료, 완료진행형

Pre-Check

P. 30

1 had cooked 2 will have cooked
3 have been cooking

Check-up

P. 31

A 1 had finished 2 had seen
3 has been driving 4 will have worked

B ① talking ② have been talking
③ have been waiting

EXERCISE

P. 32

A 1 have studied 2 had planned
3 have been 4 will have concluded
5 Has, ordered 6 had fed
7 have waited

B 1 ○ 2 had
3 has 4 will have
5 have 6 ○

C 1 will have bought a new house
2 have known each other
3 Had you checked the oil
4 (has / had) prepared a special pizza
5 The marathoners have been running

B 2 작년(과거) 이전의 일이므로 과거완료로 써야 한다.
3 어젯밤(과거) 이후로 계속 자는 것이므로 현재완료진행형을 쓴다.
4 미래의 표현(by the time)이 있으므로 미래완료가 되어야 한다.
5 1학년 이후로 계속 같은 학교에 다닌다는 의미이므로 현재완료로 쓴다.

REVIEW TEST

P. 33

A 1 How long 2 since
3 for 4 since
5 had decorated 6 have seen
7 will have reached
8 has been snowing

B 1 ⓐ 2 ⓒ 3 ⓓ 4 ⓑ
5 ⓓ 6 ⓓ 7 ⓐ

C 1 They have played in the band since they were in high school.
2 My youngest cousin has been coughing since late last night.
3 At the end of the year, he will have worked for the school for 20 years.
4 Jessica has visited me several times for 4 years.
5 Do you know how long he had been working at the company?
6 They had stayed in a nice hotel before I met them.

D ③

A 1 얼마나 오랫동안 어머니와 통화를 하고 있는 거니?
▶ '얼마나 오랫동안'이라는 표현이 와야 한다.
2 우리 가족은 여기 이사 온 이래로 동물원을 즐겨 찾고 있다.
▶ 과거의 특정 시점이 나왔으므로 접속사 since가 옳다.
3 그 소년들은 일주일 이상 캠프에 가 있다.
▶ 기간을 나타내는 전치사 for가 와야 한다.
4 뉴질랜드로 이사 온 후로 5년이 되었다.
▶ '~한 지 얼마가 지났다'에는 since를 쓴다.
5 파티가 시작되기 전에 그녀는 케이크를 장식했다.
▶ 특정 과거 시점 이전의 일이므로 과거완료를 쓴다.
6 우리는 런던의 크라운 보석가게를 여러 번 봤다.
▶ 경험을 이야기하는 현재완료가 와야 한다. 동작을 나타내는 것이 아니므로 진행형으로 쓰지 않는다.
7 그 편지는 내일 아침 8시면 도착할 것이다.
▶ 미래의 일이므로 미래완료를 쓴다.
8 며칠 동안 눈이 내리고 있다.
▶ 현재의 시점에서 말하고 있으므로 현재완료진행형이 와야 한다.

B 1 그는 피곤한 게 틀림없다. 열 시간 동안 자고 있다.
▶ 열 시간이라는 기간이 나오므로 for가 와야 한다.
2 그는 졸업하기 전 2년 동안 그 팀에서 농구를 했었다.
▶ 주절에 과거완료가 왔으므로 과거시제가 와야 한다.
3 걱정하지 마세요. 당신 차는 당신이 필요로 하는 그 날까지는 수리될 거예요.
▶ 미래의 때를 표현하는 구가 와야 한다.
4 대학을 함께 다녔던 때 이후로 그녀 소식을 듣지 못했다.

▶ '~이후로 …하지 못했다'란 뜻이다. since가 현재완료와 함께 쓰일 때는 since절에 과거 동사를 쓴다.

5 우리 할아버지 할머니는 내년이면 결혼 50주년이 된다.
▶ '내년'이라는 미래의 시점에 일어날 일을 이야기하고 있으므로 미래완료를 쓴다.

6 나는 대학에 입학하기 전에 3개월 동안 트럼펫 레슨을 받았다.
▶ 특정 과거 시점 이전에 일어난 일이므로 과거완료를 쓴다.

7 그녀는 어제 운전면허증을 분실했다.
▶ yesterday라는 과거의 특정 시점이 왔으므로 과거시제를 쓴다.

C 1 그들은 고등학교 이후로 그 밴드 활동을 해 왔다.
▶ 특정 과거 시점부터 현재까지의 일이므로 have played로 고친다.

2 가장 어린 사촌은 어젯밤 늦게부터 계속 기침을 하고 있다.
▶ 현재까지 계속 진행되는 일이므로 has been coughing으로 고친다.

3 올해 말이 되면, 그는 그 학교에서 20년 동안 일하는 게 될 것이다.
▶ 미래에 완료될 사건을 이야기하고 있으므로 will have p.p. 형태로 고친다.

4 Jessica는 지난 4년 동안 여러 차례 나를 방문했다.
▶ '지난 4년 동안'이라는 기간을 나타내므로 for로 고친다.

5 그가 얼마나 오랫동안 그 회사에서 일했는지 아는가?
▶ 기간을 묻고 있으므로 how long으로 고친다.

6 내가 그들을 만나기 전에 그들은 좋은 호텔에서 머물렀다.
▶ 과거완료가 왔으므로 과거 시제가 와야 한다.

D

그 시대의 대부분의 노동자와 마찬가지로 George Stephenson은 학교에 다닌 적이 없다. 그는 스스로 읽는 것을 배웠고 공부를 해서 잉글랜드 북동부의 석탄광산에서 기술자가 되었다. 그는 말이 끄는 마차보다 더 효율적으로 석탄을 옮기는 방법이 있을 거라고 생각했다. 그는 Richard Trevithick의 작업을 더 개선시키기로 결심했는데, Richard Trevithick은 간단한 (형태의) 기관차를 만든 사람이었다.

▶ (A) 과거의 경험을 이야기하므로 had never been (B) 과거의 일이므로 thought (C) 특정 과거 시점 이전의 일이므로 had built

FURTHER STUDY [Writing]

P. 35

1 have been to the park several times
2 have tried bungee jumping
3 He has seen *The Phantom of the Opera*
4 had been doing, you called me
5 I have not had an opportunity to study
6 will have worked for this company
7 They have been teammates
8 She will have been waiting here for an hour

WRAP-UP TEST

P. 37

1 ⓒ 2 ⓑ 3 ⓑ
4 I haven't 5 ⓐ 6 ⓒ
7 ⓑ 8 has been searching for, for
9 ⓒ 10 ⓓ

1 ⓐ 너는 얼마나 오랫동안 LA에 살았니? ⓑ 나는 전에 그를 만나 본 적이 한 번도 없어. ⓒ 이 수업을 몇 번이나 들었니? ⓓ 그는 한 달 동안 이 프로젝트를 작업하고 있다.
▶ ⓒ 현재완료 문장이므로 p.p. 형태인 taken이 와야 한다.

2 "트랜스포머"라는 영화에 대해서 들어본 적 있니?
▶ 현재완료의 경험을 나타내는 부사는 ever이다.

3 Crane 씨는 작년부터 서울에 살았다.
▶ since last year가 왔기 때문에 현재완료이다.

4 A: 방 청소 다 했니?
B: 아니요, 아직이요.
▶ 현재완료로 질문했으므로 현재완료형으로 답한다.

5 ⓐ 애완동물을 키워 본 적이 있니? ⓑ 이 회사에서 일한지 얼마나 되었나요? ⓒ 우리는 그것에 대해서 들어본 적이 없습니다. ⓓ 아빠는 2시간째 신문을 읽고 있다.
▶ 과거의 특정 시점을 나타내는 ago는 현재완료와 같이 쓰이지 않으므로 ago를 삭제한다.

6 이 학교에서 얼마나 오래 영어를 가르치셨나요?
ⓐ 여기는 내가 지금까지 가 본 장소 중에서 가장 흥미로운 곳이야. ⓑ 나는 학교에 지각한 적이 없어. ⓒ 할머니가 지난 수요일부터 병원에 계셔. ⓓ 그녀는 운전면허 시험에 여러 번 떨어진 후 마침내 합격했어.
▶ ⓐ 경험 ⓑ 경험 ⓒ 계속 ⓓ 완료

7 ⓐ 우리는 해외에 나가본 적이 없다. ⓑ 그는 이 차를 5년간 타고 다녔다. ⓒ 나는 이것보다 더 재미있는 것을 읽어본 적이 없다. ⓓ 전에 이 대회에 참가한 적이 있나요?
▶ ⓐ 경험 ⓑ 계속 ⓒ 경험 ⓓ 경험

8 Andrew는 2시간 전에 인터넷에서 정보를 찾기 시작했다. 그는 아직도 정보를 찾고 있다.
▶ 2시간 전부터 지금까지 정보를 찾고 있는 것이므로 현재완료 진행형이 적절하다. 뒤에 시간이 왔으므로 for가 적절하다.

[9-10]

남자 100미터 달리기에서 가장 좋은 점수(최단 기록)는 이제 10초 미만이다. 선수들의 기술력과 체력 향상만이 기록 갱신을 돕는 유일한 것은 아니다. 인조 트랙, 공기역학적 운동복, 그리고 현대적인 신발의 발달에 기술력 또한 도움이 되어 왔다. 출발 방법과 시간을 재는 방법이 향상되고 있고, 현대의 전자 시스템은 선수들과 관리자들이 모든 경기가 가능한 한 정당하게 치러질 거라고 확신하는 데 도움을 준다.

9 ▶ 과거부터 현재까지 진행되고 있는 것이므로 현재완료진행형이 적절하다.

10 ▶ 고영양 음식에 대해서는 언급되지 않았다.

Unit 03

조동사 can, may

Pre-Check
P. 40

1 can't　　2 can't　　3 may

Check-up
P. 41

A 1 is able to swim　　2 is not able to play
3 Are you able to read

B 1 b　　2 a　　3 c

EXERCISE
P. 42

A 1 be able to　　2 can
3 Could　　4 can't be
5 might

B 1 ⓑ　　2 ⓒ　　3 ⓐ
4 ⓒ　　5 ⓑ

C 1 이번 주말에 네가 우리와 함께 영화를 보러 갈 수 없다니 유감이야.
2 나는 오빠의 컴퓨터를 쓰는 것을 허락받았다.
3 그녀는 이 잡지에 관심이 있을지도 모른다.
4 Henry는 지금 벌을 받는 중이라서 너와 얘기할 수 없다.

B 1 엄마가 '가도 좋다'고 허락하는 내용이다.
2 '사실일 리가 없다'고 말하고 있으므로 가능성에 해당된다.
3 축구를 잘하고 못하고의 문제는 능력(ability)을 가리킨다.
4 지금 집에 없으므로 경기장에 있을 것이라고 짐작하고 있다. 이는 가능성(possibility)에 해당된다.
5 길을 가르쳐 달라고 요청(request)하는 것이다.

2 조동사 will, must, shall

Pre-Check
P. 43

Will, should, must

Check-up
P. 44

A 1 would bring　　2 Shall we sit
3 Will you mail　　4 must not drive

B ① would/used to　　② used to
③ would/used to

EXERCISE
P. 45

A 1 don't have to　　2 must
3 has to　　4 have to
5 will have to　　6 mustn't

B 1 have to　　2 must not
3 must have been　　4 ○
5 had to　　6 ○

C 1 should see this movie
2 would play soccer
3 What shall we do
4 must be kidding
5 mustn't[must not] tell

B 1 일상적인 행동을 의미하므로 had to를 have to로 고친다.
2 학교에 개를 데려오는 것은 '정책적으로 금지된 일'에 해당한다. 금지에 해당하는 must not으로 고친다.
3 '전화를 건 것'은 과거의 일이다. 따라서 과거의 추측을 나타내는 말을 써야 한다. must be를 must have been으로 고친다.
5 '~했기 때문에 …해야 했다'라는 뜻이다. must의 과거형인 had to를 쓴다.

3 기타 조동사

Pre-Check
P. 46

1 used to　　2 had better
3 would rather

Check-up
P. 47

A 1 would rather not come
2 had better bring
3 needn't[need not/don't need to]

B ① a　　② b

EXERCISE
P. 48

A 1 had better not　　2 would rather
3 You'd better　　4 would rather
5 might have opened

B 1 had better　　2 go
3 have heard　　4 ○
5 have studied　　6 shouldn't

C 1 did not need to take
2 used to go swimming
3 had better ask
4 had better hand it in
5 would rather have

B 1 had better 구문은 〈주어 + had better + V〉로 나타낸다.
2 〈would rather + not + 동사원형〉이므로 go로 바꾼다.
3 과거에 대한 추측은 〈might + have + p.p.〉로 나타낸다.
5 과거에 대한 추측은 〈must + have + p.p.〉이다.
6 내용상 '~하면 안 된다'이므로 부정문으로 고친다.

REVIEW TEST

P. 49

A 1 will 2 must be
3 would 4 would rather not
5 May 6 need not
7 should have returned
8 might have been

B 1 ⓑ 2 ⓓ 3 ⓐ 4 ⓑ
5 ⓑ 6 ⓒ 7 ⓓ

C 1 Need he pay for this right away?
2 I was able to play three instruments when I was in high school.
3 Rachel, can[could/will/would] you lend me 20 dollars?
4 I would rather not talk to her in person because she's very rude to everyone.
5 We couldn't start the game since there was no ball.

D ④

A 1 우리는 내일 오후까지 이 프로젝트를 끝낼 수 없을 것이다.
▶ 내일 오후의 일이므로 will을 쓴다.

2 봐! 응급 차량이 아주 많아. 사고가 심각한 게 틀림없어.
▶ 사건의 심각성을 미루어 짐작하는 내용이므로 추측을 나타내는 must be를 쓴다.

3 실례합니다. 이것 좀 도와주시겠어요?
▶ 상대방에게 요청할 때는 조동사 would를 쓴다.

4 영화관에 가지 않는 게 좋겠어. 해야 할 일이 매우 많아.
▶ 영화관에 갈지 말지를 선택하는 것이므로 would rather not을 고른다.

5 여권과 다른 신분증을 볼 수 있을까요?
▶ 상대방의 허락을 구하는 조동사인 may를 고른다.

6 내가 예전 것의 복사본을 가지고 있으니까 우리는 새 양식에 기입할 필요가 없다.
▶ 불필요에 해당하므로 need not이 적절하다.

7 그 휴대 전화는 결함이 있었다. 그녀는 그것을 교환했어야 했는데 그러지 않았다.
▶ 여자가 휴대 전화를 교환하지 않았음에 대한 유감을 나타내는 표현이다.

8 아직 소포를 받지 못했다. 아마도 다른 주소로 배달됐을지도 모르겠다.
▶ 소포가 잘못된 주소로 배달된 것 같다며 미루어 짐작하는 내용이다.

B 1 그가 내게 전화해 주지 않았다. 내게 화가 난 게 분명하다.
▶ 내용상 추측을 나타내는 조동사를 찾는다.

2 서두를 필요 없어. 기차 타기까지 시간이 충분해.
▶ 내용상 '~할 필요가 없다'라는 뜻이다.

3 누구나 열심히 한다면 외국어를 마스터할 수 있다.
▶ 가능성을 나타내는 조동사를 찾는다.

4 코너 근처에 주유소가 있었다. 하지만, 지금도 거기에 있는지는 잘 모르겠다.
▶ '전에는 ~했었다'라는 뜻의 조동사가 필요하다. 단, 상태를 나타내는 would는 쓸 수 없다.

5 오늘 밤 영화관에서 만날까?
▶ '우리 ~할까요?'라는 뜻이므로 shall we를 쓴다.

6 그녀는 그 사고 소식을 듣고 충격을 받았던 게 틀림없다. 그녀는 기절했다.
▶ 과거 사실에 대한 추측을 나타내는 문장이다.

7 몇몇 사람들은 일찍 떠날 수 있으니 모든 사람의 저녁 식사를 준비할 필요는 없다.
▶ 내용상 '~할 필요가 없다'라는 뜻이다. 조동사 need의 부정은 need not이다.

C 1 그는 지금 바로 이것의 값을 치러야 합니까?
▶ need가 조동사 의문문으로 쓰인 형태이다. 따라서 need 다음에는 동사원형이 와야 한다.

2 나는 고등학교에 다닐 때 세 가지 악기를 연주할 수 있었다.
▶ '고등학교에 다닐 때'는 과거의 일이므로 be동사의 과거시제인 was를 써야 한다.

3 Rachel, 나한테 20달러 빌려 줄 수 있니?
▶ 상대방에게 요청을 할 때 쓰는 조동사는 will/would, can/could 등이다.

4 그녀와는 개인적으로 얘기하지 않는 게 좋겠어. 그녀는 누구에게나 무척 무례해.
▶ would rather의 부정은 would rather not이다.

5 요전 날 우리는 공이 없어서 경기를 시작할 수가 없었다.
▶ couldn't는 과거 표현이므로 was가 돼야 한다.

D

간혹 사람들은 정치 문제로 화를 낸다. 그러나 Will Rogers는 정치를 소재로 사람들을 웃게 만들 수 있었다. 그는 유명한 미국인이며, 오클라호마 출신의 지혜롭고 재미난 카우보이였다. 그는 어떤 것에 관해서든 얘기할 수 있었고 사람들이 웃으면서 그 일에 관해 생각할 수 있게끔 했다. 그는 공식적으로 특정 정당을 지지하지는 않았다. 그는 모든 정치인들이 바른 일을 하도록 조언했다. 그는 정치인들이 말을 많이 하지 말고 열심히 일해야 한다고 말했다.

▶ (A) 과거의 일이므로 was able to (B) '이야기할 수 있었다'라는 뜻이므로 could (C) '일해야 한다'는 뜻이므로 should

FURTHER STUDY [Writing]

P. 51

1 rather find another bus schedule
2 couldn't[could not] sleep because of the lamplight
3 you mustn't[must not] sell
4 will never be able to arrive on time
5 ought to move into her new apartment
6 Shall I carry your bags
7 She would rather make a chocolate cake
8 don't have to keep the papers, had better recycle

WRAP-UP TEST

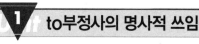

P. 53

1 ⓓ 2 ⓒ 3 ⓑ 4 ⓓ
5 ⓓ 6 ⓑ 7 ⓐ 8 ⓒ
9 over $200
10 ⓒ

1 티켓을 보여주시겠어요?
▶ 요청을 할 때 사용하는 조동사로 will, can, could는 쓸 수 있지만 should는 충고, 권유, 의무를 나타낸다.

2 속삭일 필요 없어요. 더 크게 말해 주세요.
▶ don't have to는 need not과 같은 뜻이다.

3 ▶ 금지를 나타내는 조동사는 must이다.

4 ▶ ⓐⓑⓒ는 '해야 한다'는 뜻이지만 ⓓ는 '~일지도 모른다'라는 추측을 뜻한다.

5 ⓐ 그는 이탈리아 출신임이 틀림없어. ⓑ 그녀가 Susan일 리가 없어. Susan은 파리에 갔어. ⓒ 그 파일을 다운로드 하지마. 바이러스에 감염된 것일 수도 있어. ⓓ 여기 근처에 절이 있었다.
▶ would는 과거의 상태를 나타낼 때는 쓸 수 없다. 여기서는 used to가 적절하다.

6 할아버지는 점심 식사 후에 낮잠을 주무시곤 했다. ⓐ 이 복사기를 사용하실래요? ⓑ 내 친구와 나는 방과 후에 함께 모이곤 했다. ⓒ 내가 너라면 문을 잠글 텐데. ⓓ 내가 너에게 나중에 말하겠다고 말했어.
▶ 주어진 문장의 밑줄 친 부분은 과거의 습관을 나타내고 있다. ⓑ 과거의 습관

7 ⓐ 그것이 사실일까? ⓑ John과 통화를 할 수 있을까요? ⓒ 문 좀 열어주시겠어요? ⓓ 우산 좀 빌려줄래?
▶ ⓑⓒⓓ는 부탁/요청의 뜻인데 ⓐ는 추측을 나타내고 있다.

8 A: Mark가 어디 있는지 알아?
B: ⓐ 그의 룸메이트에게 물어보는 게 좋을 것 같아. ⓑ 테니스 동아리에 갔을지도 몰라. ⓒ 그는 집에 있었어야 하는데. ⓓ 십 분 후에 여기로 올 것 같아.
▶ 〈should have p.p.〉는 과거에 하지 못한 일에 대한 후회를 나타내므로 Mark가 어디 있는지에 대한 질문의 응답이 될 수 없다.

[9-10]

많은 사람들이 에너지 절약 방법에 관해 생각해왔다. (그 중) 한 방법은 가정집에서 불필요한 전등을 끄는 일이다. 이제는 새로 나온 '발광 다이오드 전구(LED)'가 에너지를 좀 더 절약할 수 있도록 도울 수 있다. 만약 이 전구를 사용한다면 3분의 2정도 에너지를 덜 사용하게 될 것이다. 또한 (이 전구는) 10배 정도 오래 지속된다. 사람들은 이 새로운 에너지 절약형 전구를 사용해야 한다. 만약 10개의 전구를 사용한다면 당신은 일 년에 200달러의 에너지 비용을 절약하게 될 것이다.

10 ▶ '사람들이 이 새로운 전구를 사용해야 한다'는 뜻이 적절하므로 should나 must가 적절하다.

Unit 04

1 to부정사의 명사적 쓰임

Pre-Check

P. 56

To read

Check-up

P. 57

A 1 To go
2 to draw paintings
3 to put the books
4 to watch parades

B ① where to ② who to call
③ which articles to read

EXERCISE

P. 58

A 1 to be 2 to buy
3 to build 4 To go
5 to invite 6 to buy
7 to solve

B 1 buy 2 to get
3 ○ 4 ○
5 not to miss 6 to invite
7 where to go

C 1 It is important to forgive quickly.
2 It is exciting to make new friends.
3 It is great to be kind to others.
4 It is bad for your health to eat junk food late at night.
5 It is necessary to exercise regularly for a healthy life.

B 1 to부정사는 〈to + 동사원형〉이다.
2 expect는 목적어로 to부정사를 취한다.
5 to부정사를 부정할 때는 to 앞에 not을 둔다.
6 〈how many ~ to부정사〉 구문이다.
7 〈의문사 + to부정사〉의 구문이다.

2 to부정사의 부사적 쓰임

Pre-Check

P. 59

1 to do 2 to meet 3 to hear

Check-up

P. 60

A 1 to give 2 to become
3 to eat 4 to discover

B 1 ⓑ 2 ⓐ

EXERCISE
P. 61

A 1 to hear　2 to work
3 to witness　4 to lose
5 to know　6 to miss
7 to drive

B 1 so that he can stay healthy
2 in order to look fashionable
3 too young to enter the contest
4 quiet enough to sleep
5 so that she can celebrate my parents' 25th wedding anniversary

Unit 3 to부정사의 형용사적 쓰임

Pre-Check
P. 62

1 ① cold　② to drink
2 ① available　② to stay

Check-up
P. 63

A 1 to play with
2 someone to fix
3 a hotel to stay in
4 to complain about
5 are to leave

B ① b　② a

EXERCISE
P. 64

A 1 for　2 up　3 about
4 to　5 with

B 1 to do
2 to visit my sister
3 to write about

C 1 is to eat out at the Italian restaurant
2 someone positive to work with
3 is looking for a hotel to stay in
4 for the train to leave
5 big enough for us to get in

Unit 4 기타 부정사의 쓰임 & 원형 부정사

Pre-Check
P. 65

1 of　2 for　3 wash

Check-up
P. 66

A 1 paint　2 play/playing
3 (to) wash　4 jump/jumping
5 do

B 1 fix, fixed　2 squeeze, squeezed

EXERCISE
P. 67

A 1 write　2 (to) move
3 make/making

B 1 ○　2 call/calling
3 take　4 of you
5 to help　6 (to) make

C 1 made me do
2 saw the man break into
3 saw a gray mouse run into
4 useful for students to participate in
5 heard my sister talking
6 wants me to take

B 2 지각동사 hear는 목적격보어로 원형부정사나 현재분사가 온다.
3 사역동사 make는 목적격보어로 원형부정사를 취한다.
4 칭찬의 의미가 담긴 형용사의 경우, to부정사의 의미상 주어는 〈of + 사람〉으로 한다.
5 앞에서 happy가 왔으므로 to부정사의 부사적 쓰임 중 감정의 원인을 나타낸다.
6 help는 목적격보어로 원형부정사나 to부정사를 취할 수 있다.

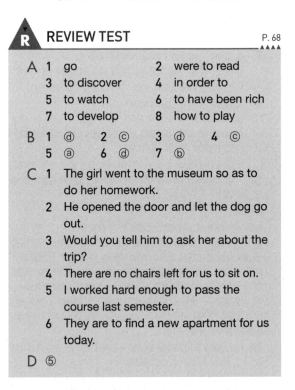

R REVIEW TEST
P. 68

A 1 go　2 were to read
3 to discover　4 in order to
5 to watch　6 to have been rich
7 to develop　8 how to play

B 1 ⓓ　2 ⓒ　3 ⓓ　4 ⓒ
5 ⓐ　6 ⓓ　7 ⓑ

C 1 The girl went to the museum so as to do her homework.
2 He opened the door and let the dog go out.
3 Would you tell him to ask her about the trip?
4 There are no chairs left for us to sit on.
5 I worked hard enough to pass the course last semester.
6 They are to find a new apartment for us today.

D ⑤

A 1 Karen은 Mike에게 가게에 가서 우유를 사 오게 했다.
▶ have동사가 '누구에게 ~하게 하다'라는 뜻의 사역동사로 쓰일 때는 목적격보어로 동사원형을 취한다.

2 우리는 캔자스시티의 의문의 산타에 관한 이야기를 읽게 되었다.
▶ 〈be to부정사〉 구문이다.

3 그 잠수부는 굴에서 아름다운 진주를 찾아내려고 했다.
▶ to부정사의 부사적 쓰임 중 목적을 나타낸다.

4 우리 오빠에게 줄 여분의 음료수 하나를 더 사 줄래요?
▶ so that이 오려면 뒤에 주어와 동사가 모두 있어야 한다.

5 그녀가 관람하기 가장 좋아하는 이벤트는 올림픽 아이스 댄싱 경기이다.
▶ 명사를 꾸미는 to부정사의 형용사적 쓰임이다.

6 그는 40대 초반에는 부유했던 것처럼 보인다.
▶ '과거에 ~했던 것으로 보인다'는 뜻이므로 완료부정사로 쓴다.

7 우리의 바람은 훌륭한 축구 선수팀을 만들어내는 것이다.
▶ 보어로 쓰인 to부정사의 명사적 쓰임이다.

8 그는 나에게 이 게임을 하는 법을 묻지 않았다.
▶ play의 목적어로 this game이 있으므로 what이 오면 안 된다.

B 1 그는 내 점심 값을 가져가서는 다시 돌려주지 않았다.
▶ to부정사의 부정은 to부정사 앞에 not[never]을 붙인다.

2 나는 이 학교에서 장학금을 받을 기회를 원했다.
▶ 앞의 a chance를 꾸며주는 형용사적 쓰임이다.

3 영화를 보면 그는 놀랄 것이다.
▶ 감정의 원인을 나타내는 형용사와 함께 쓰여 '~하다니 …이다'라는 뜻이다.

4 정오까지 거기 가려면, 전철역을 빨리 찾으세요.
▶ 의도의 〈be to부정사〉 용법이다.

5 선생님은 학생들에게 새 컴퓨터 프로그램에 대해 도와달라고 했다.
▶ 목적격보어로 원형부정사(help)가 쓰였으므로, 사역동사 let이 적절하다.

6 당신에게 할 말이 아주 많아요.
▶ talk about은 '~에 대해 이야기하다'라는 표현이다.

7 그녀는 오늘 학교에 갈 수 있다고 말했지만, 여전히 아파 보인다.
▶ 현재 아직도 아픈 것처럼 보인다고 했으므로 단순 현재 시제의 to부정사가 적절하다.

C 1 그녀는 숙제를 하기 위해 박물관에 갔다.
▶ '~하기 위해'라는 뜻의 to부정사 쓰임이므로 in order to나 so as to로 고친다.

2 그는 문을 열고 개를 밖으로 나가도록 했다.
▶ 사역동사 let은 목적격보어로 동사원형을 취하므로 go out으로 고친다.

3 그녀한테 여행에 관해 물어보라고 그에게 이야기해 주시겠어요?
▶ 〈동사 + 목적어 + to부정사〉의 구문이다. tell의 목적어로 소유격이 아니라 목적격이 와야 한다.

4 우리가 앉을 의자가 남아있지 않았다.
▶ sit at chairs가 아니라 sit on chairs가 옳다.

5 나는 지난 학기에 그 과정에 합격할 만큼 충분히 열심히 공부했다.
▶ '~할 만큼 충분히'라는 뜻이므로 〈enough to부정사〉를 쓴다.

6 그들은 오늘 우리를 위해 새 아파트를 찾을 예정이다.
▶ 〈be to부정사〉 용법 중 '예정'을 나타낸다.

D

사람들은 전 세계 곳곳에서 금을 찾아 왔다. 금을 찾는 방법에는 몇 가지가 있다. 첫 번째 방법은 사금을 파내서 체를 치는 것이다. 이것은 어렵고 시간이 많이 드는 방법이다. 이 기술로는 제한된 양의 금밖에 얻을 수 없다. 두 번째 방법이 좀 더 효과적이다. 이 방법은 강의 한 가운데 보트를 띄워서 강바닥에서 사금과 금덩어리를 진공으로 빨아들이는 것이다.

▶ (A) ways를 수식하는 to부정사의 명사적 쓰임으로 to search (B) '파는 것'이라는 뜻의 보어로 to dig (C) '진공으로 빨아들이는 것'이라는 뜻의 보어로 to vacuum

FURTHER STUDY [Writing]

P. 70

1 impossible for you to master tap dance
2 for Americans to eat turkey
3 kind of her to say
4 in order not to miss the concert
5 hard enough to win the championship
6 set the alarm, not to be late for the flight
7 She heard a cat cry/crying
8 my husband pick our daughter up

W WRAP-UP TEST

P. 72

1 to sleep 2 ⓓ 3 ⓑ
4 ⓑ 5 ⓐ
6 so easy to find his house
7 ⓒ 8 ⓐ 9 ⓑ
10 watch the actors rehearse

1 나는 네가 자는 척하고 있다는 것을 알고 있다.
▶ pretend 다음에는 to부정사가 온다.

2 ▶ postpone은 다음에는 동명사가 온다.

3 A: 오늘 밤에 영화 보러 가는 게 어때?
B: 미안한데 오늘은 나갈 수가 없어. 할 일이 매우 많거든.
A: 걱정 마. 내가 일하는 거 도와줄게.
▶ ⓑ afford 다음에는 to부정사가 온다.

4 ⓐ 나는 그가 우리가 그와 함께 가기를 기대했다는 것을 안다. ⓑ 그들은 나에게 모든 짐을 가져오게 했다. ⓒ 이 종이를 철하는 것을 도와주시겠어요? ⓓ 우리는 모두 그 문제에 대해서 분명히 설명하지 못했다.
▶ made는 사역동사로 목적격보어 자리에 동사원형이 온다.

5 그런 결정을 하다니 너는 정말 현명하다.
나에게는 규칙적으로 일기를 쓰는 것이 중요하다.
▶ 의미상의 주어를 묻고 있다. wise 다음에는 of, important 다음에는 for가 온다.

6 그의 집을 찾는 것은 쉬웠다.
▶ 가주어 It이 앞으로 올 때에는 to부정사구가 뒤에 위치한다.

7 그녀는 너무 긴장해서 운전을 할 수가 없었다.

▶ too ~ to 용법은 so that S can't로 바꿔 쓸 수 있다. 여기서는 시제가 과거이므로 couldn't가 왔다.

8 우리는 산 정상에 도착하기를 원했다.

ⓐ 그녀는 단것을 먹지 않기로 결심했다. ⓑ 나는 캐나다로 가는 비행편을 확인하기 위해 웹사이트를 방문했다. ⓒ 모두 시작할 준비 되었나요? ⓓ 냉장고에 뭔가 먹을 것이 있지 않나요?

▶ 명사(목적어) ⓐ 명사(목적어) ⓑ 부사(목적) ⓒ 부사(형용사 수식) ⓓ 형용사(부사 수식)

[9-10]

영화 제작은 굉장한 협동을 요하는 예술 형식이다. 전적으로 혼자 이미지를 창조해내는 사진사나 화가와는 다르다. 많은 사람들이 이야기를 전하는 영화를 만들기 위해 모인다. 영화 촬영기사로서, 나는 배우들이 리허설하는 것을 보고, 그 이야기의 각 순간에 알맞은 분위기를 만들어낸다. 빛과 색을 사용하여 나는 그 이야기에 맞는 눈에 보이는 언어를 창조해낸다. 나는 영화가 시각 예술 중 가장 강력한 것이라고 믿는다. 영화는 오락거리 이상인 것이다.

9 ▶ 부사적 쓰임의 to부정사가 들어가야 한다.

10 나는 촬영기사로서 무엇을 하는가?

→ 나는 배우들이 리허설하는 것을 보고 분위기를 만들어낸다.

Unit 05

1 동명사의 여러 가지 쓰임

Pre-Check P. 74

dancing

Check-up P. 75

A 1 Performing 2 reading
3 baking 4 writing

B 1 ① P ② G 2 ① G ② P
3 ① P ② G

EXERCISE P. 76

A 1 enjoy reading
2 helping me
3 forming a band
4 Having fun on weekends

B 1 ○ 2 giving
3 telling 4 ○
5 is 6 sitting

C 1 Collecting baseball cards
2 Having studied Tom's notes
3 Writing an essay
4 Being chosen president of the club
5 Seeing my baby cousin

B 2 전치사의 목적어로는 명사나 동명사가 온다.
3 keep은 동명사를 목적어로 취한다.
5 동명사구 주어는 단수 취급한다.
6 mind는 동명사를 목적어로 취한다.

2 동명사 vs. 부정사

Pre-Check P. 77

1 playing 2 to watch
3 to lock

Check-up P. 78

A 1 to be 2 sitting
3 buying 4 to go
5 doing 6 not to use

B 1 ⓑ 2 ⓐ

EXERCISE P. 79

A 1 to have 2 waiting for
3 to write 4 putting away
5 eating 6 to leave

B 1 to buy, asking 2 working, to let
3 to paint, to get 4 to delete, doing

C 1 denied informing me
2 suggested organizing a new club
3 mean to infer by that silly comment
4 gave up participating in the video game contest
5 pretended to enjoy her soup

3 동명사의 기타 쓰임

Pre-Check P. 80

1 having lunch
2 after finishing this work

Check-up P. 81

A 1 went shopping
2 worth buying
3 does not feel like playing
4 can't help complaining
5 for bringing

B 1 buying me the gift
2 wrapping the gift for me
3 paying for the gift

EXERCISE

P. 82

A 1 fishing 2 ○
3 from arriving 4 studying
5 worrying

B 1 good at heading
2 admit having cheated
3 busy helping others
4 feel like playing badminton with us
5 It is no use blaming

C 1 grumbling
2 practicing the piano
3 seeing his new movie
4 sitting in a smoking area

A 1 '~하러 가다'는 go -ing이다.
3 〈prevent+목적어+from -ing〉는 '목적어가 ~하지 못하게 하다'라는 표현이다.
4 〈be used to -ing〉는 '~하는 데 익숙하다'라는 표현이다.
5 〈can't help -ing〉의 형태로 '~하지 않을 수 없다'라는 표현이다.

REVIEW TEST

P. 83

A 1 hearing 2 to receive
3 to rent 4 playing
5 Being selected 6 taking
7 on 8 on

B 1 ⓐ 2 ⓑ 3 ⓑ 4 ⓒ
5 ⓒ 6 ⓑ 7 ⓓ

C 1 He pretended to be busy when I entered the room.
2 My best friend promised not to tell my secret to others.
3 Haven't you felt like taking a long walk recently?
4 The doctor advised my father to quit smoking as soon as possible.
5 I can't help wondering about the gift in the red box.
6 She is worried about changing the schedule after the notice.

D ⑤

A 1 선생님은 발표를 듣는 것을 다음 주 금요일까지 연기하셨다.
▶ postpone은 동명사를 목적어로 취한다.
2 학급 아이들은 졸업식에서 졸업장 받는 것을 기대하고 있다.
▶ expect는 to부정사를 목적어로 취한다.
3 나는 아내를 위해 DVD를 빌리기 위해 가게에 들렀다.
▶ 〈stop to부정사〉는 '~하기 위해 멈추다'이고, 〈stop V-ing〉는 '~하는 것을 멈추다'이다.
4 그는 선수권 대회에서 패한 후 축구 하는 것을 포기했다.
▶ give up은 동명사를 목적어로 취한다.
5 의장으로 뽑혔다는 것은 나에게는 예상치 못한 영광이었습니다.
▶ 주어가 되어야 하며, 의미상 수동의 동명사가 와야 한다.
6 당신의 즐거움 중 하나가 다른 나라로 여행을 가는 것입니까?
▶ is의 보어로 동명사가 와야 한다.
7 그 여배우는 자기가 직접 위험한 연기를 하겠다고 우겼다.
▶ 〈insist on V-ing〉는 '~할 것을 우기다'이다.
8 그 소녀는 밤새 노래를 계속했다.
▶ '계속 ~하다'는 〈keep on V-ing〉로 표현한다.

B 1 기침은 일반적인 감기의 증상으로 바이러스에 의해 야기된다.
▶ 주어의 자리이므로 To cough나 Coughing이 와야 한다.
2 나는 제때에 책을 반납하는 것을 깜빡했다. 그래서 연체료를 지불해야 했다.
▶ 반납해야 하는 것을 깜빡한 것이므로 forget 뒤에 to부정사가 와야 한다.
3 그것을 함으로써 당신은 여기서 무엇을 이루고 싶은가?
▶ 뒤에 동사원형이 왔으므로 want to가 와야 한다.
4 나는 매운 음식을 잘 먹지 못한다.
▶ be accustomed to 뒤에는 동명사가 와야 한다.
5 Kenny는 학기 마지막 날에 소풍을 가자고 제안했다.
▶ suggest는 동명사를 목적어로 취한다.
6 학생들은 야외 수업에 익숙하지 않다.
▶ 〈be used to -ing〉는 '~하는 데 익숙하다'라는 표현이다.
7 당신의 교수법을 지켜본 것이 제가 더 좋은 교사가 되는 데 도움이 되었습니다.
▶ 주어가 help보다 한 시제 앞선 것이므로 완료동명사를 쓴다.

C 1 그는 내가 방에 들어갔을 때 바쁜 척 했다.
▶ pretend는 to 부정사를 목적어로 취한다.
2 나와 가장 친한 친구는 다른 사람들에게 내 비밀을 말하지 않겠다고 약속했다.
▶ to부정사의 부정은 to부정사 앞에 부정어가 온다.
3 최근에 산책하고 싶지 않았니?
▶ 앞에 Haven't가 왔으므로 p.p. 형태가 와야 한다.
4 의사는 아빠에게 가능한 한 빨리 담배를 끊으라고 조언했다.
▶ quit은 동명사를 목적어로 취한다.
5 나는 그 빨간 상자 안의 선물이 무척 궁금했다.
▶ '~하지 않을 수 없다'는 〈can't help V-ing〉이다.
6 그녀는 공지 후에 일정을 바꾸는 것에 대해 걱정했다.
▶ 〈be worried about -ing〉 형태로 써야 한다.

D

이란 태생의 미국인인 Ansari는 그녀의 나이 16세 때 미국으로 왔다. 그녀는 과학 분야에서 자신의 열정을 이뤄내고 싶어 했다. 이제 그녀의 꿈이 이루어질지도 모른다. 그녀는 우주로 가는 최초의 여성이 되기 위해 자신이 벌어들인 많은 돈을 지불했다. 그녀는 우주여행을 하는 첫 번째 여성이 될 것이다. 그녀는 몇 가지 테스트 후에 러시아 우주 비행 임무를 띠고 우주여행을 하게 될 것으로 기대된다.

▶ (A) want는 to부정사를 목적어로 취하므로 to pursue
(B) expect는 to부정사를 목적으로 취하므로 to fly
(C) 전치사 뒤에는 동명사가 오므로 taking

FURTHER STUDY [Writing]

P. 85

1 do not feel like going to the party
2 mind seeing the movie
3 prevented me from driving
4 insisted on preparing dinner
5 clean your room after finishing your homework
6 leave without calling
7 complained about wrapping all of the boxes
8 having broken her mug

WRAP-UP TEST

P. 87

1 ⓒ 2 ⓒ 3 ⓒ 4 ⓒ
5 eating, to study
6 ⓒ 7 ⓓ 8 ⓒ 9 ⓑ
10 enjoy playing, not to use

1 A: 충치가 있는 것 같아. 정말 아파.
B: 치과에 가는 게 어때?
▶ 전치사 about 다음에는 동명사가 와야 한다.

2 그녀는 호텔 매니저와 얘기하고 싶다고 요구했다.
▶ ⓒ 전치사 다음에는 동명사가 오므로 talking이 돼야 한다.

3 ▶ 〈Do you mind ~〉는 '~해도 될까요?'라는 뜻이다.

4 ⓐ Sam은 팝콘서트에 가자고 제안했다. ⓑ Sarah는 항상 불평을 한다. ⓒ 나는 그 과정을 포기하지 않기로 결심했다. ⓓ 네 건강을 위해서 가장 좋은 것은 규칙적으로 운동을 하는 것이다.
▶ ⓒ decide는 to부정사를 목적어로 취한다.

5 우리 어머니는 저녁 식사 후에 항상 블랙커피를 마신다.
너는 올해 더 열심히 공부해야 한다.
▶ 전치사 after 다음에는 동명사가 와야 한다. need는 to부정사를 목적어로 취한다.

6 그 남자는 실정을 잘 모르면서 할 수 있다고 말했다.
나는 사람들 앞에서 연설을 하는 것에 익숙하지 않다.
▶ '~한 채로 라는 뜻으로 without이 적절하다. 〈be used to 동명사〉는 '~에 익숙하다'는 뜻이다.

7 선생님께서 영어 신문을 읽는 것은 영어를 배우는 데 도움이 된다고 했다. ⓐ 우리 모두 John 삼촌과 낚시를 가는 것을 좋아했다. ⓑ 나는 그가 제 시간에 도착할지 확신할 수 없다. ⓒ 내가 가장 좋아하는 취미는 만화책을 읽는 것이다. ⓓ 텔레비전 드라마를 보는 것은 내 취미 중 하나이다.
▶ 주어 ⓐ 목적어 ⓑ 전치사의 목적어 ⓒ 보어 ⓓ 주어

8 Jim은 그것을 성공적으로 마쳐서 만족했다.
▶ 주절이 과거시제이고 이보다 더 이전 시제를 표현하기 위해서 〈having p.p.〉 구문을 사용했다.

[9~10]
나는 다음 주에 중요한 시험이 있다. 그래서 나는 시험 전에 인터넷 사용을 자제하리라 계획했다. 나는 인터넷 게임을 즐기지만 이런 게임들은 공부에 방해가 될 수 있다. 그래서 나는 한동안 집에서는 컴퓨터를 사용하지 않기로 결심했다. 만약 공부하는 데 컴퓨터를 사용해야 한다면 대신 도서관에서 사용할 수 있을 것이다. 이렇게 하면 인터넷 서핑하기보다 공부하는 데 도움이 될 것이다.

9 ⓐ 나는 인터넷 게임을 하는 것이 익숙하지 않다.
ⓑ 나는 컴퓨터가 공부하는 것을 방해한다고 생각한다.
ⓒ 나는 TV를 보는 것보다 인터넷 게임을 좋아한다.
ⓓ 나는 시험을 통과한 후로 집에서 컴퓨터를 사용하지 않을 것이다.

Unit 06

1 현재분사

Pre-Check

P. 90

1 interesting 2 reading
3 watching

Check-up

P. 91

A 1 calling/call 2 blowing
3 running/run 4 talking/talk
5 playing

B the guy standing by the door, the cooking man

EXERCISE

P. 92

A 1 P 2 G 3 P
4 G 5 P 6 G

B 1 players practicing
2 mouse running into
3 touching play
4 girl smiling at
5 person leaning against

C 1 walking to the post office
2 rolling into the street
3 working on our computers
4 sitting on the dealer's parking lot
5 speaking at today's meeting

A 1 명사 performance를 수식하는 현재분사이다.
2 dislike의 목적어로 쓰인 동명사이다.
3 명사 family를 수식하는 것으로 현재분사이다.
4 mind의 목적어로 쓰인 동명사이다.
5 명사 sound를 수식하는 현재분사이다.
6 washing machine은 a machine for washing으로 용도를 나타내는 〈동명사 + 명사〉로 굳어진 표현이다.

Unit 2 과거분사

Pre-Check
P. 93

1 ① exciting ② excited
2 ① hanging ② hung

Check-up
P. 94

A 1 painted 2 folded
3 delivered 4 returned
5 displeased

B ① bored ② exciting
③ exciting ④ excited

EXERCISE
P. 95

A 1 practicing 2 blocked
3 burning 4 broken
5 amazed 6 delayed

B 1 invited 2 made
3 canceled 4 confused
5 mended 6 frightened

C 1 entering the event
2 stored in the wooden boxes
3 removed from the shelf
4 released camera

A 1 '내 동생은 지금 뒤뜰에서 투구 연습을 하고 있는 중이다.'라는 진행의 의미이므로 현재분사를 고른다.
2 막고 있는 길이 아니라, 막힌 길이므로 과거분사를 쓴다.
3 내용상 '불타고 있는 빌딩'이어야 한다.
4 '깨진 파이프'라는 수동의 의미를 가지므로 과거분사를 쓴다.
5 학생들이 놀라는 감정을 느끼는 것이므로 과거분사가 적절하다.
6 flight는 사물이며 스스로 연착하는 것이 아니라 외부 요인에 의해 연기되는 것이므로 과거분사인 delayed를 쓴다.

Unit 3 분사의 다양한 표현

Pre-Check
P. 96

Because

Check-up
P. 97

A 1 Walking
2 Judging from
3 Amused/Being amused
4 Entering

B 1 ⓐ 2 ⓐ

EXERCISE
P. 98

A 1 Preparing 2 Confused
3 Coming 4 holding
5 Satisfied

B 1 Because 2 After
3 As 4 While
5 Since

C 1 Being in school
2 Winning the championship
3 Considering the circumstances
4 Folding her arms

A 1 After we prepared the holiday meal together.라는 종속절을 분사구문으로 만든 것이다. '우리'와 '준비하다'의 관계가 능동이기 때문에 현재분사 형태인 preparing이 적절하다.
2 그가 혼란스러움을 느낀 것이기 때문에 수동 의미인 confused를 고른다.
3 When they came to a bus stop을 분사구문으로 바꾼 것이다. '그들'과 '오다'의 관계가 능동이기 때문에 coming이 적절하다.
4 'as she held her sick~'을 분사구문 형태로 만든 것이다.
5 '성공에 만족하여~'라는 뜻이므로 과거분사인 satisfied를 쓴다.

R REVIEW TEST
P. 99

A 1 fascinated 2 amazed
3 While 4 interesting
5 pleasing 6 Being
7 Although 8 annoyed

B 1 ⓐ 2 ⓑ 3 ⓓ 4 ⓐ
5 ⓒ 6 ⓒ 7 ⓑ

C 1 She was so worried that she forgot to say that she would be late.
2 The missing wallet wasn't stolen. I found it under the bed.
3 Generally speaking, our class is not prepared to take the test.
4 Look at the completed puzzle. It must have been exhausting to put it together!
5 The singing bird was fascinating to Sunny. She was satisfied with this amazing discovery.
6 The artist drew an interesting woman who was standing by a locked door.

D ①

A 1 교사는 학생들이 인디언 부족의 역사에 매료되었다는 것을 알았다.
▶ 학생들이 인디언 부족의 역사에 매료된 것이므로 과거분사를 사용한다.
2 서커스를 보고 감탄한 사람들은 공연자들에게 박수를 쳤다.

▶ '놀람을 당한'이라는 수동의 의미이므로 과거분사인 amazed를 고른다.

3 운전 중에는 안전벨트를 꼭 매야 한다.
▶ 두 접속사 중 이 문장의 뜻과 어울리는 접속사는 '~하는 중'이라는 의미의 while이다.

4 학생들은 신문 기사가 자신들의 에세이 주제로 쓸만큼 충분히 흥미롭다는 것을 깨달았다.
▶ 기사가 흥미로운 것이므로 능동의 interesting을 고른다.

5 그들은 친구와 친척들을 기쁘게 한 예식에 만족했다.
▶ 예식(ceremony)이 기쁘게 해 준 것이므로 능동의 pleasing을 고른다.

6 너는 학생이기 때문에 나가기 전에 숙제를 다 끝내야 한다.
▶ Since you are a student ~를 분사구문으로 만든 것이다.

7 비록 바람이 매섭긴 했지만 그 바람은 우리를 상쾌하게 만들어 주었다.
▶ 양보 부사절을 이끄는 접속사 Although가 필요하다.

8 그녀의 전화에 짜증이 난 Jack은 그녀의 질문에 대답조차 하지 않으려 했다.
▶ Jack이 그녀의 전화로 인해 짜증이 난 것이기 때문에 과거분사를 쓴다.

B 1 날씨를 고려해 볼 때 회의를 취소하고 비가 그칠 때까지 여기서 기다리는 것이 더 낫겠다.
▶ considering은 '~을 고려하면'이라는 뜻을 가진 독립분사구문이다.

2 사무실에서 일하고 있는 남자들은 전화기를 수리하고 있다.
▶ '일하고 있는 남자(능동/진행)' 라는 뜻이므로 현재분사를 고른다.

3 신고를 받지 못했기 때문에, 경찰이 너무 늦게 도착해 범인을 체포하지 못했다.
▶ 신고를 받지 못한 것이 범인 체포를 위해 현장에 도착한 것보다 시제가 빠르므로 have를 사용했고 경찰은 신고를 '받는' 것이므로 수동형을 쓴다.

4 지금 떠나시면, 교통 체증이 덜 할 거예요.
▶ 조건을 나타내는 접속사 if를 고른다.

5 피로에 지친 탐험가들은 숲에서 쉴만한 장소를 찾았다.
▶ 탐험가들이 피로에 지쳐 있는 감정을 느끼는 것이므로 과거분사 형태가 적당하다.

6 교사 회의를 기획하면서 그녀는 아주 철저했다.
▶ When she planned~라는 종속절을 분사구문으로 만든 것으로 주어(she)와 plan의 관계가 능동이므로 planning을 고른다.

7 모두들 그들을 만날 준비가 되어 있었나요?
▶ '준비되다'는 완료의 뜻을 나타내므로 과거분사가 적당하다.

C 1 그녀는 너무 걱정이 되어서 그녀가 늦을 거라고 말하는 걸 잊어버렸다.
▶ 그녀가 말하는 것을 잊어버린 것이므로 능동이다. 또한 시제에 맞춰 과거시제인 forgot을 써야 한다.

2 (내가) 잃어버린 지갑은 도둑맞은 것이 아니었다. 나는 그것을 침대 밑에서 찾았다.
▶ 지갑은 훔침을 당하는 것이므로 수동의 의미인 과거분사를 써야 한다.

3 일반적으로 말하자면, 우리 반은 시험을 볼 준비가 되지 않았다.
▶ '일반적으로 말해서'라는 뜻을 가진 분사구문은 generally speaking이다.

4 저기 완성된 퍼즐을 봐. 퍼즐 맞추는 건 힘들 일이었을 거야!
▶ 퍼즐은 이미 완성된 것이므로 완료의 의미인 과거분사를 사용한다.

5 노래하는 새가 Sunny에게는 매혹적이었다. 그녀는 이 놀라운 발견에 대해 매우 만족했다.
▶ 그녀는 이 놀라운 발견으로 인해 만족감을 느낀 것이므로 과거분사로 쓴다. satisfy는 '~를 만족시키다'라는 뜻이고 'be satisfied with'로 쓰여 '만족하다'라는 뜻이 된다.

6 예술가는 잠긴 문 옆에 서 있던 흥미로운 여인을 그렸다.
▶ '잠긴 문'은 수동의 의미이므로 과거분사가 와야 한다.

D

중세 르네상스 박람회가 미시간에서 열렸다. 그 박람회에 참가한 리포터는 그가 방문했던 주말에 대해 글을 썼다. 그 굉장한 박람회를 참가하는 동안 그는 1560년대에서 온 것처럼 행세하는 여러 명의 흥미로운 사람들을 만났다. 샌드위치 백작을 만난 후, 여왕과 그녀의 중신들을 만날 수 있는 특권이 그에게 주어졌다. 몇 명의 기사들 사이에서 마상 창 시합을 보면서, 그는 그 경기가 계획된 것이 아닐까 하는 생각이 들었다.

▶ (A) '참가하는 동안'이라는 뜻이므로 While (B) '~인 체하면서'라는 뜻의 분사구문이므로 pretending (C) '~을 보면서'라는 뜻의 분사구문이므로 Watching

FURTHER STUDY [Writing]

P. 101

1 Rushing for the bus
2 downloaded the files, turned off
3 Turning right at the first corner
4 Walking down the street, selling old albums
5 Taking down
6 been away from her country
7 Driving the car, talk/talking about our team's loss
8 Knowing, asked him (to) help

WRAP-UP TEST

P. 103

1 ⓒ 2 ⓑ 3 ⓑ
4 Frankly speaking
5 ⓑ 6 ⓓ
7 ⓐ listening ⓑ stolen
8 ⓓ 9 ⓐ 10 Judging from

1 미국 영화가 전 세계적으로 얼마나 인기가 많은지 정말 놀랍다.
▶ '놀라운 일이다'라는 뜻이므로 능동의 형태가 적절하다.

2 A: 그 소식 들었어?
B: 응, 그의 발견에 우리 모두 기뻤어.
▶ 첫 번째 빈칸에는 현재완료 의문문이므로 p.p. 형태가 적절하

며, 두 번째 빈칸에는 기쁨을 느낀 것이므로 과거분사가 적절하다.

3 새 약을 받은 환자 중 몇 명은 더 빨리 회복되었다.
▶ 환자가 약을 받는 것이므로 과거분사는 patients 뒤에 와야 한다.

4 ▶ '솔직히 말해서'라는 뜻의 분사구문인 frankly speaking이 적절하다

5 그것을 고려한 후에 우리는 회의를 취소했다.
▶ 분사구문으로 의미상 '~한 후에'가 적절하므로 접속사 after가 적절하다.

6 ⓐ 밖에 비가 오니? ⓑ 내 남동생이 그때 컴퓨터를 수리하고 있었다. ⓒ 전화기가 울렸을 때 Matthew는 책을 읽고 있었다. ⓓ 나는 어제 침낭을 샀다.
▶ ⓐⓑⓒ는 현재분사이고 ⓓ는 동명사이다.

7 클래식 콘서트 연주를 듣는 몇몇 어린이들은 잠이 들었다. 어제 도난당한 차는 서울 부산 간 고속도로 어딘가에서 발견되었다
▶ ⓐ 어린이들이 연주를 듣는 것이므로 능동의 현재분사가 와야 한다. ⓑ 자동차가 도난을 당하는 것이므로 수동의 과거분사가 와야 한다.

8 ⓐ 그는 경기 후에 매우 피곤했다. ⓑ 그는 오른쪽 차선에서 운전하는 것에 익숙하지 않다. ⓒ 식사 전에 물을 마시는 것은 건강에 좋지 않다. ⓓ 울고 있는 아이는 열이 높았다.
▶ '울고 있는 아이'라는 뜻이므로 cried가 아니라 crying이 와야 한다.

[9-10]

관람객이 예술을 듣도록 장려하는 특별한 미술 전시회가 열렸다. 눈으로 보지 않고 예술을 듣게 하는 것이 예술가들의 의도였다. 예를 들면 나무 뒤 스피커를 통해 습지대 소리가 흘러 나왔다. 다른 예술 작품에는 음악을 연주하는 전화기도 있었다. 관람객의 의견으로 판단해보면, 그들은 상반된 반응을 보였다. 어떤 사람들은 그 소리가 즐거웠다고 했고, 어떤 사람들은 불쾌했다고 했다.

9 ▶ 특별한 전시회가 '열리는' 것이므로 created가 와야 한다.

Unit 07

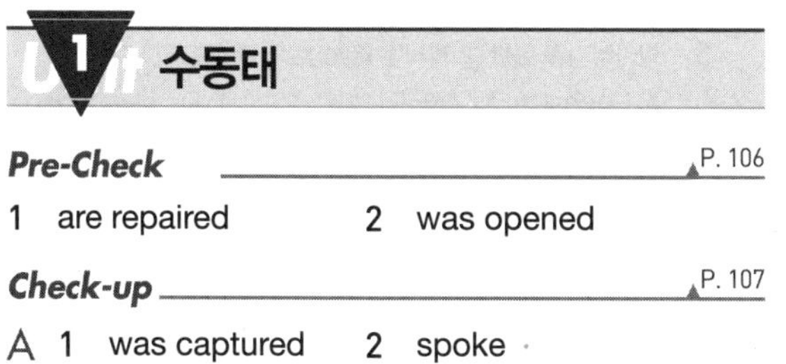

Unit 1 수동태

Pre-Check P. 106

1 are repaired 2 was opened

Check-up P. 107

A 1 was captured 2 spoke
3 was bought 4 was seen
5 moved 6 wasn't repaired

B ① bit ② have been bitten
③ sent ④ will be sent

EXERCISE P. 108

A 1 was demolished 2 was surprised
3 are taken 4 can be used
5 were frightened 6 are sent

B 1 by the police 2 was confused
3 ○ 4 were posted
5 irritated 6 will be performed

C 1 The big fire was put out
2 The broken bookcase has been fixed
3 The water pitchers are being filled
4 The operation on Tom's broken leg will be led
5 Will three more pies be baked

B 1 수동태에서 행위자는 〈by+목적격〉으로 나타낸다.
2 grandmother가 혼란스러움을 느낀(수동) 것이다. 따라서 수동태 문장이 되어야 한다. 수동태 형식은 〈be+p.p. (by+목적격)〉이다.
4 〈be+p.p.〉가 수동태 형식이다. 행위자가 일반인(we, they, people)인 경우나 행위자가 불특정하거나 확실하지 않을 경우, 문맥상의 주체가 명백한 경우는 생략이 가능하다.
5 〈be p.p.〉가 돼야 하므로 was irritated로 바꿔야 한다.
6 조동사의 수동태는 〈조동사+be+p.p.〉로 조동사는 그대로 둔다.

Unit 2 수동태의 여러 가지 형태

Pre-Check P. 109

1 The elders 2 Computer lessons

Check-up P. 110

A 1 to finish 2 was made for
3 painted 4 were fascinated by

B ① is tanned ② was burned
③ would be healed

EXERCISE P. 111

A 1 was made to prepare
2 was found by
3 have been bought
4 was felt by
5 was heard screaming
6 were satisfied with

B 1 by 2 ○
3 by him 4 by
5 It is said/People say

C 1 being treated 2 heard
3 be transferred 4 be given
5 be taught 6 was accustomed

B 1 by 이외의 전치사를 쓰는 수동태를 제외하고 수동태에서 행위자는 〈by + 목적격〉으로 나타낸다.

3 look after는 동사구이므로 한 단어로 취급한다. look after 다음에 〈by+행위자〉를 넣어야 한다.

4 The editor will correct the writing.이라는 3형식 문장을 수동태로 만든 것으로 행위자를 〈by + 목적격〉으로 나타낸다.

5 '~라고 한다'는 관용적으로 It is said (that) ~ 또는 People say(that) ~을 쓴다.

R REVIEW TEST

P. 112

A 1 was sold 2 are trained to
3 has been taught 4 to
5 making 6 to be taught
7 was covered with

B 1 ⓓ 2 ⓑ 3 ⓑ 4 ⓓ
5 ⓓ 6 ⓑ 7 ⓒ

C 1 These chocolates are made from the finest cocoa beans.
2 The children were not allowed to enter the hall.
3 I wanted to be admired like a movie star by lots of people.
4 Some books will be given to you by my father.
5 The party for her grandfather has been planned by Rachel.

D ⑤

A 1 그 공장은 1995에 그 회사에 의해 매각되었다.
▶ 1995년이라는 과거 시점이 명시되어 있으므로 과거시제를 쓴다.

2 많은 앵무새들은 3개월 안에 영어로 말하도록 훈련받는다.
▶ People train many parrots to speak ~ 이라는 5형식 문장을 수동태로 바꾼 문장이다. 목적어인 many parrots가 문장 앞으로 나가고, 동사가 〈be+ p.p.〉로 바뀌었으며 행위자가 일반인이어서 생략되었다.

3 그 남자는 새 소프트웨어를 사용하는 법을 배웠다.
▶ 가르침을 받은 것이므로 수동형을 쓴다.

4 그 이메일은 학생들이 유명 작가에게 쓴 것들이었다.
▶ The students wrote the emails to the famous author.라는 문장을 수동태로 만든 것이다. 이메일은 '그 작가에게' 쓴 것이므로 to를 고른다.

5 그 소녀가 전화 통화하는 것이 언니에 의해 목격되었다.
▶ My sister watched the girl making a phone call.이라는 5형식 문장을 수동태로 바꾼 것이다. 목적격보어가 분사인 경우에는 그대로 둔다.

6 학생들은 수업 시간에 다른 언어를 배우길 원했다.
▶ 학생들이 수업을 하는 것이 아니라, 수업을 받는 것이다. 그러므로 수동태를 고른다. want 다음에다 to부정사가 온다.

7 그 어린 소년은 젖은 운동장에서 온통 진흙을 뒤집어쓰고 있었다.
▶ be covered with는 '~로 덮여있다'라는 표현이다.

B 1 그 가게는 지난 10년 동안 문을 닫지 않았다.
▶ 시점이 10년 전부터 현재까지 이어지는 상태이므로 현재완료 시제를, 가게는 동작을 할 수 있는 주체가 아니기 때문에 수동태를 고른다.

2 지난해 전국적인 홍수로 인해 많은 사람들이 영향을 받았다.
▶ 시제는 '지난해'라고 명시되어 있으므로 과거형, 사람들이 홍수로 인해 피해를 입은 것이므로 수동태를 고른다.

3 디저트는 내일 그 요리사에 의해 만들어질 것이다.
▶ '내일'이므로 미래시제를, 디저트가 요리사에 의해 만들어지는 것이므로 수동태를 고른다.

4 이 연구는 2013년 11월부터 2014년 4월까지 계속되었다.
▶ 과거에 끝난 일이므로 과거시제를, 연구는 행위를 받는 대상이므로 수동태를 쓴다. carry on은 동사구이므로 한 단어로 취급한다.

5 당신의 비용은 다음 주에 완전히 처리될 것이다.
▶ take care of는 동사구이므로 한 단어로 취급해야 하고, 비용이 처리되는 것이기 때문에 수동태를 고른다.

6 고등학교 때부터 Green 씨는 시를 써왔다.
▶ 고등학교 때부터 현재까지 이어져 온 행위이므로 현재완료를, Green 씨는 시를 쓰는 행위의 주체이므로 능동태를 고른다.

7 사진에 관심이 있으시면, 주저하지 마시고 우리 동호회에 가입하세요.
▶ be interested in은 '~에 관심이 있다'라는 표현이다.

C 1 이 초콜릿은 최상급의 코코아 열매로 만들어진 것이다.
▶ '~로 만들어진'이라는 표현은 be made from(재료의 형태를 알아볼 수 없게 되었을 경우)과 be made of(재료의 형태를 보존하고 있는 경우)가 있다.

2 어린아이들은 강당 입장이 허락되지 않았다.
▶ let은 수동태 문장에서 쓰이지 않으므로 allowed로 바꾼다.

3 나는 영화배우처럼 많은 사람들로부터 존경받고 싶었다.
▶ 내가 존경을 하는 것이 아니라 존경을 받는 것이므로 수동태가 돼야 한다.

4 우리 아버지가 책 몇 권을 너에게 줄 것이다.
▶ 수동태에서 행위자는 〈by + 목적격〉으로 나타낸다.

5 할아버지를 위한 그 파티는 Rachel이 계획한 것이다.
▶ Rachel에 의해 파티가 계획된 것이므로 has planned를 has been planned로 고친다.

D

작년에 중국에서 영국인 동물 전문가에 의해 멸종 위기에 처한 두 종이 연구되고 있었다. 그는 인디아로리스 원숭이와 양쯔강 돌고래의 생존을 염려했다. 인디아로리스 원숭이는 멸종 위기에 처한 동물이다. 인디아로리스 원숭이는 흉조로 여겨졌다. 사람들은 그 원숭이를 두려워하기 때문에 그 원숭이를 죽이고 있다. 불행하게도, 이 동물 전문가는 양쯔강 돌고래는 한 마리도 발견할 수가 없었다. 이 돌고래 종을 살리기엔 너무 늦었는지도 모른다.

▶ (A) 연구되고 있다'라는 뜻이므로 were being studied
(B) 〈be concerned with〉 '~을 염려하다'라는 뜻이므로 with
(C) '~로 여겨지다'라는 뜻이므로 is considered

FURTHER STUDY [Writing]

P. 114

1 His face is known to
2 were excited by
3 is being treated in the animal hospital
4 are filled with
5 has been parked
6 gave, must be signed
7 Her plan will be discussed
8 was not surprised at the cost of the house

W WRAP-UP TEST

P. 116

1	ⓒ	2	is being introduced to				
3	ⓒ	4	should be paid				
5	ⓒ	6	was given, were given to				
7	ⓑ	8	ⓑ	9	ⓓ	10	ⓐ

1 A: 그 시는 언제 쓰였니?
B: ⓐ 그것은 내 동생에 의해 쓰였어. ⓑ 그것은 워드프로세서로 쓸 수 있어. ⓒ 그것은 어젯밤에 쓰였어. ⓓ 그것은 사랑에 대해 쓴 거야.
▶ when이 있으므로 시간과 관련된 부사가 있어야 한다.

2 사장님께서 비서를 모든 직원에게 소개하고 있다.
▶ 현재진행형의 수동태는 〈be + being + p.p.〉이다

3 ⓐ 그 소프트웨어는 Taylor에 의해 설치되었다. ⓑ 저녁이 Amy에 의해 준비되는 중이다. ⓒ 우리 마을에 박물관이 지어질 것이다. ⓓ '제인에어'는 Charlotte Bronte가 쓴 것이었다.
▶ ⓐⓑⓓ는 행위의 주체를 나타내는 by가 들어가야 하는데 ⓒ는 뒤에 장소가 나오므로 전치사 in이 적절하다.

4 A: 납부 기한이 언제인가요?
B: 이번 달 말까지 지불되어야 합니다.
▶ 조동사의 수동태는 〈조동사 + be + p.p.〉이다.

5 ⓐ 나는 그의 변명이 지겹다. ⓑ 네 성적에 실망하지 않았니? ⓒ 링컨 대통령은 게티스버그 연설로 유명하다. ⓓ 버스는 러시아워 시간에 많은 학생과 직장인들로 가득 찼다.
▶ 문맥상 '~으로 유명하다'가 적절하므로 be known for가 적절하다.

6 Teddy는 나에게 장미 한 다발을 주었다.
▶ 4형식 문형의 수동태이다.

[7-8]

7 ⓐ 그 작은 소년은 코트를 입었다. ⓑ 그 개가 방에 들어가는 것이 허락되었다. ⓒ 이 공문은 학장에게 쓴 것이다.
ⓓ 그 여성의 가방에서 지갑을 가져가는 것이 목격되었다.
▶ 사역동사 let은 수동태로 쓰지 않는다.

8 ⓐ 그 팀은 그 과정을 8월 4일까지 끝낼 계획이다. ⓑ 그 조사는 11월부터 12월까지 실행되었다. ⓒ 그 벽은 폭풍 때문에 붕괴되었다. ⓓ 모든 소년 소녀에게 윗몸일으키기를 하게 했다.
▶ The survey는 실행하는 것이 아니라 실행되는 것이므로 수동태가 와야 한다.

[9-10]

최근, 암사슴 한 마리가 오클라호마 호수의 얼음 위에 꼼짝없이 갇히는 사건이 발생했다. 그 불쌍한 동물은 거의 동사 직전에 있었다. 곧이어 TV 뉴스 헬리콥터가 그 겁먹은 사슴 위에 나타났고, 놀라운 일이 발생했다. 그 헬리콥터가 일으킨 바람으로 인해 사슴은 미끄러운 얼음을 가로질러 호숫가 가장자리로 밀려나기 시작했다. 암사슴은 호숫가에 다다르자 폴짝 뛰어 달아났다. 모두가 놀랐지만 운이 좋은 그 사슴으로 인해 정말 행복했다.

9 ▶ 주체가 된 everyone이 놀란 것이므로 수동태가 되어야 한다. everyone은 단수 취급한다.

10 ▶ 처음에 사슴은 동사 직전에 있었지만 헬기 덕분에 무사하게 되었다.

Unit 08

1 명사

Pre-Check

P. 118

1 My sister and I watched a movie last night on TV.
2 Have you ever been to Canada?
3 What would you like to drink, coffee or tea?
4 What is the most important thing in your life?

Check-up

P. 119

A 1 room 2 people
3 plays 4 hours
5 a lot of

B ① some ② a cup of
③ much

EXERCISE

P. 120

A 1 a lot of 2 a few
3 times 4 much
5 trip 6 lots of
7 cheese

B 1 water 2 much
3 ○ 4 ○
5 many 6 a lot of/lots of/many
7 a way

C 1 many bottles of 2 two bowls of
3 a few slices of 4 a bag of
5 a teaspoon of 6 four glasses of
7 two cartons of

B 1 '물은 생명에 필수불가결한 것이다'라고 할 때의 water는 셀 수 없는 물질명사이므로 a(n)을 쓰지 않는다.
2 '병 속에 담겨 있는 상태'에서의 wine은 셀 수 없는 물질명사이다. 따라서 셀 수 있는 명사와 함께 쓰이는 many를 쓸 수 없다.
5 '여러 번 전화했다'라는 뜻으로 전화한 것을 횟수로 셀 수 있으므로 many를 쓴다.
6 셀 수 있는 명사(books)가 왔으므로 〈a lot of/lots of/many + 명사〉의 형태로 쓸 수 있다.
7 여기서 way는 수로 셀 수 있는 '방법, 방식' 이라는 뜻이다. 동사가 단수이므로 a way가 알맞다.

Unit 2 관사

Pre-Check P. 121

1 a　　2 the
3 Ø, Ø

Check-up P. 122

A 1 Ø　　2 the
3 a　　4 the
5 the

B ① the　　② the
③ the

EXERCISE P. 123

A 1 ⓐ　　2 ⓓ
3 ⓒ　　4 ⓑ

B 1 a glass　　2 the one
3 baseball　　4 ○
5 the tool　　6 ○

C 1 soccer　　2 the time
3 car　　4 the only reason
5 the last person

B 1 '물 한 잔'을 의미하므로 glass 앞에 a를 붙인다.
2 one이 뒤에 나오는 수식어구로 한정되어 있으므로 a 대신 정관사 the를 쓴다.
3 운동 경기 앞에는 관사를 쓰지 않는다.
5 '어제 너에게 준 도구'라고 한정하고 있으므로 정관사 the를 쓴다.

Unit 3 대명사

Pre-Check P. 124

① mine　　② myself
③ us　　④ ours
⑤ your　　⑥ you
⑦ his/her/its　　⑧ they

Check-up P. 125

A 1 her　　2 Your
3 him　　4 I
5 its

B ① Dell　　② People

EXERCISE P. 126

A 1 itself　　2 his
3 my　　4 by myself
5 he　　6 himself
7 She

B 1 herself　　2 that
3 those　　4 he
5 ours　　6 myself

C 1 his　　2 ○
3 us　　4 our
5 that　　6 your
7 these boxes

C 1 him 다음에 명사가 나왔으므로 소유격 his로 바꾼다.
3 ourselves가 목적어 자리에 있으므로 목적격인 us로 바꾼다.
4 명사(team) 앞에는 소유격이 와야 한다.
5 앞에 나온 명사의 반복을 피해 that을 쓴다.
6 명사(papers) 앞에는 소유격이 와야 한다.
7 지시대명사 these에 맞춰 명사를 복수형인 boxes로 쓴다.

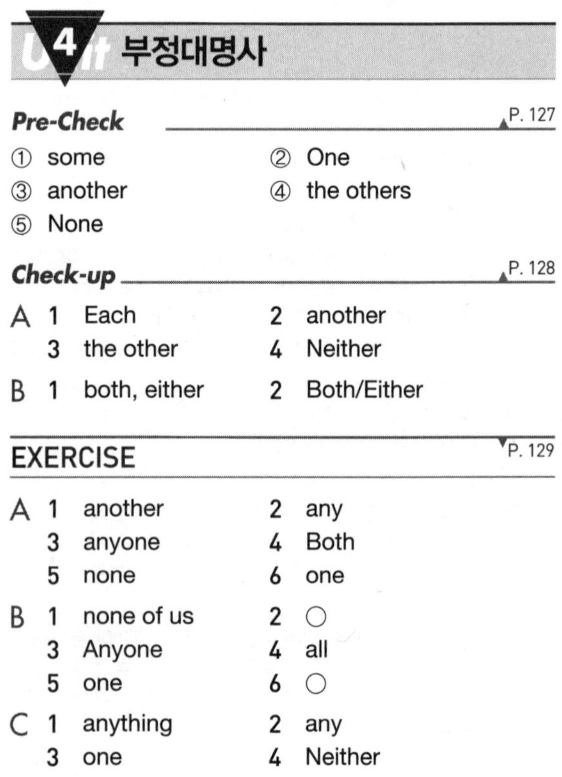

Unit 4 부정대명사

Pre-Check P. 127

① some　　② One
③ another　　④ the others
⑤ None

Check-up P. 128

A 1 Each　　2 another
3 the other　　4 Neither

B 1 both, either　　2 Both/Either

EXERCISE P. 129

A 1 another　　2 any
3 anyone　　4 Both
5 none　　6 one

B 1 none of us　　2 ○
3 Anyone　　4 all
5 one　　6 ○

C 1 anything　　2 any
3 one　　4 Neither

B 1 none of us: 우리들 중 어느 누구도
3 정해지지 않은 대상을 나타내어 '누구라도'라는 뜻으로 쓰였으므로 anyone을 쓴다.
4 내용상 '전부'라는 뜻이므로 all을 쓴다.
5 둘 중에서 어느 하나를 가리킬 때는 one을, 나머지 하나는 the other를 쓴다.

R REVIEW TEST

P. 130

A 1 A 2 this
3 my 4 others
5 others 6 her
7 it 8 them

B 1 ⓐ 2 ⓑ
3 ⓑ 4 ⓓ
5 ⓓ 6 ⓐ
7 ⓒ

C 1 There are some chocolate cookies here. Please have some.
2 Don't serve any of the dishes until Sharon and her team arrives to help you.
3 Betty bought all of these suits for Mark, but he didn't appreciate her efforts at all.
4 We put our balls in the storehouse and this suited our coach just fine.
5 Anyone has his or her chance to speak on this topic before a final decision is made.

D ②

A 1 돌고래는 매우 똑똑하고 친근한 동물이다.
▶ 대표명사를 나타낼 때는 명사 앞에 관사 a(n), the을 붙이거나 복수명사로 쓴다.
2 그런 문제를 가지고 내게 오는 것은 이것을 마지막으로 해라.
3 나는 내 말이 잘못 이해되었다니 믿을 수 없다.
▶ 뒤에 명사(words)가 왔으므로 소유격이 와야 한다.
4 우리는 다른 사람이 생각하는 것을 무시하면 안 된다.
▶ '다른 사람들'이라는 의미의 others가 와야 한다.
5 어떤 사람들은 축구를 좋아하고 일부는 야구를 좋아한다.
▶ some과 others가 나올 경우 일부는 ~하고 또 일부는 ~한다라고 해석한다.
6 Jake는 그녀에게 상황을 설명할 기회를 주지 않으려고 했다.
▶ give의 목적어가 올 자리이므로 her를 쓴다.
7 (그것을) 간단하고 쉽게 해 주세요.
▶ 문맥상 make의 목적어로 it이 적절하다.
8 우리는 여행사와 여행 일정을 얘기해 본 후에 일정 중 몇 가지는 (좀더) 고려할 것이다.
▶ these travel schedules를 받는 목적격 대명사로는 them이 적절하다.

B 1 여동생과 나는 보통 일주일에 두 번 수영하러 간다.
▶ '~마다'라는 의미일 때는 부정관사 a를 쓴다.
2 나는 당신들 둘 다 동시에 참석해야 하는 이유를 모르겠다.
▶ '~ 둘 다'라는 의미일 때는 <both of + 복수명사>의 형태를 쓴다.
3 한국은 반도인데, 이러한 지리적 위치가 한국의 역사에 영향을 주었다.
▶ 명사 앞에 3인칭 단수의 소유격 its가 와야 한다.
4 당신은 은행 계좌 개설을 위해 어떤 ID든지 제출할 수 있습니다.
▶ form이 단수 형태로 쓰였으므로 앞에 올 수 있는 것은 either뿐이다.
5 나는 Tom과 더 이상 논쟁하지 않을 것이다. 왜냐하면 Tom은 결코 다른 사람들에게 동의하지 않기 때문이다.
▶ 내용상 '다른 사람들'을 의미하는 others가 와야 한다.
6 우리 모두는 우리의 요구를 계속해서 주장하는 것이 의미 없다고 생각했다.
▶ 진목적어 to부정사 이하를 대신하는 가목적어 it을 쓴다.
7 이것은 어머니들이 왜 자녀들에게 정말 중요한지에 대한 또 하나의 본보기일 뿐이다.
▶ mothers를 받는 소유격 their를 쓴다.

C 1 여기 초콜릿 쿠키가 있습니다. 좀 드세요.
▶ 긍정문이므로 any를 some으로 고친다.
2 Sharon과 그녀의 팀이 도착해서 도와줄 때까지는 음식을 제공하지 마세요.
▶ 뒤에 명사(team)가 있으므로 she를 소유격 her로 고친다.
3 Betty는 Mark를 위해 이 모든 양복을 샀지만 그는 그녀의 노력에 전혀 고마워하지 않았다.
▶ 뒤에 명사(efforts)가 왔으므로 소유격 her로 고친다.
4 우리는 우리의 공을 창고에 넣었고 이것이 우리의 코치를 만족시켰다.
▶ 앞에 얘기한 일을 대신하는 것이므로 those를 this로 고친다.
5 최종 결정이 나기 전에 누구든지 이 주제에 대해 얘기할 기회가 있다.
▶ 단수 명사 앞이므로 these를 this로 고친다.

D

문화는 동일한 지역 내에서 일치된 동질성을 수용하는 사람들로 이루어진다. 그러나 모든 문화는 시간이 흐르면서 변화하기도 한다. 이 때문에 한 문화 내의 사람들이 그 같은 변화와 관련된 과제와 맞닥뜨리게 될 때 문제가 발생하기도 한다. 외부의 다른 문화로부터 변화를 강요받을 때는 특히나 더 그러하다. 예컨대, 동유럽의 많은 나라들은 공산주의가 몰락한 1990년대 이후로 급격한 경제 성장을 겪었다. 이와 동시에, 시장 경제로 이행하면서 야기된 광범위한 문화적 중압감도 겪게 되었다. 또한 시장 경제는 그들의 종교적, 민족적 관습의 일부와 맞서게 되었다.

▶ (A) '모든 문화'라는 뜻으로 뒤에 cultures(복수 명사)가 왔으므로 all (B) '다른 문화들'이라는 뜻이므로 others (C) 그들 문화의 '일부'라는 뜻이고 긍정문이므로 some

 FURTHER STUDY [Writing]

P. 132

1 isn't[is not] afraid of dogs or any other animals
2 Between ourselves, puts on airs
3 My grandparents live in a small village
4 a pound of flour, two cups of water
5 go to the park to play tennis
6 She complains, involves a lot of
7 some of the books, not all of them
8 None of these articles are/is helpful for

W WRAP-UP TEST

P. 134

1 ⓐ 2 ⓐ 3 ⓑ
4 three pieces of 5 ⓐ
6 ⓒ 7 ⓒ 8 ⓓ
9 ⓐ 10 ⓐ

1 그의 가족은 어제 이탈리아로 갔다.
▶ 밑줄 친 family는 집합명사이다. 보기 중에 집합 명사는 audience 뿐이다.
2 내 여동생은 하루에 우유를 (많이 / 한 잔 / 한 팩) 마신다.
▶ milk는 셀 수 없는 명사이므로 앞에 many가 올 수 없다.
3 ⓐ 그녀의 발표는 매우 성공적이었다. ⓑ Kerry와 나는 주말에 저녁을 먹은 후 배드민턴을 친다. ⓒ 문 좀 열어 주시겠어요? ⓓ 그녀는 일주일에 두 번씩 전화하겠다고 약속했다.
▶ 스포츠 경기 앞에는 관사를 붙이지 않는다.
4 ▶ a piece of 한 조각의 / three pieces of 세 조각의
5 지금 사무실 온도는 26도이다.
LA까지 차로 가는데 7시간이 걸렸다.
그가 지금 병원에 있는 것은 확실하다.
6 ⓐ Bill은 우주비행사가 되기를 원한다. ⓑ 그녀는 그녀가 가장 좋아하는 뮤지컬의 무료 티켓을 얻게 되어서 매우 기쁘다.
ⓒ 당신의 급여는 일주일에 한 번씩 지급될 것입니다.
ⓓ 나는 다음 달 여행을 위해 모자와 선글라스를 샀다.
▶ ⓐⓑⓓ: 막연한 하나 ⓒ 마다
7 ⓐ 그는 직접 비행기 모델을 조립했다. ⓑ 역사는 반복된다고 한다. ⓒ 엄마는 양배추를 썰면서 칼에 베였다. ⓓ 너 혼자 이 문제를 풀 수 있다고 생각하지 않니?
▶ 재귀대명사는 강조 용법으로 쓰일 때 생략할 수 있다.
8 ⓐ 모든 나라들은 고유의 문화와 역사가 있다. ⓑ 선생님의 질문에 어느 학생도 답하지 않았다. ⓒ 몇몇 사람들은 여름 방학 동안 해외에 간다. ⓓ 내가 어제 받은 이메일은 모두 바이러스에 감염되어 있었다.
▶ 주어가 복수(emails)이므로 동사도 복수 동사(were)가 와야 한다.

[9-10]
한국의 문자 체계인 한글은 세계에서 문자의 생성 시점이 알려진 유일한 문자이다. 세종대왕에 의해 고안된 한글은 아름다운 예술의 형태를 띠면서 매우 과학적인 음성 상의 규칙도 가지고 있다. 각각의 한글 문자는 실제 인간의 말을 정확하게 반영할 수 있도록 고안되었다. 그렇기 때문에 외국어를 발음할 때도 이상적인 문자 체계가 된다. 예를 들어 Paris는 한글로 'Parii'로 발음되는데, 이는 영어로 발음될 때보다도 훨씬 더 실제 불어 발음에 가깝다.
9 ▶ 고유명사 앞에는 관사를 붙이지 않는다.
10 ⓐ 한글의 창제일은 알려지지 않았다. ⓑ 한글은 세종대왕에 의해 고안되었다. ⓒ 한글 문자는 실제 말소리를 반영한다. ⓓ 한글 문자는 외국어를 발음하는 데 적절하다.

Unit 09

Unit 1 형용사

Pre-Check

P. 136

1 good
2 helpful
3 wise

Check-up

P. 138

A 1 used digital camera
2 miles long
3 famous writer
4 lots of
5 a few friends

B A 말할 게 있는데. 지금 시간 있니?
B 미안하지만, 오늘 아침에는 ① 시간이 거의 없어. 다른 시간으로 약속을 정할까?
A 모르겠어. 급한 일이라서.
B 흠. 나는 오후 수업 사이에 ② 시간이 약간 있을 거야.

EXERCISE

P. 139

A 1 helpful 2 endless
3 dangerous 4 foolish
5 awesome 6 delighted
7 sleepy

B 1 older 2 sleeping
3 indoor 4 alive
5 alone 6 outside
7 unhappy

C 1 seven feet long
2 tastes bitter
3 go somewhere exotic
4 some indoor exercises
5 your bad habit

Unit 2 부사

Pre-Check P. 140

1 ① beautiful ② beautifully
2 ① iced water ② very icy

Check-up P. 141

A 1 Ridiculously 2 proper
3 desperately 4 simply
5 kindly

B 1 hardly 2 softly
3 later 4 as soon as possible
5 highly

EXERCISE P. 142

A 1 부사 2 부사
3 형용사 4 형용사
5 부사 6 부사

B 1 really 2 final
3 ○ 4 carefully
5 last 6 ○

C 1 early 2 easily
3 strangely 4 capably
5 slightly

B 1 형용사 happy를 수식하는 부사 really로 고쳐야 한다.
2 명사 score를 수식하는 형용사 final로 고쳐야 한다.
4 동사를 수식하는 것이므로 형용사 careful을 부사로 고친다.
5 명사 place를 수식하기 위해서는 last라는 형용사가 와야 한다.

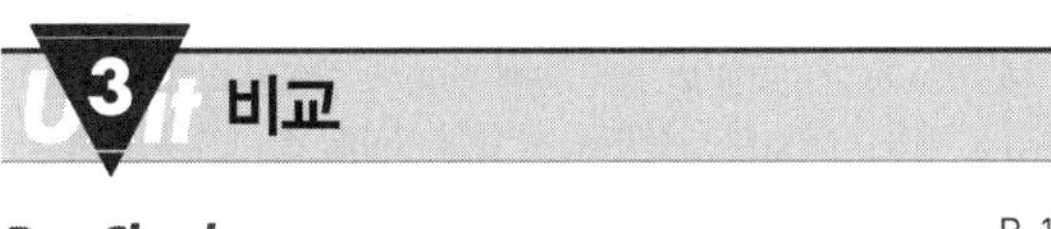

Unit 3 비교

Pre-Check P. 143

1 colder 2 less cold
3 coldest

Check-up P. 144

A 1 easier 2 more prepared
3 most selfless 4 more concerned

B ① larger ② the largest
③ the more

EXERCISE P. 145

A 1 ○
2 much[a lot/still/far/even] better
3 as much as
4 the most
5 the least

B 1 happier than
2 more and more portable
3 as simple as
4 worse and worse
5 more expensive than

C 1 as strong as
2 the largest country
3 colder and colder
4 more quickly than
5 a higher crime rate than

A 2 비교급의 강조는 비교급 앞에 much, a lot, still, far, even 등을 쓴다.
3 동등 비교 〈as + 형용사/부사 + as〉의 표현이다.
4 의미상 비교급이 아니라 최상급이 되어야 한다.
5 의미상 비교급이 아니라 최상급이 되어야 한다.

R REVIEW TEST

P. 146

A 1 little 2 costly
3 sure 4 gladly
5 aware 6 more childish
7 most probable 8 partly

B 1 ⓐ 2 ⓐ 3 ⓑ 4 ⓓ
5 ⓑ 6 ⓐ 7 ⓒ

C 1 Our product is less competitive than our competitor's.
2 It's more foolish to wait for help than to act quickly.
3 Peter is the more helpful of the two boys.
4 He is often regarded as one of the most influential directors in the U.S.
5 How many states are you going to travel through on your trip?

D ②

A 1 그는 예술적인 능력이 거의 없다.
▶ ability는 셀 수 없으므로 little이 옳다.
2 지금 행동하지 않으면, 큰 대가를 치러야 하는 실수가 될 수도 있을 것이다.
▶ costly는 '희생이 큰, 비용이 많이 드는'이라는 뜻의 형용사이다.
3 네 결정이 옳다고 확신하는 게 좋다.
▶ 주격보어 자리이므로 형용사가 와야 한다.
4 Kerry는 새로운 회사의 직급을 기쁘게 받아들였다.
▶ 동사를 수식하는 것은 부사이다.
5 그 파이프의 누수 현상이 그렇게 심각하다는 것을 아무도 깨닫지 못했다.

▶ 의미상 '깨닫는, 인식하는'이라는 뜻의 aware가 와야 한다.

6 Martin은 때때로 자기 남동생보다 더 어린애 같이 행동한다.
▶ 2 음절 이상의 형용사 비교급에는 more를 쓴다.

7 이 실험에서 나올 가장 예상되는 결과는 무엇인가?
▶ 의미상 최상급의 형태가 되어야 한다.

8 Jerry는 비를 피하려고 재킷 안으로 머리를 일부분만 숙여 넣을 수 있었다.
▶ 동사 lower를 수식하는 부사가 와야 한다.

B 1 우리는 더 좋은 사진을 (찍기) 위해 몇 가지 아이디어들을 시도했다.
▶ '착상, 고안, 아이디어'라는 뜻으로 쓰인 idea는 셀 수 있다.

2 날씨가 안 좋으면 모든 운전자들은 속력을 더 낮추어야 한다.
▶ drivers가 복수이고 의미상 '모든'이라는 수식어가 와야 한다.

3 그가 예의 바르게 행동하기 때문에 모두 그를 좋아한다.
▶ 동사(behaves)를 수식하는 것은 부사이다.

4 마지막 보고서는 처음 것만큼 거의 쓸모가 없다.
▶ 동등 비교 〈as + 형용사/부사 + as〉의 표현이다.

5 좀 더 말조심을 하지 않으면 당신은 곤란에 처하게 될 것이다.
▶ 의미상 '좀 더 주의하다'가 적절하다. 비교의 대상이 나와 있지 않지만 의미상으로 비교급을 쓴다.

6 Bella는 무슨 일이 생기더라도 자신의 직업에서 성공하리라고 단단히 결심했다.
▶ 주격보어 자리에는 형용사를 쓴다.

7 Carter는 요즘 말과 행동 모두에 훨씬 더 조심성이 없어지고 있다.
▶ '훨씬 더'라는 뜻으로 비교급을 강조할 때 쓰는 표현으로 a lot을 쓴다.

C 1 우리 제품은 경쟁사 제품보다 경쟁력이 떨어진다.
▶ 비교급 문장이므로 less로 고친다.

2 재빨리 행동하지 않고 도움을 기다리는 것이 더 어리석다.
▶ act라는 동사를 수식하는 부사 quickly로 고친다.

3 Peter는 그 두 소년 중에서 더 도움이 된다.
▶ 비교급 형태로 쓰일 수 있는 것은 형용사와 부사이다. 따라서 helpful로 고친다.

4 그는 종종 미국에서 가장 영향력 있는 감독들 중 한 사람으로 여겨진다.
▶ 빈도부사는 be동사, 조동사 뒤나 일반동사 앞에 온다.

5 여행 동안 얼마나 많은 주(洲)를 여행할 것인가요?
▶ 복수 명사를 수식하는 것이므로 much를 many로 바꾼다.

D

요즘에는 운이 좋은 많은 개들이 전자 공학적인 방법으로 집에 가는 길을 찾는다. 이 개들은 특별한 꼬리표를 단다. 아주 작은 마이크로칩이 개의 피부 속에 들어가는데, 이 마이크로칩에는 개 주인의 정보가 들어 있다. 이 마이크로칩은 사람의 손만큼 작은 기계에 의해 읽힌다. 마이크로칩에 들어 있는 정보는 해당 단체에 등록되어 있다. 그 단체에서 애완동물을 잃어버린 주인에게 재빨리 연락을 취한다.

▶ (A) 뒤에 복수명사 dogs가 왔으므로 Many (B) '사람의 손만큼 작은'이라는 뜻이므로 as small as (C) 동사 contacts를 수식하는 부사가 필요하므로 quickly

F FURTHER STUDY [Writing]

P. 148

1 as cold as yesterday
2 treated the poor very kindly
3 delightfully accept my offer
4 The higher, the colder
5 the most boring book I have ever read
6 rarely missed a day of school.
7 knows more about computers than Stephen
8 is superior to that of my previous one

W WRAP-UP TEST

P. 150

1 ⓒ 2 ⓐ
3 ⓐ 4 ⓑ
5 in 6 not as expensive
7 ⓓ 8 ⓑ
9 ⓑ
10 더 많이 저축할수록 (돈을) 더 많이 벌게 될 것이다.

1 ▶ 형용사에 -ly를 붙이면 뜻이 달라지는 경우이다.
hard(열심히) - hardly(거의 ~않다)
ⓒ high(높은) - highly(매우)

2 어떤 사람들은 혼자 살고 어떤 사람들은 그렇지 않다.
오렌지 좀 드시겠어요? 아주 맛이 있네요.
▶ some~, others ~: '일부는 ~하고, 일부는 ~하다'
빈칸 뒤에 셀 수 있는 명사가 나오므로 some이 가장 적절하다.

3 ⓐ 우리 형 알아? ⓑ 무슨 일이야? 아무도 회의에 참석하지 않았어. ⓒ 실례합니다. 정문이 어디에 있죠? ⓓ 침낭이 정말 귀엽구나!

4 ⓐ 저 개구리를 봐. 매우 높게 뛴다. ⓑ 그들은 미술 작품을 매우 아름답게 완성했다. ⓒ 점심 식사를 좀 더 빨리 마쳐 주세요. ⓓ 문제는 네가 사람을 너무 쉽게 믿는다는 거야.
▶ lovely는 '아름다운, 멋진' 뜻을 가진 형용사이다.

5 그는 우리 반에서 가장 뛰어난 학생이다.
자동차 중개인인 Walton 씨는 우리 마을에서 옷을 가장 잘 입는 사람으로 선정되었다.
▶ the 최상급 + in + 장소

6 이 스케치북은 저것보다 덜 비싸다.
이 스케치북은 저것만큼 비싸지 않다.
▶ less + 원급 + than = not as + 원급 + as

7 ⓐ 오늘은 일 년 중 가장 더운 날이었다.
ⓑ 오늘은 그 어느 날보다 더운 날이었다.
ⓒ 오늘처럼 더운 날은 없었다.
▶ ⓓ는 '오늘이 다른 날보다 훨씬 더웠다'는 뜻으로 비교급의 의미이다.

8 ⓐ 서울은 대한민국의 어느 다른 도시보다 더 오염되었다.
ⓑ 팀워크에서 화합이 개인 능력보다 중요하다. ⓒ 책을 읽는 것은 TV 드라마를 보는 것보다 훨씬 더 재미있다. ⓓ 그 남자

가 다른 어떤 코미디언보다 재미있다.

▶ ⓐⓒⓓ는 than이 들어가지만 ⓑ에는 to가 들어가야 한다.

[9-10]

젊은이들은 저축에 대해 거의 생각하지 않지만, 누구나 총수입의 10–15%는 저축해야 한다. 더 많이 저축할수록, 더 많이 이익을 얻게 될 것이다. 저축을 시작하는 가장 빠른 길은 아주 간단하다. 적은 양을 정기적으로 저축하라. 어떤 젊은 여성은 매주 비싼 커피를 마시는 것을 중단하고 그 돈을 저축했다. 그녀는 5년 동안 매주 12달러를 저축했고, 그 저축에 대해 10%의 이자를 받았다. 그녀는 5년 후에 약 4000달러를 받고는 놀랐다.

9 ▶ 빈도부사는 일반동사(think) 앞에 위치한다.

10 ▶ the + 비교급, the + 비교급: ~할수록 더 ...하다

Unit 10

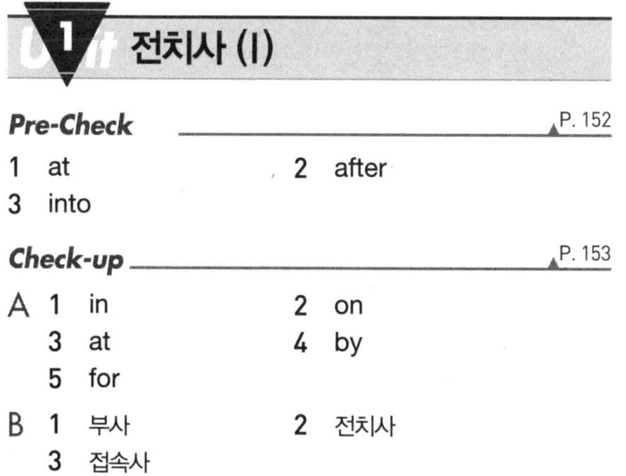

1 전치사 (I)

Pre-Check P. 152

1 at 2 after

3 into

Check-up P. 153

A 1 in 2 on

3 at 4 by

5 for

B 1 부사 2 전치사

3 접속사

EXERCISE P. 154

A 1 at 2 next to

3 until 4 on

5 through 6 past

B 1 into 2 over

3 out of 4 during

5 along 6 between

C 1 by 2 at

3 in 4 on

5 between

C 1 '~까지(시간), ~옆에(장소)'를 나타내는 전치사는 by이다.

2 '~에(시점), ~에(지점)'를 나타내는 전치사 at이 필요하다.

3 '~에서(넓은 공간 개념), ~에(계절)'와 함께 쓰이는 전치사는 in이다.

4 '~위에(장소), ~에(날이나 때)'를 나타내는 전치사는 on이다.

5 '사이에(시간), ~끼리만(분배/공유)'을 나타내는 전치사 between을 쓴다.

2 전치사 (II)

Pre-Check P. 155

1 for 2 from

3 to

Check-up P. 156

A 1 for 2 from

3 with 4 to

5 of

B 1 ① the computer

② bought

2 ① called

② the police

EXERCISE P. 157

A 1 for 2 from

3 to 4 of

5 with

B 1 on 2 of

3 to 4 by

5 with 6 for

7 from

A 1 '호화로운 식당의 값 비싼 식사 치고는(비교)' '다음 2주 동안(기간)', '과학 경시대회를 위해(이유)'이므로 전치사 for가 필요하다.

2 '1주일의 결근(부재)' '내가 쓴 노래(출처/기원)' '우리 집에서부터(시작 지점)'을 나타내므로 전치사 from이 필요하다.

3 '2시 15분 전(시간)' '학교로(방향)' '스페인에(장소)'를 나타내는 전치사 to가 필요하다.

4 '그의 활동에 관한(관계/관련)' '~이기 때문에(because of)' '~때문에(원인)'를 나타내는 전치사 of를 쓴다.

5 '손을 든 채로(동시)' '푸른 눈을 가진(소유)' '이웃들과 함께(동반)'의 뜻을 가진 전치사는 with이다.

3 전치사를 포함한 다양한 표현

Pre-Check P. 158

1 for 2 for

3 for

Check-up P. 159

A 1 to 2 with

3 between 4 for

5 of 6 of

B 1 at 2 X

3 to 4 X

5 x 6 to

EXERCISE

P. 160

A 1 with　2 to
3 to　4 for
5 about　6 for
7 on

B 1 to　2 ○
3 of　4 ○
5 for　6 between
7 on

C 1 forget about　2 cause of
3 think of　4 invitation to
5 pleased with　6 rude to

B 1 '~에 대한 손해'라는 표현은 ⟨damage to⟩이다.
3 '~이 부끄러운'이라는 표현은 ⟨be ashamed of⟩이다.
5 '~에 대해 책임이 있는'이라는 표현은 be responsible for이다.
6 '~사이의 관계/관련'이라는 표현은 connection between이다.
7 '~에 의존하다, ~에 달려 있다'라는 표현은 depend on이다.

R REVIEW TEST

P. 161

A 1 for　2 to
3 through　4 in
5 to　6 about
7 until　8 of

B 1 ⓒ　2 ⓐ
3 ⓒ　4 ⓑ
5 ⓐ　6 ⓐ
7 ⓓ

C 1 I was short of coins so I borrowed some from my sister for the parking meter.
2 Weren't the boys responsible for throwing the ball through our window?
3 The company will have to add new rooms to the hotel next year.
4 I talked to/with Ben about our exam until school was over.
5 The city of Baltimore is famous for its wonderful crab cakes.
6 The detective was searching for clues in connection with the suspicious fire.

D ③

A 1 그는 직장에서 (일어난) 그 큰 문제에 대해 설명했다.
▶ '~의 이유를 밝히다, 설명하다'는 account for이다.
2 우리 부모님이 내일 그녀를 공원에 데리고 갈 것이다.
▶ '~로'라는 뜻으로 방향을 나타내는 전치사는 to이다.
3 그 지도는 사막을 통과하는 길을 보여준다.
▶ get through는 '~을 통과하다'는 의미로 전치사 through를 포함하는 표현이다.
4 그들은 저 파란색 야구점퍼를 입은 남자를 아나요?
▶ '~를 입고 있는'이라는 뜻으로 쓰이는 전치사는 in이다.
5 아빠가 지금 막 공항까지 타고 갈 택시를 마련했다.
▶ '공항으로'라는 뜻의 방향을 나타내는 to가 알맞다.
6 올해도 내가 네 생일을 잊어버렸다니 믿을 수가 없어.
▶ '~을 잊어버리다'라는 표현은 forget about이다.
7 우리는 어두워질 때까지 밖에서 우리는 그녀를 기다렸다.
▶ by는 끝나는 지점을 언급하는 것이므로 '~ (할 때) 까지'라는 뜻을 가진 전치사 until을 고른다.
8 이 책의 각 단원은 짧고 읽기가 매우 쉬웠다.
▶ '~의'라는 뜻을 나타내는 전치사 of가 알맞다.

B 1 우리 마을은 신선한 과일로 유명하다.
▶ '~로 유명한'이라는 표현은 be famous for이다.
2 우리 오빠는 전자 제품에 대해 아는 것이 거의 없는데도, 내 라디오를 고치려고 노력 중이다.
▶ '~에 관해 알다'라는 표현은 know about이다.
3 우리 회사의 가장 인기 있는 인터넷 서비스는 세 가지 기본 특징으로 구성되어 있다.
▶ '~로 구성되다'라는 표현은 consist of이다.
4 우리 가족은 올해 내 학업 (성적) 향상에 대해 기뻐하고 있다.
▶ '~에 기뻐하다/만족하다'라는 표현은 be pleased with이다.
5 목수는 나무 의자에 난 구멍의 원인을 알아냈다.
▶ '구멍의 원인'이라는 뜻이므로 cause of가 가장 적절하다.
6 그는 손님 모두에게 저녁을 사겠다고 고집을 부렸다.
▶ '고집하다'는 의미의 insisted on을 고른다.
7 허리케인이 미국의 주택들에 큰 피해를 입혔다.
▶ '~에 대한 피해' 라는 의미의 damage to를 고른다.

C 1 나는 동전이 부족해서 여동생에게 주차 미터기에 넣을 동전 몇 개를 빌렸다.
▶ borrow from은 '~로부터 …를 빌리다'라는 뜻이다.
2 그 소년들이 우리 창문으로 공을 던진 데에 책임이 있지 않았나요?
▶ responsible for는 '~에 대해 책임이 있는'이라는 뜻이다.
3 내년에 회사는 그 호텔에 새로운 객실을 늘려야 할 것이다.
▶ 영어에는 관용적으로 전치사를 사용하지 않고 next(다음 ~에), last(지난 ~에), this(이번 ~에), that(그 ~에)처럼 부사구가 되는 것이 있다. 따라서 next year 앞에는 전치사를 쓰지 않는다.
4 학교가 끝날 때까지 나는 Ben과 시험에 대해 얘기를 나눴다.
▶ '~와 얘기하다'라는 뜻의 talk to/with가 쓰여야 한다.
5 볼티모어 시는 맛있는 게살 케이크로 유명하다.
▶ 동격을 나타내는 전치사 of(~ 의)가 필요하다.
6 형사는 그 수상쩍은 화재와 관련된 단서를 찾고 있었다.
▶ '~를 찾다, 수색하다'라는 표현은 search for이다.

D

미시간 주 디트로이트 북쪽으로 1시간 거리에서 매년 멋진 범선 경기가 열린다. 300척이 넘는 범선들이 Huron 호수에서 Mackinac이라 불리는 아름다운 섬까지 경주를 하게 된다. 그 섬은 엔진이 없는 운송 수단만 허용되는 것으로 유명하다. 해마다 약 25만 명의 사람들이 Bayview Mackinac Race와 축제에 참가한다. 본 경기 전날 밤에는 어린이들이 82년 역사를 지닌 미니 범선 경기를 시작한다. 이런이 경기는 장난감 범선들로 이루어지는데 빗물을 받는 수로에서 (이 장난감 범선들로) 서로 경쟁한다. (축제에 참가한) 모든 사람들은 그 경주를 즐긴다.

▶ (A) '~로 유명한'의 뜻이므로 be famous for (B) '~와 경쟁하다'라는 뜻이므로 compete against (C) '~에 기뻐하다'라는 뜻이므로 be pleased with

FURTHER STUDY [Writing]

P. 163

1 take the cat to the veterinary hospital at 3 o'clock
2 The dog jumped over the fence
3 be nice to you from now on
4 your opinion on [about] the matter
5 ran across the street into the building
6 taken a photograph of my boyfriend
7 They were ashamed of losing the game
8 The connection between the two painters' paintings

WRAP-UP TEST

P. 165

1 on, at, in 2 ⓓ
3 ⓑ 4 ⓐ
5 ⓑ 6 ⓐ
7 ⓒ 8 ⓑ
9 during
10 travelers planning summer vacations should get their tickets quickly

1 Jay는 9월 4일 오후 3시에 캐나다로 떠난다.
▶ 날짜 앞에는 전치사 on, 시각 앞에는 at, 오전/오후 앞에는 in이 온다.

2 Dana는 가게에 갔지만 아무 것도 사지 않고 돌아왔다.
백화점은 5번가의 극장 맞은편에 있다.
누구나 엘리베이터를 타고 에펠탑을 올라갈 수 있다.
▶ ⓐ went to ⓒ is across from ⓑ take an elevator up

3 Lisa는 Bob 옆에 앉기를 원했다.
▶ next to: ~ 옆에(=by)

4 ⓐ 들어오라고 할 때까지 여기서 기다려 주세요. ⓑ 소년은 그의 고양이가 지붕 위에서 노는 것을 보았다. ⓒ 아빠는 2시간 동안 TV를 보고 있다. ⓓ 강변을 따라서 걷는 동안 그들은 거의 빠져 죽기 직전의 한 남자를 보았다.
▶ ⓐ 의미상 들어오라고 할 때까지 기다려야 하므로 전치사 until이 와야 한다.

5 ⓐ 우리 엄마는 요리를 잘하지 못한다. ⓑ 너는 도마뱀을 무서워하지 않아도 돼. 내가 애완동물로 기르는 거야. ⓒ 큰 농장과 5층짜리 집은 Walton 씨의 소유이다. ⓓ 너는 누구를 기다리는 거니?
▶ be afraid of: ~을 두려워하다

6 네가 원한다면 리포트를 우편으로 보낼 수 있어.
그 소포는 지금까지는 도착했어야 해.
▶ 도구/수단을 나타내며, '~까지'라는 뜻을 지니기도 하는 전치사는 by이다.

7 너랑 Jennifer 사이에 무슨 일이 생긴 거야?
나는 여행을 하는 동안 많은 박물관을 방문했다.
너는 그 저축한 돈으로 무엇을 할 거야?
▶ 빈칸 다음에 you and Jennifer가 나오므로 between, 의미상 '여행하는 동안에'가 적절하므로 during, '저축을 가지고'라는 뜻이므로 with가 적절하다.

8 ⓐ 달에는 생명체가 없다고 한다. ⓑ 협조해 주셔서 정말 감사합니다. ⓒ 푸껫은 아름다운 바다로 유명하다. ⓓ 그 콘서트는 큰 성공을 거두었다. 콘서트홀은 사람들로 가득 찼다.
▶ ⓐ on the moon ⓒ be famous for ⓓ be full of
ⓑ appreciate는 타동사로 뒤에 전치사 없이 바로 목적어가 온다.

[9-10]

어떤 여행자들은 여름에 특별한 Amtrack 열차를 타고 여행하는 것을 즐긴다. 사람들은 미국의 많은 지역으로 가는 특별하게 책정된 가격의 기차표를 구매한다. 또한 가족은 보다 저렴하게 여행할 수 있다. 성인 한 명이 기차표를 구매하면, 15살 미만의 어린이 두 명에 한에서는 티켓이 무료로 제공된다. 이 가격은 여름을 제외한 다른 기간의 정상 기차표 가격과는 차이가 있다. 여름 기차표에 대한 수요는 높다. 그러므로 여름휴가를 계획하는 여행자들은 빨리 기차표를 구매해야 한다.

9 ▶ during: ~하는 동안

Unit 11

Unit 1 접속사

Pre-Check

P. 168

1 and 2 and

Check-up

P. 169

A 1 and 2 or
3 and 4 or
5 but also

B 1 1 2 2
3 2 4 3

EXERCISE

P. 170

A 1 or 2 neither
3 either 4 and
5 not only 6 but
7 both

B 1 so/and 2 not only
3 ○ 4 nor
5 and 6 but

C 1 by bus or on foot
2 so[and] he passed the exam
3 a new notebook and a dozen pencils
4 because they practiced hard this time
5 the saxophone but also the drums

B 1 '그래서, 그러므로'의 의미를 가지는 등위접속사인 so/and를 쓴다.
2 '~뿐 아니라 …도'라는 뜻의 not only A but also B를 쓴다.
4 neither A nor B는 'A도 B도 아니다'라는 뜻이다.
5 cautious와 wise를 대등하게 연결해주는 접속사 and가 필요하다.
6 '길을 잃지 않았다'와 '어디로 가는지 확신이 없었다'라는 두 개의 절은 의미상 서로 상반되므로 역접의 의미를 나타내는 접속사 but이 필요하다.

Unit 2 명사절

Pre-Check

P. 171

1 Thomas 2 Her friend
3 That her friend told her a lie

Check-up

P. 172

A 1 what 2 that
3 whether 4 that
5 where

B ① what ② that
③ what ④ that
⑤ what

EXERCISE

P. 173

A 1 who 2 where
3 whether 4 That
5 It

B 1 Jane went 2 that
3 that 4 whether/if
5 ○ 6 ○

C 1 how I can write a good essay
2 where the party will be
3 who that person in the red coat is
4 what the main topic of the discussion was
5 why the train took so long to get here

B 1 의문문을 명사절로 바꿀 때는 〈의문사 + 주어 + 동사〉의 어순이다.
2 It's certain that ~의 형태로 if를 that으로 고친다.
3 '~을 말하다'라는 뜻의 목적어절이므로 it을 that으로 고친다.
4 'Barbara가 우리 표를 가지고 있는지 아닌지'라는 뜻으로 접속사 whether/if를 쓴다.

Unit 3 부사절

Pre-Check

P. 174

1 after 2 although
3 while

Check-up

P. 175

A 1 because 2 since
3 until 4 although
5 If 6 Unless

B ⓐ, ⓑ, ⓓ

EXERCISE

P. 176

A 1 so that 2 when
3 While 4 Unless
5 but 6 although

B 1 As/Since/Because
2 Although/Even though/Though
3 In case
4 Although/Even though/Though
5 ○

C 1 because somebody turned the lights off
2 while I was sleeping
3 Although Nancy studies very hard
4 whereas Andy was in charge yesterday

B 1 '흐리고 바람이 불어서 취소됐다'는 뜻으로 이유를 나타내는 접속사 As/Since/Because로 고친다.
2 '배가 불렀다'와 '계속 먹기를 원했다'는 서로 상반되는 의미이다. 따라서 대조를 나타내는 Although/Even though/Though로 고친다.
3 내용상 '비가 올 경우'라는 조건의 의미이다. 따라서 조건을 나타내는 in case로 고친다.
4 '부유하진 않다'와 '가진 것을 나눠 준다'는 서로 상반되는 의미이다. 따라서 양보/대조를 나타내는 Although/Even though/Though로 고친다.

R REVIEW TEST

P. 177

A
1 whether 2 that
3 or 4 unless
5 Before 6 as soon as
7 if 8 Since

B
1 ⓓ 2 ⓑ
3 ⓒ 4 ⓑ
5 ⓓ 6 ⓒ
7 ⓒ

C
1 Neither Jessica nor I am responsible for the accident.
2 We don't know whether he went out or stayed inside.
3 The main problem is that I don't know what is going on in the meeting.
4 Neither Steve nor Simon contacted me, even though[although/though] I'd sent them several emails.
5 After driving for more than 14 straight hours, Camille was extremely tired.
6 Because of the heavy rain, the school was closed for the day.

D ③

A 1 Judy는 입학시험에 합격했는지 확신할 수가 없다.
▶ '~인지 아닌지'의 의미를 가진 whether가 적절하다.
2 그는 모든 문서 양식이 제대로 작성되었음을 확인했다.
▶ 동사 confirmed의 목적어 역할을 하므로 that이 적절하다.
3 Burt는 자신의 의견을 고집했고, Peter나 Sally의 말을 들으려 하지 않았다.
▶ 'A 또는 B'의 의미로 either A or B가 적절하다.
4 모든 사람들로부터 충분한 도움을 받지 못한다면 그 프로젝트는 성공하지 못할 것이다.
▶ '~하지 않으면'의 의미를 가진 접속사 unless가 적절하다.
5 인도를 여행하기 전에는 인도가 얼마나 아름다운 나라인지 알지 못했다.
▶ 의미상 '~전에'라는 의미의 Before가 적절하다.
6 이 수업에 등록하면 곧바로 영어 이름을 하나 고르세요.
▶ 의미상 '~하는 즉시'의 뜻을 가진 as soon as가 적절하다.
7 이 시험에 낙제한다면 보충 수업을 받아야 한다.
▶ 의미상 '~한다면'이라는 뜻의 if가 적절하다.
8 그는 외국어에 재능이 있기 때문에, 스페인어와 독일어를 익히는 것이 그에게는 쉬웠다.
▶ 의미상 '~때문에'를 나타내는 Since가 적절하다.

B 1 학생들이 더 이상 등록하지 않으면 이 수업은 폐강될 것이다.
▶ 조건의 부사절을 이끄는 if가 적절하다.
2 Sam이 올림픽 팀에서 가장 빠른 선수라는 것은 부인할 수 없다.
▶ 주어 역할을 하는 명사절이 필요하므로That이 적절하다.
3 어떤 식습관은 한 나라에서는 이상하게 보일지도 모르지만, 또 다른 나라에선 지극히 자연스러울 수 있다.
▶ 사용된 형용사가 strange와 natural이므로 역접을 나타내는 접속사 but이 적절하다.
4 운전 중에는 안전벨트를 매 주십시오.
▶ 의미상 '~하는 동안'이라는 뜻의 while이 가장 알맞다.
5 시간이 되실 때 당신을 만나고 싶습니다.
▶ 시간의 부사절을 이끄는 접속사 when이 적절하다.
6 그는 Susan과 Paul 둘 다 그의 지시를 잘 따르지 않는다고 느꼈다.
▶ nor와 함께 쓰여 상관접속사를 이루는 단어는 neither이다.
7 방문객들은 누구나 그 숲을 즐길 수 있도록 캠프장을 깨끗이 정리해야 한다.
▶ 목적의 부사절을 이끄는 접속사 so that이 적절하다.

C 1 Jessica와 나 둘 다 그 사고에 책임이 없다.
▶ neither A nor B는 동사와 가까운 주어(I)에 동사를 일치시키므로 are를 am으로 고친다.
2 우리는 그가 외출을 했는지 아니면 실내에 있는지 잘 모른다.
▶ whether와 함께 쓰일 수 있는 것은 or (not) 이다.
3 가장 큰 문제는 회의가 어떻게 진행되는지 모른다는 것이다.
▶ 보어절을 이끄는 접속사 that으로 고친다.
4 내가 수차례 이메일을 보냈음에도 불구하고 Steve도 Simon도 내게 연락하지 않았다.
▶ 양보의 부사절을 이끄는 접속사가 필요하다. as를 although, even though 등으로 고친다.
5 쉬지 않고 14시간 이상을 연속으로 운전한 후, Camille은 몹시 피곤했다.
▶ 분사구문으로 쓰인 문장이다. 종속절에서 생략된 주어(Camille)와 drive의 관계가 능동이므로 driving을 쓴다. 그리고 문장의 의미를 분명하게 강조하고 싶을 때는 접속사를 그대로 둔다.
6 폭우 때문에 하루 동안 학교가 휴교되었다.
▶ because는 이유의 부사절을 이끄는 접속사다. 그런데 뒤에 절이 아닌 구가 왔으므로 전치사가 필요하다. 따라서 because를 because of로 바꾼다.

D

비록 비판을 받아오긴 했지만, 원자력 에너지는 세계 에너지 문제를 해결할 수 있는 커다란 잠재력을 가지고 있다. 과거의 기록으로 판단해 볼 때, 원자력 에너지는 석탄이나 석유를 사용하는 것보다 훨씬 오염이 덜 하다. 어떤 사람들은 원자력 에너지가 안전하지 않다고 생각하지만 그것은 사실이 아니다. 전 세계적으로 원자력 발전소는 안전하게 운영되고 있다. 몇 차례 원자력 사고가 발생했던 1980년대 이후로 안전 기준도 더욱 높아졌다. 원자력 에너지가 얼마나 안전한지에 대해 전 세계 사람들이 깨닫게 해주어야 한다.

▶ (A) 동사 think 다음에 명사절을 이끄는 접속사 that (B) '안전하지 않다고 생각하지만, 사실은 그렇지 않다'라는 뜻으로 역접을 나타내는 but (C) '1980년대부터/이후로'라는 뜻으로 since + 특정 기간 (the 1980s)

FURTHER STUDY [Writing]

P. 179

1 where the bank is
2 why the bus is
3 Both, and, are major Korean port cities
4 Neither, were willing to attend the conference
5 Even though/Although/Though we ruined, didn't blame us
6 Either James or Jane will pick you up
7 Nobody expected that the Korean soccer team
8 was in a meeting when I called him

WRAP-UP TEST

P. 181

1 ⓒ 2 ⓓ
3 ⓑ 4 ⓐ
5 ⓑ 6 ⓓ
7 or you'll fail the course
8 so, that 9 ⓒ
10 해마다 미국인들이 점점 더 살이 찌면서

1 Jake는 자신이 로미오 역을 하고 싶어 했지만 아무도 그의 생각에 동의하지 않았다.
Rachel 뿐만 아니라 Julie도 나와 댄스파티에 가는 것을 거절했다.

2 ⓐ Susan과 Donna는 저녁을 만들 것이다. ⓑ 나는 스파게티와 피자 둘 다 좋아하지 않는다. ⓒ 호텔이 가득 찼기 때문에 방을 예약할 수 없었다. ⓓ 그 또는 그의 비서는 발표 준비가 되어 있었다.
▶ ⓓ either A or B 구문에서 동사의 수는 동사와 가까운 주어 B에 일치시킨다. his secretary이므로 동사는 단수 동사인 was가 적절하다.

3 ⓐ 벽에 낙서를 한 사람은 바로 너다. ⓑ 제시간에 갈 수 있도록 서둘러 주세요. ⓒ 문제는 그녀가 평소처럼 한마디의 말도 없이 약속을 취소했다는 것이다. ⓓ 우리는 그가 유명한 가수였다는 사실을 몰랐다.
▶ ⓐⓒⓓ는 명사절을 이끄는 접속사인데 ⓑ는 부사절을 이끄는 접속사이다.

4 오른쪽으로 돌면 빵집이 보일 거예요.
ⓐ 그들에게 사실인지 물어봐라. ⓑ 바쁘지 않으면 우리집으로 오세요. ⓒ 비가 오지 않으면 아버지가 세차를 할 것이다. ⓓ 좋은 성과를 내지 못하면 그 과정을 그만두라고 할 수 있습니다.
▶ 주어진 문장의 if는 '~라면'이라는 뜻의 조건을 나타내는데 ⓐ는 '~인지 아닌지'라는 뜻이다.

5 사무실을 떠나기 전에 그는 스케줄을 다시 확인했다.
▶ 분사구문으로서 의미상 '사무실을 떠나기 전에'가 가장 적절하므로 before가 적절하다.

6 그 아이는 책장 꼭대기에 손이 닿을 수 있도록 발끝으로 섰다.
▶ ⓓ although가 있기 때문에 '책장 꼭대기에 손이 닿을 수 없지만 ~'이라는 뜻이 되므로 문장의 의미가 다르다.

7 열심히 공부하지 않으면 낙제할 것이다.
▶ 명령문 + or : ~하지 않으면 ~할 것이다

8 그는 너무 게을러서 누구도 그와 함께 일하고 싶어 하지 않는다.

[9-10]
미국인들은 지구상에서 가장 부유한 사람들일뿐만 아니라 가장 비만인 사람들이 되었다. 미국인들이 먹는 음식은 대부분 칼로리가 높고, 단 음식들로 이루어져 있다. 이런 문제에도 불구하고 미국에서 정크 푸드를 규정하는 법안은 많지 않다. 해마다 미국인들이 점점 더 살이 찌면서 의사들은 이 문제가 해결되지 않을 경우 10년 내에 많은 미국인들이 당뇨병이나 심장질환 같은 병으로 고통을 받을 것이라고 경고한다.

9 ▶ 빈칸 다음에 this problem이라는 명사가 있기 때문에 빈칸에는 전치사가 들어가야 한다. 의미상 '~임에도 불구하고'를 뜻하는 Despite가 적절하다.

Unit 12

1 관계대명사

Pre-Check

P.184

1 우산을 들고 있는 소녀
2 독일산 자동차

Check-up

P.186

A 1 who/that 2 which/that
3 which/that 4 that
5 who/that

EXERCISE

P.187

A 1 which 2 whose
3 who 4 that
5 Whatever 6 what
7 that

B 1 whose 2 that
3 whatever/whichever 4 ○
5 ○ 6 who/that

C 1 the magazine which/that
2 a new recipe which/that is for
3 the musician who/that is very popular
4 (which/that) my father got yesterday
5 the woman in raincoat who/that

B 1 '그녀의 자전거'라는 의미이므로 소유격 관계대명사 whose를 쓴다.
2 선행사가 〈the + 최상급〉 구문일 때는 관계대명사는 that을 주로 쓴다.

3 의미상 whatever/whichever(무엇이든지)가 적절하다.
6 선행사가 the teachers이고 관계대명사 바로 뒤에 동사가 나오므로 who나 that을 쓴다.

Unit 2 관계부사

Pre-Check
P.188

1 yesterday
2 on a weekly basis
3 the day when he got back from vacation

Check-up
P.189

A 1 when 2 why
3 how 4 where

EXERCISE
P.190

A 1 whenever 2 where
3 when 4 why
5 when 6 how

B 1 when 2 how/the way
3 ○ 4 wherever
5 ○

C 1 where, in which
2 when, during which
3 how, in what way/the way in which
4 why, for which
5 where, from which
6 how, in what way/the way in which

B 1 시간을 나타내는 the day가 선행사이므로 when으로 고친다.
2 방법을 나타내는 관계부사 how와 the way는 같이 쓰지 않고 둘 중 하나만 쓴다.
4 선행사가 a location이고 의미상 '어디든지'라는 뜻이므로 복합관계부사인 wherever로 고친다.

REVIEW TEST
P.191

A 1 whom 2 whose
3 However 4 which
5 the reason 6 Wherever
7 the way

B 1 ⓓ 2 ⓐ
3 ⓓ 4 ⓑ
5 ⓐ 6 ⓑ
7 ⓒ

C 1 Do you know the girl who lives next door to you?
2 Will you please explain to me how [the way] the accident occurred last night?
3 I think it is the same thing that she planned on studying in school.
4 My mother found the old storybook that she used to read to me.
5 This is the place in which your grandparents moved from England.
6 Padre island is a popular location where students spend their spring vacations.

D ①

A 1 Mary가 데이트하는 사람 만나본 적 있니?
▶ 선행사가 사람이고 또한 is dating의 목적어 역할을 할 수 있는 목적격 관계대명사가 필요하다.
2 우리 아버지는 부모님이 서울에서 사업체를 운영하는 한 소녀를 알고 있다.
▶ 사물에는 of which, whose 두 가지 소유격 관계대명사를 모두 사용할 수 있으나 사람인 경우에는 whose만 가능하다.
3 아무리 그 일이 힘들다 하더라도, 그 업무를 완성하기 위해 노력할 만한 가치는 있다.
▶ '아무리 ~할지라도'라는 의미의 복합관계부사를 고른다.
4 내가 지난주에 사고를 낸 차는 아주 비싼 차였다.
▶ 선행사가 사물(the car)인 목적격 관계대명사 which가 적절하다.
5 내가 너와 영화를 보러 가지 못하는 이유는 시험 때문이다.
▶ 문맥상 이유를 나타내는 관계부사가 필요하다.
6 그녀는 어디를 가든 강아지를 데리고 간다.
▶ 문맥상 '어디를 가든지'를 나타내는 wherever가 적절하다.
7 나는 네가 내 남자친구에게 얘기하는 방식이 마음에 안 들어.
▶ 문맥상 방법을 나타내는 the way가 적절하다.

B 1 Cameron 선생님은 내가 유일하게 좋아하는 여선생님이다.
▶ 선행사가 〈the only + 명사〉일 경우 관계대명사는 주로 that을 쓴다.
2 내가 너와 함께 오페라에 가지 못하는 이유를 아니?
▶ 이유를 나타내는 선행사 the reason과 함께 쓰이는 관계부사는 why이다.
3 돌아올 때는 언제라도, 이 방법으로 공항을 찾으실 수 있을 겁니다.
▶ '방법'을 나타내는 관계부사 the way가 적절하다.
4 나는 엄마가 사 주신 빨간 모자가 더 좋다.
▶ 선행사가 사물(the red cap)이므로 목적격 관계대명사 which가 적절하다.
5 그 회사는 경영학 석사 학위를 가진 지원자를 뽑았다.
▶ 선행사가 사람(the applicant)이므로 주격 관계대명사 who가 적절하다.
6 이 학교가 우리 언니와 내가 다녔던 곳이다.

▶ attended는 목적어를 가지는 타동사이므로 attended in 이라고 쓰지 않는다. 따라서 목적격 관계대명사 which를 고른다.

7 어떤 곳을 방문하든지, 미국 인디언들에 관한 연극을 보세요.

▶ 명사 site와 어울리며 타동사인 visit의 목적어 역할을 할 수 있는 관계사 whichever가 적절하다.

C 1 너의 옆집에 사는 소녀를 알고 있니?

▶ 선행사가 사람이고, 동사 lives의 주어 역할을 할 수 있는 주격 관계대명사 who가 와야 한다.

2 어젯밤에 발생한 사고가 어떻게 일어났는지 나에게 설명해주시겠어요?

▶ 방법을 나타내는 관계부사 how와 선행사 the way는 같이 쓰지 않는다. the way와 how 중 하나만 사용한다.

3 나는 그것이 그녀가 학교에서 짠 학습 계획표와 같은 것이라고 생각해.

▶ 선행사 the same thing과 주로 같이 쓰이는 관계 대명사는 that이다.

4 엄마는 (예전에) 내게 읽어 주곤 하셨던 오래된 동화책을 발견하셨다.

▶ 타동사 found의 목적어는 ⓒ의 the old storybook이다. 그 사이에 있는 which는 필요 없다.

5 이곳이 너희 조부모님이 영국에서 이사 온 곳이다.

▶ 선행사가 the place이기 때문에, 관계부사로 where나 in which가 필요하다.

6 Padre 섬은 학생들이 봄방학을 보내는 곳으로 인기 있는 장소이다.

▶ 선행사가 a location(위치)이다. 따라서 장소를 나타내주는 관계부사 where로 고친다.

D

미시간 주(州)의 East Lansing 시는 시의 제정일 기념식을 할 예정이다. 올해로 이 도시는 100번째 생일을 맞이한다. 도시는 일 년 내내 계속되는 축하 행사를 계획하고 있다. 도시가 처음 탄생한 해는 1907년이다. 많은 사람들은 이 도시의 탄생지인 도심에서 생일을 축하할 것이다. 많은 시민들이 모여 100이라는 숫자 모양을 만들 것이다. 많은 사람들이 도심에서 친구와 이웃을 만날 것이다. 사람들로 도심이 아무리 붐빈다 할지라도, 모든 사람들이 즐거운 시간을 보낼 것이다. 시민들이 다가올 행사에 대한 정보가 필요하면 언제든지 특별 웹사이트를 방문하면 된다.

▶ (A) 선행사가 The time이므로 관계부사 when (B) 문맥상 '아무리 ~해도'를 나타내는 However (C) 문맥상 '언제든지'를 나타내는 whenever

FURTHER STUDY [Writing] P.193

1 the bicycle whose/of which the rear tire is flat
2 the freshman who(m)/that you interviewed
3 the cell phone which/that I told you about
4 introduced the new math teacher whose name is Hansen
5 how/the way the picture was painted
6 was the reason why I couldn't sleep well
7 have whatever you want
8 the time when a lot of kids visit

WRAP-UP TEST P.195

1 ⓓ	2 ⓒ
3 ⓑ	4 ⓓ
5 ⓓ	6 ⓑ
7 ⓐ	8 ⓒ
9 ⓐ, ⓑ	10 ⓐ

1 우리 모두 그가 준 것을 좋아했다.
이것이 그가 찾고 있던 것이다.

▶ 선행사를 포함하는 관계대명사 what이 적절하다.

2 그가 바로 그 사람이다. 나는 그를 정말 미워한다.

▶ the one 다음에는 관계대명사 who[that]가 생략되었다.

3 ⓐ 이곳이 우리가 야구를 하곤 했던 공원이다. ⓑ 나는 Sarah Parker라는 이름을 가진 소녀를 알고 있다. ⓒ 이것이 네가 고를 수 있는 가장 좋은 방법이다. ⓓ 나는 우리가 처음 만났던 날을 잊을 수가 없다.

▶ 소유격 관계대명사는 생략할 수 없다.

4 이것은 내가 먹어 본 스파게티 중 가장 맛이 없다.

▶ 주어진 문장, ⓐ, ⓑ, ⓒ: 목적격 관계대명사 / ⓓ: 주격

5 ⓐ 그들이 런던에 도착한 날은 비가 오고 안개가 끼었다. ⓑ 지난밤에 잠을 잘 수가 없었던 이유는 울고 있는 고양이 때문이었다. ⓒ 네가 어떻게 과학 문제를 풀었는지 말해 줄 수 있니? ⓓ 우리가 어디에서 만나기로 했는지 아무도 모른다.

▶ in which = where

6 이 근처에 세워 둔 자전거를 본 사람이 있나요? 누가 훔쳐간 것이 틀림없어요.

▶ 선행사 the bike 뒤에 관계대명사가 와야 한다.

7 ⓐ 나는 캐나다 오타와에서 온 외국인 친구가 있다. ⓑ Monica는 내가 그녀에게 빌려준 책 중 한 권을 잃어버렸다. ⓒ 그는 LA에서 산 많은 DVD를 가지고 있다. ⓓ Joanna는 항상 Anne의 집 지붕처럼 지붕이 녹색인 집에서 사는 것을 꿈꿨다.

▶ 소유격 관계대명사 다음에는 명사가 와야 한다.

8 ⓐ 당신이 원하는 것은 무엇이든지 고를 수 있습니다. ⓑ 어디를 가더라도 나는 언제나 당신과 함께하겠습니다. ⓒ 이 책이 그가 찾고 있는 책인가요? ⓓ 내 친구 중 한 명이 어젯밤에 자동차 사고를 당했는데 이로 인해 모든 반 학생들이 놀랐다.

▶ 관계대명사 that 앞에는 전치사가 올 수 없다.

[9-10]

미국의 한 회사에서 신기술을 이용해 더 안전한 도로를 만들고 있다. 이 새 도로 표면은 눈이 들러붙지 않는다. 이 도로 위에 소금이 살포되는 곳이면 어디든지 그 효과는 훨씬 좋아진다. 또한, 이 새 도로의 표면은 위험한 '검은 얼음'의 발생도 막아 준다. 검은 얼음이란 고속도로 위에 육안으로는 보이지 않는 얼음(빙판)을 말한다. 겨울에 사고가 많이 일어나는 이유도 이 때문이다. 이 새로운

도로 표면은 사고를 줄여 주는 방법이다. 심지어는 사고가 많이 발생하던 어떤 다리에서 사고율이 제로로 줄어들었다. 많은 주(州)에서 고속도로에 새 표면을 만드는 재료를 얻기를 원한다.

9 ▶ the way와 how는 같이 쓰지 않는다.

10 ▶ It은 앞문장의 black ice를 의미한다.

Unit 13

Unit 1 가정법 (I)

Pre-Check P.198

1 당신이 컵을 떨어뜨리면 그것은 깨질 것이다.
2 내가 당신이라면 그들과 함께 가지 않을 텐데.
3 그가 복권에 당첨되었다면 가난한 사람들을 도왔을 텐데.

Check-up P.199

A 1 ⓓ 2 ⓔ
3 ⓐ 4 ⓒ
5 ⓑ

B 1 ⓐ 2 ⓑ

EXERCISE P.200

A 1 will go 2 were
3 had found 4 will burn
5 won't 6 would have been

B 1 will cancel 2 were
3 would/could get 4 hadn't [had not] snowed

C 1 didn't stay, couldn't see
2 isn't, can't play
3 didn't study, was not
4 couldn't find, was late

A 1 아직 확정되지 않은 현재나 미래의 일을 나타내는 단순 조건문이다. 시간과 조건을 나타내는 부사절에서는 현재시제가 미래시제를 대신하므로 if절에서는 현재시제, 주절에서는 미래시제가 된다. 따라서 will go를 고른다.
2 가정법 과거 if절에서 쓰이는 be동사는 인칭이나 수에 관계없이 were가 쓰인다.
3 주절의 동사 형태가 가정법 과거완료이다. 따라서 if절에는 had found가 와야 한다.
4 단순 조건문이므로 will burn을 고른다.
5 단순 조건문이므로 won't를 고른다.
6 if절의 동사 형태와 내용으로 보아 가정법 과거완료임을 알 수 있다. 따라서 would have been을 고른다.

Unit 2 가정법 (II)

Pre-Check P.201

1 wish 2 wish
3 as if

Check-up P.202

A 1 helped 2 were
3 had spoken 4 would buy

B (1) I could stay here and help you
(2) we could do well together

EXERCISE P.203

A 1 were 2 had lived
3 had called 4 were
5 had set

B 1 were 2 had sent
3 hadn't bought 4 knew
5 hadn't had

C 1 made 2 is not
3 care about 4 broke
5 am not

A 1 '바보가 아니다'라는 것은 현재 사실이다. 그래서 현재 사실에 반대되는 가정법 과거를 사용한다.
2 '~에 살았던 것처럼'이라는 의미로 쓰였다. 과거 사실에 대한 반대이므로 가정법 과거완료를 쓴다.
3 과거에 일어난 일에 대한 얘기이다. 따라서 가정법 과거완료를 쓴다.
4 현재 사실을 언급하고 있다. 또한 문장의 내용상 '현재 ~였으면 좋겠다'는 의미이므로 가정법 과거를 쓴다.
5 '알람을 맞춰 놓고 잤으면 좋았을 텐데'라는 과거의 사실을 말하고 있으므로 가정법 과거완료를 쓴다.

Unit 3 일치, 특수 구문

Pre-Check P.204

1 on earth 2 do
3 the director of *Jurassic Park*

Check-up P.206

A 1 your grandmother
2 the Friday after Thanksgiving
3 a scholarship
4 Mr. Benjamin

B ① is ② are
③ is

EXERCISE

P.207

A 1 are 2 came an old horse
3 mention 4 is
5 Are 6 do

B 1 There goes 2 did I discover
3 ○ 4 Neither/Nor did I
5 has he done 6 so was I
7 ○

C 1 It was Kevin
2 It was the young boy
3 It was the soccer ball
4 It was her youngest cousin
5 It was on the afternoon flight

B 1 here, there로 시작하는 문장은 주어와 동사가 도치된다. 따라서 There goes로 고친다.
2 only 등의 부정의 뜻을 가진 말이 문두에 오면 주어와 동사가 도치되어 〈부정어 + be/do/조동사 + S + V〉의 어순이 된다.
4 nor, neither등이 문두로 나오면 주어와 동사가 도치되며 앞 문장이 부정문이므로 〈Neither did I〉나 〈Nor did I〉로 바꾼다.
5 부정어가 문두에 오면 주어 동사는 도치되는데 동사구 전체가 도치되는 것이 아니라 조동사만 도치된다. 따라서 has만 주어와 도치되어야 한다.
6 앞문장의 내용을 받는 so, neither, nor가 문두로 나오면 주어 동사가 도치된다. 그래서 so was I로 바꾼다.

R REVIEW TEST

P.208

A 1 have gone 2 will fly
3 could buy 4 had said
5 want 6 wouldn't have been
7 disagree 8 is

B 1 ⓓ 2 ⓓ 3 ⓑ 4 ⓐ
5 ⓑ 6 ⓒ 7 ⓐ

C 1 If it were not for snow, we could go for a drive now.
2 Both he and she wore the same sweater to the amusement park yesterday.
3 If she had arrived on time, we might have gotten a table.
4 While he and I were baking bread, the phone rang in the bakery.
5 It was the English literature composition that my brother wrote.
6 The chemistry teacher, Mr. Cortez, helps me with my science project all the time.

D ⑤

A 1 그들이 나를 초대했었다면 나도 어젯밤에 그들과 함께 갔었을 텐데.
▶ 과거 사실에 반대되는 내용이므로 가정법 과거완료를 쓴다.
2 새장이 열리면 그 카나리아는 날아갈 것이다.
▶ If절에 현재시제를 써서 아직 확정되지 않은 현재나 미래의 일을 나타낸 단순 조건문이다.
3 내게 5달러가 있다면 너에게 아이스크림을 사 줄 수 있을 텐데.
▶ if절의 동사가 과거로, 현재 사실에 반대되는 가정법 과거 형태의 문장이다.
4 그녀는 내가 뭔가를 잘못 말한 것 같은 표정을 지었다.
▶ as if 가정법으로 과거 사실에 반대되는 의미이다.
5 나는 그것이 Tara와 Doris가 나에게 얘기하려고 한 것이라고 생각한다.
▶ I imagine은 삽입어구이다. 이 문장의 동사의 시제가 현재이므로 종속절의 동사도 현재(want)를 고른다.
6 그녀가 내 경고를 들었더라면, 그때 그런 문제를 겪지 않았을 텐데.
▶ 과거 사실의 반대인 가정법 과거완료 문장이다.
7 우리 학교의 대부분의 학생들이 내 의견에 반대한다.
▶ most students는 복수명사이므로 동사의 수를 복수형에 일치시켜야 한다.
8 수학은 내가 가장 좋아하는 과목이다.
▶ 학과명은 단수동사를 쓴다.

B 1 내가 그 상을 받았다면, 선생님께서 놀라셨을 텐데.
▶ 과거 사실의 반대되는 내용을 가정하는 가정법 과거완료 문장이다.
2 아침에 날씨가 좋지 않으면, 나와 오빠는 수영하러 가지 않을 것이다.
▶ 조건을 나타내는 단순 부사절이다. 따라서 주절에 미래시제를 쓴다.
3 얼마 지나지 않아 나는 그녀가 그에게 파티에 대해서 얘기했다는 걸 알게 되었다.
▶ 부정어구가 문장 앞으로 오면 주어 동사가 도치된다. 〈부정어 + be/do/조동사 + S + V〉의 어순이다.
4 식탁 아래에 있는 내 지갑을 발견한 사람은 웨이터였다.
▶ 〈It ~ that ...〉의 강조 구문이다.
5 나는 그의 것과 같은 새 핸드폰을 가지고 싶다.
▶ 현재 사실에 반대되는 내용인 가정법 과거 문장이다.
6 사람들은 자신들이 비싼 선물을 받을 수 없다는 데 동의했고, 나 역시 그랬다.
▶ so, neither, nor 등을 써서 앞의 내용을 받을 때는 주어와 동사가 도치된다. 여기서는 부정의 내용을 받은 것이므로 neither가 와야 한다.
7 강아지를 데리고 한 남자가 빌딩 밖으로 걸어 나왔다.
▶ 장소 부사가 문장 앞으로 나올 때 주어와 동사는 도치된다.

C 1 눈이 내리지 않으면 지금 드라이브를 갈 텐데.
▶ If it were not for ~ 구문이다.
2 어제 놀이공원에 갔을 때 그와 그녀는 똑같은 스웨터를 입고 갔었다.
▶ 〈both A and B〉 구문이므로 동사를 복수 형태로 한다. 또한 yesterday는 과거 시점이므로 wears를 wore로 고친다.

3 그녀가 제시간에 도착했더라면, 우리가 자리를 잡을 수 있었을 텐데.
▶ 내용상 과거 사실과 반대되는 가정법 과거완료 문장임을 알 수 있다. 따라서 arrived를 had arrived로 고친다.

4 그와 내가 제과점에서 빵을 굽고 있는 동안 전화가 울렸다.
▶ 내용상 과거에 일어난 일이다. 종속절의 시제가 과거이므로 주절에도 과거시제가 와야 한다.

5 내 동생이 쓴 것은 영문학 작품이었다.
▶ 〈It ~ that ...〉 강조 구문이다. 따라서 what을 that으로 고친다.

6 화학 교사인 Cortez 씨는 항상 내 과학 숙제를 도와준다.
▶ 화학 교사와 Cortez 씨는 동격이다. 따라서 주어는 3인칭 단수가 되므로 help를 helps로 고친다.

D

오늘은 우리 오빠의 생일이다. 오빠를 위해 다른 선물을 샀었더라면 좋았을 것 같다. 왜냐고? 방금 난 오빠가 정말로 갖고 싶어 하는 것이 무엇인지 알아냈다. 오빠는 새로운 게임 CD를 갖고 싶어 한다. 오빠는 미치 나를 마음을 읽을 수 있는 능력이 있는 사람처럼 대한다. 오빠는 해마다 생일 선물로 무엇을 받고 싶어 하는지 내게 알아맞히게 한다. 그리고 그의 생일인 오늘에서야 자신이 무엇을 갖고 싶어 하는지 말한다. 매년 이런 식이다. 내가 더 나이가 많다면, 그에게 매년 생일 선물 '알아맞히기 게임'에 대해서 내가 어떻게 생각하는지 말해줄 것이다. 하지만 그렇게 하는 대신 나는 오빠의 친구들이 오기 전에 새로운 게임 CD를 사러 가야 한다.

▶ (A) I wish 가정법으로, 현재 사실에 반대되는 가정법 과거이므로 had bought (B) as if 가정법으로, 현재 사실에 반대되는 가정법 과거 (C) 가정법 과거 문장으로, if절에 쓰이는 be동사는 인칭에 관계없이 were

FURTHER STUDY [Writing]

P.210

1 were rich, would travel around the world
2 had come with me, could have met him
3 had read the map, could find the station
4 wish I spoke [could speak] Spanish
5 as if he had stayed at the library
6 is my favorite subject
7 is all I have
8 The number of people at the free concert was

WRAP-UP TEST

P.212

1 ⓐ
2 were
3 ⓐ
4 ⓑ
5 ⓐ
6 didn't do anything wrong
7 ⓓ
8 ⓐ
9 If he hadn't been a former sports star
10 ⓑ

1 A: 내일 비가 오면 뭐 할 거야?
B: 수영 대신에 쇼핑하러 갈 거야.
▶ 단순 조건문으로 내일 무엇을 할지 미래시제로 답하는 것이 적절하다.

2 • 내가 너라면 일을 그만두고 로마로 갈 거야.
• 그녀의 도움이 없었더라면 거기에 제시간에 갈 수 없었을 거야.
▶ 가정법 과거의 if절에서 be동사는 were를 쓴다.

3 ⓐ 네가 그녀를 사랑한다면 그녀에게 청혼해야 해. ⓑ 내가 너라면 그 신발을 살 텐데. ⓒ 그는 CSI 요원인 것처럼 행동한다. ⓓ 나도 네 것과 같은 카메라가 있다면 좋을 텐데.
▶ ⓐ: 단순 조건문 ⓑ, ⓒ, ⓓ: 가정법

4 그때 우리가 기차를 탔더라면 지금쯤 해변에서 수영을 하고 있을 것이다.
▶ 혼합가정법으로 과거에 일어난 일이 현재까지 영향을 미치는 경우이다. by now를 통해서 알 수 있다.

5 ⓐ 1년 반은 나에겐 그렇게 긴 시간이 아니었다. ⓑ 당뇨병은 요즘 가장 흔한 질병 중 하나이다. ⓒ 나는 생선을 날 것으로 먹어 본 적이 없다. ⓓ Jim 뿐만 아니라 나도 테니스를 잘 친다.
▶ ⓑ diabetes는 병명으로 단수 취급(are → is)
ⓒ 부정문+동사+주어(I had → had I)
ⓓ not only A but also B (are → am)

6 그녀는 내가 그녀에게 무언가 잘못한 것처럼 행동한다.
▶ as if + 가정법 과거완료: 과거의 사실과 반대
'사실, 나는 그녀에게 잘못한 것이 없다'의 의미가 된다.

7 모두가 __________에 대해서 동의했다.
▶ 주절이 과거(agreed)이므로 종속절에는 과거, 과거완료가 올 수 있다.

8 ⓐ 내가 산 오렌지의 대부분은 시었다. ⓑ 신입생의 수가 매년 줄어들고 있다. ⓒ 수학과 정치는 내가 가장 좋아하는 과목이다. ⓓ 우리 아버지뿐만 아니라 어머니도 선생님이다.
▶ ⓐ most of + 복수 명사(oranges) + 복수 동사(were)
ⓑ the number of + 복수 명사 + 단수 동사

[9-10]

어느 유명한 전직 축구 선수가 미국 텔레비전 쇼에 출연했다. 그가 출연한 쇼는 'Survivor'이다. 그는 자신이 생존 경쟁 게임에서 이긴다면, 백만 달러를 받게 된다는 것을 알고 있었다. 그는 그 상금을 받기를 원했다. 만약 그가 유명한 전직 축구 선수가 아니었다면 그 게임에 출연도 못했을 것이다. 그는 그 게임에 대비해 운동을 했다. 전에는 흰개미와 도토리도 결코 먹어 본 적이 없었다. 생존 게임을 하는 동안, 그는 더위와 부족한 음식 때문에 몸무게가 30 파운드나 빠졌다. 전에 유명 인사였던 Gary Hogeboom은 최후 승자가 되지는 못했지만, 과테말라 'Survivor'시리즈에서 마지막 남은 7명 중의 한 명이었다.

9 ▶ 가정법 과거완료: if+S+had p.p., S+would have p.p.

10 ▶ 게임 생존자 중 한 명으로, 게임 중에 있으므로 아직 백만 달러를 받지 못했다.

Workbook 정답 ▸▸

Unit 01

1 현재 & 현재진행형

P. 2

A

1 have　　2 arrives/is arriving
3 is applying　　4 grow
5 is dripping　　6 are looking
7 don't own

B

1 ○　　2 remember
3 carry　　4 is studying
5 have　　6 needs
7 believe

C

1 I like many flavors
2 Do you usually clean
3 The Michigan economy isn't declining
4 My computer skills aren't increasing

내신 FOCUS

A 1 ⓑ　　2 ⓒ
B 1 ⓑ　　2 ⓓ
C 1 ⓓ　　2 ⓓ
D 1 resembles his grandfather
2 does not belong to me
3 starts at 2 pm
4 until I call you

2 과거 & 과거진행형

P. 4

A

1 placed
2 received
3 heard
4 was paying
5 are taking

B

1 told　　2 participated in
3 wrote　　4 lived in
5 was　　6 ate

C

1 met　　2 had
3 heard　　4 ○
5 ○　　6 wanted

내신 FOCUS

A 1 ⓑ　　2 ⓓ
B 1 ⓓ　　2 ⓑ
C 1 ⓑ　　2 ⓑ
D 1 wrote the song
2 left the office
3 was snowing, wasn't raining
4 was meeting a person

3 미래 & 미래진행형

P. 6

A

1 are going to rent
2 is not going to enter
3 is going to repair
4 Are you going to make

B

1 미래
2 미래
3 현재진행
4 미래
5 현재진행

C

1 is going to
2 ○
3 ○
4 is going to bring

내신 FOCUS

A 1 is going to be
2 is arriving
B 1 ⓓ　　2 ⓓ
C 1 ⓒ　　2 ⓐ
D 1 will[are going to] stay here
2 is about to leave
3 will be waiting

Unit 02

1 현재완료 (I)

P. 8

A

1 Have you ever baked
2 Did you lose
3 How long
4 have been

B

1	since	2	How long
3	hasn't	4	for
5	always visit	6	○
7	lived	8	○

C

1 has purchased
2 has taken
3 have flown
4 have known

내신 FOCUS

A 1 for 2 since
B 1 ⓒ 2 ⓑ
C 1 ⓓ 2 ⓐ
D 1 have not seen Fred since last Christmas
2 have you played the violin
3 have you ever tried sushi

2 현재완료 (II)

P. 10

A

1	have lost	2	haven't started
3	hasn't planned	4	has moved

B

1	○	2	have
3	○	4	has
5	repaired	6	given

C

1 has purchased good meat
2 have prevented some robberies
3 have just finished
4 have not used the calculator
5 has warned the students

내신 FOCUS

A 1 went, has gone
2 did not do, have not done
B 1 ⓑ 2 ⓒ
C 1 ⓒ 2 ⓓ
D 1 has gone to England
2 have left my keys
3 have sold my computer

3 과거완료, 미래완료, 완료진행형

P. 12

A

1 has just finished
2 will have completed
3 had performed
4 had spent
5 has not set
6 will have landed

B

1 ○
2 had moved
3 ○
4 will have been
5 for
6 had never heard

C

1 will have destroyed many homes
2 has studied geography
3 will have picked up the cat
4 had met several times before
5 has already been working
6 had never visited

내신 FOCUS

A 1 will have seen
2 has been doing
B 1 ⓓ 2 ⓓ
C 1 ⓓ 2 ⓐ
D 1 had cleaned her room, arrived
2 will have worked for 30 years by next year
3 has been eating dinner for one hour

Unit 03

조동사 can, may

P. 14

A

1 be able to　2 may
3 can　4 couldn't
5 Could　6 may

B

1 ⓒ　2 ⓐ
3 ⓑ　4 ⓑ
5 ⓒ

C

1 이번 주말에 경기에 참여할 수 있겠니?
2 학교 축제에 쓸 새 포스터를 만들어 주시겠어요?
3 Sam은 아마도 식료품점에 있을 거야.
4 당신은 여기에 주차하실 수 있어요.

내신 FOCUS

A 1 can　2 can't
B 1 ⓑ　2 ⓒ
C 1 ⓓ　2 ⓐ
D 1 may/might drop by here
2 Could/Can/Would/Will you give me a ride
3 can't[cannot] cost that much

조동사 will, must, shall

P. 16

A

1 would　2 had to
3 must not　4 will not
5 must be　6 should have

B

1 ○　2 had to
3 (will) have to/must　4 must not/should not
5 ○　6 will

C

1 저를 위해서 이 소포를 우체국에 가져가 주시겠어요?
2 버스 운전기사가 운전을 하는 동안에는 그를 방해해서는 안 된다.
3 그가 요리사가 될 거라고? 믿을 수 없어!
4 그 소프트웨어가 어떻게 작동되고 있는지 눈여겨봐야 한다.
5 수요일 밤 오페라 티켓을 살까요?

내신 FOCUS

A 1 ⓐ　2 ⓐ
B 1 ⓓ　2 ⓒ
C 1 ⓐ　2 ⓓ
D 1 would[used to] take a walk after dinner
2 must[should] not talk on the cell phone
3 should have apologized to him

3 기타 조동사

P. 18

A

1 need not　2 had better
3 used to　4 could have
5 must have

B

1 would rather　2 didn't
3 used to　4 ○
5 ○　6 ought to

C

1 had better clean up
2 would rather go shopping
3 must not have seen
4 must have found out
5 had better play

내신 FOCUS

A 1 You'd better not cancel
2 I would rather not drink
B 1 ⓓ　2 ⓐ
C 1 ⓑ　2 ⓓ
D 1 used to be slim
2 would rather go with you
3 must have seen me

Unit 04

to부정사

P. 20

A

1 to swim　2 to tell
3 To collect　4 to play

5 to find

B

1	wear	2	to fix
3	○	4	To own
5	to change	6	○

C

1 It is difficult to choose which way to go.
2 It is wise to hear Tom's ideas
3 It is easy to send an email
4 It is sometimes important to speak slowly to non-native speakers.
5 It is challenging for young men and women to become astronauts.

내신 FOCUS

A 1 to come 2 to raise
B 1 ⓑ 2 ⓑ
C 1 ⓑ 2 ⓓ
D 1 to read a detective story
2 to be a great teacher
3 to cook Italian food
4 haven't decided what to wear

Unit 2 to부정사의 부사적 쓰임

P. 22

A

1	to stay	2	to be
3	to start	4	to read
5	to get	6	to receive

B

1 too tired to drive to the park
2 if they see the aquarium
3 too late to see the doctor
4 in order to discuss the complaint with her
5 so worried about the exam that he can't think about the party

내신 FOCUS

A 1 enough 2 too
B 1 ⓑ 2 ⓑ
C 1 ⓑ 2 ⓓ
D 1 not to wake up the baby
2 laughed loudly to see her funny hat
3 hard enough to get an A

Unit 3 to부정사의 형용사적 쓰임

P. 24

A

1 to play with
2 to talk about
3 to fill out

B

1 to remind us about the test
2 to collect 100 baseball cards
3 to talk about a new agenda

C

1 is to sit down
2 are to fly to
3 has nothing to discuss
4 something sweet to eat

내신 FOCUS

A 1 with 2 in
B 1 ⓓ 2 ⓑ
C 1 ⓒ 2 ⓒ
D 1 good news to tell
2 needed someone to talk to
3 wanted something cold to drink
4 have houses to live in

Unit 4 부정사의 기타 쓰임 & 원형부정사

P. 26

A

1	to eat	2	seemed to
3	help	4	hit/hitting

B

1	○	2	for
3	to understand	4	describe

C

1 seem to be completing
2 not good for dogs to spend
3 smelled something burn
4 her to keep taking
5 everyone to come to the party
6 helped me do

내신 FOCUS

A 1 ⓒ 2 ⓒ
B 1 ⓒ 2 ⓓ
C 1 ⓐ 2 ⓓ

D 1 easy for me to finish the work
2 to have been late again
3 had the students carry the luggage
4 watched the stars move

Unit 05

동명사의 여러 가지 쓰임

P. 28

A
1 creating 2 cleaning
3 reading 4 Making
5 Having 6 performing

B
1 entering
2 ○
3 feed
4 Owning/To own
5 ○

C
1 Reading mystery novels
2 Becoming a veterinarian
3 teaching sculpture
4 Buying a new cell phone
5 repairing broken cars

내신 FOCUS

A ⓐ
B 1 ⓒ 2 ⓓ
C 1 ⓑ 2 ⓓ
D 1 liked his acting
2 telling me the truth
3 is writing scenarios
4 Writing an essay is

동명사 vs. 부정사

P. 30

A
1 to solve 2 swimming
3 chasing 4 speaking
5 making 6 to change
7 to ski

B
1 taking, to remain
2 having, to cooperate
3 to see, to report
4 identifying, to access

C
1 request to modify the contract
2 practiced running for a marathon
3 decided to build a new building
4 suggested parking in a parking lot

내신 FOCUS

A 1 ⓑ 2 ⓓ
B 1 ⓐ 2 ⓑ
C 1 ⓐ 2 ⓒ
D 1 began learning[to learn] English
2 puts off cleaning his room
3 forgot to bring a swimming suit

Unit 3 동명사의 기타 쓰임

P. 32

A
1 me
2 discussing
3 to making
4 not informing
5 trying
6 eating

B
1 him
2 from attending
3 my
4 ○
5 ○
6 Fishing

C
1 can't help looking at
2 succeeded in completing
3 kept on complaining
4 fearful of changing
5 feel like doing more homework

내신 FOCUS

A 1 ⓑ 2 ⓒ
B 1 ⓒ 2 ⓐ
C 1 ⓓ 2 ⓑ

D 1 after arriving home
2 dreams about going abroad
3 insisted on doing it
4 prevented us from seeing

Unit 06

Unit 1 현재분사

P. 34

A

1 P 2 G
3 G 4 P
5 P 6 G
7 P

B

1 is dripping
2 competing/compete for
3 flooding
4 shining
5 is reloading

C

1 calling from the hallway
2 coming toward me
3 knitting on the park bench
4 showing at the theater

내신 FOCUS

A 1 boring
2 confusing
B 1 ⓒ 2 ⓐ
C 1 ⓒ 2 ⓒ
D 1 earthshaking news
2 very interesting
3 wearing the black suit

과거분사

P. 36

A

1 looking 2 disappointed
3 fallen 4 fixed
5 heard 6 wearing

B

1 lost 2 held
3 hidden 4 flying
5 trusted

C

1 opened box
2 spoken to the team
3 taken to the tent
4 scared kitten
5 flowers painted on every advertisement

내신 FOCUS

A 1 ⓓ 2 ⓓ
B 1 ⓒ 2 ⓒ
C 1 ⓓ 2 ⓐ
D 1 fixed computer broke down again
2 a ring fallen on the grass
3 a book written in Japanese

Unit 3 분사의 여러 다양한 표현

P. 38

A

1 Waiting 2 Finding
3 being 4 Depending
5 Since 6 Not knowing

B

1 If
2 While
3 After
4 Because

C

1 Generally speaking
2 Passing the market
3 Considering the alternatives
4 Judging from his fans' response

내신 FOCUS

A 1 ⓒ 2 ⓐ
B 1 ⓒ 2 ⓒ
C 1 ⓑ 2 ⓑ
D 1 Having no money
2 Jumping rope
3 Cleaning the computer screen

Unit 07

수동태

P. 40

A

1 was taken
2 were scared
3 will be taught
4 was purchased
5 will be maintained

B

1 released　2 be designed
3 be listed　4 been owned
5 ○

C

1 The foundation of the large building was prepared
2 The computer in the library was being used
3 A special cake is being baked
4 A new curriculum will be presented
5 The vase has been filled
6 The good news about her is known

내신 FOCUS

A 1 ⓒ　2 ⓑ
B 1 ⓑ　2 ⓒ
C 1 ⓒ　2 ⓑ
D 1 was built in 1996
2 was written by Karen
3 will be held

수동태의 여러 가지 형태

P. 42

A

1 was allowed to drive
2 is written to me
3 was being watched
4 was sold
5 were made to
6 will be taught

B

1 run　2 be written
3 to　4 ○
5 was called

C

1 smells　2 be paid
3 be found　4 was given

내신 FOCUS

A 1 from　2 to
B 1 ⓓ　2 ⓓ
C 1 ⓓ　2 ⓐ
D 1 was given a book by Jane
2 was taken care of by
3 were made to clean our room by

Unit 08

1 명사

P. 44

A

1 some　2 a slice of
3 The basket of　4 hope
5 several　6 a box of
7 Europe

B

1 Australia
2 a bowl of rice
3 little time
4 ○
5 any/much
6 a golden opportunity

C

1 a cup of　2 a slice of
3 many　4 two pounds of
5 a tablespoon of　6 a carton of

내신 FOCUS

A ⓐ
B 1 ⓒ　2 ⓑ
C 1 ⓑ　2 ⓐ
D 1 without sugar or cream
2 your last chance
3 as an archaeologist
4 two bottles of water

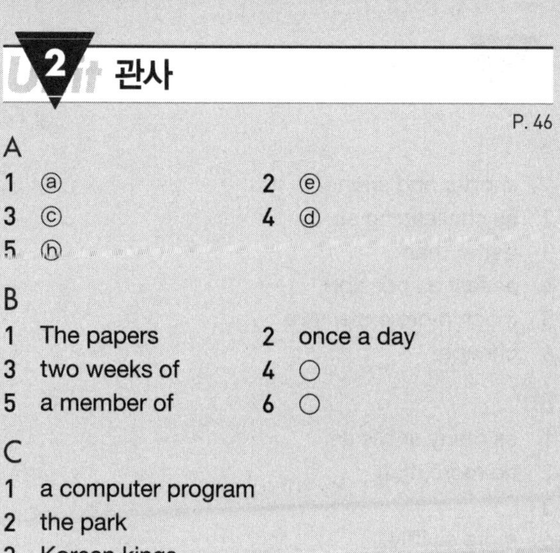

Unit 2 관사

P. 46

A

1 ⓐ 2 ⓔ
3 ⓒ 4 ⓓ
5 ⓗ

B

1 The papers 2 once a day
3 two weeks of 4 ○
5 a member of 6 ○

C

1 a computer program
2 the park
3 Korean kings
4 a classical music concert
5 Alaska

내신 FOCUS

A 1 an 2 the/The
B 1 ⓑ 2 ⓐ
C 1 ⓐ 2 ⓓ
D 1 take an hour
2 once an hour
3 The hot chocolate
4 the man stole my wallet

Unit 3 대명사

P. 48

A

1 him 2 her
3 myself 4 It
5 These 6 They
7 Steven's

B

1 those 2 ○
3 she 4 my
5 ○ 6 my

C

1 ourselves 2 him
3 this 4 She
5 those 6 it

내신 FOCUS

A 1 We 2 mine, Brandon's
B 1 ⓑ 2 ⓐ
C 1 ⓒ 2 ⓑ
D 1 with a friend of hers
2 with his family last week
3 from my house
4 those in the city

Unit 4 부정대명사

P. 50

A

1 both 2 One
3 some 4 none
5 another 6 Either

B

1 Both 2 the old ones
3 None 4 ○
5 the other one 6 ○

C

1 the other 2 some
3 most 4 another

내신 FOCUS

A 1 one, the other 2 another
B 1 ⓓ 2 ⓐ
C 1 ⓑ 2 ⓒ
D 1 Most of the books
2 the other is rotten
3 None of our mistakes
4 Someone should clean the table

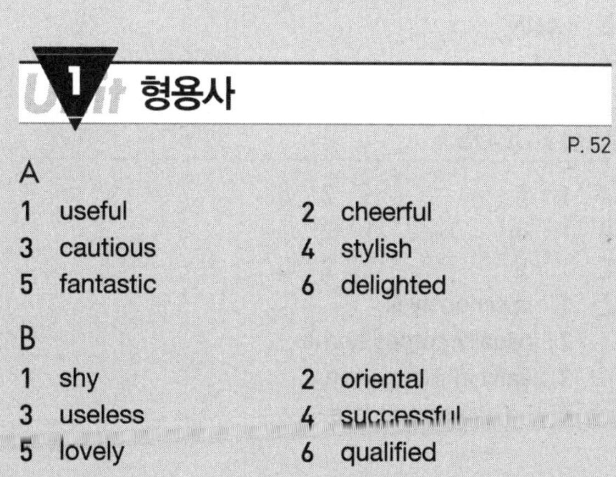

Unit 09

Unit 1 형용사

P. 52

A

1 useful 2 cheerful
3 cautious 4 stylish
5 fantastic 6 delighted

B

1 shy 2 oriental
3 useless 4 successful
5 lovely 6 qualified

C

1 colorful flowers
2 a new card game
3 any Mexican restaurants
4 a dental appointment
5 much experience at

내신 FOCUS

A 1 successful 2 childish
B 1 ⓑ 2 ⓑ
C 1 ⓑ 2 ⓒ
D 1 was upset at the noise outside
2 this new program useful
3 anyone capable of speaking French
4 your present address

Unit 2 부사

P. 54

A

1 부사 2 형용사
3 형용사 4 부사
5 부사 6 형용사
7 부사

B

1 ○
2 ○
3 quietly
4 sometimes
5 some
6 too late
7 hard

C

1 usually
2 viciously
3 Lastly
4 fast

내신 FOCUS

A 1 ⓐ 2 ⓓ
B 1 ⓑ 2 ⓓ
C 1 ⓑ 2 ⓓ
D 1 is seriously ill
2 usually comes home
3 early in the morning
4 he arrived too late

Unit 3 비교

P. 56

A

1 shorter and shorter
2 as challenging as
3 better than
4 as fast as possible
5 much more expensive
6 cheaper

B

1 as many shells as
2 no more than
3 ○
4 more swiftly
5 more and more

C

1 better than
2 more and more
3 more money than
4 as tall as

내신 FOCUS

A 1 farther than 2 senior to
B 1 ⓓ 2 ⓐ
C 1 ⓒ 2 ⓒ
D 1 as many CDs as
2 twice as expensive as
3 bigger and bigger

Unit 10

Unit 1 전치사 (I)

P. 58

A

1 until 2 behind
3 from 4 at
5 during 6 on
7 through

B

1 into 2 after
3 next to 4 down
5 out of 6 at

C

1 on 2 at
3 in 4 before
5 until

내신 FOCUS

A 1 ⓓ 2 ⓓ
B 1 ⓑ 2 ⓐ
C 1 ⓑ 2 ⓒ
D 1 fell off the bed
2 goes through
3 during my college years

Unit 2 전치사 (II)

P. 60

A

1 for 2 with
3 from 4 to
5 of

B

1 at 2 in
3 from 4 of
5 on 6 for
7 by 8 to

내신 FOCUS

A 1 ⓒ 2 ⓑ
B 1 ⓓ 2 ⓐ
C 1 ⓐ 2 ⓓ
D 1 suffered from
2 for one week
3 a quarter to seven

Unit 3 전치사를 포함한 다양한 표현

P. 62

A

1 of 2 to
3 of 4 on
5 with 6 between
7 for

B

1 of 2 ○
3 on 4 with
5 from 6 with

C

1 responsible for 2 cause of
3 damage to 4 pleased with
5 forget about 6 in connection with

내신 FOCUS

A 1 from 2 to
B 1 ⓑ 2 ⓐ
C 1 ⓒ 2 ⓑ
D 1 forgot about
2 consists of
3 be ashamed of
4 in connection with

Unit 11

Unit 1 접속사

P. 64

A

1 Not only 2 Neither
3 and 4 either
5 but 6 or

B

1 ○ 2 and
3 or 4 because/for
5 or 6 but

C

1 (Both) Jim and Sam
2 because we wanted to go to the Blarney Stone
3 so I took an aspirin
4 that I am at the doctor's now
5 Neither my sister nor I

내신 FOCUS

A 1 ⓐ 2 ⓐ
B 1 ⓒ 2 ⓑ
C 1 ⓓ 2 ⓓ
D 1 young but wise
2 or go out
3 Either David or I am

Unit 2 명사절

P. 66

A

1 Whether　　2 It
3 that　　4 who
5 where　　6 what

B

1 ○　　2 What
3 that　　4 what
5 ○

C

1 where the new city park is
2 what that spot on his arm is
3 who the race car driver on TV is
4 what you want to do now
5 where I could buy that book

내신 FOCUS

A 1 what you are
　2 if/whether he is coming
B 1 ⓓ　　2 ⓐ
C 1 ⓒ　　2 ⓑ
D 1 that she is your cousin
　2 that there's life on Mars
　3 that he will accept the offer

Unit 3 부사절

P. 68

A

1 when
2 but
3 so
4 unless
5 while
6 Although

B

1 ○　　2 but
3 because　　4 If
5 Because　　6 If possible

C

1 if you hold onto the string
2 As the lake was very beautiful
3 such a large box that I couldn't
4 so that we could get to the train station on time
5 Since my brother fixed my car quickly

내신 FOCUS

A 1 While　　2 until
B 1 ⓐ　　2 ⓑ
C 1 ⓒ　　2 ⓒ
D 1 If you want my support
　2 because/since he wants to buy his own car
　3 Even though/Although/Though I knew it was my mistake

Unit 12

Unit 1 관계대명사

P. 70

A

1 whose
2 who
3 that
4 Whoever
5 Whichever
6 which
7 Whatever

B

1 who(m)　　2 with whom
3 ○　　4 who(m)
5 who　　6 ○

C

1 which
2 the books which/that
3 my new car whose
4 new customers who
5 whichever TV

내신 FOCUS

A 1 ⓑ, ⓓ　　2 ⓒ, ⓓ
B 1 ⓑ　　2 ⓑ
C 1 ⓓ　　2 ⓐ
D 1 who/that lives next door
　2 that excited us
　3 who didn't recognize me
　4 What I want is

Unit 2 관계부사

P. 72

A

1 why
2 where
3 Wherever
4 how
5 when
6 whenever
7 when

B

1 Whenever
2 ○
3 where
4 ○
5 However

C

1 at any time when
2 at any place where
3 No matter how
4 in which

내신 FOCUS

A 1 in which
  2 in which
B 1 ⓐ 2 ⓑ
C 1 ⓓ 2 ⓑ
D 1 The time when
  2 the church where
  3 the way we can

Unit 13

Unit 1 가정법 (I)

P. 74

A

1 had arrived
2 were
3 would
4 would
5 make
6 had worked

B

1 could send
2 doesn't see
3 would/might go shopping
4 could/might play with

C

1 call, won't get
2 isn't, can't go
3 doesn't have, can't drive
4 didn't bring, couldn't return
5 is, don't

내신 FOCUS

A 1 had woken up
  2 were not
B 1 ⓑ 2 ⓐ
C 1 ⓐ 2 ⓒ
D 1 will meet
  2 if you were rich
  3 had studied harder

Unit 2 가정법 (II)

P. 76

A

1 could play 2 couldn't have
3 buy 4 had given
5 couldn't

B

1 had 2 could find
3 had gone 4 had locked

C

1 isn't 2 has
3 isn't 4 haven't visited
5 don't want to

내신 FOCUS

A don't have
B 1 ⓒ 2 ⓒ
C 1 ⓐ 2 ⓒ
D 1 had taken his advice
  2 as if she had been a psychologist
  3 had taken the medicine
  4 couldn't finish

Unit 3 일치, 특수 구문

P. 78

A

1 is
2 appear
3 came
4 was
5 will be
6 was fought

B

1 Nor/Neither
2 know
3 ○
4 met
5 Is
6 were
7 ○

C

1 It was Mr. Johnson from his office
2 It was economics
3 It was in the park
4 It was Tom

내신 FOCUS

A ⓑ

B 1 ⓑ 2 ⓓ

C 1 ⓐ 2 ⓑ

D 1 Five dollars is
2 All of the men in this room are
3 The number of the participants is
4 she is learning Japanese